ST. LUCIA: SLAVERY, EMANCIPATION AND FREEDOM

Description of the culture as well as of the
social, legal and economic situation of St. Lucia's black population under
British dominion in the 19th century
A contribution to the ethno-history of the Caribbean

English version with amendments of my Theses in German from the year
1985 at the University of Vienna, Austria, Europe
Institute for Social and Cultural Anthropology

German title:

ST. LUCIA: SKLAVEREI, EMANZIPATION UND FREIHEIT

*Beschreibung der Kultur sowie der sozialen, rechtlichen und wirtschaftlichen
Situation der schwarzen Bevölkerung St. Lucias unter
Britischer Herrschaft im 19. Jhdt.
Ein Beitrag zur Ethnohistorie der Karibik*

Author: KOLAR Ernestine
2019

Content

P R E F A C E

This work is an elaboration in English of my theses in German from the year 1985, which mainly refers to documents of the former PUBLIC RECORD OFFICE at Kew/London (see also chapter "9. Biography of the Author Dr. Ernestine Kolar", p.453). It gives a specific view of the culture as well as of the social, legal and economic situation of St. Lucia's black population during the 19th century, especially before and after the abolition of slavery, i.e. between the years 1834 and 1838.

St. Lucia was colonized in the 17th and 18th century mainly by the French. From the beginning of the 19th century the British took over this island and administered it till its independence in the year 1979.

The aim of my theses was to establish a dynamic ethno-historical cultural picture of the black population of St. Lucia under British dominion before and after the abolition of slavery.

In the year 1844 the British colonial government servant BREEN published a book with the title "St. Lucia: Historical, Statistical & Descriptive", which gives among other things a general survey of the culture and living conditions of the black population of St. Lucia. This publication is a standard work in St. Lucia today. Other book publications of the 19th century refer only sporadically to cultural, social or economic aspects regarding the black population of St. Lucia.

With the collecting of material I started in the year 1983 within the scope of a co-operation project between the INSTITUT FÜR VÖLKERKUNDE (Institute of Ethnology, Chair II)[1] of the University of Vienna Austria and two St. Lucian institutions engaged in the field of local cultural research and development, namely the Folk Research Centre (FRC) and the National Research and Development Foundation (NRDF), formerly Caribbean Research Centre (CRC). The project concentrates on research in ethnography and ethno-history of St. Lucia and the application of the research results in a developmental context (compare KREMSER/WERNHART 1986 pp. 11-36).

From March 20th till April 18th, 1983, I worked in Castries, St. Lucia, in the following archives and libraries:

- St. Lucia Archaeological and Historical Society (National Trust)
- Folk Research Centre
- Morne Educational Complex Library and
- Castries Central Library

---

[1] The name changed to "Institute of Social and Cultural Anthropology Vienna"

In these institutions I mainly found literature of the 20th century.

Through a scholarship granted by the Austrian Federal Ministry for Science and Research it was possible for me to work in archives and libraries in London for four months (July and August 1983 as well as February and March 1984). A further necessary stay in London for three weeks (May 1985) was financed by myself.

I found the greatest amount of material in the PUBLIC RECORD OFFICE at Kew/London. There is the original version of the correspondence between the British colonial government of St. Lucia and the British government in London. Further I worked in the following libraries in London:

- British Library: Department of Printed Books, Department of Manuscripts, Official Publications Library and Newspaper Department
- Royal Commonwealth Society
- Institute of Commonwealth Studies and
- Foreign and Commonwealth Office

For supporting me I thank Prof. Dr. Karl R. WERNHART and ao. Prof. Dr. Manfred KREMSER as well as the Austrian Federal Ministry for Science and Research for granting me the scholarship.

1 Introduction

1.1 Geography, climate, flora and fauna

The volcanic island of St. Lucia belongs to the Windward islands of the Lesser Antilles and is situated between Longitude limits of 60° 53′ and 61° 05′ West and the Latitude limits of 13° 43′ and 14° 7′ North. St. Lucia lies approximately half-way between St. Vincent to the south and Martinique to the north. The island is 27 miles long and by 14 miles wide. The area is approximately 233 square miles. The middle part of St. Lucia is mountainous; there is a longitudinal main ridge; offset spurs run down to the coast on either side. "Morne Gimie" (3.145 ft.) is the highest peak. The most spectacular mountains, however, are the Pitons of Soufrière; Gros Piton (2.619 ft.) and Petit Piton (2.461 ft.).

(JESSE 1964: IX-X) describes the landscape as follows:

> "Much less mountainous are the Northern and Southern ends of the island. The Northern part consists mostly of small hills or "mornes", few of which are over 400 ft. By contrast, the Southern part, Vieux Fort, is a nearly flat plain, about 4 square miles in area; it is slightly raised above sea-level, and ends in a bold promontory, Moule à Chique.
>
> Between the off-shoots of the main ridge of mountains broad, flat valleys spread out toward the sea. In the Western and South-Western districts, and in the Vieux Fort area, there are also valleys, but they are narrow and deep. Numerous rivers and streams intersect the mountains and spurs. As might be expected under these conditions, the coast-line of the island is deeply indented. Between the bays or "anses" the hillspurs have been broken down by marine erosion, and vertical cliffs are seen along the coast in many places, particularly between Canarias and Soufrière."

The climate of St. Lucia is characterized by constant north-easterly trade winds. The average temperature of the year varies from 26° to 28° Celsius. The average rainfall amounts to approximately 2000 mm per year whereas the rainfall within the island varies according to the sea level. The rainy season lasts from June to November. The dry period is from December to May. The relative humidity varies between 60% and 90%. Between July and November hurricanes can occur.

Map Caribbean Islands

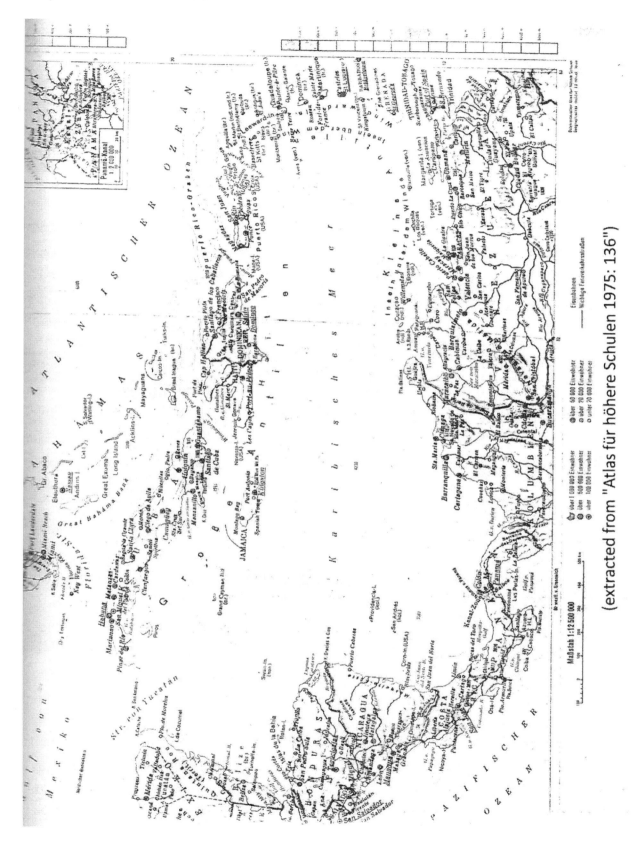

(extracted from "Atlas für höhere Schulen 1975: 136")

SAINT LUCIA

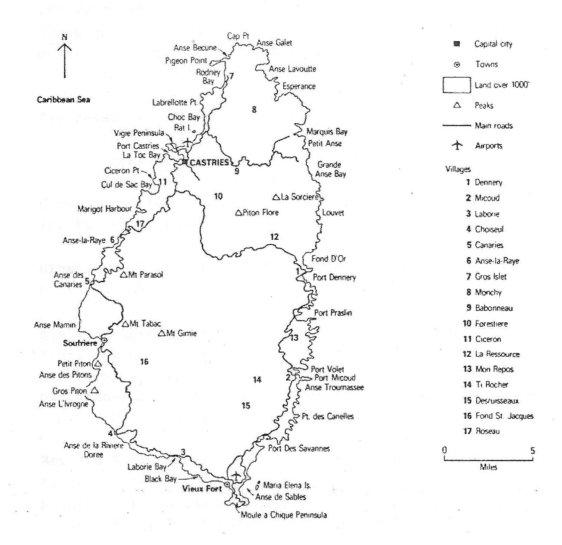

(extracted from BROCK 1984: 1)

Regarding the flora and fauna of St. Lucia BREEN (1844: 150-154) informs as follows:

Principal spices:

"Cinnamon, ginger, vanilla, cloves, pimento, nutmeg, indigo, logwood, cassia, aloes, castor-oil,…"

Provisions:

"Yams, edoes, sweet potatoes and cassada are produced in great abundance. The other leguminous plants and esculents are cabbages, cucumbers, peas, parsnips, beans, carrots, salads, radishes, egg-fruit, beet-root, celery, mountain-cabbage, sorrel, spinage, pumpkin, tomatoes, succory, ocros, and calalou."

Fruits:

"All the delicious fruits of the West Indies and many valuable exotics grow to perfection in St. Lucia. The most attractive are the pine-apple, cocoa-nut, grape, melon, date, fig, sappodillo, orange, shaddock, lemon, lime, citron, guava, plantain, fig-banana, mango, star-apple, pomegranate, plum, cherry, mamee, granadilla, water-melon, avocado-pear, chestnut, tamarind, bread-fruit, cashew, papaw, bread-nut, custard-apple, golden-apple, sugar-apple and soursop."

Forest trees:

"St. Lucia is covered with forest trees of every form and of endless variety. They are, with few exceptions, indigenous to the soil. Many of them furnish valuable materials for building, and some, excellent specimens of fancy wood. The locust, or native mahogany, grows in great produsion. The other principal trees are the palm tree, trumpet tree, oak, white cedar, black cedar, bully tree, poplar, orange tree, cotton tree, sandbox, cinnamon tree, Indian fig tree, bamboo, sandal wood, cocoa-nut tree, satinwood, mango tree, tamarind tree, cashew tree, bread-fruit tree, calabash tree, citron tree, date tree, mamee tree, manchineel, soap tree, rosewood, avocado-pear tree, ironwood, guave tree, laurel, bois immortal, bois diable, sour-orange tree, willow, sea-side grape, simaruba, lignum vitae, acacia, logwood, bois riviere, boistan, acoma, grisgris, angelin, gommier, chatanier-grand' feuille, pois doux, bois violon, bois sept ans, bois pian, barabara, bois d'inde, bois flambeau, galba, mangrove, macata, rose mahaut, bois fourmi, fromager, balisier, latanier, paletuvier, and fougere."

Animals:

"The domesticated animals are the same as those of Europe, whence they were originally imported. Of the horse, ass, ox, mule, cow, hog, sheep, goat, duck, cock, hen, turkey, cat, dog, rabbit, goose, pigeon, and guinea bird, there are various species, and they all thrive admirably. The woods are inhabited by the wild ox, musk rat, wild hog, iguana, and agouti, … The most remarkable birds are the partridge, dove, wild pigeon, plover, parrot, snipe, banana bird, egret, trush, humming-bird, quail, water hen, crabbier, hawk, galding, ground dove, goat-sucker, swallow, cuckoo, wild *duck, booby, frigate, trembler, white-throat, nightingale, woodcock, curlew, and yellowlegs.*

The markets exhibit an abundance of fish of excellent quality: the rivers teem with it, and the sear coast, maugre the depredations of sharks and whales, is no less plentifully supplied. The choicest fishes are the sprat, cutlass, eel, dolphin, anchovy, herring, sole, flounder, mullet, ray, mackerel, doctor, flying fish, baracouta, captain, king-fish, parrot-fish, snapper. Crabs, crawfish, and lobsters are in great abundance ..."

BREEN mentions a yellow serpent, which is domiciled in St. Lucia and Martinique. She is between 6 and 8 feet long and a bite is usually deadly. This serpent is the "Fer de Lance", also mentioned by DURHAM/LEWISOHN (1971: 17) and designated in St. Lucia with the special name "Bothrops caribbaeus". Both authors also refer to the "Boa constrictor" in St. Lucia.

According to CROWLEY governor DES VOEUX introduced mongooses from India to St. Lucia in 1869 to combat the "Fer de Lance". He established a bounty for each "Fer de Lance" head turned over to the government. The mongooses killed many snakes but they also rapidly developed a taste for poultry. In his article CROWLEY describes a snake and mongoose fight held in St. Lucia in commemoration of the days of trouble with the snakes and mongooses.

The flora of St. Lucia is described by DURHAM/LEWISOHN (1971: 10) as follows:

"The gardens give a nut-shell review of the flora of the island: lilies, poinsettia, bougainvillea, bamboo, chenille plant, heliconia, hibiscus, ixora, oleander, gloriceda, cassia, frangipani, breadfruit, cotton tree, sea grape, cashew, ad infinitum. Even the smallest home has some decorative plant."

1.2 History of settlement and policy

1.2.1 Indians

The first settlers of St. Lucia were Indians. One can distinguish three groups, Ciboneys, Arawaks and Caribs, who reached St. Lucia in three big waves of immigration.

FRIESINGER/DEVAUX (1983: Fig. 24) suggest the following Indian settlement of St. Lucia:

ARCHAEOLOGICAL CHRONOLOGY FOR ST. LUCIA

A.D.	CULTURE	PERIODS	REGIONAL SERIES	LOCAL STYLES	HISTORIC EVENTS
2000					
	PERIOD IVa / CREOLE CARIB		CREOLE SERIES	MARTINIQUE STYLE	
1663					ENGLISH TREATY WITH THE CARIBS
	PERIOD IV / MODIFIED ISLAND CARIB	SAUZOID COMPLEX	LAVOUTTE SERIES	FANIS STYLE	EUROPEANS ENTER
1500					
	PERIOD IIIa / ISLAND CARIB				
1250					CARIBS ESTABLISHED / ARAWAKS EXTERMINATED
	PERIOD III		COMORETTE SERIES	CHOC STYLE	CARIBS ENTER
1050		TERMINAL SALADOID	CALIVINY SERIES	MICOUP STYLE	MIXING OF CULTURES
950					CLIMAX OF THE ARAWAKS
				GRAND ANSE STYLE	
		MODIFIED SALADOID (BARANCOID)	PEARLS SERIES		
700					EXPANSION
	PERIOD II / ARAWAK			TROUMASSE STYLE	
500					PERMANENT SETTLEMENTS / ORGANIZED SOCIAL STRUCTURES
		INSULAR SALADOID	SIMON SERIES	CANELLES STYLE	PLANTER-FISHER-HUNTER
200					START OF THE CERAMIC CULTURE / ARAWAK MIGRATION
	PERIOD I / CIBONEY (MESOLITHIC)	PRE-CERAMIC COMPLEX			FISHER-HUNTER
0					BEGINNING OF AGRICULTURE
	(PALAEOLITHIC)				FISHER-HUNTER

(extracted from FRIESINGER/DEVAUX)

A map from DEVAUX dated in the year 1975 show that mainly the southern part of the island had been settled by the Indians:

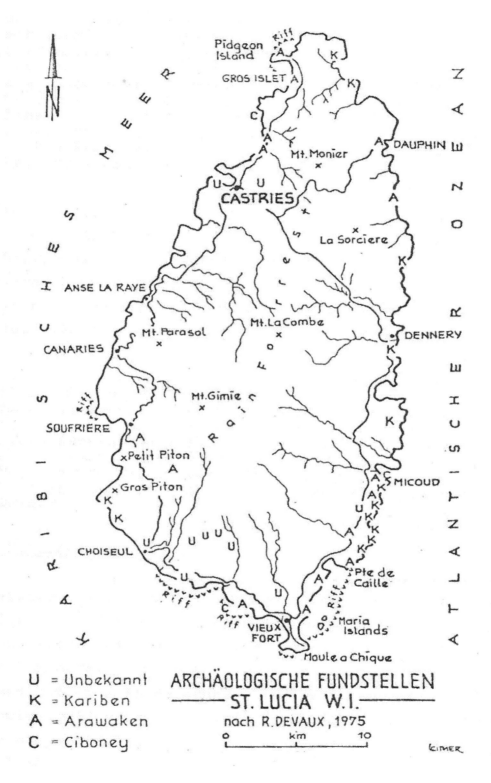

U = Unbekannt   ARCHÄOLOGISCHE FUNDSTELLEN
K = Kariben   ———— ST. LUCIA W.I. ————
A = Arawaken   nach R.DEVAUX, 1975
C = Ciboney

(extracted from FRIESINGER/DEVAUX 1983)

FRIESINGER/DEVAUX (1983: 228) mention that the oldest traces of the Ciboneys can be proved with a fair probability by artefacts found in the sea (today up to approximately 14 feet deep). The settlements of the Arawaks and Caribs were mainly in the vicinity of the sea shore. Numerous single discoveries – beneath exclusively stone axes – were made in the interior of the island. But these discoveries relate more to wood-cutting activities than to settlement.

Austrian excavations under the leadership of Prof. Dr. FRIESINGER (Institute of Prehistory and Early History of the University of Vienna) started in the year 1983 upon the invitation of the St. Lucia Archaelogical and Historical Society. An aim was to correlate archaeological and ethnological data.

1.2.2 Europeans

The circumstances of the European discovery are controversial. Regarding a discovery by Columbus there are three different versions. But not one version can be proved by historical documents. The data refer to a discovery on December 13th, 1498, in June 1502 as well as on December 13th, 1502. Another unconfirmed theory refers to wrecked French seamen who discovered St. Lucia "some time after 1502".

The first mention of St. Lucia in a document was in a "Spanish Cedula" dated 1511. The island was designated "Sancta Lucia" and shown as Spanish crown property (JESSE 1964: 13-14).

The principal data on the history of settlement and policy of St. Lucia are as follows:

1605:   On August 23rd the ship "Oliph Blossome" landed in St. Lucia under the command of Captain Nicholas St. John with 67 persons. After attacks of the Caribs 19 settlers who were still alive had to take to the sea in an open boat.

1638:   The British Captain Judlee arrived with about 300 men. But after two years the settlement had to be given up because of attacks by the Caribs.

1643:   the French settled in St. Lucia

1664:   Invasion by the British from Barbados; a settlement was erected but was abandoned two years later because of the Caribs and because of sickness.

1667:   Peace of BREDA: St. Lucia became French.

1674:	St. Lucia became a dependency of Martinique.
1722:	On June 20th the island was granted by the King of England to the "Duke of Montague". On December 16th a British settlement was set up but because of French opposition the British had to leave.
1723:	Treaty of CHOC; St. Lucia became neutral. The French settlers stayed on the island.
1744:	The French established a garrison under the command of M. de Longueville.
1748:	The Treaty of AIX LA CHAPELLE again declared St. Lucia neutral, but until 1756 the island remained a French colony.
1762:	On February 25th the British occupied the island.
1763:	The Treaty of PARIS put St. Lucia back into the hands of the French.
1778:	Under the command of General Grant the British occupied St. Lucia.
1783:	By the Treaty of VERSAILLES it was eventually agreed that the island should pass into French hands; it was thus delivered up to the French Governor-General de Damas in January 1784.
1794:	The British occupied St. Lucia. One year later they had to leave the island because of the opposition of the French Republicans.
1796:	Again the British occupied St. Lucia. Then followed the period of the BRIGAND-Wars, but before the end of 1797 the Brigands were defeated by the British.
1802:	Treaty of AMIENS: St. Lucia became a French territory.
1803:	Last battle between the British and the French for the island. The British won.
1814	The island remained in British hands until it was finally ceded to Britain by the Treaty of PARIS. The island was administered as a separate territorial unit.
1838	St. Lucia was administered within the Government of the Windward Islands. The Windward formation was dissolved on December 31st, 1959.

1960:	The island was once again administered as a separate island.
1967:	St. Lucia became an Associated State with full control over all her internal affairs, and Britain having responsibility for her defence and foreign affairs in consultation with the island's government.
1979:	On February 22nd St. Lucia became independent member of the Commonwealth of former British Empire territories.

(ST. LUCIA YEAR BOOK 1982: 13-17)

1.3 Language

According to BREEN (1844: 184-185) mainly French and Patois (a mixture of French and African languages) were spoken in St. Lucia in the middle of the 19th century. With the erection of the British MICO-Schools[2], from the year 1838, the influence of the English language became more important. This information follows from two reports of the STIPENDIARY MAGISTRATE of the 1st district of St. Lucia (Castries, Anse la Raye)[3] of the year 1845 as follows:

> *"The agricultural labourers have, in all respects, much improved, and are progressively improving in civilization; and with the advantages of the schools of the Mico Establishment, the rising population are making a proficiency in the English language which was not known heretofore, and of which they are very proud."*
>
> (CO 253/83/8: 17/1/1845)[4]

> *"I again bear most willing testimony to the good effects of the schools of the Mico establishment; they have been the means of spreading a knowledge of the English language amongst the peasantry which was heretofore altogether unknown; there are few children either in the town or country who do not speak a little English, and a large number fluently."*
>
> (CO 253/83/10: 14/7/1845)

The above mentioned great influence of the English language seems to be a little exaggerated as at that time the school attendance was very low (compare chapter 6.7.1. School education, p. 399).

---

[2] The designation of these schools traces from a lady MICO who left a fortune in the 17th century. After the abolition of slavery this fortune was made available by trustees for the education of former slaves. The first MICO-School was opened in St. Lucia on June 11th, 1838 (6. 7.1. School education p. 399)

[3] In the year 1837 St. Lucia was divided into five districts (cp. Chapter "3.2. Records of the Public Record Office", p. 28)

[4] Regarding the quoting compare pp. 39-42

It further follows from a report of the "St. Lucia Public Library" in Castries from February 28th, 1854, that 1.315 persons of St. Lucia's total population spoke English (CO 253/114/2: 28/2/1854). According to a report of the year 1855 the total population of St. Lucia amounted to 25.230 persons (CO 258/51/1:1855/"Population"). From these figures it follows that only about 5% of the population of St. Lucia spoke English at that time.

Today in St. Lucia English and Patois (Kréyòl) are spoken.

2 Miscellaneous

2.1 Theoretical position, methodology and objective

As already mentioned in the preface the aim of my thesis was to establish a dynamic ethno-historical cultural picture. Some remarks on ethno-history in Vienna were taken from an article of Prof. Dr. WERNHART from the Institute of Ethnology in Vienna (Chair II) published in 1986 as follows:

> *"Ethnohistory is a part of the regional ethnology, considering particularly written documents (i.e. manuscripts), pictures and illustrations, oral traditions, artifacts and field research data. The basic requirements for the use of the above mentioned sources are their criticism and sequence in the light of interpretation and the concepts of hermeneutics. In this way the ethnohistorian attempts a presentation of dynamic patterns. Ethnohistory is of importance in dealing with questions of transformation of cultures (social, economic and religious questions of culture change) in the applied as well as political anthropology.*
>
> *From the methodological point of view, ethnohistory in Vienna is the adequate application of historical methods within ethnology, using diachrony and an exact conception of time. The criticism of sources and their sequence have to be taken strictly into account, the historical unity of time and area being the fundamental principle. By "sequence of sources" we understand the presentation of a successive continuation of sources dealing with a special ethnic group or subject, in order to come to an understanding of cultural manifestations specific to time and area. This particular approach of considering the diachrony allows for the recognition of cultural changes or cultural constancies. The studies of cultural changes and acculturation processes are only efficient if they are based on an historical validity. The presentation gives a historical picture of cultural manifestations of an ethnic group, specific to time and area, and founded on the sequence of sources. The source material, thematically arranged, gets in movement by the chronological sequence and thus makes allowance for the dynamic, cultural and social change. We call this conceptualisation, developed in our institute, the "dynamic ethnohistorical cultural picture" (ethnohistorisch dynamisches Kulturbild) WERNHART 1981 : 238, 240). Another possibility of presenting historical ethnographic data is the "concept of phases" (Phasenkonzept); it can only be used if there exist sufficient historical sources in short intervals on a specific ethnic group. In its fundamental structure, the concept of phases also corresponds to the diachronic aspect of history and takes into account the dynamic and changes."*

The following work is divided into three main parts:

1. The period of slavery and emancipation (end of 18th century – 1838)
2. The period after emancipation (1838 – end of 19th century)
3. Special subjects

The first part begins with the revolutionary effects of the French Revolution in St. Lucia, the wars of the Brigands and the final conquest of the island by the British in 1803 and ends with the termination of the emancipation period in 1838.

The second part opens with the end of the emancipation period. The chapters concerning population and economy give a general review till 1870. The chapter regarding the living conditions of St. Lucia's labour population is very detailed and comprises the first twelve years after the emancipation. Immigrations to St. Lucia started during the emancipation period and ended in the year 1893.

The part "Special subjects" refers generally to the 19th century.

2.2 Glossary

APPRENTICE:
In the emancipation period the former slaves were designated APPRENTICES. In this work former field slaves are referred to as FIELD-APPRENTICES and other slaves as NON-FIELD-APPRENTICES. In some sources the term "Praedials" was used for FIELD-APPRENTICES and for NON-FIELD-APPRENTICES the term "Non-Praedials".

BLACK POPULATION: People of mixed colour are also included under this term.

FREE NON-WHITES: This is the group of people of mixed colour and blacks who were free. In many sources this group is referred to as "Free Coloured".

MASTER:
This term refers specifically to slave owners and managers of estates.

PROCUREUR GENERAL/DU ROI: In the sources there is also the term ATTORNEY GENERAL/OF THE KING.

STIPENDIARY MAGISTRATE: In the sources the terms "Special Magistrate" or "Special Justice" are also mentioned.

2.3 List of used British measuring and weight units

Linear measures:	1 ell	60-80 centimetres
	1 inch	2,54 centimetres
	1 foot/ft.	30,48 centimetres
	1 mile	1,609 centimetres
	1 cord	1,9 metres
Nautical measures:	1 nautical mile	1,852 kilometres
Square measures:	1 square foot	929,029 square centimetres
	1 square mile	2,59 square kilometres
	1 acre	4.046,8 square metres
Measures of capacity:	1 pint	0,568 litres
	1 quart	1,136 litres
	1 gallon/gall.	4,5459 litres
	1 barrel/bbl.	163,656 litres
	1 hogshead	238,456 litres
Commercial weight:	1 pound/lb.	453,59 grams
	1 long ton	1.016,05 kilograms

(BROWNE 1899: 118-122)[5]

| Linear measure of French origin: | 1 carré | about 3 British "acres" (about 12.000 square metres) |

(CO 253/3/2: 24/7/1805)

---

[5] The mentioned measures and weights were fixed with the „Weights and Measures Acts" dated 1878 and 1889. They correspond with the current British measuring and weight units (cp. EVERYMAN'S ENCYCLOPAEDIA 1978: 249-250).

3 Sources

The analysis of the sources was done according to WERNHART (1971: 60) and SZALAY (1983: 91-128) with slight modifications.

3.1 Book publications

COLERIDGE, Henry Nelson
      1826   Six Months in the West Indies in 1825,
                  London

In the year 1825 this author visited the following Caribbean islands: Barbados, Trinidad, Grenada, St. Vincent, St. Lucia, Martinique, Dominica, Montserrat, Nevis, Anguilla, Antigua and Barbuda. In St. Lucia he stayed only three days (12th – 15th of April).

COLERIDGE had decided to undertake this journey for reasons of health on the one hand, but on the other because of his spirit of adventure.

His remarks on St. Lucia (p. 117-128) concern the geography and the fauna of the island as well as general information from colonial officers. Of special interest is his observation about boats on page 120:

> *"I was much amused too with a flotilla of fishing or passage boats, which, as we were going rapidly in a contrary direction, shot by us like lightning. These boats are very long, narrow and light, having two and even sometimes three masts upon which they carry so much sail that the men are obliged to sit on the weather bulwarks to keep them from oversetting."*

JEREMIE, John, Esq.
      1831   Four Essays on Colonial Slavery,
                  London

On February 28th, 1825, JEREMIE was appointed to the FIRST PRESIDENT of the court of appeal of St. Lucia. The British government had ordered him to revise the slave laws of St. Lucia. JEREMIE was successful in introducing the measures for ameliorating the living condition of the slaves and he helped the FREE NON-WHITES to get more civil and political rights. His activities raised a fierce opposition against him in St. Lucia and after six years of active and useful work as a legislator, a statesman, and a judge, he retired from the colony on the 1st May 1831 (BREEN 1844: 328-331).

His four essays describe slavery in general and the situation of slaves in St. Lucia.

INHABITANT OF ST. LUCIA,
      1832   Mr. Jeremie's Pamphlet,
                 London

This anonymous publication of an inhabitant of St. Lucia is a reply to JEREMIE's book published in 1831 on the situation of slaves in St. Lucia. On page 19 JEREMIE's book is described as:

> "...abounding with egregious misstatements and gross exaggerations, as regards St. Lucia;"

STURGE J. /HARVEY T,
      1838   The West Indies in 1837, being the Journal of a visit to Antigua, Montserrat, Dominica, St. Lucia, Barbados and Jamaica,
                 London

On October 17th, 1836, four British gentlemen, Joseph STURGE, Thomas HARVEY, John SCOBLE and William LLOYD joined the "Skylark Packet" at Falmouth. All the travellers excepting John SCOBLE were members of the "Society of the Friends".

On November 12th, 1836, the ship "Skylark Packet" reached Barbados. Shortly after their arrival in Barbados William LLOYD and John SCOBLE separated themselves from the other two and went to British Guiana. John STURGE and Thomas HARVEY stayed at first in Barbados. Then they went to Antigua, Montserrat, Martinique and St. Lucia. Afterwards they returned to Barbados. They reached St. Lucia on December 24th, 1836, and left after two days on the evening of the 26th December, 1836.

Back in England they published a book. The relevant article on St. Lucia comprises eleven pages and refers to reports made to the authors as well as observations made by them, such as on the cutting of sugar cane on an estate in St. Lucia.

BREEN, Henry, H.,
      1844   St. Lucia: Historical, Statistical & Descriptive,
                 London

BREEN was born in Ireland in the year 1805. After a general education in that land he studied philosophy, theology and French literature in Paris (College St. Esprit). About the year 1829 he went to Martinique. From 1831 he lived in St. Lucia and had the following functions:

-   From March 1832:   Deputy Registrar of the Royal Court of St. Lucia

-	From April 1833:	Registrar-in-chief and Registrar of Deeds and Mortgages
-	From November 1835 Till September 1838:	Member of the Executive and Legislative Council of St. Lucia
-	From June 1840 to May 1842:	Colonial Secretary and Treasurer
-	From November 1842:	Vice President of the African Institute of Paris
-	27th February 1851:	Selection to the Mayor of Castries
-	From September 1855:	Colonial Secretary and Chairman of the Trustees of the St. Lucia Public Library and Museum and
-	From May/September 1857: to September 1861:	Governor of St. Lucia

After this 30 years' public activity in St. Lucia BREEN moved to St. Vincent, where he was appointed to Provost-Marshall in April 1862. On November 2nd, 1881, he died at the age of 76 years in St. Vincent (JESSE 1968: 1-10).

BREEN's book is very comprehensive and deals with the following subjects:

- Geography
- Historical facts of the 17th and 18th century
- The war period in the last decade of the 18th century
- Climate, fauna and flora
- Population: general, FREE NON-WHITES, refugees from Martinique, customs and languages
- Religion
- Agriculture
- Administration

As BREEN also refers to time periods before his arrival in St. Lucia his book cannot be handled as a totally primary source. In any case his book is an important addition to the records of the PUBLIC RECORD OFFICE.

MARTIN, R. Montgomery, Esq.,
    1851-57   The British Colonies; their History, Extent, Condition, and Resources,
                London

MARTIN is a British historian who was never in St. Lucia. He published four volumes about the British colonies. His remarks on St. Lucia are mainly based on BREEN but also contain other information.

COMINS, D.W.D.,

    1893   Note on Emigration, From the East Indies to St. Lucia,
                    Calcutta

This author was a British surgeon-major who stayed twelve days in St.
Lucia (12th – 24th May 1891). His publication deals with the immigration of
Indians to St. Lucia. It is mainly based on documents of the immigration
office of St. Lucia as well as on his own observations.

REA, J. T.,

    1898   Building in St. Lucia,
                    Iverness

REA was a surveyor with the Royal Engineer Establishment in England. He
visited St. Lucia and made a detailed report of house-building in St. Lucia
in March 1897. This report was published by the Association of Surveyors
of H.M. Service in the year 1898.

DES VOEUX, William, G.,

    1903   My Colonial Service in British Guiana, St. Lucia, Trinidad,
                    Fiji, Australia, New-Foundland, and Hong Kong
                    with interludes,

DES VOEUX was governor of St. Lucia from 1869 to 1876. He published
two volumes in which he describes his stays in the above mentioned
colonies. Regarding St. Lucia the author gives a survey of the population
as well as general observations about the situation in the colony.

3.2 Records of the PUBLIC RECORD OFFICE

The written documents (manuscripts) about St. Lucia are kept in the PUBLIC RECORD OFFICE under the following shelfmarks:

CO 253: Letters from the Governor of St. Lucia to the SECRETARY OF STATE in London with various enclosures for the period from 1709 to 1838 as well as letters from the Governor of Barbados to the SECRETARY OF STATE in London with various enclosures from the year 1838 to 1873 bound in 150 volumes; in 1838 when St. Lucia was annexed to the Windward formation which was headed by the Governor of Barbados the letters of the Governor of St. Lucia were transferred via Barbados to London.

The letters of the Governors of St. Lucia and Barbados respectively after 1873 were bound under "WINDWARD ISLANDS" on the shelfmarks CO 376, CO 377 and CO 321.

CO 254: Letters of the SECRETARY OF STATE in London to the Governor of St. Lucia for the period from 1794 to 1872 bound in 19 volumes. Further documents of the SECRETARY OF STATE in London, especially on administrative subjects, are found under the shelfmark CO 381/69.

CO 255: Ordinances, proclamations and ORDERS IN COUNCIL which were publicly proclaimed in St. Lucia for the period from 1818 to 1960 bound in 23 volumes.

CO 256: Minutes of the PRIVY, EXECUTIVE AND LEGISLATIVE COUNCIL of St. Lucia respectively for the period from 1820 to 1960 bound in 55 volumes.

CO 257: "Government Gazettes" for the period from 1857 to 1961 bound in 94 volumes

CO 258: "Miscellanea"
Vol. no. 1-2: Newspaper "The Palladium" for the period from 1838 to 1856
Vol. no. 3-4: various correspondence
Vol. no. 5-15: Reports of the PROTECTOR OF SLAVES for the period from 1826 to 1834
Vol. no. 16-17: Police-reports
Vol. no. 18-136: BLUE BOOKS for the period from 1821 to 1940

All the above mentioned documents were used by the author for the period from 1709 to 1873.

Most of the documents are hand-written. Often printed letters of the Governor of St. Lucia and Barbados respectively with enclosures for the British Parliament as well as answers of the SECRETARY OF STATE in London were additionally bound to the original hand-written documents. Further proclamations, ordinances and ORDERS-IN-COUNCIL were also printed partly. Sporadically newspaper articles, printed circular letters of the Governor or printed general reports were found in the correspondence files.

Very informative were the volumes under the shelfmark CO 253. In them the respective letters of the Governor to the SECRETARY OF STATE with enclosures were bound in chronological order. By classifying these sources the following picture resulted:

- <u>Letters of the Governor of St. Lucia to the SECRETARY OF STATE in London</u>

  Especially in the period of slavery the Governors made tours them. In September 1829 for example Governor STEWART of St. Lucia visited most of the estates of the island and observed beside the general labour situation and the maintenance of the slaves also the clothes of the women. In general these letters refer to the financial and economic situation of the colony, the situation of the planters and slaves as well as to special events. Often they are summaries of enclosures. In these cases only the original reports or letters were used by the author.

- <u>Letters of the Governor of Barbados to the SECRETARY OF STATE in London</u>

  Only in cases when the Governor of Barbados visited St. Lucia could the relevant documents be used. The other letters were short summaries of the reports sent from St. Lucia.

- <u>Enclosures:</u>

- <u>Other letters of the Governor of St. Lucia</u>

  The Governor also contacted the British colonial servants in St. Lucia by letters. But as these documents mostly deal with administrative subjects, they were only used in some cases. A very informative source regarding the refugees from Martinique to St. Lucia is the correspondence between the Governor of St. Lucia and the Governor of Martinique.

- <u>Letters and reports of the British colonial servants in St. Lucia</u>

Reporters to the Governor of St. Lucia were:

- the COLONIAL SECRETARY
- the PROCUREUR GENERAL; from 1826 PROTECTOR OF SLAVES
- the PROCUREUR DU ROI
- the COLONIAL TREASURER
- the SENESCHAL
- the STIPENDIARY MAGISTRATE
- several JUDGES
- Servants of the SECRETARY's OFFICE
- Servants of the CUSTOM HOUSE, as for example the slave registrator
- Servants of the IMMIGRATION OFFICE as well as
- the PRIVY, EXECUTIVE AND LEGISLATIVE COUNCILs

The reports of the STIPENDIARY MAGISTRATES are the most informative source for the first years after the abolition of slavery. DOOKHAN (1983: 95-96) reports about the STIPENDIARY MAGISTRATES as follows:

The office of the STIPENDIARY MAGISTRATE was fixed in the law for the abolition of slavery which came into force in the British colonies on August 1st, 1834. According to Lord Stanley, the STIPENDIARY MAGISTRATES should be "men uninfluenced by local assemblies, free from local passions". Accordingly, most of them were appointed from Britain, and since one of the intentions of the British government was to keep down costs, the great majority were appointed from among retired army and naval officers living on half-pay. In addition to these men, a smaller number of non-officials from Britain, as well as some people from the Caribbean not associated with the planter or merchant class, were appointed. STIPENDARY MAGISTRATES were expected to administer justice and to assist in preventing social and economic disturbance.

From a letter of Governor DUDLEY HILL of St. Lucia to the SECRETARY OF STATE GLENELG, dated August 7th, 1835 (CO 253/49/7: 7/8/1835)[6] follows, that at the beginning of the period of emancipation three STIPENDIARY MAGISTRATES, who came from Great Britain, were appointed. As the first of these servants arrived in St. Lucia only in 1834, Governor DUDLEY HILL felt obliged to appoint inhabitants of St. Lucia as STIPENDIARY MAGISTRATES on short term at the time of the abolition of slavery.

---

[6] Regarding the quotation cp. Chapter „3.6. Quoting of sources" pp. 39-42

In St. Lucia every STIPENDIARY MAGISTRATE was in charge of one district. At the beginning of the emancipation period St. Lucia was divided into the following three districts:

1. District: Castries, Gros Islet, Dauphin, Anse La Raye,
2. District: Soufrière, Choiseul, Laborie and
3. District: Vieux Fort, Micoud, Praslin, Dennery

(BREEN 1844: 12)

In July 1837 this division was altered according to BREEN (1844: 12-13) as follows:

1. District: Castries, Anse La Raye,
2. District: Gros Islet, Dauphin,
3. District: Soufrière, Choiseul,
4. District: Vieux Fort, Laborie and
5. District: Micoud, Praslin, Dennery

Graphic representation of the mentioned districts:

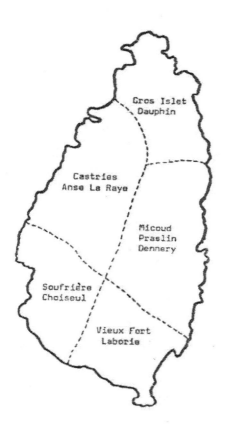

Division of districts extracted from a map of St. Lucia of the year 1847 – BPP/CG/4/1: 1847, p. 518 – regarding the quotation cp. pp. 39-42)

This alteration of the districts also caused a rise in the number of the STIPENDIARY MAGISTRATES from three to five.
Reports regarding the period from 1834 to 1845 were bound under the above mentioned shelfmark CO 253. From 1836 there are monthly reports with interruptions and from 1843 to June 1845 there are half-yearly reports. Reports up from June 1845 were bound under the shelfmark CO 258.

Deserving of special mention are the reports for the period from 1840 to 1845 which inform about social and economic aspects, the maintenance, the free time and the clothes of the black population as well as about the flower festivals LA ROSE and LA MARGUERITE or Obeah.

The letters and reports of the other British colonial servants (officers) give a wide range of information. According to the duty of the officers the reports refer to economic, social or legal situations of planters and slaves. There are also population tables compiled in most cases by the Secretary's Office.

- Other letters and reports

These are letters from the SECRETARY OF STATE in London to St. Lucia and letters of planters as well as newspaper articles.

- Petitions and protest letters

These sources refer mainly to the bad financial and economic situation of the planters in the period of slavery as well as to general protests of the free population of St. Lucia against the laws regarding the amelioration of the living conditions of the slaves. There are also petitions of the FREE NON-WHITES concerning legal assimilation in status with the whites during the 1820's. Generally these petitions were addressed to the Governor of St. Lucia or directly to the British government (parliament, king).

- Proclamations, Ordinances, ORDERS IN COUNCIL

These documents are laws which were passed by the colonial government in St. Lucia. It is from these sources especially, that the legal situation of the slaves as well as the development of the laws regarding the amelioration of the living conditions of the slaves was worked out.

An important law is the Slave Law of St. Lucia which was passed by the PRIVY COUNCIL of St. Lucia on February 8th, 1826, and which came into force on June 1st, 1826. This law was transferred from

Governor MAINWARING of St. Lucia to the SECRETARY OF STATE in London on February 9th, 1826 (CO 253/22/4: 1/6/1826)[7]

A great part of the proclamations, ordinances and ORDERS IN COUNCIL were bound in chronological order under the shelfmark CO 255.

Special mention should be made also of the documents under the shelfmark
CO 258. The volumes 5-15 comprise reports of the PROTECTOR OF SLAVES which were in general submitted half yearly during the period from 1826 to 1834. These reports had to be made on the basis of forms which were divided into various sections and which concern the following subjects:

- Punishment of slaves on the estates (number of punishments, kind of offence)
- Complaints of slaves
- Marriages
- Number of slaves' manumissions
- Property of slaves as well as
- General remarks on the slave population

Along with these reports of the PROTECTOR OF SLAVES, in some cases the letters of the Governor of St. Lucia to the SECRETARY OF STATE in London, as well as the answer of the SECRETARY OF STATE were also bound in the same file.

One can also mention the half-yearly reports of the STIPENDARY MAGISTRATES regarding the period from July 1845 to December 1853, which are bound in chronological order in the volumes 16 and 17. They are forms which were filled in by the STIPENDIARY MAGISTRATES per district. Additionally the STIPENDIARY MAGISTRATE of the 1st district always made a summary. The several sections of the forms mainly refer to education, church, number of land-owners, informs, immigrants, emigrants and economic aspects.

A further important source are the BLUE BOOKS which are available for the period from 1821 to 1940 and which comprise the volumes from 18 to 136. The BLUE BOOKS are yearly reports of the Colonial Secretary of St. Lucia and mainly contain figures informing of the financial situation of the colony, taxes, population, economy, education and the church, etc.

Under the above mentioned shelfmark CO 258 is also bound "The Palladium" newspaper (Volume 1 and 2). This newspaper is available for the period from 1838 to 1856 and refers on the one hand to important

---

[7] Regarding the quotation cp. Chapter „3.6. Quoting of sources" pp. 39-42.

events abroad and on the other hand to actual events happening in St. Lucia. The exact title of the newspaper in the period from 1838 to 1843 was "The Palladium and St. Lucia Free Press" and in the period from 1844 to 1847 "St. Lucia Palladium and Public Gazette". From this source information about the economy and labour conditions as well as about superstition (Obeah) and the flower festivals LA ROSE and LA MARGUERITE were taken.

Minutes of the PRIVY, EXECUTIVE and LEGISLATIVE COUNCIL of St. Lucia, which are bound under the shelfmark CO 256, were also used in some cases.

3.3 Printed documents of the OFFICIAL PUBLICATIONS LIBRARY

As already mentioned in the previous chapter (cp. p. 29) parts of the correspondence between the Governor of St. Lucia and Barbados with the SECRETARY OF STATE in London were printed for the British Parliament. This correspondence as well as laws of the Parliament regarding St. Lucia are bound together with reports of other British colonies in the Parliamentary Papers "Slave Trade" vol.-no. 61-87 for the period from 1799 to 1838. The majority of the correspondence regarding St. Lucia concerns the period from 1820 to 1838.

Of special information is an English abstract of the CODE DE LA MARTINIQUE which was done by the secretary of Governor BLACKWELL of St. Lucia on October 25th, 1825, and sent to the SECRETARY OF STATE BATHURST in London on October 25th, 1825 (BPP/ST/71/2: 24/10/1825)[8] This abstract comprises all slave laws of St. Lucia valid at that time.

Parts of the correspondence from the year 1838 are bound in the Parliamentary Papers "Colonies General" from vol.-no. 1.

From these printed documents some laws, tables as well as two letters were used beside the above mentioned abstract of the CODE DE LA MARTINIQUE.

Other laws were taken from the collection "Bills Public" as well as from the book "St. Lucia: Ordinances enacted by His Excellency the Lieutenant-Governor, no. 1 of 1853 – no. 17 of 1935" under the shelfmark C.S./F 246.

3.4 Newspapers

As main source "The Palladium" newspaper was used; already mentioned in chapter "3.2. Records of the PUBLIC RECORD OFFICE", p. 28.

Further, the newspaper "The independent Press" was used. One number dated September 4th, 1839, is available in the newspaper department of the BRITISH LIBRARY under the shelfmark C.misc. 425 (2). In this number there is special reference to the economic situation of St. St. Lucia.

Another informative newspaper is "The London Gazette" which sometimes contains laws and petitions concerning St. Lucia. It is available in the OFFICIAL PUBLICATIONS LIBRARY.

---

[8] Concerning the quotation cp. pp. 39-41

3.5 General critical analysis of the sources

3.5.1 Outer criticism

Authenticity:

The book publications were all in the original English version. The author of this work didn't use any translations. They were also complete regarding the number of pages. Regarding the authors of the books see chapter "3.1. Book publications", pp. 24-27.

The hand-written documents of the PUBLIC RECORD OFFICE used as sources are available in original. On many documents, however, was the note "Copy" or "Duplicate" although the documents were obviously signed with an original signature. As the author of this work tried in vain to get original documents dated earlier than 1880 in St. Lucia the sources of the PUBLIC RECORD OFFICE were therefore the only available. Moreover that institute gave the assurance it was the sole depository for the original correspondence between the British colonies and the government in London.

Moreover there were copies marked with "True Copy" by the Governor or the Colonial Secretary of St. Lucia.

Regarding the writers of the several documents see chapter "3.2. Records of the PUBLIC RECORD OFFICE", pp. 28-34.

In addition, all printed documents of the correspondence files are also available in hand-written form. An examination by spot-checks regarding completeness, exactness, abridgements and extinctions showed, beside the capitalization and the use of small letters, no deviations. Ordinances, proclamations and ORDERS IN COUNCIL are partly printed and partly hand-written. All printed documents used in this work are marked in the bibliography as "printed".

The used newspaper articles were all written by anonymous authors.

Semantic judgement

The risk of misunderstanding a text is in general as great as the distance between the culture of the author, the source and its user. The older a document is the greater is the probability of misunderstanding it. Terms and words vary in the course of time and in their application. For that reason, and in order to present the ethnographic material as objectively as possible and independent of the author's perspective, the principal extracts of sources were quoted word by word.

Localisation of sources

The ethnographic material consists of written documents which refer to the respective chronological, spatial and ethnic scope. The chronological localisation is noted before or after the quotations (mention of date of issue). The spatial scope is the island of St. Lucia, if not otherwise stated. The ethnic scope is the black population of St. Lucia which consists of different African ethnic groups.

Some exceptions are pictures and illustrations from which the respective scope follows either directly from the source or from the enclosed letter.

Relationship of sources

It is important to examine whether a source is original or dependent upon other sources. The value of a derived source will be in proportion to the degree of the dependence. That dependence can be very different.

This work is based on original reports. Derived sources were only used as additional literature.

3.5.2 Inner criticism

Reliability

The problematic nature of this work is the fact that the sources were written by whites, persons who didn't belong to the culture of the blacks. Exceptions are petitions of FREE NON-WHITES. The sources used in this work are therefore to be seen from the perspective of the whites, especially of the British colonial government.

The geographical nearness to the subject is necessarily given because of the relatively small size of the island. But it should be noted that observation reports were preferred.

A problem was in the case of statistical data, as for example, population or export figures. The deviation among them is very high and the writers of the reports often designated the figures as doubtful, but as the only available ones. These remarks are noted when mentioning such figures.

The ethnographic material concerns in general economic, social, legal and religious aspects as well as superstition, obeah, the flower festivals LA ROSE and LA MARGUERITE, clothes and house-building.

The main part of these sources can be designated as official reports of British colonial servants. There are also reports of other persons, for example planters. Other sources are laws, newspaper articles and book publications.

Known motivations of the authors of the book publications were described in chapter "3.1. Book publications", pp. 24-27). They are partly explainable from the profession of the author.

The education, profession and social status of the several authors as well as their interests in the respective subjects were mentioned in the chapters "3.1.-3.4", pp. 18-28, or in the text.

Validity

To examine the validity of the sources the ethno-historian can only compare different sources which refer to the same subject and which originate from different people. When there is an agreement in these sources then the validity can be assumed.

When comparing sources and the sources confirming each other are different, the degree of validity is high. Sources of the same kind can more easily have the same errors as sources of very different kind. The several sources can be written documents (manuscripts), pictures and illustrations, oral traditions, artefacts and field research data.

For this work in many cases only reports of different British colonial servants were available for comparing. But often other written documents, such as reports of planters, complaints of slaves as well as newspaper articles could be compared with the reports of the colonial servants.

3.6 Quoting of sources

The bibliography is divided into the following sections:

Sources:

- Book publications
- Records of the PUBLIC RECORD OFFICE
- Printed documents of the OFFICIAL PUBLICATIONS LIBRARY and
- Newspapers

Literature

The published books are quoted as follows: author, publication year and page.

The documents of the PUBLIC RECORD OFFICE and the OFFICIAL PUBLICATIONS LIBRARY as well as the newspapers are sorted according to shelfmarks and volume-numbers. For these documents some special declarations are necessary:

Records of the PUBLIC RECORD OFFICE

Quotations from the sources of the PUBLIC RECORD OFFICE are indicated by the shelfmark, volume, a consecutive number, the date of establishment of the document, and in some cases, also by the page number or the designation of the enclosure.

- The documents under the shelfmark CO 253:

    The letters of the Governor of St. Lucia, and from 1838, the letters of the Governor of Barbados to the SECRETARY OF STATE in London with enclosures, are bound in chronological order and in most cases summarized in a register at the end of the volume. These documents are quoted as follows:

    (CO 253/10/2 : 16/10/1816)

CO 253	shelfmark
10	volume-number
2	consecutive number under which the document can be found in the bibliography of this work within the volume-number
16/10/1816	date of the document

39

In some volumes there was also numbering by pages. In these cases the page number is noted additionally after the date.

The kind and the author of the document is mentioned in the text.

The letters of the Governor of St. Lucia till 1838 are mentioned in the bibliography in full wording (name of the Governor, name of the SECRETARY OF STATE – if noted – and date of issue).The letters of the Governor of Barbados (from 1838) are only mentioned with their consecutive number, because these documents were not directly used as source but only the enclosures therefrom.

In addition to the letters of the Governor of St. Lucia and of Barbados respectively a section "Miscellaneous" was yearly made. It consists of letters and reports of colonial servants or laws and which are also divided into various sub-sections, for example, "Treasury" or "Mr. Jeremie". These sub-sections are mentioned in the bibliography.

- <u>Proclamations, ordinances, ORDERS-IN-COUNCIL under the shelfmark CO255 as well as Minutes of the PRIVY COUNCIL under the shelfmark CO 256</u>

are bound in chronological order. They are quoted in the same manner as the documents under the shelfmark CO 253.

- <u>The documents under the shelfmark 258</u>

The reports of the PROTECTOR OF SLAVES in general were made half-yearly and are bound in chronological order (volumes: 5-15). They are quoted in the same manner as stated before except that in this case the time period to which the report refers is quoted instead of the date. Also especial sections "A-I" respectively "General Observations" (GO) are mentioned:

(CO 258/12/1: 1/7/1832-31/12/1832/Section A).

The various sections are registered at the beginning of each volume.

The half-yearly reports of the STIPENDIARY MAGISTRATES (volumes: 16-17), also bound in chronological order, are quoted in the same manner as stated above, except that here pages are mentioned instead of sections.

The yearly reports of the BLUE BOOK for one year were bound in one volume. The used data are, on the one hand, population figures, and on the other, export figures. In this case they are referred to the respective sections "Population" or "Agriculture":

(CO 258/18/1: 1821/"Population").

Both sections are registered at the beginning of each volume.

Printed documents of the OFFICIAL PUBLICATIONS LIBRARY

The used documents were divided into the sections "OPL" and "BPP". "OPL" is the abbreviation of the library. Under this designation two ordinances with the shelfmark C.S./F 246 are mentioned. The quoting is as follows:

(OPL/C.S./F 246/1: 21/7/1858).

The number after the shelfmark is the consecutive number under which the document can be found in the bibliography. The ordinances are bound in chronological order.

"BPP" is the abbreviation for "British Parliamentary Papers". The documents used by the author can be divided into three groups:

- "BP": "Bills Public"
- "CG": "Colonies General"
- "ST": "Slave Trade"

Citation is as follows:

(BPP/BP/
    CG/
    ST/77/1 : 2/2/1830

After the group designation follows the volume number and the consecutive number under which the document can be found in the bibliography within the volume number. All these documents have page numbers. The respective page is stated in the bibliography and in some cases also in the text.

Newspapers

In general all quotations of newspaper articles in this work are marked with "N". As the newspapers are kept in different libraries and archives the different shelfmarks are as follows:

- N/BL/ND/C.misc. 425 (2):   BRITISH LIBRARY/Newspaper Department/

                            Shelfmark

-	N/CO 28/171: OFFICE	Shelfmark of the PUBLIC RECORD
		(Correspondence of Barbados/ volume number
-	N/CO 258/1: PALLADIUM	Shelfmark of the newspaper
		in the PUBLIC RECORD OFFICE/ volume number
-	N/OPL/LG:	OFFICIAL PUBLICATIONS LIBRARY/ London Gazette

After the shelfmark and the volume number follows the consecutive number under which the article can be found in the bibliography, the date of the article as well as the page.

4 The period of slavery and emancipation (end of 18th century – 1838)

4.1 The effects of the French Revolution in St. Lucia, the wars of the Brigands and the final conquer by the British

When taking over the Bastille in Paris in the year 1789, the principle of the French Revolutionists was "Freedom, Equality and Fraternity". These revolutionary ideas produced positive reactions among the most of the inhabitants of St. Lucia. The white planters welcomed the news as giving them a chance of power in Martinique and even in France. The free non-white inhabitants, mostly engaged in commerce, saw in the events an opportunity for complete equality with the whites, and the slaves hoped that the new ideas would bring them freedom (GACHET 1975: 61-64).

At the beginning of the year 1791 two republican agents, MONTDENOIX and LINGER, hoisted the tricolour-flag on the Morne Fortune in the south of the town of Castries which was the seat of the then French governor GIMAT. The French governor had to leave St. Lucia.

In September 1792 the Republic was proclaimed in France. In December that same year the republican captain LA CROSSE arrived in St. Lucia. He was entrusted with the mission of circulating the new philosophical doctrines amongst the Antilles. Whereas in Martinique and Dominica LA CROSSE had had no success, he was received with open arms in St. Lucia. His influence was soon noticeable: the slaves discontinued the work on the estates and discussed the rights of men. Anarchy and terror prevailed.

On February the 4th, 1794, the abolition of slavery was promulgated in the French Antilles.[9] On April the 4th of the same year the British conquered St. Lucia. The slaves just freed by the French retired into the woods – by British law slavery still existed in the island – and were joined by a number of French soldiers who had succeeded in making their escape. Jointly they carried on a war against the British supported by the republicans of Guadeloupe.

In the middle of February 1795 troops from Guadeloupe landed in St. Lucia and the French under the command of GOYRAND succeeded in conquering the British who on June 18th, 1795, were forced to evacuate St. Lucia. But already one year later, on April 26th, 1796, British troops landed again in St. Lucia and on the 26th of May, 1796, the republicans laid down their arms. General MOORE was appointed Governor of St. Lucia and although the regular military operations ceased on the surrender of

---

[9] In the year 1802 slavery was again introduced by the French emperor NAPOLEON. The final abolition of slavery took place in France in the year 1848 (cp. BERNER 1984 : 171-173)

the military base of MORNE FORTUNE, the rest of the island remained unsubdued.

The population of St. Lucia was split into two parties:

- The "friends of law and order" who formed the majority of the inhabitants and
- The "disaffected of every class", all hostile to the British connection as involving the destruction of their cherished projects. This group received the appellation of BRIGANDS.

(BREEN 1844: 77-99)

The majority of these BRIGANDS were apparently slaves who were freed under French rule and who refused to be enslaved again by the British. They retired to the woods and kept up guerrilla warfare against the British. BREEN (1844: 105-107) writes thereof:

"They made repeated excursions from their fortresses; murdered the inhabitants without distinction of age or sex; plundered the houses; burned plantations; and committed numerous deeds of cruelty."

General MOORE tried to communicate with the BRIGANDS. He thought it advisable to use the influence of a certain MARIN PADRE, who was the chief of the BRIGANDS of St. Vincent and who had surrendered upon terms in that island. But after a tedious correspondence LACROIX, the chief of the BRIGANDS in St. Lucia, rejected the proposed terms and the negotiation was broken off. But at the end of 1797 the successor of General MOORE, Colonel DRUMMOND, succeeded in conquering the BRIGANDS. As the black prisoners stipulated that they didn't want to get enslaved again, they were formed into a regiment which was sent to Africa (BREEN 1844: 105-107).

At the end of 1798 the British Governor of St. Lucia, PREVOST, reported:

"It is with great satisfaction I have the honour of announcing your Grace the tranquillity of returning prosperity of this unfortunate Colony, ...

This misfortune of intestine commotions almost unparalleled for cruelty and excesses which have been devastated the country, destroyed a great part of the Inhabitants and reduced the working Negroes to 3100 Males and 5060 Females, ..."

(CO 253/2/1: 22/11/1798, p. 3)

Three months later Governor PREVOST pointed to a further improvement of the situation:

> "I feel myself particularly happy in having it in my power to assure your Grace that daily experience evinces the confidence with which the Inhabitants now rely on the British Government & that every appearance denotes a return of ... & prosperity equal to their highest expectations ...
>
> At the time this Island was last captured by His Majesty's forces the then Commander in Chief finding it deserted by all the most respectable Inhabitants, & that those who remained were from their prejudices & bad inclinations likely to prove troublesome subjects, judged a Government entirely military to be the most efficacious & which still continues.
>
> On my arrival to take command in July last, several respectable Inhabitants who had been driven away, returned. I found the disposition of the people much changed & the Brigands who remained in the woods, so much reduced, as by a little exertion with the stationed Troops, to render them no longer to be dreaded."

(CO 253/2/2: 2/2/1799, p. 13)

On March 25th, 1802, St. Lucia became again a French colony by the contract of AMIENS, but one year later, on June 22nd, 1803, the British reconquered St. Lucia. From this time on St. Lucia was ruled by the British up to its Independence in the year 1979.

4.2 British Slave Policy in St. Lucia (1803-1834)

4.2.1 Detailed Description

At the beginning of the 19th century the rights and duties of the slaves in St. Lucia were ruled by the CODE DE LA MARTINIQUE. This collection of laws contained laws of the CODE NOIR from the year 1685 which had been partly altered by French enactments, ordinances or proclamations. These laws were taken over by the British and renewed in some cases.

The main provisions of the above mentioned CODE DE LA MARTINIQUE can be summarized as follows:

Disability Clauses:

- Slaves were considered as moveable and as such liable to mortgage.
- Slaves could possess nothing independent of their masters.
- Assemblies of slaves of different estates were only possible with the sanction of the PROCUREUR DU ROI.

- Slaves were not allowed to be appointed to office of to any public situation or to be concerned in commerce. They were further not allowed to compose or distribute remedies or to undertake the cure of any description of disorder with the exception of the bite of serpents.
- They were forbidden to sell certain products as for example sugar canes, coffee or cotton. Other products like fruits or vegetables could only be sold with the consent of their masters.
- Slaves were not allowed to possess arms of any kind, except they were sent out shooting by their masters.
- Slaves could not be parties in civil matters, either as plaintiffs or defendants. Their evidence in court was used except for or against their masters.
- A slave who struck his master, his master's wife or children in the face or causing bleeding was to be punished by death. Also thefts of horses, mules or canes could be punished with death.

Beneficent Clauses:

- Masters were to supply each slave with provisions, clothes as well as medical care.
- Slave owners were prohibited to put their slaves to torture, to mutilate or kill them, but they were permitted to flog them or put them in chains.
- Slaves had the right to make their complaint to the PROCUREUR DU ROI.
- Masters of twenty years of age and over could manumit their slaves.
- When slaves were sold, families were not to be broken up.

Furthermore it should be mentioned that slaves were to be converted to Christianity. They could also marry with the consent of their master.

(BPP/ST/71/2: 1685-1819, p. 184-212)

On January 1st, 1808, the British law for the abolition of the slave trade came into force (DOOKHAN 1983: 85). In the year 1814, when St. Lucia was finally ceded to the British, an ORDER IN COUNCIL was enacted which provided for the registration of all slaves (CO 253/8/1: 24/9/1814).

A most noticeable feature in the struggle against slavery between 1807 and 1834 was the attempt to improve the conditions under which slaves lived.
This policy stemmed from representatives of slave owners in London. They sought to kill adverse criticism by kindness. The idea found favour with the British government which, after 1815, became preoccupied with domestic social unrest and reform, and sought to promote the amelioration plan in the colonies. In the year 1823 the "Society for the Gradual Abolition of Slavery" or "Anti-Slavery-Society" was formed. In the

same year Lord BATHURST, the SECRETARY OF STATE for the colonies conveyed a despatch to all governors of the British colonies in which certain clearly specified objectives of the policy of amelioration were specified (DOOKHAN 1983: 86-87).

The main suggestions were as follows:

- More religious education and promotion of Christian marriages between slaves
- Evidence of slaves in court
- Concessions concerning the manumission of slaves as well as social measures for children, disabled and sick freed slaves
- Slaves families should under no circumstance be broken up. Also the habit of selling slaves for the payment of their owners' debts was to be discontinued.
- Measures concerning the punishment of slaves: the prohibition of flogging women and of the use of the whip in the field, the prevention of any domestic punishment whatever until the day following that on which the offence may have been committed, the prohibition of punishments exceeding three lashes; a regular entry should be made in a plantation book to be kept for that purpose.
- The granting of the right to possess property as well as the establishment of a savings-bank

(BPP/ST/68/1: 9/7/1823, p. 278)

In a report of the PROCUREUR GENERAL, SENESCHAL and PROCUREUR DU ROI of St. Lucia, dated December 1st, 1823, it is stated that some proposals, as for example the right of the slaves to give evidence in a court, were already considered in the local laws. Other proposals such as the establishment of a savings-bank for slaves were considered superfluous and refused. Regarding concessions of punishment it is mentioned that such changes would give the death blow to the subordination of slaves and would essentially compromise the safety of the masters (BPP/ST/68/1: 1/12/1823, p. 278).

On May 15th, 1824, Governor BLACKWELL of St. Lucia informed the SECRETARY OF STATE BATHURST that some of the recommended measures could not be carried into effect with safety. He saw an endangering of the white population as they were a numerical minority and the military of St. Lucia could not secure an efficient defence. Thereto he referred also to the geographical situation of the colony which made the possibilities of communication between the districts difficult. Also the ecclesiastical establishment of the island which according to the opinion of the governor *"would so powerfully operate to the maintenance of tranquillity"* he referred to them as *"in a state of perfect infancy"*. Furthermore he pointed to a rumour existing among the slaves in 1823 because of a misunderstanding by the slaves of the resolutions of the

House of Commons regarding the amelioration of the living conditions of the slaves. On this occasion he expressed his opinion as follows:

> "With respect to the Slaves, the state of ignorance and simplicity in which Major Gen. Mainwaring has declared them to be may be supposed to have rendered them last year less apt to receive an ill-impression from the Resolutions of the House of Commons than those of any other Colony – Having however notwithstanding this ignorance received an impression, vaguely perhaps, in the distant quarters, but positively that their freedoms had been sent out to them, and were detained from them by the Local Government, or their Masters; it will strike your Lordship at once that this impression is infinitely more dangerous in the uncultivated minds of the Slave Class of this Colony than it would be in the minds of the more civilized Slave of Barbados, Antigua, or indeed of any other: for St. Lucia in this respect is unquestionably the last."

(CO 253/18/1: 15/5/1824)

On February 28th, 1825, Mr. JEREMIE was appointed First President of the Court of Appeal. His mission was a revision of the slave laws. In a letter of February 1825 he wrote to the Governor of St. Lucia:

> "We are unquestionably required to adopt the full spirit of Earl Bathurst's Instructions to the local circumstances of this colony, and to give the Slave the advantage of every benefit intended for him; …
>
> It is useless to ameliorate the Slaves' condition in some points, whilst many harsh and long since obsolete laws may be revived to their injury."

(CO 253/19/2: 18/2/1825)

On February 8th, 1826, a new Slave Law was passed by the PRIVY COUNCIL of St. Lucia. It considered the suggested amelioration measures of Lord BATHURST and came into force on June 1st, 1826 (CO 253/22/1: 9/2/1826).

By desire of Lord BATHURST the new Slave Law was slightly altered on April 24th, 1827, with an ORDER IN COUNCIL (CO 255/1/2: 24/4/1827).

With a letter dated July 28th, 1827, Mr. JEREMIE informed the SECRETARY OF STATE in London about the effects of the new slave law:

> "In every respect, except in the discipline of some of the gangs, I should say without hesitation and am prepared at all times to prove facts, that it has been productive of unmingled benefit. The holding of property, their right of giving evidence, of being allowed to be parties to suits and the regulations respecting the hours of labour together in short with every Clause in that law amounting to 122 excepting the Compulsory Manumission, those relating to discipline and Sunday markets, I have never heard an objection, even from Planters and I believe as far as this Colony goes, no kind of objection is likely to be started."

But according to a petition of "certains Planteurs" of July 1827 (CO 253/23/1: July 1827) there were objections. The planters objected against the appointment of a PROTECTOR OF SLAVES. This title was given to the PROCUREUR GENERAL to whom the slaves could complain because of unjustified treatment by their owners. The planters were of the opinion that a slave should only have his master as protector. A PROTECTOR OF SLAVES who had the right to supervise the slave owners would give rise to a feeling of hatred and enmity between master and slaves. Next they referred to the limitation of their power to punish slaves. They also mentioned the regulations for working slaves in the night. They found such regulations superfluous as they saw therein an allegation that they would overwork their slaves without them.

According to a letter of Governor STEWART of St. Lucia from March 1829 the planters complied with the new laws:

> *"I have much satisfaction in stating, that, so far as I have seen, matters go on well. The laws are obeyed, the Instructions with regard to the slave population and other subjects are strictly attended; and in the short experience I have had, I have every reason to believe that the Planters are well disposed to accommodate themselves to the recent changes in the Slave Laws; …"*

(CO 253/26/2: 10/3/1829)

But objections on the side of the planters existed. In a Petition of "certains Planteurs et Propriétaires de St. Lucie" to the Governor of St. Lucia, dated June 1829 it is stated:

> *"Les nègres interprétent mal les dispositions de la loi à leur égard, se sont formé l'idée (et cette opinion se progage journellement parmi eux) que leur emancipation immediate est une mesure que le Gouvernment a en vue; mais que leurs Maìtres s'y opposent.*
> *De là, le découragement qui se fait remarquer dans quelques atteliers; de là, les désordres, l'arrogance, l'insubordination qui se sont manifestés dans d'autres. Il est en effet de toute notoriété que des Esclaves connus autrefois par leur attachement et leur dèvouement à leur maître se sont, depuis ces Ordonnances, refusés aux travaux ordinaires de l'Habitation, et mème, à fournir au propriétaire les objets journaliers et de première nécessité.*

(CO 253/26/3: June 1829)

Governor STEWART referred to the above mentioned petition in a letter to the SECRETARY OF STATE MURRAY in London as follows:

"..., but I may be permitted to say that altho' the apprehensions and anticipations of these Gentlemen incline them to take too gloomy a view of the subject, I have found them well disposed, and ready to obey the law in all its provisions; and altho' that their statements with regard to the influence the law has on the disposition and conduct of the Slaves, are in substance correct."

(CO 253/26/4: 25/6/1829)

On February 2nd, 1830, the British government enacted an ORDER IN COUNCIL which concerned further provisions for ameliorating the living conditions of slaves (BPP/ST/77/1: 2/2/1830, p. 27). This law was discussed and accepted by the PRIVY COUNCIL of St. Lucia on April 20th, 1830 (CO 256/2/1: 20/4/1830).

The planters of St. Lucia protested against these laws also because of economic losses:

"In consequence of the Slave Laws enforced by His Majesty's Ministers the Crops of this Colony have been yearly diminishing and are now reduced to a quantity hardly adequate to pay the expenditure of Estates at the ruinous rate for which West India Produce is selling and has been for the last three years."

(CO 253/30/1: 31/10/1831)

On November 2nd, 1831, the British government enacted another ORDER IN COUNCIL (BPP/ST/79/1: 2/11/1831). The principle provisions were:

- The extension of the power of the PROTECTOR OF SLAVES
- The general shortening of the daily working time to nine hours (Sundays and holidays were free: compare chapter "4.7.5. Labour conditions on the plantations", pp. 168-184)
- The alteration of the stipulations regarding the providing of the slaves. An important point was the self-providing of the slaves with provisions. They should generally get a piece of land for planting their own provisions.

This ORDER IN COUNCIL was proclaimed by Governor BOZON of St. Lucia on December 24th, 1831, and came into force on January 7th, 1832 (CO 255/2/1: 24/12/1831, p. 106).
This law caused vehement protests. "Planters, Merchants and other Inhabitants" wrote in January 1832 as follows:

"That the Order in Council of the 2nd November is utterly destructive of our rights and property in our slaves! Vests an individual in the character of a slave protector, with an inquisitorial and despotic power over every free inhabitant, which they have never exercised over their slaves! Deprives the planter of the means of reaping the produce of his land; yet compels him to furnish his labourers daily with double the quantity of provisions supplied to the King's troops, and to give them clothing such as their masters are, in many instances, themselves destitute of.

That the inhabitants, convinced of the impracticability of carrying into effect this unjust and ruinous measure, find themselves forced to oppose, by every constitutional means, the execution of these enactments."

(CO 253/37/4: 4/1/1832)

Another protest by 23 "Managers and Others" was as follows:

"That your Memorialists approach your Excellency with feelings of the deepest sorrow and despondency, on being apprised that it is your Excellency's determination to enforce the execution of the late Order of His Majesty in Council, for the government and management of slaves and properties in this island.

That your Memorialists are fully aware of the ruin that must follow the operation of several clauses of that Order in Council, to the slaves themselves, as well as to the estates to which they are attached; as it will be impossible for the estates to give the extravagant quantity of provisions specified in the case of giving rations; and in the case of giving land, which must be the case on all estates in this island, the slaves are sure to fall into despondency and die, when they find themselves entirely dependent on the produce of their gardens for subsistence, and deprived of their weekly allowance of salt provisions, which was their greatest support and comfort, and which can never be made up to them by substituting frivolous articles of wearing, which they do not make use of in this climate, and of which they do not feel the least want.

That the abridgment of the hours of labour by the said Order in Council, deprives your Memorialists of the power of manufacturing the crops of the estates under their charge, inasmuch as that manufacture absolutely requires a continual attendance, with but very short interruptions, during its process, which, according to the said abridgments, cannot be accomplished.

That the said Order in Council having subjected the government and management of slaves and properties to the decision and judgment of officers entirely unacquainted with the intricacies and peculiarities of the subjects placed under their control, the Memorialists, by the smallest act of nonconformity to these absurd and perplexed regulations, would be liable to enormous penalties, which would deprive them of the means of existence.

That your Memorialists, convinced that under the operation of many clauses of that Order in Council, and from its tenor as a whole, it will be utterly impossible to conduct the estates under their charge with any advantage to their employers, or safety to themselves; and that the execution of the said Order in Council will immediately drive them, however reluctantly, to the necessity of giving up their situations, although their only means of subsistence, unless they are guaranteed against such a cruel and vexatious law.

Your Memorialists, therefore, most humbly implore your Excellency to avert the ruin that must fall upon them, and upon the properties under their charge, from the said Order in Council, by delaying to enforce the execution of the said Order in Council until His Majesty's gracious pleasure is known thereupon, in answer to the humble representations of the inhabitants of this colony on their most perilous and unhappy situation."

(CO 253/37/5: Jan. 1832)

In spite of these protests the said ORDER IN COUNCIL came into force – as already mentioned – on January 7th, 1832. With a strike of all store- and shopkeepers of Castries – from January 16th 1832 on all shops were kept closed – the protests reached their height. On this occasion Governor BOZON published the following proclamation:

"Whereas it has appeared to me that some evil disposed Individuals have conspired and combined to impede and oppose the measures of the Executive Government of this Colony, and have induced others by their influence and example to co-operate in such measures:

And whereas under the influence of such illegal combination, the several Stores and Shops of this Town have been closed since the morning of Monday 16th instant – all business suspended – and all classes of the Inhabitants exposed to serious and distressing privations by such proceedings:

And whereas such measures are not only calculated, but evidently intended to render inoperative His Majesty's Order in Council of the 2nd of November last, for ameliorating the condition of the Slaves in this Colony, by affording a pretext to inconsiderate or designing persons of evading His Most Gracious Majesty's humane and benevolent intentions towards the Slave population of this Colony, under the plea of inability to obtain supplies of food and clothing for that portion of His Majesty's subjects:

And whereas such conduct is calculated to produce excitement among the Slave population and most injurious consequences to the community at large, and to afford a pretext of representing the Slave population as undeserving of His Majesty's favour and protection.

Now, I, MARK ANTHONY BOZON, Senior Officer Administering the Government of Saint Lucia, acting under the power and authority in me vested, do hereby proclaim that all persons who have heretofore entered into or may hereafter enter into such illegal combination will be held responsible to the Laws for high crimes and misdemeanours, and be punished accordingly. And I do hereby order and command all Merchants, Shopkeepers, and all other persons in this Town, and throughout this Colony, concerned in such illegal combination, to reopen their Stores and Shops, and legally resume their several callings on or before Monday Morning the 23rd instant, under pain of the consequences: And I do hereby order and recommend all His Majesty's Loyal subjects within this Colony, to govern themselves according to this Proclamation."

(CO 253/37/1: 18/1/1832)

A further protest of March 27th, 1832 was published in the "London Gazette" in May 1832:

"The Lords of your Majesty's Privy Council have advised your Majesty to promulgate, in this Colony, an Order in Council, dated the 2nd of November last, which, under the specious pretext of ameliorating the condition of the slaves, is subversive of the rights, and destructive to the property, of their owners. ...

Wherefore, we humbly pray your Majesty, as the guardian of the laws and the fountain of justice in your dominions, either altogether to repeal the Order in Council of the 2nd November last, or to cause the following reasonable modifications to be made therein: ..."

(Z/OPL/LG: 27/3/1832, p. 1219)

The suggestions for modification were as follows:

- The limitation of the power of the PROTECTOR OF SLAVES
- The increase of the daily working time in the crop time from nine hours to ten for agricultural labour and to twelve hours for manufacturing labour. (On Sundays and holidays slaves were not obliged to work).
- Demand for an examination if the new regulations respecting food and clothing are sufficient to secure the comfort of the slaves

With the increase of the daily working time to twelve hours in the crop time Governor FARQUHARSON of St. Lucia complied with the wishes of the plantation owners in a proclamation dated January 3rd, 1833 (CO 255/2/4:3/1/1833,p.181).

From a report of the first prison judge of St. Lucia it follows that the new laws were not generally obeyed:

"The first Prison Judge is clearly of opinion that the law of 2nd November 1831 is not generally obeyed throughout the Colony. The Protector of Slaves brought before him eleven complaints against individuals accused of contravention to the law. In nine of these cases the offender was found guilty and a penalty imposed on him."
(CO 253/43/1: 3/1/1833)

In a record of the "Proprietary Body" of St. Lucia dated in January 1833 the effects of the now ORDER IN COUNCIL were described very negatively:

"6thly. That for twelve months the Inhabitants of this unfortunate Colony have suffered under every species of tyranny and vexation. By obstinate attempts to force into operation the absurd regulations of the King in Council of the 2nd November, the Slaves have been totally estranged from their Owners: unexampled insubordination reigns amongst the gangs; the cultivation has been so greatly neglected, that the Crop, now on the ground, will not exceed that of the past year; robberies are daily committed by the Slaves, to an extent unexampled in the Colony – even the working cattle are not safe from their depredations, which pass with impunity."

(CO 253/43/3: 28/1/1833)

On February 23rd, 1833, Governor FARQUHARSON referred to the comment of the "Proprietary Body" and argued against it as follows:

"With respect to the 6th resolution I have known of nothing deserving the name of Insubordination, except on two Estates; the slaves on the one were brought to a sense of duty by the Commissary Commandant, …, and the desired end was attained without difficulty of any occurrence worthy of further notice in either case.

… the present Crop will exceed considerably that of the past year. I am not aware that daily robberies are more numerous, or committed with more impunity, than at any other period heretofore, because all the laws, Civil and Commercial, are, and have been for a length of time in full force."

(CO 253/43/4: 23/2/1833)

4.2.2 Summary

As the British conquered St. Lucia in the year 1803, they took over the French Slave Laws which were part of the CODE DE LA MARTINIQUE. These French Laws were renewed in some cases by British enactments (ordinances, proclamations) and were valid up to the year 1826. On January 1st, 1808, the British law for the abolition of the slave trade came into force.

According to a movement in Britain to ameliorate the living conditions of the slaves the British government took measures in the colonies. The first suggestions of amelioration reached the colonial government in St. Lucia in the year 1823 by a letter of the SECRETARY OF STATE BATHURST. These suggestions became law in St. Lucia on June 1st, 1826. Further extensive amelioration laws were enacted in St. Lucia in the years 1830 (April 20th) and 1831 (December 24th).
Between the slave owners of St. Lucia and the British colonial government and the British government in London, there were discussions about the amelioration measures as the slave owners of St. Lucia often protested very vehemently against the directed measures. But because of the political system of St. Lucia the amelioration measures were enforced by the British government with ORDERS IN COUNCIL.

4.3 Abolition of slavery and beginning of the emancipation period

4.3.1 Detailed description

This chapter describes the abolition of slavery in St. Lucia and examines also the reactions of the slave owners to this event. Moreover the main legal provisions which were valid in the following four year-emancipation period are pointed out.

On June 26th, 1833, Governor FARQUHARSON of St. Lucia confirmed the receipt of a resolution of the HOUSE OF COMMONS concerning the abolition of slavery dated May 14th, 1833 (CO 253/44/1: 26/6/1833). In a letter dated August 1833 with which the governor acknowledged the receipt of further resolutions of the HOUSE OF COMMONS he reported the opinion of the slave owners of St. Lucia concerning the abolition of slavery:

> *"All proprietors and managers of Slaves in this Colony appear to me extremely anxious to learn the ultimate decision of both Houses of Parliament upon this momentous measure, to the wisdom of which they appear calmly resigned, ..., they seem apprehensive only that the apprentice will not give them a sufficient quantity of labour to enable them to bring their Crops to market."*

Furthermore he referred to the general tranquil situation:

> *"On the other hand I am happy in having to state that generally speaking the Slaves in this Colony have shown no insubordinate disposition since His Majesty's gracious intentions towards them have become publicly known, although upon some of the Estates an evident relaxation in their labour did manifest itself amongst a few of each gang."*

(CO 253/44/2: 2/8/1833)

In August 1833 the British Parliament enacted the final law for the abolition of slavery:

**"Act for the Abolition of Slavery throughout the British Colonies;
for promoting the Industry of the Manumitted Slaves;
and for compensating the persons hitherto entitled to the Services
of such Slaves"**

This law came into force on August 1st, 1834. The main provisions of this law were as follows:

- From August 1st, 1834, slavery was to be abolished
- Slave children under six years of age and all children born to slaves were to be free
- All other slaves were to serve a period of apprenticeship to their masters; in the case of field slaves until 1st of August 1840 and non-field slaves until 1st of August 1838
- APPRENTICES (the name for the slaves in the emancipation period) were to work for three-quarters of the working week for their masters
- The apprenticeship might be brought to an end before the specified time either by voluntary discharge by the master or by purchase by the APPRENTICE
- The APPRENTICE was to continue to be provided by his master with food, clothing, lodging and medicine as he was accustomed to have during slavery
- The superintendence of the APPRENTICES and jurisdiction over them was entrusted to STIPENDIARY MAGISTRATES
- Slave owners were to be compensated for the loss of their property in slaves and grant of 20 million Pounds was allocated by the British government for this purpose

(DOOKHAN 1983: 89-90)

Regarding the obligation of the field slaves for working till August 1st, 1840, it shall be mentioned that the emancipation period for field slaves was abridged to the 1st August 1838, the same date as for the non-field slaves (cp. "Chapter 4.4.2. Abridgement of the emancipation period for FIELD-APPRENTICES: general reasons, p. 61")

On July 12th, 1834, a new Governor, DUDLEY HILL, took over the government in St. Lucia (CO 253/46/1: 1/8/1834). After his appointment he made a journey round the colony to inform the slaves personally of the new regulations. This speech to the slaves was published in the newspaper "St. Lucia Gazette" on July 30th, 1834, as follows:

"My Friends, - You are aware that I have recently arrived from England to be Governor of this Colony. You see, I lose no time in coming amongst you; and my reason is, that I know you have been for a length of time past expecting some great benefit to be conferred upon you. I have come to tell you, you are right. – The King and the People of England, with your Masters in this Country, have mutually made sacrifices in order that you should enjoy the blessings of Freedom.

On the 1st day of next month, the name of Slave is to be forgotten – no man is to call another a Slave – You are no longer to be Slaves – You are free – not idle free people, but industrious free people, bound to labour moderately for your Masters in return for allowances which your Masters, as they have hitherto done, will be bound to furnish you. Now, my friends, attend to what I say – believe what I say – I am here in this Country representing the Great and Good King of England, who, with his People, is *your Friend; therefore, my duty is also to be your Friend; - for your own sakes, believe and trust the words I speak.*

The benefits which you are to have from the 1st of next month are very great. Whilst you are slaves, your children and your children's children are slaves; - on the 1st of next month all children under 6 years of age are free – all born after the 1st next month are born free. As slaves, you had to work for your Masters 9 hours every day or 54 hours every week; - as free apprenticed labourers, you are to work 7 ½ hours per day or 45 hours per week.

As slaves, you were to work these 9 hours every day of every week of your whole lives; - after the 1st next month, you are to work these 7 ½ hours per day for six years, or, if you are domestics, for four years only. The domestics have the shorter term allotted to them because their services are without remission. You can release yourselves by purchase, at a fair valuation, from the service of your apprenticeship, in like manner as hitherto you had the right of buying your freedom from slavery. Yet during apprenticeship you are to receive from your employers the same allowances as when they had from you your full time.

As a slave your master can order you to be punished; - as a free apprenticed labourer, you are not subject to this authority – The King has appointed Special Justices to decide on all differences that may arise between you and your masters, with authority to prevent any wrong being done to you, and also to punish you when you do wrong; and he alone has this power. These Officers have not yet arrived, but this Gentleman, by my appointment, is to be your Magistrate until the other does arrive. Obey him – respect him – for he has my authority.

Do not deceive yourselves: every man in this world must work; GOD, who made us all, has ordered that we should live by the sweat of our brow. Let me warn you against so great a mistake as supposing, because your master has no longer the power of punishing you that therefore no punishment at all can happen to you. The Magistrate has full power to punish you for every fault you commit – has full power to make you perform the 7 ½ hours of labour you owe to your master – has full power to punish you, if you are lazy, careless, negligent, absent from work, impudent or disobedient.

As the good things of which I have been before telling you are secured to you and your children, to be sure you in your turn shall receive punishment if you do not honestly and fairly work for your masters the whole time to which by law he is entitled whilst the apprenticeship lasts. Some people tell me, that perhaps you will try not to work at all. I cannot believe you to be such fools, or so ungrateful, or so wicked. Work you must, the moderate time required from you by law. If any of you dare to resist the law, and think that by combining together you can evade or set it at defiance, be assured I shall instantly come amongst you – not as now, to do you good and advice you, but severely to punish the offender. My duty is to have the law obeyed – to protect all men and their properties. This duty, depend upon it, I will fully perform, if but one single act of general insubordination take place amongst you, whereby your master's property is endangered and the public peace disturbed – That moment, I will be on the spot, with the King's Troops and other His Majesty's loyal subjects. But, my friends, I trust, (and indeed, from the first moment of my coming amongst you, my confidence on the score is increased) that your conduct will not be such as to require my presence for any purpose of visiting the guilty.

For your magistrate and from your masters too, you may learn many other things relating to your rights and to the duties you are to perform. There is but one other duty and one other privilege which I shall now mention; the duty is a very sacred one – the penalty for its non-performance very severe. As your children are free, they must be supported as free children are supported, that is, by their parents; and for this among other reasons, was the difference of labour between 7 ½ and 9 hours per day granted to you. If, however, your children are left destitute, they may by law be apprenticed, that is, bound to labour until they are 21 years of age.

The privilege of which I have to make mention, is, that at your own free will and pleasure, with denial or interruption whatsoever, you may on every Sabbath day perform Religious Worship at any Church of Chapel in the island; and, my friends, not only when you may next meet at any Place of Worship, but when you leave this spot to-day and return to your domiciles and are in the midst of your children, go down on your knees and thank the Great GOD for the blessings of freedom which I have told you are to be yours in part and your children's altogether after the 1st of next month.
Be grateful to the people of England, who have paid a great deal of money to make you free – be obedient to the laws – and on all occasions you shall have their protection.

Now, my friends, in conclusion, let me once more remind you of all the advantages you derive from this great measure:

1st, That all grown-up persons are required to perform a moderate labour of 7 ½ hours per day, in lieu of 9 hours per day as before; and these 7 ½ hours are for six years only, instead of for all your lives.
2ndly, That in like manner as you could purchase freedom when you were slaves, so now you may purchase release from apprenticeship.
3rdly, That children under 6 years of age, and all born after the 1st of next month, are free.
4thly, That the power of inflicting punishment is no longer arbitrary with your Masters, but depends upon the decision of the Magistrate.
5thly, That the most entire liberty is given to you to frequent on Sundays any Place of Worship you please.

And, my friends, I have to tell you that by proclamation I have appointed the 1st of next month, the day from which all these great things take effect, to be a day of general thanksgiving to GOD for these blessings, which, most heartily and sincerely I hope you may for ever enjoy your peace, content, and happiness."

(Z/CO 253/46/1: 30/7/1934)

On August 1ˢᵗ, 1834, Governor DUDLEY HILL proclaimed the abolition of slavery in St. Lucia:

> *"I do hereby proclaim and make known that by virtue of an Act of Parliament passed in the session held in the 3ʳᵈ and 4ᵗʰ Years of the reign of His Most Gracious Majesty King WILLIAM the IV., Slavery ceased on this present 1ˢᵗ day of August and by virtue of the said Act it is now abolished in this Colony henceforth and forever and I do further proclaim that from and after this day praedial labourers are to become apprentices for six years and non-praedial labourers for four years and I do strictly exhort, enjoin, and commend all such apprenticed labourers as aforesaid to be obedient to their masters and those in authority to be industrious to their habits and submissive to the law."*
>
> (CO 255/2/2: 1/8/1834, p. 268)

On the same day in the evening the Governor informed the SECRETARY OF STATE in London about the proclamation and the tranquil situation:

> *"... that the announcement which took place in my presence and in that of the principle inhabitants of the Island, was received with the most hearty and grateful expression of loyalty and that the public tranquillity remains most perfectly undisturbed at the late hour of the day at which I have the honour to transmit this Despatch."*
>
> (CO 253/46/1: 1/8/1834)

On August 16ᵗʰ, 1834, Governor DUDLEY HILL published a proclamation in which he cautioned against the spreading of unfounded rumours concerning commotions in the district of Micoud:

> *"Whereas various false reports respecting the state of the population in distant parts of the Island are prevalent and amongst other mischievous summons there is now current one to the effect that the Militia of the Quarter of Micoud had been under the necessity of rising fire-arms against His Majesty's free subjects, the apprentices of the said quarter, and having every reason to believe the same to be unfounded."*

He further confirmed the willingness of working of the APPRENTICES as well as the general tranquil situation in the colony:

> *"I have thought fit to issue this my proclamation for the purpose of reassuring the public mind and of making generally known that the recent visits which I have paid to the respective districts of the Colony, have fully satisfied me of the loyalty of the labouring population and have insured me with the fullest confidence that their legal services will henceforth continue to be performed with diligence and the public tranquillity maintained as it hitherto has been wholly undisturbed, ..."*
>
> (CO 255/2/3: 16/8/1834, p. 276)

With a letter of August 26ᵗʰ, 1834, Governor DUDLEY HILL informed the SECRETARY OF STATE SPRING RICE in London about the general situation in St. Lucia:

> "... that the Abolition of Slavery excited in this Island no other emotions amongst the parties most interested than those which so happy and great an event would naturally produce, ..., nor has there been exhibited since (the abolition) any demonstration of public feeling which could give me serious uneasiness respecting the preservation of tranquillity throughout the Colony."

Then he referred to an imprudent behaviour of the white population who were of the opinion that the general peace was only possible with more militia. The governor saw such a measure as superfluous because of the tranquil behaviour of the APPRENTICES. Further he reported about rumours concerning commotions under the workers which were spread by the white population. Because of his personal investigation he referred to these rumours as "imaginary danger". Concerning the labourers he wrote:

> "I had the pleasure to observe that there were no exceptions to the general good behaviour of the labourers, save those which arising from simple misapprehension of the new rights could be remedied gradually and temporarily and except also those breaches of discipline which amongst a large body of people would occur under any system of compulsory labour and which were not less frequent under that just abolished."

He finished his letter as follows:

> "I feel indeed fully warranted by present appearances in allowing His Majesty's Government to entertain an expectation that Saint Lucia will continue free from those emotions to which I learn with regret the tranquillity of Trinidad, St. Christopher and other Islands has been temporarily exposed and I beg you to be assured that I shall not fail to devote all my energies to realize this expectation."

(CO 253/46/3: 26/8/1834)

In November 1834 Governor DUDLEY HILL confirmed again the tranquil conduct of the APPRENTICES:

> "... to inform you that the tranquil and orderly conduct of the apprenticed labourers fully justifies my giving you an assurance which cannot fail be gratifying to His Majesty's Government and that is that the Abolition of Slavery has not up to this period interrupted the industry which was customary previously to that happy event, ..."

(CO 253/46/4: 3/11/1834)

4.3.2 Summary

In summary it can be said that the abolition of slavery in St. Lucia was carried out without special events. Among the slave owners there were suspicious feeling regarding the behaviour of the slaves as they were anxious about the continuity of the work of the slaves as well as about their own security. According to the references not only before the 1st of August 1834 but also after this date there were no interruptions in work and also no commotions.

4.4 The end of the emancipation period

4.4.1 Introduction

The law for the abolition of slavery provided for FIELD-APPRENTICES a six-year and for NON-FIELD-APPRENTICES a four-year emancipation period. Shortly before the end of the four-year emancipation period of the NON-FIELD-APPRENTICES the British government decided to limit the emancipation period for FIELD-APPRENTICES also to four years.

This chapter deals in the first section with the common reasons of the British government for limiting the emancipation period generally to four years. Then the following points will be considered: the general feeling of the APPRENTICES before the end of the emancipation period, the classification problems between FIELD- and NON-FIELD-APPRENTICES as well as the discussion about the general ending of the emancipation period in St. Lucia. The last section refers to the common course of the 1st August 1838.

4.4.2 Abridgement of the emancipation period for FIELD-APPRENTICES: general reasons

By a law of April 1838 the British government decided to end the emancipation period for all APPRENTICES in general from 1st August 1838. As reasons for this decision DOOKHAN (1983: 99-100) point to the following facts:

- Some planters envisaged definite gains. It would no longer be necessary to provide the APPRENTICES with food, clothes, medical care and housing. Also they would pay the lowest wages which would be necessary to attract just the number of labourers required for work.
- The British government was beginning to have doubts about the benefits of apprenticeship and that the scheme was not providing

the APPRENTICES with the kind of training for freedom which was envisaged.

- The "Anti-Slavery-Society" began to criticize the emancipation system.
- The humanitarians were arguing that it was time the APPRENTICES should be free.
- All APPRENTICES – field as well as non-field workers – were looking forward to being free. To withhold freedom from the FIELD-APPRENTICES could have led to much dissatisfaction and possibly violence.
- In some colonies it was difficult to differentiate between the FIELD- and NON-FIELD-APPRENTICES. As a result of the shortage of field labourers it was necessary to supplement the labour force by recruitment from among the domestics.

4.4.3 The situation among the APPRENTICES in St. Lucia in the first half year of 1838

In addition to the following reports it should be mentioned that in St. Lucia the abridgement of the emancipation period for FIELD-APPRENTICES was publicly proclaimed on 13th July 1838 (cp. chapter 4.4.5. Discussion for the general ending of the emancipation period for all APPRENTICES with 1st August 1838 in St. Lucia, pp. 66-67). All of the following reports were made before the 13th July 1838.

In March 1838 Governor MEIN of St. Lucia addressed a circular letter to the STIPENDIARY MAGISTRATES in which he expressed his apprehensions that the FIELD-APPRENTICES had imagined that they would be emancipated in August 1838. He requested the STIPENDIARY MAGISTRATES to make relevant reports as well as to inform him if disturbances were to be expected (CO 253/64/1: 22/3/1838).

From the following reports of the STIPENDIARY MAGISTRATES it follows that in general there were no special reasons to apprehend a disturbance:

1st district (Castries, Anse La Raye)

> "As far as my experience extends, I beg to observe that the purport of your letter gives the first allusion to such a subject that has ever come to my knowledge.
> Nor have I reason to think that any excitement tending to insubordination will occur at that period; at least judging from the tranquillity and apparent contentment at present evinced by both classes of the apprentices in the district under my care."
> (CO 253/64/2: 10/4/1838)

2nd district (Gros-Islet, Dauphin)

In this report the STIPENDIARY MAGISTRATE refers to the war period at the end of the 18th century when the slaves were freed by the French in the year 1794 and enslaved again by the British two years later (cp. also chapter 4.1. The effects of the French Revolution in St. Lucia, the wars of the Brigands and the final conquer by the British, pp. 43-45).

> *"... that in my visits throughout the second district I made the most minute inquiry as to the feelings entertained by the apprentices who are praedials attached, to be emancipated with the non-praedials in August next, and have ascertained that they are generally well acquainted with the position in which they are placed under the Act for the Abolition of Slavery.*
>
> *In some few cases the apprentices appear even to be doubtful as to their being finally emancipated in 1840, and this feeling has arisen from occurrences during the French revolution, still fresh in the recollection of many of the old apprentices, when the slaves were declared free, and were compelled after a short period again to relapse into a state of slavery. In my communications with several of the non-praedials who have lately purchased the unexpired term of their apprenticeship, I have asked the reason of their not preferring to wait until the 1st of August next, as the period was so near at hand, when they would be freed without the expense of purchasing, and have invariably been answered that they prefer buying their freedom, in consequence of obtaining a paper (meaning the Act of affranchisement), which would make their freedom more secure; this I believe to be a general feeling. On the liberation of the non-praedials, on the 1st of August next, there may be some trifling ebullition of feeling evinced by the praedials attached, but I do not apprehend the occurrence of anything of such a nature as to create any apprehension as to the result on the part of government."*

(CO 253/64/3: 8/4/1838)

3rd district (Soufrière, Choiseul)

> *"I have the honour to report, in reply to your letter of the 22nd instant, that there does exist in the minds of the majority of the praedial apprentices in this district, an idea that they will be freed on the 1st of August next, together with the personals; but I do not anticipate any serious disturbing at that period, inasmuch as the idea which they appear to entertain is a vague and indefinite one, and I am quite sure that no combined or concerted measures have been at all contemplated by the apprentices, tending to insubordination, on the 1st of August next. They may, perhaps, for a few days be disinclined to work as usual, but as far as my humble opinion goes, I think the authority of the magistrates will be quite sufficient to put down any slight disorder arising from the above mentioned cause."*

(CO 253/64/4: 28/3/1838)

4th district (Vieux Fort, Laborie)

"In reply to your confidential communication of the 22nd ultimo, I have the honour of stating for His Excellency's information that, after minute inquiry, I have no good reason to suppose that the praedial attached apprenticed labourers have imagined that they will be emancipated with the non-praedials in August next.

Some months ago a few alarmists circulated a report of a similar nature, which caused much unnecessary apprehension, and which, on investigation by order of His Excellency Colonel Bunbury, had in my opinion no real foundation. Although, as far as my information goes, there exists at present no excitement in the minds of the apprenticed population tending to insubordination, nor in my opinion any great likelihood of its occurrence at the period above mentioned, ..."

(CO 253/64/5: 9/4/1838)

5th district (Micoud, Praslin, Dennery)

"In reply to your confidential letter of the 23rd instant, I have the honour to state that I am not aware of any disposition on the part of the apprenticed labourers of the 5th district to insubordination on the approaching 1st of August."

(CO 253/64/6: 28/3/1838)

Graphic representation of the mentioned districts:

Division of districts extracted
From a map of St. Lucia from
The year 1847 (BPP/CG/4/1:
1847, p. 518)

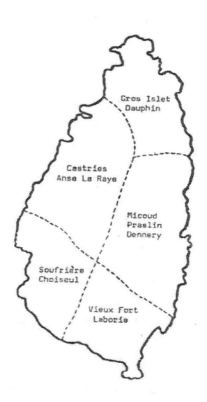

At the beginning of June 1838 the STIPENDIARY MAGISTRATES of the 1st, 2nd and 5th district confirmed a tranquil feeling under the APPRENTICES (CO 253/64/7-9: 1/, 2/, resp. 4/6/1838). Other situations were described by the STIPENDIARY MAGISTRATES of the 3rd and 4th district:

3rd district (Soufrière, Choiseul)

> "I have the honour to report that in this District the Praedial Apprentices begin to manifest symptoms of uneasiness respecting the Emancipation of the Personal & Trade Apprentices on the 1st of August next – On several Estates they are not working with the same cheerfulness as heretofore – and many of the inhabitants, (and I think not without some reason) unto anticipate considerable disturbance on the Estates at that period – in other respects all appears going on as usual –"
>
> (CO 253/64/10: 1/6/1838)

4th district (Vieux Fort, Laborie)

> "The conduct of the apprenticed labourers has not been during the last month as satisfactory as it was wished to be. Considerable excitement prevails on several Estates in the district on account of a report spread about by some evil disposed persons that all apprentices, to whatever class belonging, will be freed indiscriminately on the 1st August next. This is the more to be regretted as till very lately the Praedials were perfectly contented and had no idea or expectation that they were to be freed sooner than 1st August 1840, which was so fully explained to them at the commencement of the Apprenticeship by His Excellency Sir Dudley Hill."
>
> (CO 253/64/11: 1/6/1838)

One month later the situation in the 4th district had been calmed down. The STIPENDIARY MAGISTRATE reported respecting the APPRENTICES: "conduct good" (CO 253/64/12: 2/7/1838).

4.4.4 Classification problems of the APPRENTICES in St. Lucia

The fact of the difficult classification between FIELD- and NON-FIELD-APPRENTICES mentioned by DOOKHAN (cp. pp. 61-62) applied to St. Lucia.

On September 4th, 1837, Governor BUNBURY of St. Lucia pointed in his instructions to the STIPENDIARY MAGISTRATES to the following:

> "On the second point, I anticipate much confusion from the disputes likely to arise regards classification, for, I apprehend that many persons who have hitherto been considered and returned as domestics have been subsequently improperly designated Praedials attached, thereby depriving them of their just rights;"
>
> (CO 253/56/1: 4/9/1837)

He instructed the STIPENDIARY MAGISTRATES to examine this matter.

In February 1838 the governor published a proclamation in which he pointed also to grievances concerning the designation of the APPRENTICES. He requested the inhabitants of St. Lucia to assist the STIPENDIARY MAGISTRATES in clearing up this matter (CO 255/3/1: 13/2/1838), p. 131). In the same month the British government enacted for St. Lucia an ORDER IN COUNCIL which demanded a correction of the classification of the APPRENTICES. An extract therefrom is as follows:

> "And whereas, there is reason to believe that Apprentices properly "Non-Praedials" have been in some instances erroneously registered as "Praedials" and it is expedient that provision should be made for the correction of such erroneous classification in all cases in which the fact can be clearly established;"
>
> (CO 253/65/1: 15/2/1838)

Further sources concerning this classification problem were not available to the author.

4.4.5 Discussion for the general ending of the emancipation period for all APPRENTICES with 1st August 1838 in St. Lucia

The law regarding the ending of the emancipation period of FILED-APPRENTICES enacted by the British government in April 1838 produced protests in St. Lucia. In a petition of May 1838 (CO 253/61/1: 24/5/1838) "Planters, Merchants and other Inhabitants" of St. Lucia wrote as follows:

> "Your petitioners denounce this attempt as a breach of good faith. The Act of Parliament of 1834 secured to them the services of the praedial apprentices for the full term of six years, as an integral part of the price for which they were compelled to surrender their properties, and they solemnly protest against any abridgement of the term as a violation of a great and solemn national compact, and as an act of unqualified spoliation. ...
>
> Many of your petitioners have made extensive purchases of property, and stand pledged for themselves and on behalf of others (to whom they have made advances) to the payment of very large sums of money. Property to an immense amount has been disposed of under judicial sale, and loans have been obtained from your Majesty's Government, from whence has arisen a variety of new contracts and engagements, for the punctual fulfilment of which the contracting parties stand pledged in their properties and persons. ...
>
> Suddenly roused from a peaceful and contented acquiescence in their present lot into a state of unexpected freedom, they will not fail to consider the change as a release by superior authority from the irksome

tax daily labour in the service of their employer; and instead of remaining on the estates, to continue the regular cultivation of the properties to which they are attached, the evil-disposed will be found wandering through the country, and crowding to the town, indulging in the habits of idleness and vice, with only an inefficient police force at command, wholly insufficient to suppress their disorderly conduct; others will seek, by the cultivation of waste land, abounding in all parts of the colony (and from which it will be impossible to exclude them), the means of procuring a precarious subsistence; the aged and infirm, for whom no adequate provision has yet been made, will be exposed to all the horrors of indigence and want, whilst only a few better disposed may remain upon the estates, whose labour, however, will be wholly insufficient to carry on the cultivation."

Also the EXECUTIVE AND LEGISLATIVE COUNCIL of St. Lucia opposed the preposition of the British government with the exception of one vote (CO 253/61/2: 28/5/1838).

In spite of these protests the British government enforced a law and with a proclamation dated 13th July 1838 the emancipation period for all FIELD-APPRENTICES was abolished with 1st August 1838 by the Governor of the Windward-formation, Mac GREGOR:

"... That all and every the Persons who on the First day of August in the present Year of Our Lord, One Thousand Eight Hundred and Thirty-eight, in, under, and by virtue of the Act of the Imperial Parliament first above mentioned[10] were and were to be taken and considered as Apprentices for and during a certain period therein limited, to wit, until the First Day of August, in the Year One Thousand Eight Hundred and Forty, under the Classification and Denomination of Praedial Apprenticed Labourers, shall be and they are hereby declared and pronounced to be to all intents and purposes from and after the said First day of August, in the present Year One Thousand Eight Hundred and Thirty-eight, absolutely free and discharged of and from all manner of Apprenticeship and Obligations whatsoever, (in regard to his, her or their present Masters or Employers) imposed by the said Act."

(CO 255/3/2: 13/7/1838, p. 138)

---

[10] The Governor referred to the law for the abolition of slavery of August 1833; cp. chapter "4.3. Abolition of slavery and beginning of the emancipation period", pp. 55-59.

4.4.6 The 1st August 1838

According to the reports of the STIPENDIARY MAGISTRATES the 1st August 1838 passed in a tranquil atmosphere. Extracts therefrom are as follows:

2nd district (Gros-Islet, Dauphin)

"It is pleasing for me to have it in my power to record the orderly and becoming manner in which the newly emancipated labourers converted them sober on the 1st August; although the weather was very unfavourable, great numbers of them attended divine Service at the Protestant and Catholic Churches in the Town of Castries, ...

... there was not one single instance of misbehaviour on the part of any of the newly liberated Apprentices either in the Town of Castries or this District."

(CO 253/62/1: 3/8/1838)

3rd district (Soufrière, Choiseul)

"The Roman Catholic Churches were crowded by the newly Emancipated Subjects, who are chiefly of that persuasion, and cannot be denied that no description of Persons could have conducted themselves in a more orderly and becoming manner; during the whole of the day there was not a single instance of disturbance, they returned to their homes in the same peaceable manner."

(CO 253/62/2: 2/8/1838)

4th district (Vieux Fort, Laborie)

"... that the important 1st Aug. has passed over in this District without the slightest disturbance; in fact the "Labourers" (lately Apprentices) conduct on that day does them infinite credit, not one drunken man was seen in the Streets of Soufrière, hundreds applied to me to explain to them fully the change in their position in Society."

(CO 253/62/3: 1/8/1838)

The STIPENDIARY MAGISTRATE of the 5th district (Micoud, Praslin, Dennery) designated the behaviour of the APPRENTICES *"with order and regularity* (CO 253/62/4: 4/8/1838).

4.4.7 Summary

The emancipation period was limited to generally four years for FIELD- and NON-FIELD-APPRENTICES by the British government. Originally the emancipation period for FIELD-APPRENTICES should have lasted six years. But for several reasons it was assimilated to that of the NON-FIELD-APPRENTICES. The common reasons for this decision mentioned by DOOKHAN (1983: 99-100) don't correspond in one point exactly with the events in St. Lucia. DOOKHAN mentioned for the first reason a positive feeling of some planters regarding the abridgement of the emancipation period for FIELD-APPRENTICES: it would no longer be necessary to provide the APPRENTICES with food, clothes, medical care and housing. Also the planters would pay the lowest wages which would be necessary to attract just the number of labourers required for work. In St. Lucia, however, the planters protested against this abridgement for fear of the loss of the working power of the APPRENTICES.

Although the abridgement of the emancipation period for FIELD-APPRENTICES was refused by the slave owners as well as by the EXECUTIVE AND LEGISLATIVE COUNCIL in St. Lucia the British government enforced a law for the general ending of the emancipation period with 1st August 1838.

Shortly before the ending of the emancipation period there was a restless feeling under the APPRENTICES in some areas of St. Lucia. But the 1st August 1838 was described by the STIPENDIARY MAGISTRATES as a tranquil day.

4.5 Population

4.5.1 Introduction

BREEN divides the population of St. Lucia in whites, coloured and blacks. He wrote as follows:

> "The population of St. Lucia is formed of the most heterogeneous elements, and comprises every caste and colour under the sun. The chief classification is that of whites, coloured people, and blacks. The whites are divided into creoles and Europeans: the creoles are subdivided into natives of the island and West Indians; and the Europeans into English and French. The English include Irish and Scotch, and the French – Germans, Italians, and Savoyards. The coloured population is no less confused and complicated, being composed of persons from every Colony in the West Indies, and of every grade and denomination from the Carib to the Quadroon. The blacks are natives of the island with a sprinkling of Africans and Martinique refugees."
>
> (BREEN 1844: 158-159)

Regarding the original Indian population it is to be noticed that, except as quoted above, Indians are not especially mentioned in the sources used by the author of this work, neither as people of pure-blood nor of mixed race[11].

In the first section of this chapter the development and the structure of the population in the period from 1772 to 1838 is shown by means of tables, diagrams and reports. The second section refers to the distribution of the sexes of the black population which is shown by means of a table and common reports. In the last section the distribution of the population in the colony is shown. Especially here tables and diagrams are in the foreground.

4.5.2 Development and structure of population

4.5.2.1 Overview of population figures

In the available population reports the population was made up of whites, free non-whites (people of mixed race as well as of blacks) and slaves up to the year 1835. For the free non-whites the following different designations were used: "Coloured", "Free Coloured", "Free People of Colour", "Libres" and "Free Blacks". The slaves ("esclaves") in French were also mentioned as "blacks".

---

[11] According to statements of Prof. Dr. K. WERNHART (Institute of Ethnology Vienna) who conducted research in St. Lucia in the years 1982 and 1983 – there are still pure descendants of Indians, but they are of mixed race.

From the year 1836 the population was divided into whites and "Coloured Population" according to the BLUE BOOKS.

In the following a survey of the available population figures from 1772 to 1838 is given by means of tables and a diagram. The population estimates often vary strongly. In the tables of the BLUE BOOKS additional errors had been made sometimes which were not adopted by the author of this work. In some cases therefore the shown totals diverge slightly from that of the BLUE BOOK. The relevant totals of the BLUE BOOKS are shown in brackets for information (see footnotes).

YEAR	WHITES	%		FREE-NON-WHITES	%		SLAVES	%	TOTAL	SOURCE
1772	2.018	13	"Coloured"	663	4	"Blacks"	12.795	83	15.476	BREEN 1844: 165
1777	2.397	17	"Coloured"	1.050	7	"Blacks"	10.752	76	14.199	MARTIN 1851-57: IV, 125
1789	2.164	10	"Free Coloured"	1.630	7	"Slaves"	18.445	83	22.239	CO 253/14/1: 1/11/1820
1789	2.198	10	"Coloured"	1.588	7	"Blacks"	17.992	83	21.778	BREEN 1844: 165
1799	1.195	7	"Free People of Colour"	1.364	9	"Slaves"	13.391	84	15.950	CO 253/2/3: 1799
1803	1.267	8	"Free People of Colour"	1.749	10	"Negroes and Coloured Slaves"	13.690	82	16.706	CO 253/3/1: 1803
1805	1.533	8	"Free People of Colour"	4.053	21	"Slaves"	13.300	70	18.886	CO 253/3/2: 24/7/1805
1807	1.214	7	"Libres"	1.896	10	"Esclaves"	14.967	83	18.077	CO 253/7/2: 30/11/1811
1810	1.210	7	"Libres"	1.878	11	"Esclaves"	14.397	82	17.485	CO 253/7/2: 30/11/1811
1810	1.210	7	"Coloured"	1.878	11	"Blacks"	14.397	82	17.485	BREEN 1844: 165
1812	1.218	9	"Free Coloured Popul."	2.626	18	"Slave Population"	10.440	73	14.284	CO 253/19/1: 8/8/1825
1813	1.140	8	"Free Coloured Popul."	2.737	19	"Slave Population"	10.179	72	14.056	CO 253/19/1: 8/8/1825
1814	1.148	7	"Free Coloured Popul."	2.812	18	"Slave Population"	12.097	75	16.057	CO 253/19/1: 8/8/1825
1815	1.219	8	"Free Coloured Popul."	2.844	18	"Slave Population"	12.080	75	16.143	CO 253/19/1: 8/8/1825
1816	1.218	8	"Free Coloured Popul."	2.850	18	"Slave Population"	11.828	74	15.896	CO 253/19/1: 8/8/1825
1824	1.194	6	"Free Blacks"	3.659	20	"Slaves"	13.742	74	18.595	CO 258/21/1: 1824/"Popul."
1825	1.194	6	"Coloured"	3.871	21	"Blacks"	13.530	73	18.595	BREEN 1844: 165
1827	1.010	6	"Free Blacks"	3.983	22	"Slaves"	12.922	72	17.915	CO 258/23/1: 1827/"Popul."
1828	972	6	"Free Blacks"	3.721	21	"Slaves"	12.967	73	17.660	CO 258/24/1: 1828/"Popul."
1829	972	6	"Free Blacks"	3.718	21	"Slaves"	12.967	73	17.657	CO 258/25/1: 1829/"Popul."
1830	955	5	"Free Blacks"	4.374	23	"Slaves"	13.529	72	18.858	CO 258/26/1: 1830/"Popul."
1831	897	6	"Free Blacks"	2.631	18	"Slaves"	11.371	76	14.899	CO 258/27/1: 1831/"Popul."
1832	866	6	"Free Blacks"	2.828	20	"Slaves"	10.459	74	14.153	CO 258/28/1: 1832/"Popul."
1833	863	6	"Free Blacks"	2.797	20	"Slaves"	10.196	74	13.856	CO 258/29/1: 1833/"Popul."
1834	2.180	15	"Free Blacks"	2.657	18	"Slaves"	9.954	67	14.791	CO 258/30/1: 1834/"Popul."
1834						Abolition of slavery	13.348		-	BREEN 1844: 169
1834	2.310	13	"Coloured"	2.657	15	"Blacks"	13.248	73	18.215	MARTIN 1851-57: IV, 125
1835	881	6	"Free Blacks"	3.919	27	"Slaves"	9.748	67	14.548 [1]	CO 258/31/1:1835/"Popul."
1836	990	6	"Coloured Population"	14.340	94		-		15.330 [2]	CO 258/32/1: 1836/"Popul."
1837	1.023	7	"Coloured Population"	13.095	93		-		14.118 [3]	CO 258/33/1: 1837/"Popul."
1838	1.109	7	"Coloured Population"	14.896	93		-		16.005 [4]	CO 258/34/1: 1838/"Popul."

1) (14.544) 2) (15.370) 3) (14.284) 4) (16.017)

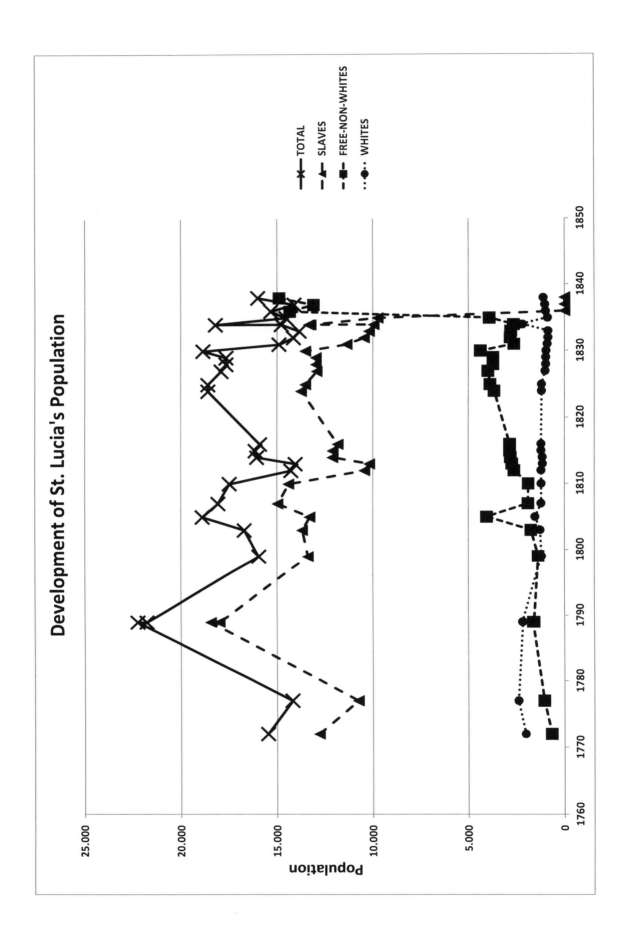

Development of St. Lucia's Population

4.5.2.2 Slave population

The increase of the slave population from the year 1772 up to the year 1789 is confirmed by BREEN (1844: 167):

> "From 1772 to 1789, when the slave trade flourished in all its enormities, there was an increase of 5,197 persons."

Because of the war in the last decade of the 18th century and the suppression of the slave trade by the British, the slave population of St. Lucia was reduced to approximately 13.000 persons according to BREEN (1844: 167).

The figures shown in the table on page 71 are as follows:

Year	number of slaves	
1789	18.445	
1789	17.992	
	18.218,5	(average)
1799	13.391	
	4.827,5	(difference)

According to these figures there was a decline of 26.5 % in the slave population for the period from 1789 to 1799.

A decline of the slave population for that time is also mentioned in a letter of Governor PREVOST of St. Lucia from October 1798:

> "The misfortune of intestine commotions almost unparalleled for cruelty and excesses which have devastated the country, destroyed a great part of the Inhabitants and reduced the working Negroes to 3.100 Males and 5.060 Females, ..."
>
> (CO 253/2/1: 22/11/1798, p. 3)

The population list for the year 1799 shows similar figures:

Slaves:	Men:	3.319	
	Women:	5.604	
	Children:	4.468	
		13.391	(CO 253/2/3: 1799, p. 55)

Governor PREVOST in his letter of 19th June 1799 informed the SECRETARY OF STATE in London of the reasons for the reduction in the slave population:

> "... many having fallen in the field – several having been taken in arms and shipped off the Island and others sent to augment the Republican Forces at St. Vincent, ..."
>
> (CO 253/2/4: 19/6/1799, p. 24)

In his letter of November 1799 to the SECRETARY OF STATE in London Governor PREVOST pointed to a further reason for the above-mentioned reduction. In connection with the transfer of population statements he wrote:

> *"The misfortunes of internal commotions almost unparalleled for cruelty and excesses which have devastated the Country, destroyed a great part of the Inhabitants and reduced the negroes to one half of their original number, renders it impossible to lay before your Grace so correct a Statement as the House of Commons requires, in fact that which I now send must be deprived of its weight when I credibly assure your Grace that many of the unfortunate negroes who died in 1796, 1797 & part of 1798 were victims to the famine created by the abandon of all Cultivation in the Colony during those periods."*
>
> (CO 253/2/5: 12/11/1799, p. 49)

For the period from May 1796 to October 1799 a report of the SECRETARY's OFFICE in St. Lucia shows the following death- and birth-figures; the birth-figures were about one third of the death figures:

Death-figures:	imported "Nègres"	1796	460	
		1797	203	
		1798	148	
		1799	138	949
	"Nègres Créoles"	1796	463	
		1797	322	
		1798	281	
		1799	157	<u>1.223</u>
	TOTAL			**2.172**
Birth-figures:		1796	104	
		1797	119	
		1798	228	
		1799	279	
	TOTAL			**730**

(CO 253/2/6: 1799, p. 54)

After the final taking over of St. Lucia by the British in the year 1803 the population increased slightly. This can be seen from the table made on page 71 and from the following two letter extracts from Governor BRERETON of St. Lucia:

> *"The increase of the population since the last capture of Saint Lucia particularly in the Capital Castries has been 33 White people, 53 people of Colour and 353 Slaves – there has also been an increase in the other quarters of the Island but not in the same ratio as in the capital."*
>
> (CO 253/3/2: 24/7/1805)

"The population, Commerce & Produce have continued to increase,..."

(CO 253/3/3: 21/9/1806)

The sudden decrease of the slave population figures shown in the table from 14.397 in the year 1810 to 10.440 in the year 1812 can probably be explained by inadequately made estimates. In the report from which the low figures were taken the following was mentioned:

"In the whole the return of Slave Population is most inconvenient even for the years previous to 1817 as it was upwards of 16.000 at the first official registration of 1816."

(CO 253/19/1: 8/8/1825)

For the period from 1824 to 1834 the slave population decreased according to the data of the BLUE BOOKS from 13.742 to 9.954 persons; this corresponds to a decrease in the slave population of 3.788 persons. On the other hand BREEN (1844: 165, 169) mentions 13.530 slaves for the year 1825 and 13.348 persons for the year 1834. This shows a decrease of the slave population of only 182 persons. Also MARTIN (1851-57: IV, 125) mentions for the year 1834 a slave population figure of above 13.000.

In order to examine the slave population figures for this period in detail the following table was made by means of the reports of the PROTECTOR OF SLAVES for the period from June 1826 to June 1833. These reports give the amount of births and deaths concerning the slave population.

Source/Period	Section	Births	Deaths	Increase	Decrease
CO 258/5/1: 1/6/1826-31/12/1826/	B	247	246	1	
CO 258/5/2: 1/1/1827-30/6/1827/	B	170	145	25	
CO 258/5/3: 1/7/1827-31/12/1827/	B	144	137	7	
CO 258/5/4: 1/1/1828-30/6/1828/	B	159	110	49	
CO 258/5/5: 1/7/1828-31/12/1828/	B	200	103	97	
CO 258/5/6: 1/1/1829-30/6/1829	B	191	121	70	
CO 258/5/7: 1/7/1829-31/12/1829/	A	168	173		5
CO 258/6/1: 1/1/1830-31/3/1830/	A	59	59		
CO 258/6/2: 1/4/1830-30/9/1830/	E	153	128	25	
CO 258/7/1: 1/10/1830-31/12/1830/	E	64	66		2
CO 258/8/1: 1/1/1831-30/6/1831/	E	150	138	12	
CO 258/9/1: 1/7/1831-5/11/1831	E	77	107		30
CO 258/11/1: 1/1/1832-30/6/1832	E	142	223		81
CO 258/12/1: 1/7/1832-31/12/1832/	E	115	106	9	
CO 258/13/1: 1/1/1833-30/6/1833/	E	208	148	60	
	TOTAL			355	118

Increase in population	237	

Common remarks of the PROTECTOR OF SLAVES on the figures mentioned in the table are as follows:

In his report for the first half year of 1829 the PROTECTOR OF SLAVES attributed the increase in birth to the measures of the government for ameliorating the living conditions of the slaves as well as to the tranquil situation in the colony:

> "Now when it is considered that the increase has been so progressive, that the Returns are confined to estates on which there are at least six working slaves, that slaves on small estates and domestics were ever on the increase, and when these unquestionable facts are contrasted with the former state of the island with regard to slave population, it seems to me that the only fair inference is that this change is owing to an amelioration in their condition, resulting principally from these regulations, and next from the re-establishment or rather establishment of order generally in the island."

(CO 258/5/6: 1/1/1829-30/6/1929)

From another report of the PROTECTOR OF SLAVES dated in March 1833 it follows that the preponderance of the deaths in the period from July 1831 to June 1832 is due to a hurricane of 11th August 1831 (CO 253/44/3: 23/3/1833).

Further reports referring to the period concerning the afore-mentioned table are as follows:

Chief Justice JEREMIE wrote in the year 1827:

> "...that the non-increase of the slave population is as much owing to the practice of procuring abortion as to any other cause, it is done openly avowedly. Enquire the reason, these females will answer: "Our Children are for our Masters, why should we add to their stock?"

(CO 253/24/1: 28/7/1827)

Two years later he informed:

> "That under the present system as cultivation has increased, also has population, ..."

(CO 253/26/5: 30/5/1829)

Also Governor STEWART mentioned a slight increase in population:

> "In every plantation there is more than the usual proportion of children; while the apparent increase is not great. This, no doubt is owing to the number of Africans brought here before the Abolition. These people are not inclined to the married state, and their constitution & indolent habits are never properly assimilated to the climate, nor reconciled to labour; and are therefore more subject to mortal diseases."

(CO 253/26/6: 29/9/1829)

Summing up it may be said that according to the table as well as to the available reports there could not have been a strong decrease in population in the period from 1826 to 1833 as shown in the BLUE BOOKS. The table on page 75 shows an increase in population of 237 persons. From the mentioned reports it also follows that there was a slight increase in population. Therefore it can be assumed that the data of BREEN with 13.530 slaves for the year 1825 and 13.348 for the year 1834 respectively and those of MARTIN for 1834 with 13.248 slaves were the nearest to the actual level of slave population.

From the year 1836 the FREE NON-WHITES and the APPRENTICES were combined in the BLUE BOOKS in one section with the title "Coloured Population". For these people the stated figures vary for the period from 1836 to 1838, about 14.000.

Concerning the number of the APPRENTICES there are the following reports:

According to a report of the colonial government for the period from 1st August 1834 to 31st July 1835 the total number of the APPRENTICES was 9.366; 4.353 were males and 5.013 females.

In a letter of 23rd November 1835 Governor DUDLEY HILL of St. Lucia noticed:

> *"The whole of the working classes do not exceed 10.000."*
>
> (CO 253/49/2: 23/11/1835)

After a visit to St. Lucia the bishop of Barbados reported in his letter from May 1836 that the total population figure of St. Lucia was about 20.000 and the number of the APPRENTICES with their children about 14.000 (CO 253/51/2: 12/5/1836).

Assuming that the population figure of the slaves was above 13.000 in the year 1834 the statement of the bishop of Barbados with 14.000 for all APPRENTICES seems possible. According to the other two reports the figure of the APPRENTICES able to work was about 10.000. The missing figure of 4.000 could have embraced the children of the APPRENTICES and old persons.

Regarding the population estimates in general the STIPENDIARY MAGISTRATE of the 1st district (Castries, Anse La Raye) noticed in January 1844 as follows:

> *"Registrations of baptisms, burials and population returns, have been so imperfectly kept and collected in this Colony, that we have no sure data to guide us, in making comparison as to the rate of mortality previous and*

subsequent to complete emancipation, and I cannot obtain any documentary evidence authentic enough for me to form a decided opinion on this subject."

(CO 253/82/1: 10/1/1844)

4.5.2.3 Construction of the development of the slave population

In the period from 1772 to 1789 the population figure increased from 10.752 to about 18.000 and decreased afterwards until the beginning of the 19th century to above 13.000. From 1803 a slight increase in population was reported. The figure of 14.397 mentioned by BREEN for the year 1810 seems to be the nearest to the actual level of population. In the period from 1825 to 1834 the slave population of St. Lucia was subjected to only slight variations. With 13.530 slaves for the year 1825 and 13.348 for the year 1834 the statements of BREEN seem the most reliable ones. The number of the APPRENTICES between 1834 and 1838 might have been about 14.000.

In summary the following table was made. The stated figures are similar to those mentioned by BREEN:

Year	number of slaves/ APPRENTICES
1772	12.795
1789	18.000
1799	13.391
1810	14.397
1825	13.530
1834	13.300
1838	14.000

4.5.2.4 FREE NON-WHITES

According to the table on page 71 the number of FREE NON-WHITES increased in the period from 1772 to 1789 from 663 to about 1.600 persons. During the war years of the last decade of the 18th century there was a decrease of 15 %.

Year	number of free non-whites
1789	1.630
1789	1.588
	1.609 (average)
1799	1.364
	245 (difference)

From the beginning of the 19th century the number of the free non-whites increased again. Concerning the high figure of 4.053 mentioned for the year 1805 there are no further statements in the sources. Relating to the criticism of sources concerning the population figure of the slaves it is assumed that in the following the statements of BREEN were the nearest to the actual figures. Accordingly the number of the free non-whites was in the year 1810 1.878 and in the year 1825 already 3.871.

At the time of the abolition of slavery there are the figures 2.657 for the year 1834 and 3.919 for the year 1835. In conformity with the statement of BREEN for the year 1825 with 3.871 free non-whites the figure of 1835 with 3.919 might be the nearest to the facts.

Summing up there is the following table:

Year	number of free non-whites
1772	663
1789	1.600
1799	1.364
1810	1.878
1825	3.871
1835	3.919

4.5.2.5   WHITE POPULATION

Concerning the white population BREEN (1844: 166) mentions an increase till 1789. Then as a result of the war in the last decade of the 18th century the number of the whites was reduced by half. Afterwards this number remained quite steady.

According to the statements in the table on page 71 the population figure amounted 2.018 in the year 1772 and increased to about 2.180 by 1789. The decrease in population during the war years was 45%.

Year	number of whites
1789	2.164
1789	2.198
	2.181 (average)
1799	1.195
	986 (difference)

For the year 1810 BREEN mentions 1.210 persons and for the year 1825 1.194 persons, which approximately corresponds with the statements of other sources.

For the time of the abolition of slavery MARTIN mentions the high figure of 2.310 whites which is very near to the statement in the BLUE BOOK with 2.180 whites. But in the year 1835 only 881 whites were mentioned. A reason for this variation does not follow from the sources. For the year 1838 in the BLUE BOOK the number of 1.109 whites was mentioned.

Summing up there is the following table:

Year	number of whites
1772	2.018
1789	2.181
1799	1.195
1810	1.210
1825	1.194
1834	2.200
1838	1.109

4.5.2.6   Summary

Year	WHITES	%	FREE NON-WHITES	%	SLAVES	%	TOTAL
1772	2.018	13%	663	4%	12.795	83%	15.476
1789	2.181	10%	1.600	7%	18.000	83%	21.781
1799	1.195	7%	1.364	9%	13.391	84%	15.950
1810	1.210	7%	1.878	11%	14.397	82%	17.485
1825	1.194	6%	3.871	21%	13.530	73%	18.595
1834	2.200				13.300		
1835			3.919				
1838	1.109				14.000		

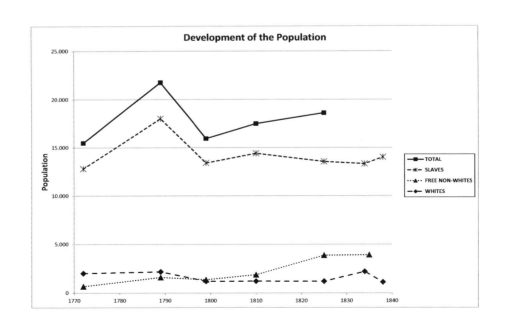

80

4.5.3 Distribution of the sexes of the non-white population

For the year 1799 there are the following figures:

<u>Slave population:</u>   13.391
Men: 3.319 – 25%
Women: 5.604 – 42%
Children: 4.468 – 33%

(CO 253/2/3: 1799, p. 55)

According to the available figures in the BLUE BOOKS the following table was compiled:

YEAR	FREE NON-WHITES		SLAVES		TOTAL					
	Men	Women	Men	Women	Men	%	Women	%	TOTAL	Source
1824	1.576	2.083	6.216	7.526	7.792	45	9.609	55	17.401	(CO 258/22/1: 1824/"Popul.")
1827	1.745	2.238	5.945	6.977	7.690	45	9.215	55	16.905	(CO 258/23/1: 1827/"Popul.")
1828	1.714	2.007	5.839	7.128	7.553	45	9.135	55	16.688	(CO 258/24/1: 1828/"Popul.")
1829	1.714	2.004	5.839	7.128	7.553	45	9.132	55	16.685	(CO 258/25/1: 1829/"Popul.")
1830	2.020	2.354	6.024	7.505	8.044	45	9.859	55	17.903	(CO 258/26/1: 1830/"Popul.")
1831	1.214	1.417	5.242	6.129	6.456	46	7.546	54	14.002	(CO 258/27/1: 1831/"Popul.")
1832	1.297	1.531	4.903	5.556	6.200	47	7.087	53	13.287	(CO 258/28/1: 1832/"Popul.")
1833	1.251	1.546	4.685	5.511	5.936	46	7.057	54	12.993	(CO 258/29/1: 1833/"Popul.")
1834	1.239	1.418	4.601	5.353	5.840	46	6.771	54	12.611	(CO 258/30/1: 1834/"Popul.")
1835	1.845	2.074	4.405	5.343	6.250	46	7.417	54	13.667	(CO 258/31/1: 1835/"Popul.")
1836	-	-	-	-	6.645	46	7.695	54	14.340	(CO 258/32/1: 1836/"Popul.")
1837	-	-	-	-	6.375	49	6.720	51	13.095	(CO 258/33/1: 1837/"Popul.")
1838	-	-	-	-	6.859	46	8.037	54	14.896	(CO 258/34/1: 1838/"Popul.") *)

*) Children were not especially mentioned in the source.

From this table it follows that there was a surplus of women in St. Lucia for the period from 1824 to 1838. This surplus is confirmed by the following reports:

Governor DUDLEY HILL of St. Lucia wrote:

> "... the female population being considerably above that of the male (in some districts 3 to 2) ..."

(CO 253/51/1: 15/3/1836)

Also two travellers (STURGE/HARVEY 1838: 108) referred in their published book to a surplus of women in St. Lucia. During their stay in St. Lucia in December 1836 they asked a certain Dr. Robinson the reasons of this surplus:

> "The number of females considerably preponderates in this as in the other islands which we have visited. Dr. Robinson mentions the only probable explanation we have yet heard of this anomaly. He believes that an inspection of the registry of slaves, from 1815 to 1834, would show that half the males died before attaining the age of twenty, while not a third of the females died within the same period, - a disparity which he accounts

for by supposing that the severe labour to which both sexes are subjected at the same age is less destructive to the female constitution, in consequence of its being more early matured."

4.5.4 Distribution of population in the colony

In this chapter the development of the distribution of the population in St. Lucia is shown by figures from the years 1799 (CO 253/2/3: 1799, p.55) and 1835 (CO 258/31/1: 1835/"Population"). In the following the available figures are compared by means of a table and graphic representations:

DISTRICT	WHITES				FREE NON-WHITES				SLAVES									TOTAL POPULATION			
	1799		1835		1799		1835		1799					1835				1799		1835	
	Figure	%	Figure	%	Figure	%	Figure	%	Male	Female	Children	Total	%	Male	Female	Total	%	Figure	%	Figure	%
Gros Islet	94	8	28	3	176	13	219	6	407	649	456	1.512	11	367	478	845	9	1.782	11	1.092	7,5
Castries	108	9	353	40	181	13	1.170	30	331	416	454	1.201	9	790	920	1.710	18	1.490	9	3.233	22
Anse La Raye	107	9	18	2	69	5	179	5	160	289	217	666	5	295	373	668	7	842	5	865	5,9
Soufrière	346	29	265	30	192	14	599	15	617	1.232	980	2.829	21	1.094	1.248	2.342	24	3.367	21	3.206	22
Choiseul	94	8	54	6	170	12	371	9	240	377	360	977	7	265	335	600	6	1.241	8	1.025	7
Laborie	133	11	57	6	152	11	622	16	365	614	553	1.532	11	488	621	1.109	11	1.817	11	1.788	12
Vieux Fort	166	14	66	7	157	12	138	4	388	690	520	1.598	12	409	464	873	9	1.921	12	1.077	7,4
Micoud/Praslin	77	6	22	2	158	12	364	9	452	749	537	1.738	13	407	463	870	9	1.973	12	1.256	8,6
Dennery	26	2	13	1	16	1	74	2	94	172	118	384	3	210	273	483	5	426	3	570	3,9
Dauphin	44	4	5	1	93	7	183	5	265	416	273	954	7	80	168	248	3	1.091	7	436	3
TOTAL	1.195	100	881	100	1.364	100	3.919	100	3.319	5.604	4.468	13.391	100	4.405	5.343	9.748	100	15.950	100	14.548	100

(compiled by Ernestine Kolar by means of the sources
CO 253/2/3: 1799, p. 55 and CO 258/31/1: 1835/"Population")

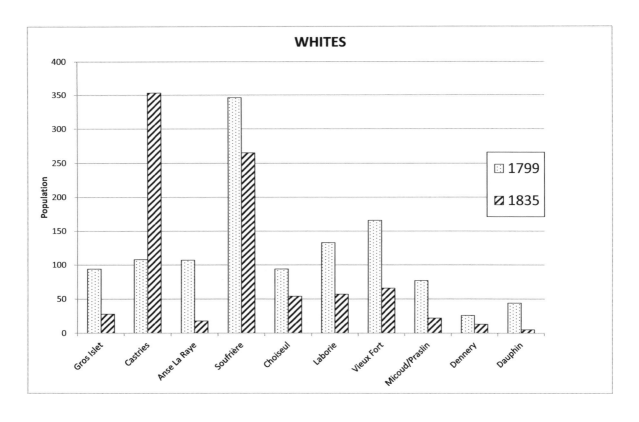

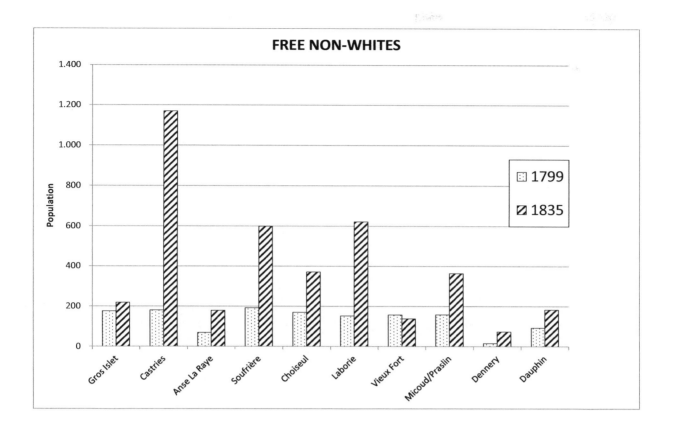

FREE NON-WHITES

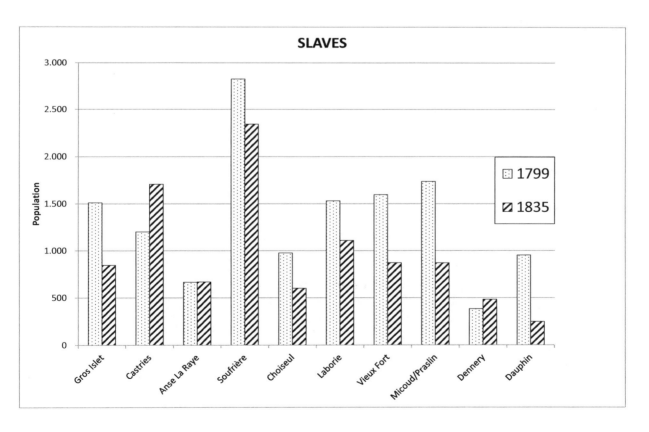

SLAVES

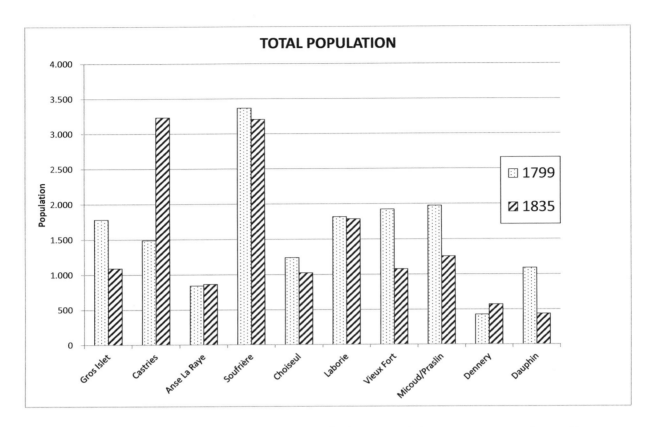

TOTAL POPULATION

According to the table on page 82 and the graphic representations the following result can be seen:

Total population:

In the year 1799 Soufrière with 21% had the highest portion of the population of St. Lucia. The areas Gros Islet, Vieux Fort, Laborie and Micoud/Praslin showed an average from 11% to 13%. The most sparsely populated areas were Castries with 9%, Choiseul 8% , Dauphin 7%, Anse La Raye 5% and Dennery with 3%.

In the year 1835 Soufrière still showed a high portion of the population: 22%. But Castries also became a main settlement area with 22%. The other areas had variations in population from +1% to -5% absolute. The most sparsely populated areas were Dennery with 4% and Dauphin with 3%.

Slaves

In both years of comparison Soufrière had the main portion of the slave population: In the year 1799 with 21% and in the year 1835 with 24%.

The well populated areas in the year 1799 were Micoud/Praslin with 13%, Vieux Fort and Laborie with 12% and Gros Islet with 11%. Sparsely populated areas were Castries with 9%, Dauphin and Choiseul with 7% , Anse La Raye with 5% and Dennery with 3%.

In the year 1835 Castries had the second highest percentage of slave population with 18%. The other areas had variations of population from +2% to -4% absolute.

Free non-whites

In the year 1799 Soufrière had the highest percentage of free non-withes: 14%. The areas Castries and Gros Islet followed with 13%, Choiseul, Micoud/Praslin and Vieux Fort with 12% and Laborie with 11%. The most sparsely populated areas were Dauphin with 7%, Anse La Raye 5% and Dennery with 1%.

In the year 1835 Castries was the main settlement area with 30% of the free non-white population. Laborie with 16% and Soufrière with 15% followed. The other areas showed variations of population from +1% to -8% absolute, whereas Gros Islet with 7% and Vieux Fort with 8% had the greatest decline in population.

Whites

In 1799 the greater part of the white population, 29%, lived in the area of Soufrière. Vieux Fort with 14% and Laborie with 11% followed. The areas Castries, Anse La Raye, Gros Islet, Choiseul and Micoud/Praslin showed 9% and 6%. The most sparsely populated areas were Dauphin with 4% and Dennery with 2%.

In the year 1835 the position of the highest portion of the white population (40%) had shifted from Soufrière to Castries. Soufrière showed then 30%. The remaining areas had a decline in population from 1% to 7% absolute.

Summing up, it can be said that at the turn of the 18th century Soufrière was the main settlement area in St. Lucia. This is also confirmed by a letter of Governor BRERETON of St. Lucia from the year 1805. The Governor wrote:

> *"There is no doubt but a great deal of produce has been smuggled off this Island from the several out Posts particularly from that of Soufrière the most populous Quarter and where the greatest quantity of land is in cultivation of any other in the Island."*
>
> (CO 253/3/2: 24/7/1805)

Up to the year 1835 Castries had been developed to an equivalent settlement area.

4.6 Economic development

4.6.1 Introduction

Until about the middle of the 17th century there were few settlers in St. Lucia. They lived from fishing and hunting. In the middle of the 17th century the population began to increase and the cultivation of tobacco, ginger and cotton was introduced.[12]

At the beginning of the 18th century these produces were almost entirely displaced by coffee and cocoa. At this period the cultivation of produces was confined to the west coast of the island and it was not until 1736 that some adventurers from Martinique came and settled in the windward districts.

In the year 1763 Grenada and St. Vincent became British. At that time several respectable French planters immigrated with their families to St. Lucia, and consequently a considerable amount of capital was introduced and an impulse given to trade and agriculture. In every part of the island plantations were extended, large uncultivated tracts reclaimed, establishments formed and the cultivation of cotton, until then of little importance, soon spread all over the island.

The first sugar establishment was commenced in the quarter of Vieux Fort on the 15th April 1765. A year or two later another was formed in the quarter of Praslin. In the year 1780 no less than thirty sugar estates had been established and upwards of twenty others were in an advanced state. In this year a tremendous hurricane destroyed most of the estates' works and threw a damp upon industry and enterprise, from which, followed as it was soon by the still more discouraging effects of the revolution, the inhabitants were unable to recover for a series of year (BREEN 1844: 275-277).

In the following a review of the economic development of St. Lucia from the war period in the last decade of the 18th century till the end of the emancipation period in the year 1838 is given.

---

[12] Regarding an earlier cultivation of cotton by Indians who settled in St. Lucia there were no statements in the sources used by the author.

4.6.2 The economic situation in the last decade of the 18th century

With the intrusion of republicans from France into St. Lucia in the year 1791 a period of commotion and wars began. It ended with the conquest over the BRIGANDS by the British in the year 1797 (cp. chapter "4.1. The effects of the French Revolution in St. Lucia, the wars of the BRIGANDS and the final conquer by the British", pp. 43-45).

During this period the economic situation of St. Lucia was miserable. Governor BRERETON of St. Lucia wrote in November 1803:

> *"The losses to the planters soon after the French Revolution were almost the whole of their male slaves and stock, which reduced many to abandon their properties and many to ruin."*
>
> (CO 253/3/4: 14/11/1803)

In a letter of Governor PREVOST dated November 1798, the following is written:

> *"At the commencement of the present War the Planters of this Island were considerably indebted of chiefly to British Merchants residing in the neighbouring Colonies for Slaves, etc. I believe I may correctly state to the amount of upwards of £ 500.000 Currency …*
>
> *… The misfortune of intestine commotions almost unparalleled for cruelty and excesses which have been devastated the country, destroyed a great part of the Inhabitants and reduced the working Negroes to 3.100 Males and 5.060 Females, together with being three times captured have rendered it impossible for them to take any measures towards liquidating these demands, in fact, the approaching crop is the only one on which the Planters could depend with any certainty for their dread of the Brigands was so great as to prevent their residing on their property and at present above one half the Island is left uncultivated for want of means."*
>
> (CO 253/2/1: 22/11/1798, p. 3)

Governor PREVOST tried to increase the number of settlers. In June 1799 he wrote to the SECRETARY OF STATE in London:

> *"As far as the state of things and the public calamities permitted I endeavoured to follow the rules established at Martinique. I thought it most advisable to rent the Estates and Negroes,…*
>
> *By causing them to be hired to the best bidder at public outcry, I have not only considerably increased their value but induced several respectable persons to become settlers."*
>
> (CO 253/2/4: 19/6/1799, p. 24)

4.6.3 The economic development of St. Lucia from the beginning of the 19th century till the end of the emancipation period in the year 1838

4.6.3.1 Tabular review and diagrams of exports

In order to review the development of the export produces of St. Lucia two tables were made. The first table covers the period from 1804 to 1838. The figures from 1804 to 1820 were taken from the correspondence of the colonial government. The figures up from 1821 originate from the BLUE BOOKS. Regarding the reliability of the statements in the BLUE BOOKS a British official wrote in the BLUE BOOK from the year 1839:

> "It is impossible to get accurate returns, the ignorance of the Police men and wilful misrepresentations made by many of the proprietors present even an approach to the truth, for instance, in one or two instances, 5000 lbs of Sugar have been returned as the Crops of last year, where I am certain nearly two times that quantity have been made."

(CO 258/35/1: 1839/"Agriculture")

The second table covers the period from 1826 to 1838. It was extracted from BREEN and serves as source of comparison.

Further the development of the export produces sugar, coffee, cocoa, cotton, rum, logwood, molasses and cassava is shown by means of diagrams.

Year	Sugar lbs. 1)	Coffee lbs.	Cocoa lbs.	Cotton lbs.	Rum galls 1)	Molasses galls.	Source
1804/05	5.944.943	619.827	438.915	656.118	31.472	89.175	(CO 253/3/2: 24/7/1805)
1817	6.255.520	247.272	117.293	11.025	29.400	83.400	(CO 253/12/1: 31/7/1818)
1818	4.591.086	178.217	33.779	3.350	32.600	112.000	(CO 253/12/1: 31/7/1818)
1819	7.555.670	249.772	48.443	1.025	71.700	-	(CO 253/14/1: 1/11/1820)
1820	5.994.260	316.828	34.281	5.479	72.704	122.325	(CO 253/15/1: 1820)
1821	8.332.088	207.135	38.433	8.751	65.690	117.441	(CO 258/18/1: 1821/"Agricul."
1822	8.233.100	168.816	48.742	5.907	46.300	118.890	(CO 258/19/1: 1822/"Agricul."
1823	6.061.702	362.129	45.881	7.950	30.950	198.900	(CO 258/20/1: 1823/"Agricul."
1824	7.658.541	297.539	256.381	4.830	22.680	169.856	(CO 258/21/1: 1824/"Agricul."
1825	9.113.726	-	143.039	3.155	27.736	259.908	(CO 258/22/1: 1825/"Agricul."
1828	8.633.000	280.550	48.820	3.150	149.188	225.415	(CO 258/24/1: 1828/"Agricul."
1829	8.633.240	-	41.820	3.150	120.982	225.415	(CO 258/25/1: 1829/"Agricul."
1830	7.962.000	130.740	31.100	2.350	135.002	238.522	(CO 258/26/1: 1830/"Agricul."
1831	5.561.815	149.571	33.515	-	90.687	224.700	(CO 258/27/1: 1831/"Agricul."
1832	5.061.500	187.520	26.277	20	67.202	135.692	(CO 258/28/1: 1832/"Agricul."
1833	5.365.943	233.294	36.176	-	77.759	162.219	(CO 258/29/1: 1833/"Agricul."
1834	6.530.638	107.394	37.617	200	109.710	192.997	(CO 258/30/1: 1834/"Agricul."
1835	5.861.379	104.888	38.908	1.050	101.028	144.684	(CO 258/31/1: 1835/"Agricul."
1836	4.318.010	163.486	43.640	800	68.187	74.455	(CO 258/32/1: 1836/"Agricul."
1837	4.663.900	183.640	39.560	150	52.910	104.773	(CO 258/33/1: 1837/"Agricul."
1838	5.822.000	82.012	38.550	300	82.054	136.360	(CO 258/34/1: 1838/"Agricul."

1) 1 Pound (lb.) = 453,59 grams, 1 Gallone (gall.) = 4.5459 litres; cp. Chapter "2.3 List of used British measuring and weight units", p. 23)

Year	Sugar lbs. 1)	Coffee lbs.	Cocoa lbs.	Rum galls 1)	Molasses galls.	Logwood tons 1)	Cassava brls. 1)	Cotton lbs.
1826	9.070.273	227.311	98.343	35.200	225.050	1.514	-	1.735
1827	8.531.828	230.584	79.275	47.680	255.440	1.164	8	3.220
1828	9.815.144	217.146	75.275	33.910	263.017	1.211	814	1.000
1829	8.957.870	385.359	93.793	57.785	219.097	1.277	279	2.300
1830	11.239.814	377.262	153.340	40.523	230.123	708	99	-
1831	7.671.723	193.087	98.090	34.544	210.150	972	59	334
1832	5.154.982	297.165	51.925	5.450	139.960	967	-	800
1833	4.898.040	235.164	91.048	12.130	142.320	784	-	50
1834	7.008.678	242.370	60.620	8.520	194.542	595	713	450
1835	5.553.585	106.665	49.218	16.228	155.573	402	-	-
1836	3.732.600	121.598	47.950	2.000	83.840	171	-	-
1837	4.687.200	85.740	48.591	15.800	106.614	118	-	-
1838	5.533.320	135.008	38.590	6.930	110.002	109	-	-

(extracted from BREEN 1844: 319)

1)1 Pound (lb.) = 453,59 grams, 1 Gallone (gall.) = 4.5459 litres, 1 long ton = 1.016,05 kilograms, 1 barrel (brl.) = 163,656 litres ; cp. Chapter "2.3 List of used British measuring and weight units", p. 23)

It is to mention that the export data of rum are on one side inconsistent between the two sources and on the other side no explanation of the increase in 1828 in the sources of the colonial government could be found.

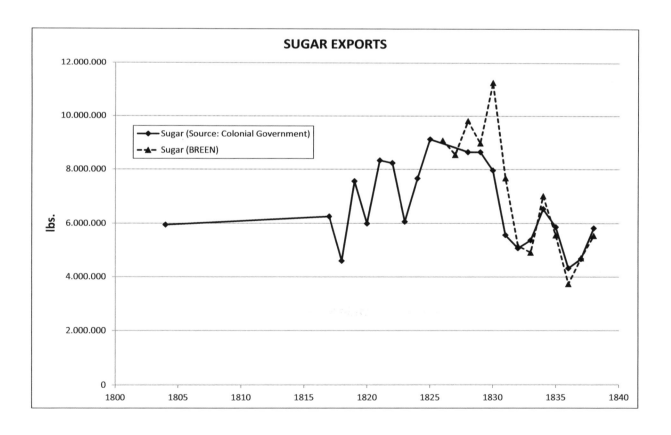

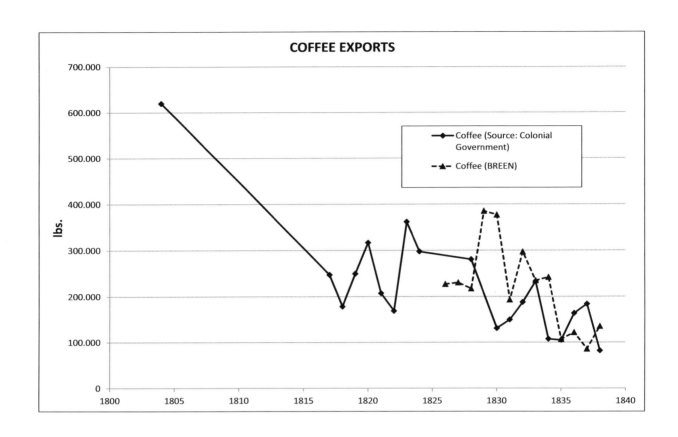

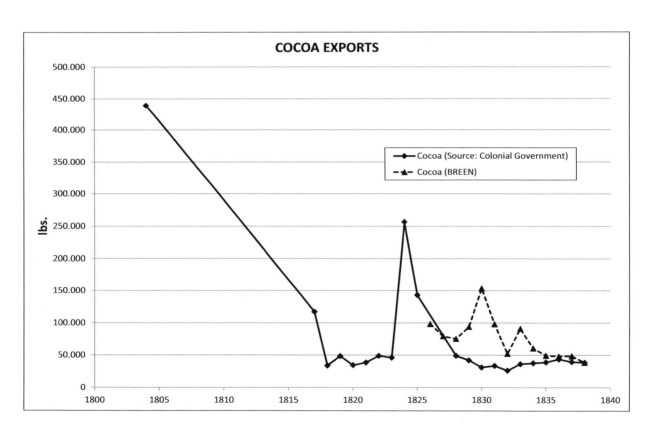

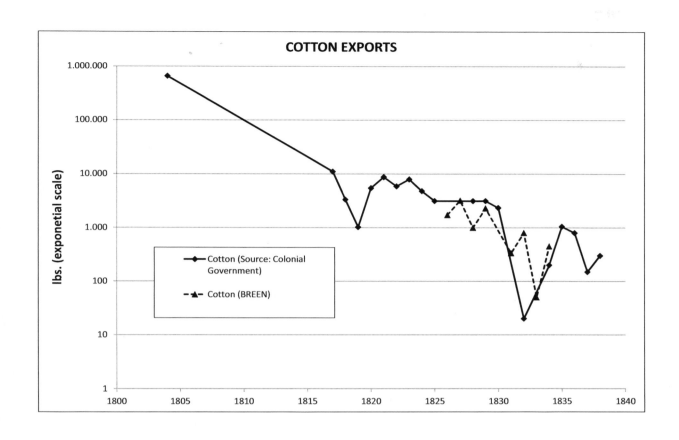

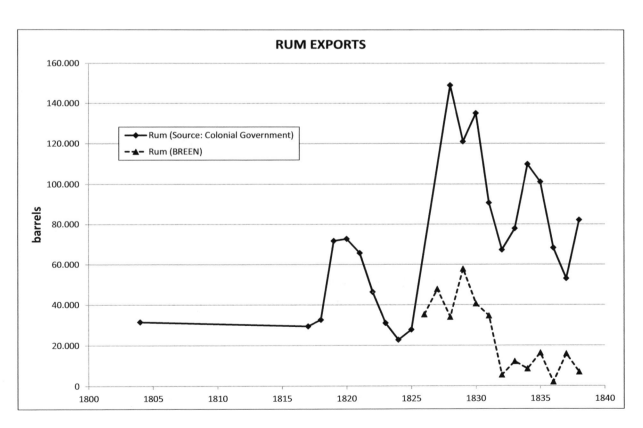

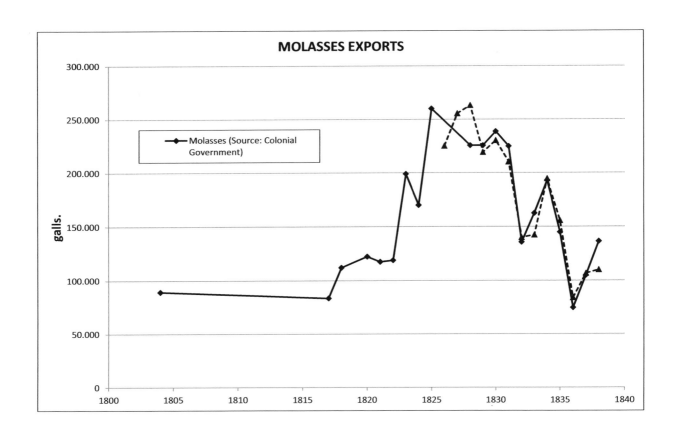

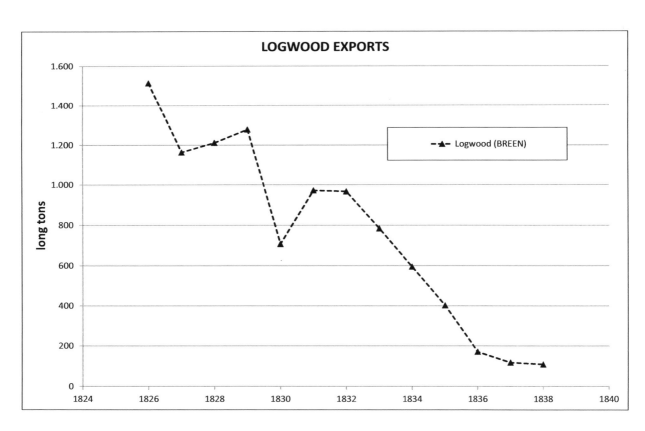

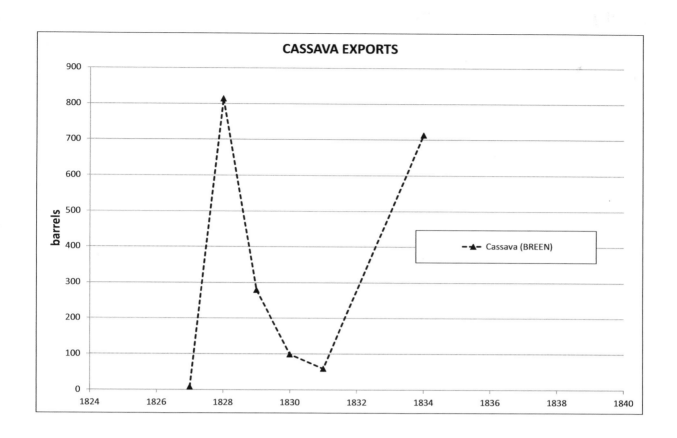

From these tables it follows that the main export produces were sugar, coffee, cocoa and cotton as well as molasses and rum. In the period from 1805 to 1817 coffee, cocoa and especially cotton decreased in significance. In this period sugar became by far the main export produce of St. Lucia.

As already mentioned on page 86, cotton was the main produce of St. Lucia in the second half of the 18th century. According to a letter of Governor BRERETON of St. Lucia dated November 1803 cotton was also at the beginning of the 19th century the main export produce of St. Lucia:

> "In addition to the other Calamities the Cotton Crop of this year which is the Staple produce of this Island has almost totally failed and many of the Estates yielding this commodity have not made as much as would pay the necessary Expenses."

> (CO 253/3/4: 14/11/1803)

The development of the significance of the export produces is also recognizable by means of the estates mentioned in the sources.

According to BREEN (1844: 277) there were already 30 sugar estates in St. Lucia in the year 1780. But in the same year many of these estates were destroyed by a hurricane.

For the year 1789 BREEN (1844: 291) mentions 43 sugar estates. The distribution of these estates within the colony was as follows:

Castries:	6 estates
Anse La Raye:	4 estates
Soufrière:	9 estates
Choiseul:	0 estates
Laborie:	5 estates
Vieux Fort:	8 estates
Micoud:	1 estate
Praslin:	3 estates
Dennery:	1 estate
Dauphin:	2 estates
Gros Islet:	4 estates
Total	43 estates

Graphic representation of the mentioned districts:

(Division of districts extracted from a map of St. Lucia from the year 1847 – BPP/CG/4/1: 1847, p. 518 as well as from BROCK 1984: 30)

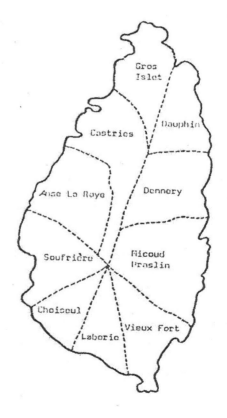

In the year 1789 the number of coffee estates was 143 according to BREEN (1844: 292). Further he wrote:

"... in those days every garden that displayed a coffee bush was dignified with the name of a coffee plantation;"

Altogether there are the following figures:

Year	Sugar estates	Coffee estates	Cotton estates	Cocoa estates	
1780	30	-	-	-	(BREEN 1844: 277)
1789	43	143	-	-	(BREEN 1844: 291-292)
1789	42	180	57	88	(CO 253/14/1: 1/11/1820)
1799	41	118	318	67	(CO 253/2/3: 1799)
1819	102	81	16	6	(CO 253/14/1: 1/11/1820)

This table confirms the gain in significance of sugar as well as the loss in significance of coffee, cotton and cocoa from the beginning of the 19th century.

In the year 1830 there were already in the district of Castries alone 30 sugar estates. Further three coffee-estates, one coffee and cotton-estate and one provision-estate were mentioned for this district (CO 253/29/1: 31/3/1830).

4.6.3.2   General economic development

After the annexation to Britain in the year 1803 the economic situation of St. Lucia was very bad.

In November 1803 Governor BRERETON of St. Lucia informed the SECRETARY OF STATE in London as follows:

> "I have learnt from a Respectable Merchant a Mr. McDowall at Glasgow who lately came here in search of considerable debts due to his House from several of these unfortunate planters that he was not able to get payment even from their Crops.
>
> … that there are many British Merchants in the same situation; and if the properties of these planters were brought to sale which these Creditors have in their power to do, the Purchase money arising therefrom could not be anything equal to clearing their encumbrances."

(CO 253/3/4: 14/11/1803)

According to a further letter of Governor BRERETON dated in July 1805 about 10% of St. Lucia was cultivated. The largest cultivated area was Soufrière:

> "The whole Island I judge may contain 200.000 English Acres, about one length of which 20.000 Acres may have been settled and put into a state of cultivation…

There is no doubt but a great deal of produce has been smuggled off this Island from the several out Posts particularly from that of Soufrière the most populous Quarter and where the greatest quantity of land is in cultivation of any other in the Island."

(CO 253/3/2: 24/7/1805)

Because of the period of war at the end of the 18th century there was a shortage of slaves in St. Lucia and many estates had been abandoned. Governor DOUGLASS wrote in October 1816 to the SECRETARY OF STATE in London as follows:

"One of the consequences of the French Revolution in this Island was the abandonment of many valuable Estates from want of population and some very fine plantations have recently been forsaken, the proprietors having concentrated their slaves on other Estates which had also too few Negroes to cultivate them."

(CO 253/10/2: 16/10/1816)

In January 1817 Governor SEYMOUR of St. Lucia proclaimed an ordinance with which the exportation of slaves from St. Lucia to other British colonies was limited. The governor informed the SECRETARY OF STATE as follows:

"I have thought it my Duty for the good of this Colony to issue the enclosed proclamation prohibiting the exportation of Slaves in large numbers from hence to other British Colonies, a Practice which if allowed to continue would depopulate the Island of St. Lucia in a very few years, and consequently render it of no value to His Majesty.-"

He mentioned further:

"... that upwards of Two Hundred Plantations have been abandoned in this Island during the last eighteen years for want of hands to cultivate them."

(CO 253/11/1: 20/1/1817)

In the year 1819 the PRIVY COUNCIL of St. Lucia decided to allow a premium to every person above 14 years of age who should import at least ten slaves from the other British colonies to St. Lucia (CO 253/14/2: 10/6/1819).

In the years 1817 and 1819 hurricanes destroyed the agriculture of St. Lucia. A report of the members of the PRIVY COUNCIL of St. Lucia for the year 1817 shows the following:

"Loss: Colonial Money: 1101,615.44.4
*   Amount in Sterling Money: 550,807.12.2*
In above are included forty six slaves killed, one hundred and sixty mules & Horses, and upwards of three hundred heads of horned cattle, together with an immense number of Sheep & Hogs."

(CO 253/11/2: 1817)

The effects of the hurricane of 13th, 14th and 15th October 1819 were described in a letter of Governor KEANE of St. Lucia on the 27th October 1819:

> "... overflow of the rivers which have not only destroyed all the ground provisions throughout the Island but have swept away or overwhelmed whole fields of produce and in many quarters works and buildings and negroes.
>
> And having moreover satisfied myself by personal observation in the neighbouring quarters of the very extraordinary and unprecedented losses experienced in the late storm by the inhabitants generally but more especially by the Planters who have not only been deprived of the means of feeding provisions but have at the same time suffered most severely in their prospects for the ensuing crop which will in all cases be most seriously diminished and in many entirely lost to them."

(CO 253/13/1: 27/10/1819)

Regarding the death of slaves as well as of the loss of slaves' houses the SECRETARY's OFFICE in St. Lucia made the following table in 1820:

Districts	Number of plantations	Number of slaves before hurricane	Loss in slaves	Loss in slaves' houses
Castries	29	635	1	53
Gros Islet	25	1.237	3	8
Anse La Raye	16	715	20	49
Micoud	11	635	-	78
Dauphin	8	570	-	10
Soufrière	59	1.907	52	155
Dennery	13	628	1	159
Vieux Fort	17	947	-	197
Choiseul	34	751	9	32
Laborie	23	1.136	1	12
TOTAL	235	9.161	87	753

(extracted from a table made by the
SECRETARY's OFFICE of St. Lucia; CO 253/14/3: 1820)

The loss in coffee, cotton and cocoa was put at 303.950 pounds and 200.000 trees respectively.

In 1831 a further hurricane reached St. Lucia. Governor BOZON of St. Lucia wrote on August 18th, 1831 as follows:

> "... on the morning of the 11th inst. This Island experienced a most violent hurricane which has occasioned more damage and loss than the hurricane

of the year 1817. Few lives have been lost, but the Plantations to the Windward & Southward side of the Island have suffered severely."

(CO 253/29/2: 18/7/1831)

At this time the economic situation was according to a petition of "Proprietors, Planters, Merchants and other Inhabitants of St. Lucia" very bad. For example they wrote:

"They beg to make known to Your Excellency that they find their condition at this moment reduced to the lowest state of wretchedness from a series of misfortunes too long to enumerate and which no other Colony has had so often to contend with. In consequence of the Slave Laws enforced by His Majesty's Ministers the Crops of this Colony have been yearly diminishing and are now reduced to a quantity hardly adequate to pay the expenditure of Estates at the ruinous rate for which West India Produce is selling and has been for the last three years."

(CO 253/30/1: 31/10/1831)

On the above mentioned Slave Laws enforced by the British government compare chapter "4.2 British Slave Policy in St. Lucia 1803-1834", pp. 41-50.
William MUTER, a member of the PRIVY COUNCIL of St. Lucia, made the following petition in April 1832:

"... that every proprietor in the Island is now reduced to the lowest state bordering upon despair. There is yet time to save many from total ruin by prompt efficacious measures of relief but if that relief be longer withheld the total ruin of every proprietor in this Island must inevitably be the result."

(CO 253/38/1: 30/4/1832)

This general bad economic situation he especially attributed to the hurricane of August 1831 as well as to the ORDER IN COUNCIL of November 2nd, 1831, which fixed measures of ameliorating the condition of the slaves.

One month later "Merchants and Householders" of St. Lucia referred to the distress in the colony:

"... that the state of extreme distress to which this Colony is reduced and the destruction of so large a portion of the Sugar and Coffee Crop, ..., has rendered it impossible for the Planters to make their accustomed payments to the Merchants ..."

(CO 253/39/1: 15/5/1832)

Governor FARQUHARSON of St. Lucia reported in July 1832:

"... that the Crop in this Colony has this season fallen short about one half."

(CO 253/39/2: 25/7/1832)

To the already-mentioned reasons for the decrease of the crop yields (the laws for ameliorating the condition of the slaves as well as the hurricane of 1831) Mr. ROBINSON, a member of the PRIVY COUNCIL, adds in September 1832:

"... regularly progressive has been the injury done to this Colony by Orders in Council framed in the Mother Country, the average Crops of the years 1825, 1826, 1827, 1828 and 1829 being from 9,000.000 to 10,000.000. Crops which could only have been kept up under the withering influence of the first Slave Law of 1826, by the almost entire abandonment of the Coffee and consequent removal of the Slaves to Sugar Culture. But that resource having failed, the result of these Orders in Council shows a regular decrease in the Crops. A decrease further augmented this year by the effects of the Hurricane of August 1831."

(CO 253/40/1: 19/9/1832)

At the beginning of the emancipation period St. Lucia was in a very bad financial situation. Governor DUDLEY HILL of St. Lucia wrote in a letter of October 1834 as follows:

"... I embraced the earliest possible opportunity after carrying into effect the great and important measure of Slavery Abolition to inquire most minutely into the finances of this Colony and although I was in some measure prepared for their being in anything but a prosperous situation yet I never could have supposed that any Island should have reached the very aim of poverty."

(CO 253/46/2: 1/10/1834)

In a petition of January 1835 "Planters and other Persons" complained because of their financial difficulties:

"That your Petitioners from the general ruinous depreciation of all West India Property, the many calamitous events which have depressed more particularly this unfortunate Colony, the recent diminished labour of apprentices and the increased expense to be incurred on their behalf in consequence of the Order in Council of 5th June 1834 find themselves totally unprovided with the means of carrying on the cultivation of their Estates or the manufacturing of their produce."

(CO 253/48/1: 17/1/1835)

The mentioned law of 5th June 1834 concerns the law of the abolition of slavery.

A letter of Governor DUDLEY HILL dated November 1835 gives a general review of the economic situation at that. The Governor was replying a letter of the SECRETARY OF STATE SPRING RICE from London concerning questions regarding the effects which free labour as a result of the apprenticeship of the slaves was likely to produce upon the pursuits of profitable industry in the British colonies. At first the Governor referred to the export produces and the working morale of the APPRENTICES:

> "The present articles of produce for exportation are chiefly sugar, coffee, cocoa and dye or logwood; and those raised for consumption consist of various description of provisions, most of them indigenous to the soil, and are always in such abundance as to enable the negroes to dispose of great quantities to the small crafts trading to and from the island. There is no doubt that as the planters and proprietors generally perceive the new measure to be working well, I think I may venture to say successfully, and so very different from what they had anticipated, they will be induced to augment their estates, ..."
>
> (CO 253/49/2: 23/11/1835)

Further he reported about exports of sulphur:

> "A gentleman arrived here some short time ago for the purpose collecting sulphur in the quarter of Soufrière where there are considerable quantities, and I learn that his undertaking is likely to prove successful, the first exportation of 80 tons being now about to be made."

Regarding exports of sulphur BREEN (1844: 319) mentions the following figures:

Year	sulphur exports in tons [13]
1836	540
1838	60
1840	160

As obstacles to the expansion of industry Governor DUDLEY HILL cited a shortage of workers and financial means:

> "I should certainly say that I do consider there are obstacles which most forcibly affect the extension of industry. St. Lucia neither possesses pecuniary means nor population in any manner equal to its extent and internal resources ...
>
> The whole of the working classes do not exceed 10,000, and I know of no estate which even possesses a full complement of labourers, and the planters are always anxious to employ aliens or any persons they can procure for the cultivation of the soil."

---

[13] Sulphur springs are situated in the South West of St. Lucia, a few miles away from the town of Soufrière (ST. LUCIA YEAR BOOK 1982: 19).

He pleaded for the immigration of working people:

"I would therefore respectfully submit that if emigration could be introduced into this colony, there is not one of His Majesty's possessions in the West Indies where persons who may be desirous of settling themselves could be more favourably provided for, whether as hired labourers on estates or in the working of land which would be allotted to them. There is perhaps not a twentieth part of the island in cultivation, and as the soil throughout is excellent and susceptible of labour of almost every description, great benefit would be deprived by the colony, as well as the mother country should the measure of emigration now recommended be carried into effect."

From the year 1836 there was a positive turn in the reports about St. Lucia's economy.

The STIPENDIARY MAGISTRATES forecasted in their reports of September and October 1836 respectively a very good crop. Extracts from these reports are as follows:

1st district (Castries, Gros Islet, Dauphin and Anse La Raye):

"The prospects of the ensuing Crop are very good. The general state of cultivation is forward and the season has been favourable."

(CO 253/52/1: Sept. 1836)

2nd district (Soufrière, Choiseul and Laborie):

"The prospects of the ensuing Crop are better than they have been for many years. The Estates are all well cultivated and in good order."

(CO 253/52/2: 2/9/1836)

3rd district (Vieux Fort, Micoud, Praslin and Dennery):

"The prospects of the ensuing Crop are most gratifying, the Hurricane months being at an end, the Planter reckons himself secure of what is on the ground. Altogether the Island has attained a state of prosperity unknown to it for many years and rather singular, but the negroes are happy and the planters contented."

(CO 253/52/3: 31/10/1836)

In December 1836 Governor DUDLEY HILL made a tour through St. Lucia. He informed the SECRETARY OF STATE GLENELG in London as follows:

"... that in every part which I visited, appearances were highly favourable and on many of the principal Estates the manufacturing of Sugar (the staple commodity of the Island) had already commenced under the most promising auspices and as the dangerous season is I trust gone by, I have

every reason to hope that under divine providence the prospects of an abundant harvest now everywhere perceptible will soon be fully realized."

(CO 253/52/4: December 1836)

Also the two British travellers STURGE and HARVEY who visited St. Lucia in December 1836 mentioned the good crop prospects (STURGE/HARVEY 1838: 114). The Governor of St. Lucia told them that the island's large debt was nearly liquidated (STURGE/HARVEY 1838: 106).

The crop prospects for the year 1838 were also good. The respective extracts from the reports of the STIPENDIARY MAGISTRATES are as follows:

1st district (Castries, Gros Islet, Dauphin and Anse La Raye):

> *"The prospect of the Crop is favourable – The season has been rather well."*

(CO 253/56/2: 1/9/1837)

2nd district (Soufrière, Choiseul and Laborie):

> *"The prospects of the ensuing crop are the best known for some years."*

(CO 253/57/1: 1/12/1837)

3rd district (Vieux Fort, Micoud, Praslin and Dennery):

> *"The weather still continues favourable, the Coffee Crop is almost finished, it has turned out an excellent one. The Sugar Crop will commence in a month and this also promises to be a very good one."*

(CO 253/57/2: 1/12/1837)

In February 1838 Governor BUNBURY of St. Lucia confirmed these good crop prospects:

> *"... that notwithstanding continued rains and the most boisterous weather within the recollection of the oldest inhabitants at this season of the Year, under the influence of Divine Providence the industrious and well disposed Colonists are likely to be rewarded with abundant Crops."*

(CO 253/64/13: 7/2/1838)

4.6.4 Sugar plantations, cultivation of sugar-cane and the manufacture of sugar: a review regarding the whole Caribbean islands

A general review of the above mentioned subject gives DOOKHAN (1983: 51-54):

Caribbean sugar estates varied in size from a few hundred to several thousand acres, according to soil, climatic and physical geographical conditions. An average estate measured about five hundred acres and was laid out according to an almost regular pattern.

The estate land consisted of a number of clearly defined parts:

- Land for sugar-cane cultivation
- Land for cultivation of provisions
- Woodlands
- Land for pasturing of livestock
- Buildings and works

Sugar-cane land was usually divided into sections or fields in order to facilitate land use, that is, one part could be planted while another was reaped.

The main buildings were the mills for crushing the canes, the boiling-house, the curing-house, and, if rum was distilled, the still-house. Further there were workshops for skilled wheelwrights, carpenters, coopers, blacksmiths and masons. In addition, there was usually a hospital for the sick and a small gaol for slaves in punishment. Sheds were constructed for livestock and to store bagasse. And store-rooms were built to keep produce and equipment.

Near the factory buildings were the houses occupied by the estate manager, overseers and book-keepers. The estate owner or his attorney, if resident, usually lived apart in grander style in the estate's "Great house". The slave quarters were set apart from the residences of the whites.

DOOKHAN (1983: 52) gives the following plan of a sugar estate:

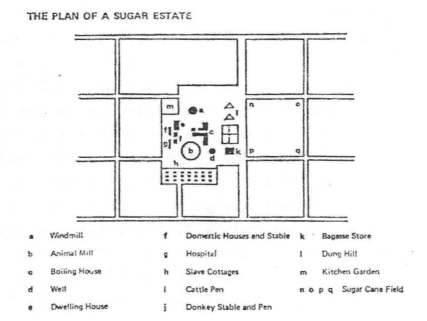

THE PLAN OF A SUGAR ESTATE

a	Windmill	f	Domestic Houses and Stable	k	Bagasse Store
b	Animal Mill	g	Hospital	l	Dung Hill
c	Boiling House	h	Slave Cottages	m	Kitchen Garden
d	Well	i	Cattle Pen	n o p q	Sugar Cane Field
e	Dwelling House	j	Donkey Stable and Pen		

(extracted from DOOKHAN 1983: 52)

Regarding the cultivation of sugar-cane and the manufacture of sugar DOOKHAN (1983: 53-54) reports as follows:

"Before sugar-cane was cultivated the land had to be prepared. The ground had to be cleared of bush, shrubs and grass, and where necessary, drainage and irrigation canals dug. On hillsides, in order to prevent soil erosion, it was sometimes necessary to terrace the land before cultivation. The ground was then marked off for tilling.

Because ploughs were not introduced until late during slavery, if at all, tilling was done by slaves with heavy digging holes, in a process called "holing". Holes were dug about four feet square and from six to nine inches deep. Into each hole some animal manure was dumped over with soil. Rows were usually parallel to each other. Planting was usually done just before the start of a rainy season. While the cuttings grew, they were "moulded" by refilling the holes with the soil originally removed.

Planting in the same field was done only periodically since, after the first year, the canes were allowed to grow from the portion of stem which was left after the cane was reaped. This process was known as ratoon cultivation and might be allowed for five to seven or more years depending on the fertility of the soil.

While the sugar-cane was growing, the rows were kept free of weeds which would hamper its growth. Three or more weeding were usually done. As the sugar-cane grew bigger, weeding became less necessary since less sunlight penetrated to the ground to nourish the weeds there.

In twelve to fifteen months, the crop was ready for reaping. Usually the canes which grew from ratoons ripened earlier than those which grew from tops. Cutting was done by slaves using cutlasses or machetes. Cut canes were tied into bundles and transported to the factories in carts.

At the factory, the canes were passed through the mills consisting of a number of rotating iron rollers. The juice, or liquor, was extracted and conveyed by gutters into receptacles called siphons. The cane trash or "bagasse" was collected, dried and used as fuel under the various boilers. In the siphons the juice was clarified by heating and the addition of a small amount of lime. The impurities were skimmed off and later used with molasses in the distillation of rum. From the siphons the liquor was transferred to the first and largest of three boilers or "coppers" where it was boiled for some time. After a certain amount of evaporation had taken place, the contents were emptied into a second and smaller copper where boiling continued but at a higher temperature. After more condensation had taken place, the liquid was transferred to the last and smallest copper. Here it was heated until it became so thick that a drop would stretch between one's fingers. This sticky substance was called teaché.

The teaché was emptied into large shallow coolers where it remained until it was almost cold. It was then put into hogsheads with perforated bottoms, which were placed on sloping platforms in the curing house. There they remained for about three weeks during which the molasses dripped out leaving the sugar crystals in the hogsheads. These were then sealed and sent off to be shipped to their European or American market."

In the book of CLAYPOLE/ROBOTTOM (1983) two interesting illustrations are shown. On the first one can see a water-driven mill:

Nig 13.1 *A water-driven mill from an eighteenth-century book. The slave in the centre is pushing cane between the rollers so that* the juice will fall into the trough below and will be carried to the boiling house along the gutter leading to the right.

(extracted from CLAYPOLE/ROBOTTOM 1983: 96)

The other illustration shows the cutting of cane in Trinidad:

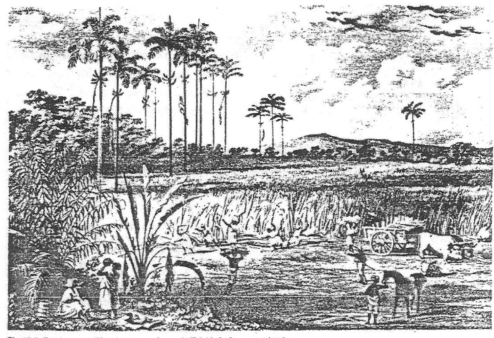

Fig 13.5 *Cutting cane. The picture was drawn in Trinidad after emancipation.*

(extracted from CLAYPOLE/ROBOTTOM 1983: 101)

4.6.5 Cutting of sugar-cane in December 1836 in St. Lucia according to an observation report

The two British travellers STURGE and HARVEY who visited St. Lucia in December 1836 observed the cutting of sugar-cane on the plantation of Mr. MUTER (Member of the PRIVY COUNCIL of St. Lucia) on December 26th. The plantation was situated to the south of the town of Castries:

> "We also went into one of the cane-pieces, where a gang of about fifty negroes, chiefly women, were employed in cutting the canes ...
>
> Here, as in Dominica, the cane is of more luxuriant growth than in Antigua or Barbados. It is reaped by two strokes of a sort of cutlass: the one taking it off about the middle, and the other close to the ground. The negro then cuts off the leaves and the plant, which consist of the one or two incipient joints at the top of the cane. The cane, the plant, and the leaves, are thrown into separate heaps, to be carried away on the backs of mules. In the cultivation of the cane, the season for planting and reaping is the same, and lasts from one-third to half of the year. ... On this estate the piece which was being planted was not holed in the usual manner, but hoed into ridges, in which the plants were inserted about twelve inches asunder, in rows running east and west, that they might sustain the least injury from the wind. The rows are five feet apart, so as to admit of the growing plants being weeded with the plough or horse-hoe. This we believe is the mode in use in Mexico. It has been partially tried on this estate, and with success. The persons employed to feed the mill and carry away the bagasse, or pressed cane-trash, were chiefly women and young persons. There were six men and one woman employed as criminals, in the severe labour of carrying the bundles of canes from the place where they had been deposited by the mules, up to the mill."

(STURGE/HARVEY 1838: 110-111)

4.6.6 Summary

From the beginning of the 19th century there was a significant change as regards the export produces of St. Lucia. Cotton which was the main export produce of St. Lucia fell in importance. The export figures of coffee and cocoa also fell. The main export produce of St. Lucia became sugar.

According to the available sources the economic situation of St. Lucia in the period of slavery under British rule from the end of the 18th century till the emancipation period was very bad. Reasons given were the wars at the end of the 18th century, shortage of slaves, hurricanes and from 1826 the measures of the British government for ameliorating the living-conditions of the slaves. Only in the emancipation period good crop prospects and an improvement of the general financial situation were reported.

4.7 Living conditions and general situation of the slaves

4.7.1 Introduction

This chapter shows the living conditions and the general situation of the slaves from the beginning of the 19th century till 1838. The chapters "4.7.2. Status of a slave", "4.7.3. General restrictions", "4.7.4. Protective laws", "4.7.5. Labour conditions on the plantations" and "4.7.6. Subsistence of Slaves and APPRENTICES" begin with the legal condition at the beginning of the 19th century and give a review of the legal developments regarding the amelioration of the living conditions of the slaves. The laws for ameliorating the living conditions of the slaves are compared with the reactions of the slave owners and other inhabitants of St. Lucia. Further observation reports about the slaves as well as slave evidences at court are mentioned.

The emancipation period will be especially mentioned in the chapters "4.7.4.4.3. Discharge of apprenticed labourers", "4.7.5.3. Situation of labour in the emancipation period" and in the chapter subsistence of slaves and APPRENTICES "4.7.6.2. Emancipation period".

4.7.2 Status of a slave

The respective laws in the CODE DE LA MARTINIQUE were as follows:

> "Art. XLIV.-Slaves considered moveables, and as such liable to mortgage."
>
> (BPP/ST/71/2: 16/3/1685, p.187)

> "Art. XII.-Children born of Slaves, although married, are still considered Slaves, and belong to the Master of the female Slave, should they have different Masters.
>
> Art. XIII.-If the slave-husband marries a free woman, the children, whether males or females, are of the condition of the mother, and considered free, notwithstanding the father be a Slave. If the father is free, and the Mother a Slave, the children are Slaves."
>
> (BPP/ST/71/2: 16/3/1685, p.185)

> "Art. IX.-Free persons who beget children with slaves, as well as the owners of such slaves permitting it, are subject to a penalty of 2000 lbs. of sugar. If the master of the slave be the father of the children, he is deprived of slave and children, who become confiscated for the good of the hospital, and lose the right of ever being freed. If, however, the father be unmarried, by marriage with his slave (if his property) she becomes free, and the children legitimate."
>
> (BPP/ST/71/2: 16/3/1685, p.184)

According to the available sources these clauses were not altered until the abolition of slavery.

4.7.3 General restrictions

4.7.3.1 Prohibition of possessing property

According to the CODE DE LA MARTINIQUE the slaves had no right to possess property:

> "Art. XXVII.-Slaves can possess nothing independent of their Masters. All that they may acquire by industry, or through the liberality of other persons, or otherwise, belong in full right to their Masters, without the children of such Slaves, their fathers, mothers, or their families, or others, pretending any right to the same, either by succession, gift, or otherwise; declaring all gifts, promises, or obligations, made by Slaves, to be null and void, and as having been made by persons incapable of acting or contracting and disposing for themselves."

> (BPP/ST/71/2: 16/3/1685, p.186)

When the British government started to ameliorate the living conditions of the slaves the SECRETARY OF STATE BATHURST proposed in a letter dated in July 1823 to all Governors of the British colonies:

> "The last subject to which I propose at present to advert, is the necessity of insuring to the Slave the enjoyment of whatever property he may be able to acquire. For this purpose Savings Banks should be established under legislative authority, upon the model of those in England, but with this alteration, …"
> (BPP/ST/68/1: 9/7/1823, p.289)

To this proposal Governor MAINWARING of St. Lucia replied:

> "There will I should fear be a great difficulty here in establishing a Savings Bank, and if there were no other I am persuaded it will take a very long time to induce the Slaves to place their savings in any public office; I have invariably remarked that the Slave is both extremely mistrustful and injudicious in his confidence."
> (CO 253/17/3: 25/8/1823)

Also the PROCUREUR GENERAL, PROCUREUR DU ROI as well as the SENESCHAL of St. Lucia were of a similar opinion:

> "The institution in question is impracticable, by reason of the dissipation, want of foresight, and mistrust of the Slaves;"
> (BPP/ST/68/1: 1/12/1823, p.289)

Regarding the possession of property for slaves in St. Lucia they reported:

"... but it is only a piece of justice due to the inhabitants to say that they always respect the little properties of those of their Slaves, who have any such, during their lifetime, and that they transmit them with fidelity to the children, relatives, or wives of these persons when deceased."

With the new slave law which came into force on June 1st, 1826, the slaves got the right to possess property:

60: "The Peculium, is all the property belonging to a Slave. It consists of the proceeds of their provision grounds, of the produce of their industry, when exempted either by law or by permission of the owner, from working for their owners, of such property as they may have acquired by gift or inheritance, of the fruits and profits arising from property obtained by any of the above methods and property obtained by barter or purchase for their own account with any part of the same."

With the consent of their owners slaves could even possess other slaves:

61: "Any kind of property real or personal may form part of their peculium, but Slaves cannot be allowed to possess other Slaves unless they obtain the owner's consent in writing, which consent shall be irrevocable."

The slaves could dispose of their property freely:

62: "A Slave has the full & entire property of his Peculium, he possesses it in his own name, he disposes of it at pleasure either with or without the knowledge or consent of his owner, who can neither administer or employ it without the Slave's consent, so that a Slave may enter into valid & effectual contracts & engagements with his owner respecting it; he may sue & be sued at law for all matters relating to it, he may dispose of the same by will, and, in short, with respect to the administration and disposal of his private property, the Slave is to be considered as free."

(CO 253/22/4: 1/6/1826)

About the habit of saving money by slaves Governor STEWART of St. Lucia wrote in May 1829:

"While the Slaves on estates are, so I have described, well disposed and comfortable, and by the sale of their spare produce from their industry, are comparatively rich, and save what in their circumstances, may be ... considerable sums of money, by which many have purchased their own freedom, there are on other Estates people of every different Caste; without industry, ..."

(CO 253/26/6: 29/9/1829)

The PROTECTOR OF SLAVES reported in the year 1830:

"The only Slave known to the Protector as having accumulated any money is the slave Jean Louis, who it appears, possesses upwards of 500 Dollars with which he is about to purchase his freedom …

Without being able to state any positive facts as to the amount of actual accumulations of money by slaves it is here generally understood that a considerable deal of property in money is possessed by many of them which they are in the custom of burying it in secret places. This fact alone accounts for the limited knowledge possessed by the Protector on this head.

The extensive tracts of abandoned land throughout the island, which the negro may occupy and cultivate afford even to the least industrious profitable returns for the produce thereof."

(CO 258/6/2: 1/4/1830-30/9/1830/Section G)

In a further report concerning the first half year 1831 the PROTECTOR OF SLAVES mentioned a slave with the name NELSON MC. DOWALL:

"The only case of accumulation of property which has come out to the protector's knowledge is that of Nelson Mc. Dowall, a plantation slave and a natural son of the late Mr. Mc. Cullon who showed the protector a receipt for 230,- Spanish Dollars which he had just deposited in the hands of Mr. Catterson, a respectable and wealthy merchant in Castries with the view to purchasing his freedom. There is owing to the same slave the further sum of 100 Dollars being his salary as overseer on the estate to which he is attached as a slave and which his good conduct and knowledge of reading and writing have procured to him from Mr. John Miller, the manager. The age of this slave is about 21."

He also referred to the establishment of a Savings Bank:

"The establishment of a Savings Bank would be productive of much benefit to the Slave. The Treasurer of the Island might be asked to afford his assistance in setting it on foot."

(CO 258/7/1: 1/1/1831-30/6/1831/Section G)

On September 27th, 1831, three members of the PRIVY COUNCIL of St. Lucia reported of a possibility for slaves to earn money:

"In the article of Logwood alone, an occupation exclusively carried on by them, a sum of no less than sixteen thousand Spanish Dollars is annually paid to them in this very limited community."

(CO 253/30/2: 27/9/1831)

The report of the PROTECTOR OF SLAVES for the first half of the year 1832 contains general information about the possibility for slaves to accumulate money rapidly – *"more indeed than any other species of property"*:

> *"Such accumulations are chiefly facilitated*
>
> *1st: By the extreme fertility of the soil in St. Lucia and the little difficulty in obtaining any quantity which may be wished for cultivation, … by the extreme high prices of the markets in the Colony.*
>
> *2nd: By the abundance of fish on the Coast; and the proximity of almost every settled part to the sea.*
>
> *3rd: By the great quantity of logwood, growing wild on waste land; which always finds a ready market for Europe, Martinique and America.*
>
> *Hence it will appear that such accumulations are chiefly made by Plantation Slaves."*

(CO 258/11/1: 1/1/1832-30/6/1832/Section G)

On August 13th, 1832, Governor FARQUHARSON of St. Lucia proclaimed an ordinance which fixed the stipulations for establishing a Savings Bank. An extract from the preamble is as follows:

> *"…, it is expedient that a Savings Bank should be immediately established in this Island for a better preserving the property of slaves with a view of enabling the industrious slave by laying aside in a safe place of deposit a portion of the earnings to effect the purchase of a freedom or for any other desirable purpose and likewise to discourage the inconvenient practices of slaves lending and depositing the amount of savings with any free person for security sake but who are frequently either unfit or unwilling to restore and pay back the same when required so to do."*

(CO 255/2/5: 13/8/1832, p. 146)

From the 1st September 1832 a Savings Bank would be opened in the town of Castries. In order to give all slaves in the island the possibility to deposit money in the Savings Bank of Castries special officials were appointed who were responsible for the money transfer from the slave to the Savings Bank.

For the year 1833 there exists a detailed report regarding the property of slaves made by the PROTECTOR OF SLAVES (CO 258/14/1: 1/7/1833-31/12/1833/Section G):

> *"That habits of industry are continuing to gain ground rapidly with the great proportion of the slave population. This he would still attribute to the diminution, by law, of the hours in which their labour is dedicated by*

compulsion to the service of others and to the facility of employing them by the general fertility of the soil and the abundance of waste land in the immediate neighbourhood of every estate."

"In support of this position he advances the notorious fact that within the last three years the articles of negro produce have fallen in price from 1/3 to ½ in the Castries' market."

As negro produce he mentioned: cassava, charcoal, firewood, forage, fish and vegetables of every description. He further mentioned:

"The export of logwood to Martinique, America and England affords a sure supply of ready money when required, even to the less steadily industrious negro."

"The general wealth is decidedly with the praedial slaves as a class. The largest accumulation of individual property have however been made by artisans, ..., tradesmen, coopers, carpenters and masons."

He gave three examples:

"Slave Neptune, property of a ship-carpenter, sold lately on his own account a small sloop which he had built in his own hours."

"The mason Joe attached to a large sugar-estate in this Island has seldom less than 10 free persons including his apprentices at work under him on his own account and has sometimes received 200 Dollars a month for himself and his workmen from planters, with whom he contracts for the repair and even erection of their buildings. The slave has purchased his wife and her child by another slave but will not purchase himself. He pays his owners a certain sum per month in consideration of being allowed to dispose of his own time."

"Another Slave Jules Vigis belonging to the succession of the late Franaces Vigis, a coffee planter in the heights of Soufrière, an excellent blacksmith and planter is in partnership with a free man in the only forge at Soufrière, and the slave's man stands first in the firm."

In conclusion the PROTECTOR OF SLAVES remarked:

"that since Slave property has been effectually secured by law a taste for comfort is becoming general among the negroes who are consequently fast giving up their former plan of burying in their gardens or elsewhere their money as they made it."

Summing up it can be said that slaves could earn money by selling cultivated produces, fish as well as logwood and by trade activities; especially from the year 1826 when they got the legal right to possess property. It was the habit of slaves to bury their earnings in the earth or to give it to free persons for depositing. In order to curtail this kind of saving, a Savings Bank for slaves was established in the town of Castries on September 1st, 1832.

4.7.3.2   Prohibition of Assemblies

The relevant clauses in the CODE NOIR were as follows:

> *"Art.XVI.-Forbidding Slaves, belonging to different Masters, to assemble together at night, at the dwelling of either Master or elsewhere, under pretext of weddings, or otherwise, nor in the high roads or by-ways, under pain of corporal punishment, which cannot be less than flogging and the fleur-de-lis; and in case of frequent repetitions, and under aggravated circumstances, they can be punished with death, at the discretion of the Judges."*

> *"Art.XVII.-Masters, convicted of having permitted or tolerated such assemblies, composed of others than their own Slaves, shall be condemned to repair any injury caused by such assembly, to pay a fine of ten livres for the first offence, and double in case of repetition."*

> (BPP/ST/71/2: 16/3/1685, p. 185)

The mentioned clauses were confirmed with laws of 9th February 1765 (BPP/ST/71/2: 9/2/1765, p.196) and 25th December 1783 (BPP/ST/71/2: 25/12/1783, p.205). From the last mentioned law follows that with the consent of the PROCUREUR DU ROI assemblies of slaves were possible:

> *"Art. XLIX.-Masters who shall be convicted of having permitted assemblies of Slaves, or having lent their dwellings for that purpose, without a commission from Commandant visaéd by the Procureur du Roi, (which is not to be permitted but seldom even during carnival, from disorders which ensue) to be condemned as follows: -Masters who shall have given permission, to a fine of 100 livres, and those who shall have lent or hired their houses, to 300 livres."*

Also in the slave law of the year 1826 the clause regarding the prohibition of assemblies was fixed. A punishable act was:

> *84: "Slaves attending meetings of Slaves belonging to different Masters held without sanction of a public officer."*

> (CO 253/22/4: 1/6/1826)

In the year 1832 it was already possible for slaves to meet only with the sanction of their owner. According to an ordinance of June 1832 the following actions were punishable:

> *"Holding Meetings or dances without permission of the Manager, or being present thereat, without such permission, ...*

Crowding or being masked on the Public Places, Streets or Wharves to be obstruction, annoyance of passangers or other persons."

(CO 255/2/6: 16/6/1832, p.133)

4.7.3.3 Prohibition of professions

In the CODE NOIR the following clause was fixed:

"Art.XXX.-Slaves not allowed to be appointed to office, nor to any public situation, nor to be appointed agents to others than their Maters, nor to be concerned in commerce, nor act as arbitrators or witnesses, ..."

(BPP/ST/71/2: 16/3/1685, p.186)

The French law of 1st February 1743 contains the following prohibition:

"Forbidding all Slaves of either sex from composing or distributing remedies made up in powders, or in any other manner, with the exception of the bite of serpents, under pain of corporal punishment; even death, if the case requires it. Slaves, who under pretext of preparing remedies for bites of serpents, should apply them to other purposes, shall be condemned to the penalties hereby laid down."

(BPP/ST/71/2: 1/2/1743, p.192)

These prohibitions of professions were also fixed in the slave law of 1826, with slight alterations:

74: "Slaves are incapable of holding public offices, and public commissions, and of being arbitrators or appraisers."

75: "Slaves shall not prepare or distribute any drugs or medicines, or undertake the cure of sick persons without the Masters' permission on pain of severe corporal punishment which may under circumstances of aggravation even extend to one hundred lashes."

(CO 253/22/4: 1/6/1826)

4.7.3.4 Prohibition of selling several products

According to the CODE DE LA MARTINIQUE the following law was valid:

"Art.XVIII.-Forbidding Slaves to sell sugar canes, even with their Masters' permission, under pain of flogging for the Slaves; a fine of ten livres tournois against the Master; and the like sum against the buyer.

Art.XIX.-Forbidding Slaves to expose for sale either in the market or at private houses any kind of produces, not even fruits, vegetables, or grass, for feeding cattle, without a written permission from their Masters. Articles so sold to be reclaimed by masters without repayment, and a fine of six livres against the buyer."

(BPP/ST/71/2: 16/3/1685, p.185)

A law dated in 1734 provided the following:

"Art. III.-Prohibiting Planters, under any pretext, from selling coffee by their Slaves.
Art. IV.-Forbidding Slaves from selling coffee, even by order of their Masters, under pain of being flogged, and the coffee confiscated.
Art. V.- Forbidding persons of all descriptions from buying coffee of Slaves, even should they have their Masters' permission."

(BPP/ST/71/2: 7/1/1734, p.191)

By an ordinance dated in April 1735 the dispositions of the above mentioned law were extended to the sale of cotton (BPP/ST/71/2: 15/4/1735, p.191).

The selling of cattle was also forbidden for slaves:

"Art. IV.-Forbidding Slaves of either sex from merchandising or purchasing cattle, either in country or town, or on board of vessels, either on their own account, or on that of their Masters.

Art. V.- Forbidding equally Masters thus to employ their Slaves on their own account, or on account of others, under pain of confiscation of the Slaves and cattle which they may have purchased, and a fine of 500 livres against the Master."

(BPP/ST/71/2: 11/7/1744, p.193)

Another prohibition concerned the trade with meat:

"Art. III.-Forbidding Slaves from following the trade of butchers, or re-selling meat bought by them of butchers, under pain of being flogged and pilloried, and also confiscation of the Slaves to the benefit of the King, if it shall be proved that the Master authorized them to do so. Slaves, however, allowed selling pork as usual."

(BPP/ST/71/2: 1/9/1763, p.195)

These were the stipulations at the beginning of the 19th century.

In the Slave Law of 1826 the following was punishable:

84: "Slaves selling Sugar Canes, Cocoa, Indigo, Cotton or Logwood, without their Master's permission.

(CO 253/22/4: 1/6/1826)

According to an ordinance of Governor FARQUHARSON of St. Lucia dated on 16th June 1832 the following was punishable for slaves:

> *"Slaves having in their possession, or traffic ring in Sugar, Coffee, Cocoa, in quantity exceeding one pound avoir du pois; Rum exceeding one imperial quart; Molasses exceeding one half Gallon; Sugar canes, Logwood, Indigo, or offering for Sale, Gold, Silver, or Jewellery, Wares or Merchandize, without a written permission from their owner, or giving a satisfactory account of the same when required."*

(CO 255/2/6: 16/6/1832, p.133)

4.7.3.5 Prohibition of possessing arms

The laws respecting the possession of arms concerning the slaves valid at the beginning of the 19th century were fixed on 25th December 1783 as follows:

> *"Art. XLIII.-Slaves sent out shooting by their Masters, to be bearers of permission in writing, which are to specify the nature of the arms given to the Slaves together with the quantity of powder, which is never to exceed half a pound under penalty of one hundred livres against the Master. Forbidding also all shopkeepers from selling powder and shot to Slaves without their Master's order in writing, which is to be left in the possession of the shopkeeper who will give another to the Slave specifying the quantity of powder delivered. Forbidding Slaves from shooting between March and end of July, under pain of flogging and pillory for three days.*
>
> *Art. XLIV.-Slaves found with fire-arms, powder, shot, and balls, without their Master's permission, to be arrested, conducted to prison, flogged, and pilloried.*
>
> *Art. XLV.-Forbidding Slaves from keeping arms in their houses under any pretext whatever, and if, on visiting, any should be found, the Slave to be seized and put in the pillory, the Master condemned to a fine of 100 livres."*

(BPP/ST/71/2: 25/12/1783, p.204)

For runaway slaves who were found with arms the punishment was more severe:

> *"Art. XXXVIII.-Slaves arrested as runaways, and found with side or fire-arms of any description, to be punished with death. Those found with cutlasses or knives other than those called jambette (like a garden-knife) to suffer corporal punishment, even death if necessary."*

(BPP/ST/71/2: 25/12/1783, p.204)

This prohibition of possessing arms was valid till the abolition of slavery. In the Slave Law of 1826 the following clause was fixed:

84: *"Slaves purchasing or carrying muskets, swords, or any other offensive weapons, or gunpowder without permission.*

... shall be subject to the penalties which shall be provided in the various police ordinances or regulations which may from time to time be enacted by the Governor in Council, provided the said penalties and punishments do not in any case exceed one hundred and fifty lashes, and three years hard labour in the chain-gang against Slaves, ..."

(CO 253/22/4: 1/6/1826)

4.7.3.6   Evidence of slaves before court

According to the CODE DE LA MARTINIQUE the slaves had no right to give evidence before court:

"Art. XXX.-Slaves not allowed to be appointed to office, ..., nor act as arbitrators or witnesses, either in civil or criminal matters; and, in the event of their being called upon as witnesses, their depositions can only serve to assist the Judge, without being considered as a presumption or admission of proof."

Their general status before court was as follows:

"Art. XXXI.-Slaves cannot be parties in civil matters, either as plaintiffs or defendants, nor be civil parties in criminal matters, reserving, however, to their Masters to act for and defend them, and to demand in their behalf, in criminal matters, reparation for any ill-treatment received by their Slaves."

"Art. XXXII.-Slaves can be prosecuted criminally, without their Masters becoming parties, unless they be accomplices, and they are judged, in first instance, by the ordinary Judges, and in appeal by the Sovereign Council (Conseil Souverain), with the same formalities as are observed in the cases of free persons."

(BPP/ST/71/2: 16/3/1685, p.186)

On July 15th, 1738 the slaves got the following right:

"Notwithstanding the 30th Article of the Ordinance of March, 1685, it is ordered, that in default of whites, the Evidence of Slaves shall be taken in all cases, except against their Masters."

(BPP/ST/71/2: 15/7/1738, p.192)

When the British government started to ameliorate the living conditions of the slaves the SECRETARY OF STATE BATHURST proposed in a letter dated July 1823 to all Governors of the British colonies:

"..., a law should be passed declaring that the evidence of a Slave shall be received in all, except perhaps certain cases, if upon appearing in Court to give testimony, he shall produce, under the hand of some of the parochial

clergymen, or of the religious teacher authorized by the master or overseer to instruct him, a certificate, stating that the proposed witness has been so far instructed in the principles of religion, as, in the judgment of the party certifying, adequately to understand the obligation of an oath. The cases to be considered must be those in which the master of the Slaves is directly concerned, and such as would affect the life of a white person."

(BPP/ST/68/1: 9/7/1823, p.280)

To this proposal Governor MAINWARING of St. Lucia replied in August 1823 as follows:

"By the law which governs this colony, the evidence of Slaves is received, excepting for or against their masters, therefore to render a qualification necessary or to increase the number of exceptions, would be to deprive them of a privilege enjoyed under the old French law since the 15th July 1738;"

(CO 253/17/3: 25/8/1823)

The PROCUREUR GENERAL, PROCUREUR DU ROI as well as the SENESCHAL of St. Lucia reported on the occasion of the proposal of the SECRETARY OF STATE:

"In conformity with the laws which rule the island of Saint Lucia, and especially an Ordinance of the King of the 15th July 1738, Slaves are admitted to give evidence in Justice, in default of white witnesses. Even, in the case when white witnesses are in sufficient number, the testimony of Slaves is nevertheless admitted in jurisprudence. The only limit in this respect is that Slaves cannot be admitted as witnesses against their masters."

(BPP/ST/68/1: 1/12/1823, p.280)

This situation was also fixed in the Slave Law of St. Lucia of the year 1826:

72: "Slave Evidence is admissible in all cases civil and criminal, except against the Slave's Master."

(CO 253/22/4: 1/6/1826)

One year later this clause was altered as follows:

"It is hereby ordered that slavery shall not operate as a disqualification for a witness, except in cases where his master has an interest and that in such cases, the evidence of a slave shall not be received either for or against the master."

(CO 255/1/2: 24/4/1827)

With the ORDER IN COUNCIL dated November 2nd, 1831, which came into force in St. Lucia on January 7th, 1832, the slaves were assimilated in status to the free persons regarding the giving of evidence before court:

"LXXXVII.-And it is further ordered, That no person shall henceforth be rejected as a witness, or be, or be deemed to be, incompetent to give evidence in any Court of Civil of Criminal Justice, or before any Judge or Magistrate, or in any civil or criminal proceeding whatsoever in any of the said Colonies, by reason that such person is in a state of Slavery; but the evidence of Slaves shall in all Courts, and for all purposes, be admissible, and be received in the said Colonies in the same manner and subject to the same regulations as the evidence of free persons."

(BPP/ST/79/1: 2/11/1831, p.93)

4.7.3.7   Summary

According to the legal situation at the beginning of the 19th century the slaves were bound to the following restrictions:

- Prohibition of possessing property
- Assemblies of slaves of different masters were only possible with the consent of the PROCUREUR DU ROI
- Slaves were not allowed to be appointed to office nor to any public situation, nor to be appointed agents to others than their masters, nor to be concerned in commerce, nor to compose or distribute remedies or to undertake the cure of any description of disorder with the exception of the bite of serpents
- Prohibition of selling several produces like sugar-cane, coffee or cotton; other produces like fruits or vegetables could be sold with a written approval of the slave's owner
- Prohibition of possessing arms
- Slaves could not give evidence before a court against their owner

When ameliorating the living conditions of the slaves they got the following rights:

- With the Slave Law dated in June 1826 the slaves got the right to possess property
- From the year 1832 for slave assemblies the consent of the slave's owner was sufficient
- From 1826 the composition or distribution of remedies as well as the cure of any description of disorder was possible for slaves with the consent of their owners
- With the Slave Law of 1826 the general prohibition of selling sugar cane, coffee and cotton was cancelled. These produces could be sold with the consent of the slave's owner. With the ordinance of June 1832 the selling of sugar-cane, coffee, cocoa, rum and molasses up to a certain amount was possible without the consent of the slave owner

- Regarding the giving of evidence before court the slaves were assimilated in status to the free persons with the ORDER IN COUNCIL dated 2nd, 1831.

4.7.4 Protective laws

4.7.4.1   Maintenance of slaves

4.7.4.1.1 Legal situation at the beginning of the 19th century

<u>Nourishing</u>

The relevant clause in the CODE DE LA MARTINIQUE was:

> "Art. XXII.-Masters to allow to their Slaves, from ten years of age and upwards, the following rations of provisions weekly: two and a half pots (Paris measure) of farina manioc, or three cassavas, each weighing two pounds and a half at least, or its equivalent, with two pounds salt beef, or three pounds fish, or other things in proportion; and to infants, from the time being weaned, until they shall have attained ten years, half of the above allowance."
>
> (BPP/ST/71/2: 16/3/1685, p.185)

Besides receiving food from their owners the slaves could also cultivate small gardens:

> "Art. II - A small portion of ground on the estate to be given to each Slave, to be cultivated for their profit and advantage. Owners, attorneys, and managers, to see that these Negroes' gardens are kept in proper order. Each Slave to receive weekly the quantity of provision necessary for subsistence, in salt-fish, salt-beef, farina, syrup, and vegetables, exclusive of any provision which the Slaves may have raised in their own gardens, which are never to enter as compensation for a lesser allowance."
>
> (BPP/ST/71/2: 15/10/1786, p.206)

<u>Clothes</u>

The laws in the CODE DE LA MARTINIQUE were as follows:

> "Art. XXV.-Masters to allow to each Slave yearly two suits of clothes, or four ells of linen."
>
> (BPP/ST/71/2:16/3/1685, p.185)

> "Art. III. -Slaves to receive two changes of clothes yearly, for the men, shirts and trousers, for the women, shifts and petticoats, and for children, shirts."
>
> (BPP/ST/71/2: 15/10/1786, p.206)

Other obligations

A clause in the CODE DE LA MARTINIQUE was:

> "Art. XXVII.-Slaves, infirm either from age, sickness, or otherwise,
> whether the disorder may be incurable or not, shall be fed and maintained
> by their Masters; and, in the event of their being abandoned, the said
> Slaves shall be sent to the hospital, and the Masters obliged to pay ten
> sols per diem for the maintenance of each Slave."

(BPP/ST/71/2: 16/3/1685, p.185)

An ordinance of October 15th, 1786, said:

"Art. IV.-A building to be appropriated solely for a hospital, to be situated
in any airy and healthy spot, and to be cleanly kept. To be furnished with
camp-beds, mats, and coarse coverlets. Forbidding Masters to suffer their
Slaves to lie on the floor."

(BPP/ST/71/2: 15/10/1786, p.206)

Regarding accommodation of slaves no clause could be found in the CODE
DE LA MARTINIQUE.

4.7.4.1.2 Maintenance of slaves from the beginning of the 19th century till the end of the emancipation period

As already mentioned in chapter "4.6. Economic development", pp. 86-
107, the planters of St. Lucia were in a difficult financial as well as
economic situation at the beginning of the 19th century. This situation
affected the maintenance of the slaves.

On January 8th, 1812, the members of the appellate court of St. Lucia
signed a petition to the British parliament in which they proclaimed the
wretched condition of the colony:

> "La cour d'appel de Sainte-Lucie, pleine de Respect et de confiance dans
> les membres qui composent votre chamber, prend la liberté de metre sous
> vos yeux l'état deplorable de cette infortunée colonie, qui tend rapidement
> à la ruine –"

(CO 253/7/3: 8/1/1812)

Among other things they pointed out that it was no more possible to
maintain the salves as ordered. There was a lack of nourishment, clothes
and medicine:

> "La misère des habitants de cette colonie est quelle, qu'ils ne peuvent plus
> fournir à leur esclaves tout la conservation, …, les salaisons nécessaires
> pour leur nourriture, les vètmens et les médicamens dont ils ont besoin;"

In the year 1817 a hurricane destroyed the ground provisions of the island. Governor O'HARA of St. Lucia wrote to the SECRETARY OF STATE in London as follows:

> "... if some measure is not immediately adopted for relieving the slave population, I fully believe the consequence will be, that a famine must take place in the Island, the ground provisions having been totally destroyed by the Hurricane, a supply of which (the produce of the Colony) cannot be expected in less than eight months."

> (CO 253/12/2: 18/4/1818)

Further the Governor mentioned:

> "Slaves of the smaller Planters were anxious from the want of Shelter so long after the Hurricane but how particularly from the reduced allowance of food paid them by their masters, in consequence of the destruction of their small coffee and cocoa plantations which has deprived them of the means of paying the high price demanded for provisions by the resident Merchants, who speculate on their wants without mercy, ..."

Two years later another hurricane devastated the island. This was on October the 13th, 14th and the 15th, 1819. Governor KEANE of St. Lucia wrote as follows:

> "... overflow of the rivers which have not only destroyed all the ground provisions throughout the Island but have swept away or overwhelmed whole fields of produce and in many quarters works and buildings and negroes.

> And having moreover satisfied myself by personal observation in the neighbouring quarters of the very extraordinary and unprecedented losses experienced in the late storm by the inhabitants generally but more especially by the Planters who have not only deprived of the means of feeding the negroes by the utter destruction of their ground provisions but have at the same time suffered most severely in their prospects for the ensuing crop which will in all cases be most seriously diminished and in many entirely lost to them."

> (CO 253/13/1: 27/10/1819)

In the year 1824 Governor BLACKWELL of St. Lucia described the general situation of the maintenance of the slaves:

> "... and that from every observation, and the most minute enquiry which I could make, it was evident to me that they in most instances, were well and regularly clothed, fed, and attended to in every respect."

> (CO 253/18/2: 6/8/1824)

In the Slave Law of 1826 the clauses regarding nourishing were as follows:

29: "All Slaves upwards of ten years of age, shall receive for their subsistence two Pots of Farina of manioc, or three cassavas, weighing each two pounds and a half, or an equivalent in good vegetable food, and two pounds and a half of dried Cod-fish weekly, and Children half that quantity, exclusively of the produce of their Provision Grounds. But when the master shall allow his Slaves to work in their Provision Grounds during one whole day in every week out of Crop, and half a day in Crop (besides Sundays) he shall be required to furnish only a pound and a quarter of Cod-fish and no other provisions."

(CO 253/22/4: 1/6/1826)

28: "Every Slave shall have a small portion of the Plantation given him for his own use as a Garden which he is to cultivate as he thinks proper. The Master shall see that the Garden grounds are kept in good order."

31: "The Slaves shall not be removed from their Gardens at a less warning than one year."

Concerning clothes and medical care there were the following clauses:

26: "Every Slave without exception shall receive a thick linen or woollen dress twice in each year, the dress shall consist for the Men, of a Shirt and Trousers, for the Women, of a Chemise and Petticoat and a Shirt for the Children, and every Slave shall be furnished with a Hat or Cap once a year."

34: "Sick and infirm Slaves whether the malady be incurable or otherwise, shall be supported by their owners. If deserted by them, they shall be adjudged to the colony, and the owner shall pay it fifty sous per day."

33: "Every plantation shall have its Hospital attached to it. The building intended for that purpose shall be erected as nearly as may be on the most airy and healthy situation of the estate. It shall be kept clean, and supplied with Camp Beds, Mats, and coarse Linen."

For the accommodation of the slaves the law said the following:

27: "The planter shall build his Negro-huts in a healthy situation and see that they are kept in good repair. The Slaves shall not be allowed to sleep upon the ground."

In May 1829 Governor STEWART of St. Lucia rode round the island. By the end of September he informed the SECRETARY OF STATE:

"During the month of May I rode round this Island, and visited and examined every plantation supporting thirty negroes and upwards; but not forgetting the smaller ones with fewer numbers, only taking less time.

I saw much to approve and much to disapprove; but it is satisfactory to be able to say, that the latter is small in comparison to the former: I saw on many plantations the negroes happy and contented - ... On these Estates the people are well fed, as their appearance fully proves, and for which the abundance of fertile land affords every facility. In that respect, this Colony has a great advantage over Barbados and other basser islands. The negroes here have another advantage in being allowed a quantity of fertile land for their own cultivation, the spare produce of which they send to market, and are thus enabled to supply themselves with many comforts. The effect of this is seen in the good and often gay dresses (particularly among the females) which they purchase."

(CO 253/26/6: 29/9/1829)

Regarding the medical care he wrote:

"... and no less important a consideration that the aged and the sick are well attended to, with comfortable hospitals for the latter, and dedicines and medical attendance."

Further he informed as follows:

"This is the state in which I found thirty nine plantations. On seventeen others, there is less appearance of comfort, but no want of provisions, or the real necessaries, altho' there is nothing of that neatness about their houses, or attention to dress - ...

Proceeding with my report, I found on several Estates great appearances of distress – indeed, of poverty; as was seen by the dilapidated state of the sugar works, principal Dwelling houses; as well as those of the negroes – with the clothing of the latter very scanty. In defence of this very defective state of comparative comfort and prosperity, it was stated, that being much involved in debt, so much of the annual income was required to pay the interest, that little surplus remained."

Governor STEWART concluded his report with the following sentences:

"Of the conduct of Planters to their slaves, I have found; as already stated, no reason to disapprove, so far as regards an abundant supply of food; and other comforts, with the exception of those who endeavour to excuse themselves on the score of poverty, and their obligations to pay over all the produce of their crop to their Creditors."

In March 1830 an "Abstract of the condition and particular management of plantations in the 1st District" was made. The following table follows from this abstract regarding the district of Castries:

Object	Evaluation								Number of plantations	Other judgements		Total
	very good		good, plenty		tolerable, sufficient		insufficient, bad					
	figure	%	figure	%	figure	%	figure	%		figure	description	
Hospital	1	4	23	92	0	-	1	4	25	10	Building, chamber	35
Accommodation	1	3	27	82	3	9	2	6	33	2	under repair	35
Slave grounds	1	3	34	97	0	-	0	-	35	0		35
Provisions	0		34	97	1	3	0		35	0		35
Clothing	0		0		0		0		0	35	Laws were observed	35

(compiled by E. Kolar based on a committee report of St. Lucia; CO 253/29/1: 31/3/1830)

From this table follows that the maintenance of the slaves in the 1st district was mostly good. The percentages for "good, plenty" vary from 82 to 97.

In an ordinance of Governor FARQUHARSON of St. Lucia dated in May 1830 the stipulations regarding the slave accommodations were exactly specified:

> "11. Every proprietor or possessor of a plantation shall provide the slaves attached thereto with good and comfortable huts, well wattled and thatched, so as to be perfectly wind and water tight, to be afterwards kept in repair by the slaves themselves. The head or chief of every family shall have a hut for himself and his family, separated into two or more apartments, according to the number of that family, and there should be cabanes or bed-places in those apartments, raised at least 18 inches, to preserve them from the dangerous effect of sleeping on the ground. Young slaves of fourteen and upwards, who have no family, shall be lodged at the rate of three or four to a hut, and they are to have their cabanes raised 18 inches from the ground as aforesaid …
>
> The slaves shall be allowed to enclose their huts with a fence or hedge, to form a little yard for their poultry and other small stock, and defend them from the incursions of the cattle in the pasture."

(BPP/ST/77/2: 3/5/1830. Pp. 369-370)

On December 24th, 1831, Governor BOZON of St. Lucia proclaimed an ORDER IN COUNCIL, which was passed by the British government on January 7th, 1832. It came into force on January 7th, 1832.

Regarding the food for the slaves the slave owners could choose whether to maintain their slaves by the cultivation of ground appropriated to them or by an allowance of provisions:

"First,-Every such owner or manager of Slaves, shall within the first week of January in each and every year, deliver or cause to be delivered to the Protector of Slaves, or to the Assistant Protector of the District in which such Slaves are resident, a written Declaration in the form prescribed in the Schedule to this Order annexed, specifying whether it is the intention of such owner or manager during the year next ensuing to maintain his Slaves by the cultivation of ground to be to them appropriated for that purpose, or by an allowance of provisions."

(BPP/ST/79/1: 2/11/1831, p.124)

If the slave owner decided to maintain his slave by an allowance of provisions the following clauses were valid:

"Fifthly,-Every owner or manager who shall by such declaration as aforesaid, propose to maintain his Slaves by an allowance of provisions, shall be, and is hereby bound and required to supply such provisions to the amount, and of the kinds following, that is to say: Each and every Slave above the age of ten years, shall receive in each week not less than twenty-one pints of Wheat flour, or of the flour or meal of Guinea or Indian Corn, or fifty-six full grown Plantains, or fifty-six pounds of Cocoas or Yams; and also seven Herrings or Shads, or other salted Provisions equal thereto; and every Slave below the age of ten years shall be supplied with one half of the before mentioned allowance in each week, which allowance shall be delivered to the mother or nurse of every such infant Slave."

"Eightly,-Any owner or manager of Slaves who may be unable or unwilling to procure such provisions as are hereinbefore mentioned, may, with the authority in writing of the Protector or Assistant Protector of the District in which such Slaves are resident, substitute for the same any other kind of provisions, provided that such substituted provisions shall, in the judgment of such Protector or Assistant Protector be equivalent to, and equally nutritious with those hereinbefore directed and prescribed."

(BPP/ST/79/1: 2/11/1831, p.125)

If the slave owner chose the other method – to maintain his slaves by the cultivation of ground appropriated to them – there were the following clauses:

"Eleventhly.-Every owner or manager of Slaves who shall by such declaration as aforesaid, propose to maintain the Slaves under his management by the appropriation of ground, to be by them cultivated for that purpose, shall be, and is hereby bound and required to set apart for every Slave so to be maintained, and being of the age of fifteen years and upwards, half an acre of land properly adapted for the growth of provisions, and not more than two miles distant from the place of residence of such Slave; and in respect of every Slave so to be maintained, and being under the age of fifteen years, every such owner or manager is hereby bound and required to set apart for the father or reputed father, or mother of every such infant Slave, one quarter of an

127

acre of like ground; or if such infant shall have no parent, being the property of the same owner, then such quarter of an acre shall be set apart for some other Slave who shall be charged with the cultivation of the same for the benefit of such infant."

"Twelfthly,-Every such owner or manager shall be, and is hereby bound and required to supply every Slave for whom any such ground shall be so appropriated, with such seeds, and with such implements of husbandry, as may be necessary for the cultivation of such ground on the first entering of such Slave on the occupation thereof."

"Fifteenthly,-Every Slave for or in respect of whom any ground shall be so appropriated and set apart, shall in each year be allowed forty days at the least for the cultivation thereof in forty successive weeks, so that from the commencement thereof one Sunday at the least may intervene between every two successive days until the entire number of forty days shall be completed, and of such forty days shall be understood to consist of twenty-four hours, commencing at the hour of six in the morning, and terminating at the hour of six of the next succeeding morning."

(BPP/ST/79/1: 2/11/1831, pp.126-127)

The stipulations regarding the clothes were as follows:

"XCVII. And it is further ordered and declared, That it is and shall be the duty of every owner or manager of Slaves, within the said Colonies, once, that is to say, either in the month of January, or in the month of June in each year, and he or she is hereby required to deliver to every such Slave for his or her use, either in the month of January or in the month of June, in each and every year, the following articles, that is to say, to every male Slave of the age of fifteen years or upwards, one hat of chip, straw, or felt, or other more durable material, one cloth jacket, two cotton check shirts, two pair of Osnaburgh trousers, one blanket, and two pairs of shoes, one knife, and one razor. To every female Slave of the age of thirteen years and upwards, one chip or straw hat, two gowns or wrappers, two cotton check shifts, two Osnaburgh petticoats, two pairs of shoes, one blanket, and one pair of scissors. To or for the use of every male Slave below the age of fifteen, one hat, one cloth jacket, one pair of Osnaburgh trousers, and one pair of shoes; and to every female Slave under the age of thirteen years, one chip or straw hat, one gown or wrapper, one check shift, one Osnaburgh petticoat, and one pair of shoes; and to and for the use of each family of Slaves in each year, one saucepan, and one kettle, pot or cauldron for the cooking of provisions."

(BPP/ST/79/1: 2/11/1831, pp. 129-130)

The PROTECTOR OF SLAVES could authorize a commutation of the prescribed articles.

The stipulations regarding the medical care were as follows:

"CIV. And it is further ordered, That every person in the said Colonies having under his or her management forty Slaves or upwards, shall and is hereby required to engage a Medical Practitioner to visit such Slaves in such his medical capacity, one at the least in each fourteen days; and it shall be the duty of such Medical Practitioner, and he is hereby authorized and required, to keep a journal of the health of each gang of Slaves so placed under his medical superintendence, in which journal he shall once in each fourteen days record what is the general state of health of such gang, and shall also enter the name of each Slave then labouring under sickness, distinguishing such Slaves as are thereby disqualified for labour, and such as are disqualified for the ordinary amount of labour, and prescribing such medicines or articles of diet as may in his judgment be necessary for the restoration of the sick; and it shall be the duty of every such Medical Practitioner once in each fortnight to deliver a copy of the entries so made by him in his journal to the owner or manager of such Slaves, which owner or manager shall be, and is hereby required to supply such Slaves with such medicines or nourishment, and to allow to such Slaves such relaxations of labour as may be such Medical Practitioner be so recommended and prescribed; and in reference to every Slave for whom any such nourishment may be provided, the rules hereinbefore contained respecting the food of Slaves, shall be and are hereby suspended; and every such Medical Practitioner shall and is hereby required, in obedience to any requisition to him for that purpose made in writing, by any such Protector or Assistant Protector such his Journal; and it is further ordered, That in case of any acute or dangerous disease of any Slave or Slaves, the owner or manager of such Slave or Slaves shall and is hereby required to employ, at his own costs and charges, a Medical Practitioner for the cure and medical treatment of such Slave."

(BBP/ST/79/1: 2/11/1831, p.132)

Immediately after publishing these stipulations the free inhabitants of St. Lucia protested against it. In January 1832 the "Managers and Others having the Administration of Estates in St. Lucia" wrote as follows:

"That your Memorialists are fully aware of the ruin that must follow the operation of several clauses of that Order in Council, to the slaves themselves, as well as to the estates to which they are attached; as it will be impossible for the estates to give the extravagant quantity of provisions specified in the case of giving rations; and in the case of giving land, which must be the case on all estates in this island, the slaves are sure to fall into despondency and die, when they find themselves entirely dependent on the produce of their gardens for subsistence, and deprived of their weekly allowance of salt provisions, which was their greatest support and comfort, and which can never be made up to them by substituting frivolous articles of wearing, which they do not make use of in this climate, and of which they do not feel the least want."

(CO 253/37/5: Jan. 1832)

In a further remonstrance of January 1832 merchants and planters of St. Lucia referred to the inequality of the allowances of food which were designed as equivalent:

"Twenty one Pints of Flour as the weekly allowance is more than equal to 3 lbs of Bread per day while the quantity of Plantains whose they can be had is not more than sufficient but Eight pounds for a day's allowance of Cocoa or Yams is as has been observed by the London Committee perfectly absurd. Yams and Cocoa (if we rightly understand what is meant by the latter) are as nutritious as Potatoes, the regulation authorizing the substitution of other Provisions brings no remedy, the quantity being defined an equivalent is ordered, so much for those who give rations –"

(CO 253/37/2: Jan. 1832)

Of the stipulations regarding the maintenance of the slaves by the cultivation of ground appropriated to them the merchants and planters had the following opinion:

"In the present state of the Slave Population few families of slaves have any Father or reputed Father to take charge of and cultivate the land allotted to infant Slaves – and therefore this task must fall on the Mother and how is the Mother of two, three, four, or five children to cultivate provisions to fill so many mouths if the scale of rations laid down by the preceding regulations be supposed necessary."

The objection regarding the provisions for clothing the slaves referred to the kind of clothes:

"The objections to this allowance of Clothing is confined to those articles which are unfitted to the Climate and which would subject the Master to a ruinous expense without equivalent benefit to the Slave –"

Regarding the food for the slaves they were of the opinion:

"The discretionary power of the Protector is again brought into operation to the disadvantage of the Master's Substitution of other articles as in the case of Food, is sanctioned but without defining. Is the equivalent in this case to be measured by the utility in the price of the substituted articles?"

Finally they mentioned:

"Shoes are useless to the slave but enormously expensive to the Masters."

In March 1832 the "Proprietors, Merchants, Planters and other Inhabitants" of St. Lucia signed a petition which was published in the newspaper "London Gazette" on May 29th, 1832:

"That the regulations respecting food and clothing be referred to your Majesty's Council in this island. The proprietors being ready to make such

allowances in both these respects, as, after a fair and impartial
examination, that body shall deem amply sufficient to secure the comfort
of the negro."

(Z/OPL/LG: 27/3/1832, p.1219)

At least up to this time it was, according to the following reports, common in St. Lucia that the slaves maintained themselves by the cultivation of ground appropriated to them. On the occasion of a meeting of the PRIVY COUNCIL of St. Lucia in August 1832 a statement of the PROTECTOR OF SLAVES was reported as follows:

"The Protector of Slaves considered that the almost universal practice in
this Colony was to allow land and time to the slaves in lieu of provisions."

(CO 253/40/2: 20/8/1832)

From a report of the PROTECTOR OF SLAVES regarding the second half of the year 1832 concerning the rise in population it also follows that the slaves maintained themselves mainly with produces of their own gardens:

"Yet, unprejudiced reflection based on practical observation induces me to
venture to express my conviction that the real foundation of our present
augmentation in Saint Lucia is to be found in the now shortened hours of
labour operating thus on the physical constitution and on the mental
energy of the Slaves, improving their food by giving them both time and
inclination to cultivate more sedulously their provision gardens from which
the Saint Lucia Slaves derive their chief support and enabling them to
purchase those luxuries and acquire those comforts which must gradually
elevate their moral condition."

(CO 253/44/3: 23/3/1833)

Governor FARQUHARSON of St. Lucia reported in March 1833:

"On every part which I visited the flourishing state of negro-gardens
convinced me that the Slaves in general were plentifully supplied with food
and that few or non of them could have any just cause of complaint, ..."

(CO 253/43/5: 7/3/1833)

Regarding the compliance with the legal regulations there exists a report of the PROTECTOR OF SLAVES according to which between 1st of February and 27th of May 1833, 44 proprietors and managers of diverse estates of St. Lucia were punished for having refused or neglected to comply with the regulations respecting the food and maintenance of slaves. The fines varied from £ Sterling 3,-- to 32,-- (CO 258/13/1: 1/1/1833-30/6/1833/Section H).

Governor DUDLEY HILL who made a tour of the island in July 1834 reported in a circular to the STIPENDIARY MAGISTRATES as follows:

"I regret to observe, that in my inspection on several estates, I have not found that attention paid to the comfort of the negro that the owner's interest would insure him a return for;"

(CO 253/49/3: 28/7/1834)

Regarding the medical care of the slaves he instructed the STIPENDIARY MAGISTRATES:

"In the inspection I have made of the hospitals on the different estates, I am by no means satisfied with their arrangements or cleanliness; and a general want of comfort is obvious. I wish you would convince the planter or manager that it is his own interest the sick should be properly treated, as with proper care they will become sooner effective in his gang."

The abolition of slavery on 1st August 1834 had no influence on the legal stipulations regarding the maintenance of slaves. Governor DUDLEY HILL told this to the slaves in June 1834:

"You are no longer to be Slaves – You are free – not idle free people, but industrious free people, bound to labour moderately for your Masters in return for allowances which your Masters, as they have hitherto done, will be bound to furnish you, ..."

(Z/CO 253/46/1: 30/7/1834)

With an ordinance of 1st August 1834 the APPRENTICES (former slaves) got an allowance of five hours per week for the cultivation of their gardens.

"1. That every praedial apprenticed labourer for or in respect of whom any ground shall be appropriated and set apart for his support, shall, out of the annual time during which such praedial apprenticed labourer is by the said recited Act required to labour after the rate of forty-five hours per week, be allowed five hours per week for the cultivation of such ground."[14]

(CO 255/2/7: 1/8/1834)

Regarding the medical care in general and the care of the children Governor DUDLEY HILL wrote to the SECRETARY OF STATE GLENELG in December 1836:

"I attentively examined into the state of the hospitals and treatment of the sick, infirm and children and had every reason to be satisfied that generally their comforts were properly attended to and that medical attendance was afforded. Where any neglect was apparent I did not hesitate to express my disapprobation."

(CO 253/52/4: December 1836)

---

[14] The said „Act" is dated with 5th June 1834 and fixed the final abolition of slavery at 1st August 1834.

4.7.4.1.3 Summary

According to the CODE DE LA MARTINIQUE the slave owners were obliged to maintain their slaves with food and clothes. Another obligation was the medical care of the slaves. In addition to the food the slaves received from their owners, they could also cultivate grounds appropriated to them by their owners.

At the beginning of the 19th century the planters of St. Lucia were in a difficult financial as well as economic situation which of course affected the maintenance of slaves. There exists a petition from the year 1812 in which the members of the Appellate Court of St. Lucia proclaimed that because of the wretched condition of the colony the inhabitants of St. Lucia were no more able to maintain their slaves as ordered. There was a lack of nourishment, clothes and medicine. In the years 1817 and 1819 hurricanes destroyed the ground provisions of the island. So the planters were deprived of the means of feeding their slaves. In the year 1824 Governor BLACKWELL described a generally good situation of the maintenance of the slaves. Further reports of the years 1829 and 1830 confirm this statement.

On January 7th, 1832, a law regarding the amelioration of the condition of the slaves came into force in St. Lucia. The free habitants of St. Lucia protested vehemently against the following stipulations: rations of food, maintenance of the slaves by the cultivation of grounds appropriated to them and kind of clothes.

According to reports from the year 1832 it was common in St. Lucia that the slaves maintained themselves by the cultivation of grounds appropriated to them. In the year 1833 Governor FARQUHARSON of St. Lucia reported on the flourishing state of the grounds appropriated to the slaves.

Regarding the emancipation period it should be noted that the legal stipulations regarding the maintenance of the slaves were adopted from those of the period of slavery.

4.7.4.2   Treatment of slaves

4.7.4.2.1 Legal development and discussion

The clauses in the CODE NOIR were:

"Art. XLII.-Masters, when they consider their Slaves deserve punishment, permitted only to chain them, and flog them with rods or cords. They are prohibited from putting them to torture, or mutilating their limbs, under pain of confiscation of the Slaves, and of the Master being proceeded against extraordinarily.

Art. XLIII.-Masters or Commandeurs, (Drivers), who kill a Slave under their orders or protection, to be prosecuted criminally, and punished according to the nature of the offence."

(BPP/ST/71/2: 16/3/1685, p.187)

In the year 1786 the number of the lashes was limited:

"Forbidding Masters, on any pretext whatever, to give their Slaves more than fifty lashes, or to beat them with sticks, or to mutilate them, or to make them perish by any kind of death."

(BPP/ST/71/2: 15/10/1786, p.207)

When disregarding these legal stipulations the following punishment was valid:

"Art. II.-Owners, Attorneys, and Managers, convicted of having given to their Slaves more than fifty lashes or having beaten them with sticks, to be for the future condemned to a fine of 2000 livres for the first offence, and for the second, to be declared incapable of owing Slaves, and to be sent to France.

"Art. III.-Independently of the fine above-mentioned, should they be convicted of having mutilated their Slaves, they shall be noted with infamy and shall suffer capital punishment, if convicted of having caused, in any way, the death of a Slave, in such cases they are to be prosecuted as murderers at the Diligence of the Procureur du Roi."

In the year 1804, one year after the final cession of St. Lucia to the British, Governor MEYERS of St. Lucia proclaimed the following law:

"... that if any Master or Mistress, Owner, Possessor, or other person whatsoever, shall, at his, her or their own will and pleasure, or by his, her or their discretion, knowledge, sufferance, privacy, or consent, mutilate or dismember any Slave or Slaves, he, she, or they being convicted thereof, shall be liable to a fine of One Hundred Pounds Sterling, and to imprisonment not exceeding Twelve Months, for every Slave so mutilated

or dismembered, and in very atrocious cases, when the Owner of such Slave or Slaves shall be convicted of such offence, the Court before whom such offender shall have been tried, if they think fit, may declare such Slave or Slaves free, and discharged of all manner of servitude, to all intents whatever; and they may order the said fine of One Hundred Pounds for each Slave so mutilated or dismembered, to be paid to the Justice and Vestry of the Parish to which such Slave or Slaves belonged, to the use of the said Parish; in consideration whereof, each slave so mutilated or dismembered, shall receive from the said Parish, Ten Pounds a year for his support during life...

And I do hereby further notify and proclaim that if any person shall wantonly, or willingly or bloody mindedly, kill, or cause to be killed, any Negro or other Slave, such person so offending, shall on conviction be adjudged guilty of felony, without benefit of Clergy, and shall suffer Death accordingly for such offence."

(CO 253/7/4: 10/12/1804)

On July 21st, 1823, there was a discussion in the PRIVY COUNCIL of St. Lucia: Governor MAINWARING referred to a letter of Earl BATHURST of May 28th, 1823, in which instructions were given for preparing the slave proprietors to expect an ORDER IN COUNCIL which absolutely prohibited the infliction of punishment of flogging female slaves under any circumstances and which fixed the cessation of the existing practice of driving slaves to the work by the sound of the whip and the infliction of it by the driver as a stimulus to labour (CO 256/1/1: 21/7/1823).

The members of the PRIVY COUNCIL of St. Lucia protested against these two measures which were passed by the HOUSE OF COMMONS on May 15th, 1823:

"Wherefore we do most respectfully, but most solemnly protest as proprietors of near one thousand two hundred slaves,..., and as members of His Majesty's Privy Council, in behalf of our fellow colonists, and all concerned in their properties and welfare, against any injury or mischief which may arise to their or our persons, and against any loss, damage, or deterioration, which may arise to their or our properties, from the resolutions of the House of Commons of the 15th May last, or from any measure which His Majesty's government may please to found thereupon."

(CO 253/17/1: 8/8/1823)

With a circular letter of July 1823 addressed to the Governors of the British colonies having local legislatures, the SECRETARY OF STATE BATHURST added two other measures:

"On the subject of the punishment of Slaves, I have already in some degree anticipated the object of the present dispatch, by directing that Legislative measures should be proposed for preventing the punishment of flogging in every case where the offender is a woman; I also pointed out

the necessity of prohibiting the use of the whip in the field. I have now, in addition to those instructions, to direct that you will cause some effectual law to be submitted to the Legislature for preventing any domestic punishment whatever until the day following that on which the offence may have been committed, and even then, except in the presence of one free person, besides the person under whose authority the punishment may be inflicted. If the punishment should exceed three lashes, it should be provided that a regular entry should be made in a plantation book to be kept for that purpose."

(BPP/ST/68/1: 9/7/1823, p.288)

Governor MAINWARING of St. Lucia answered to these proposals in a letter to the SECRETARY OF STATE as follows:

"But the unanimous opinion of all with whom I have conversed here is, that the whip or martinet must be reserved as a punishment in terrorem for the females; they unanimously declare that the women are infinitely more difficult to manage than the men; and I have had a special report from one quarter of the island, that since the whip has been discontinued for the women, the men make use of their wives to convey to their owners all sorts of insolent and insubordinate requests and observations...

With regard to the abolition of the use of the whip in the field the planters are exceedingly apprehensive that without this badge of office, the commander will not be able to enforce his orders, they, however, have very generally discontinued it;"

(CO 253/17/3: 25/8/1823)

On 1st December 1823 the PROCUREUR GENERAL, PROCUREUR DU ROI as well as the SENESCHAL of St. Lucia reacted negatively to the proposed measures:

"According to the laws of the colony the punishment of Slaves by their masters has been limited, and Slaves are authorized to complain to the King's attorney, when excessive punishments have been dealt to them. The proposed changes are therefore superfluous: but it is not enough to say that they are superfluous, it ought to be added that they could not be executed in many cases; such, for instance, as keeping a register on the part of masters, who neither know to read nor to write, and who possess not the means to pay a clerk, ...

It ought to be stated that such changes would give the death blow to the subordination of the Slaves, and would essentially compromise the safety of the masters. In short, the total subversion of the colony would be the inevitable result of such innovations."

(BPP/ST/68/1: 1/12/1823, p.288)

In spite of these objections the proposed measures of the SECRETARY OF STATE were considered in the Slave Law of 1826:

38: "The Master is not to allow the Drivers, or any other person, to carry the whip into the Field during the hours of labour.

39: The punishment of flogging shall not be inflicted by or in behalf of the Master upon Females above twelve years of age except in execution of the sentence of a Court or of an Order from the Procureur du Roi or Commissary Commandant.

Such punishment is replaced with regard to Females by the Stocks, by handcuffs and solitary confinement.

40: The Master may inflict cumulatively or separately, the punishment of the Stocks and handcuffs for six hours in each day, and solitary confinement for eight days."

(CO 253/22/4: 1/6/1826)

In the sources about St. Lucia two kind of stocks are mentioned: field-stocks and house-stocks.

JEREMIE (1831: 7) described the field stocks as follows:

"They are in the shape of a pillory, the hands of the slave are inserted in grooves, which may be raised to any height above the head, and the feet are inserted in other grooves at the bottom of the instrument, the toes alone being made to touch the ground: the body is thus suspended in mid-air, its whole weight resting on the wrists and toes."

Further he noticed that leaden weights were fixed to the wrists of the punished slave to intensify the punishment. This statement was denied from an inhabitant of St. Lucia who published a book in the year 1832. This book is an answer to JEREMIE's book which was published in 1831. The inhabitant of St. Lucia wrote as follows:

"That leaden weights are fixed to the wrists is a mere creation of Mr. Jeremie's fancy. Sometimes the "grooves" for the wrists are so large that the hands are pulled through; to prevent this, a piece of sheet lead or leather is nailed on with pump-tacks, to lessen their diameter;"

(INHABITANT OF ST. LUCIA 1832: 26)

Further information regarding field-stocks comes from the evidence of the slave MATHURINE before the court in March 1832.

"That there are nails, leather and lead in the holes of the Field Stocks, so as to tear the flesh of those who are punished, ..."

(CO 258/11/1: 1/1/1832-30/6/1832/section B)

137

The house-stocks were not described in the sources. It is assumed that here the general stocks are meant. These general stocks are described in the ENCYCLOPAEDIA BRITANNICA as follows:

> *"STOCKS, a wooden structure formerly in use both on the continent of Europe and in Great Britain as a method of punishment for petty offences. The culprit sat on a wooden bench with his ankles, and sometimes his wrists or even neck, thrust through holes in movable boards, generally for at least several hours."*
>
> (ENCYCLOPAEDIA BRITANNICA 1768: XXI, 426)

Further it is mentioned that the stocks were employed for punishing slaves in the southern states.

Another clause in the Slave Law of 1826 obliged the plantation owners to keep a plantation book:

> *41: "Upon every plantation containing at least two quarrées of Land, and to which are attached six Slaves of the age of ten Years at least, shall be kept a Plantation Book, or Journal, in which shall be daily and regularly entered and recorded the births and deaths of the Slaves, with the cause of the deaths attested by a medical practitioner or respectable Planter, and in another part of the book the names of the Slaves upon whom shall have been inflicted a punishment exceeding six lashes in the Stocks or handcuffed, or forty-eight hours in solitary confinement, together with the nature of Offence, the time when, and place where the same was committed, the number of lashes applied, the name of the free person present where there has been a free person present or otherwise the six slaves present and the length of time during which the Offender remained in confinement, in the stocks, or handcuffed."*
>
> (CO 253/22/4: 1/6/1826)

The execution of a general punishment for men was bound to the following provisions:

> *37: "If a Male Slave has committed an offence of such a nature as to render it absolutely necessary that he be punished, such punishment must be inflicted with reason and without cruelty or passion: the punishment to be enforced by and on behalf of the proprietor, may not exceed at the utmost twenty-five lashes, nor shall it be lawful to inflict on any Male Slave any corporal punishment until after sun-rise of the day next following that on which the Offence has been committed, for or in respect of which any such punishment or correction may be so inflicted, or without the presence of one person of free condition, or of six Slaves to witness the infliction of such punishment, other than and besides the person by or by the authority of whom the said punishment shall be inflicted. But in case six Slaves are substituted for one person of free condition, it shall be incumbent on the person or persons ordering the punishment to prove, if required so to do, that it was not in his power to procure the attendance in their twenty four hours, of a person of free condition. No punishment shall be inflicted but at or near the buildings of the Estate, nor shall it be repeated on the same*

day, nor until the delinquent shall have fully recovered the effects of any former punishment nor with any other instrument but a Cat or Martinet.

Provided nevertheless, that nothing herein contained shall extend to any punishment which may be inflicted on any Slave, under or by virtue of any sentence or Judgement of any Court of competent jurisdiction within the said Colony or in pursuance of any Order of the Procureur du Roi or Commissary Commandant."

The clauses regarding the punishment of slave owners who mutilated or killed a slave were adopted from the CODE DE LA MARTINIQUE as well as from the proclamation of Governor MYERS of the year 1804:

47: "Every master or other free person guilty of mutilating or maiming a Slave shall be fined from five thousand to ten thousand Livres and condemned to twelve months' imprisonment. The Court may and in all cases in which the master shall be the Offender shall also declare free and discharge from all servitude the Slave thus mutilated or injured. The said fine shall in such case be paid into the Colonial Treasury and the Colony shall allow the Slave a life annuity of five hundred Livres. The Offender may also be declared incapable of governing Slaves and sent out of the Colony and the Estate shall be put under the management of a Curator.

Upon a second conviction the fine and imprisonment shall be doubled, the Slave declared free and the Offender shall be deemed incapable of holding or governing Slaves and banished for life from the Colony."

48: "The Offence of homicide committed upon a Slave, whether by a free person or another Slave, whether with or without malice, shall be punished in the same manner as if the deceased had been free."

In a petition of July 28th, 1827, "certains Planteurs" from St. Lucia complained against their legal limitation of punishing slaves (CO 253/23/1: 28/7/1827). In a petition of June 1829 "certains Planteurs et Propriétaires de St. Lucie" wrote as follows:

"C'est que les chatiments ordonnés par les Tribunaux sont ordinairement infligés en lieux publics; la susceptibilité du caractère du nègre, la violence de ses sentiments, son amour-propre ainsi humilié, l'entraínent souvent à commettre les excès viennet d'ètre cites …

Qu'au surplus, les chatiments, ainsi ordonnés, sont genéralement imposés sans examen préalable de la force physique, des sentiments et du charactère du sujet. La loi a assigné telle peine pour tel délit; elle n'a pas fait d'execption. Mais le maitre qui connait les facultés tant morales, que physiques de ses Esclaves, sait faire les differences utiles à son proper intéret: il sait qu'une punition légère impose à tel nègre, produira le meme effet, qu'une autre plus sévère sur tel autre, pour un délit de meme nature;"

(CO 253/26/3: June 1829)

Further they protested against the prohibition to use the whip in the field.

In his report of the year 1829 the PROTECTOR OF SLAVES informed of a normalization of the situation:

> "Masters have occasionally complained of their not being allowed to carry the cat or martinet into the field. I admit, when the law was first introduced, proprietors had reason to complain of relaxation in the field labour, from the driver being divested of every badge of authority; but latterly the complaints on this head have been very few, ..."

> (CO 258/5/6: 1/1/1829-30/6/1829, p.9)

Governor STEWART of St. Lucia reported in September 1829 as follows:

> "Public punishments of slaves are more frequent than formerly, and more severe than those inflicted by masters. This principally proceeds from the operation of the new Slave act, which on the whole, works well; but there are a few clauses which might be altered to advantage. The first is, the Process, and consequent delay in punishing females: This is well understood by them, and they avail themselves of it in a manner very injurious to the good order and conduct of the males; by the example they shew of disobedience to the orders of their masters, who find themselves obliged to overlook such acts, on account of the loss of time and difficulty in bringing them to punishment. Indeed, the behaviour of these Women is frequently most provoking, idling their time, and neglecting their work, and often injuring their master's property, when their labour is most in request ...

> By another clause, no slave can be punished in less than 24 hours after the Commission of the Offence; thus the beneficial effects of prompt punishment are lost ...

> The next point of which Planters complain, is, depriving the overseers and drivers on their badge of Office – the cat or whip. This is only objectionable as being perhaps too suddenly done. So revolting to their feelings, as a practice must be, of keeping people to their work by compulsion and fear of punishment, it cannot be too soon removed; but in so doing, great caution is required as with the fiery, stubborn dispositions of many negroes."

> (CO 253/26/6: 29/9/1829)

By the end of the year 1830 the PROTECTOR OF SLAVES wrote in his report:

> "It is but fair to state that respectable slave owners complain that the slave does not work with that energy as formerly and that the females generally are obstreperous and insubordinate, the latter fact I believe to be correct since the field stocks have substituted the punishment of the lash ...

The owners declare that the punishment of the stocks is very severe, because when released from the punishment, the wrists and ankles of the culprit are so pained and benumb as to incapacitate them from continuing their labour. The negroe woman turn it in their version "La Soee/Soie" indeed it cannot but be viewed as the rack of modern days and there is no controlling power as to the mode of attaching the offender. The supplementary Ordinance, Section 5, allows 6 hours of the Field Stocks whereas the Protector can affirm that at the end of ½ hour the patient is nearly exhausted. The subject of the Field Stocks is therefore brought under the consideration of the Right Honourable Secretary for the Colonies."

(CO 258/7/1: 1/10/1830-31/12/1830/section GO)

With an ordinance dated May 26th, 1832, the punishment of women with the field stocks was declared as unlawful. The lawful means for punishing women were the house-stocks, the pillory, hand-cuffs and confinement:

"III. And, it being hereby expressly declared, That the use of an Instrument of Punishment for Women, commonly called the Field Stocks, is unlawful, I do hereby order and proclaim, that all and every Offence and Offences which may be committed by any Female Slave or Slaves in the said Colony of Saint Lucia, and which under the said last mentioned Order of the Second of February, 1830, were punishably by Domestic Authority, shall henceforth be punished by someone or other of the Modes of Punishment hereinafter immediately specified as lawful, and by none other: - That is to say,

Confinement in the House-Stocks, for the Feet only, for a space not exceeding twelve hours.
Confinement in the Pillory, for the Hands only, with or without a dress of disgrace, for a space not exceeding six hours – such Pillory being either fixed at, or near, the Works or principal Buildings, or moveable, so as to be used in the Field or elsewhere on the Plantation.
Confinement in a Pillory, for the Hands and Head, with or without such dress as aforesaid, for a space not exceeding two hours; such Pillory being fixed or moveable as aforesaid.
Hand-cuffs, not exceeding one pound in weight and attached before the body of the offender, for a space not exceeding six hours.
Confinement, solitary or otherwise, during the Slaves' own time, with Field or other customary labour, for a space not exceeding three days.
Confinement, solitary or otherwise, without labour, for a space not exceeding eight days."

(CO 255/2/8: 26/5/1832, p.124)

With the ORDER IN COUNCIL of November 2nd, 1831, the maximum lashes for punishing men were limited from 25 to 15 lashes. The period of one day which should elapse between the offence and the punishment was limited to six hours. All other stipulations were not changed (BPP/ST/79/1: 2/11/1831, p.104).

In January 1832 merchants and planters of St. Lucia protested against the abridgement of the maximum limit of the lashes:

"The Regulations respecting punishments are objectionable in as much as the number of lashes being limited to fifteen, none of the reasonable objections against Corporal punishment at all are thereby removed, sufficient is left for exasperating the refractory slave, not enough to correct him, for it is not pretended that domestic discipline can be disposed with."

(CO 253/37/2: January 1832)

In a petition of March 1832 "Proprietors, Merchants, Planters and other Inhabitants of St. Lucia" requested:

"4. That the right of domestic punishment be limited, as now, to twenty-five stripes, and no more."

(Z/OPL/LG: 27/3/1832, p.1219)

According to the available sources the government didn't comply with these requests.

Regarding the working of the slaves in chains Governor FARQUHARSON of St. Lucia wrote to the SECRETARY OF STATE GODERICH in London in July 1832:

"I have pleasure in informing your Lordship that the practice of working Slaves in chains upon their Master's Estate has been prohibited by me …"

(CO 253/39/3: 4/7/1832)

This statement is confirmed by a report of the PROTECTOR OF SLAVES as follows:

"The field stocks and working in chains in the Owner's Estate are effectual abolished."

(CO 253/44/3: 23/3/1833)

On April 11th, 1833, the female slave PETRONILLE died during punishment in the pillory. With a letter dated 12th April 1833 the PROTECTOR OF SLAVES was informed by the commissary commandant of the quarter of Dennery as follows:

"Yesterday afternoon, a female slave the property of Hardy du Bocage Esqu. was strangled by having been placed in the Pillory upon the Fond D'Or Estate in the Quarter of D'Ennery."

(CO 253/44/4: 12/4/1833)

From the report of the coroner dated 13th April follows:

> *"… that the deceased had not presented herself to work with the … Gang as she had been ordered to do. Mr. Du Bocage observed "This negro woman will not do anything for me."*
>
> (CO 253/44/5: 13/4/1833)

Before court the verdict "accidental Death" was passed (CO 258/13/1: 1/1/1833-30/6/1833/section B).

On the occasion of this event there was an excitement among the slaves on the said estate. Governor FARQUHARSON of St. Lucia informed the SECRETARY OF STATE in London as follows:

> *"As this circumstance was reported to me to have created an excitement among the Slaves, I judged it proper to send a military detachment to the Estate under the Command of … and I am happy in having to report that the excitement completely subsided in the course of the following day when the troops returned to their quarters."*
>
> (CO 253/44/6: 1/5/1833)

Still in April 1833 Governor FARQUHARSON of St. Lucia published a proclamation prescribing certain regulations to be observed in the punishment of female slaves by the pillory:

> *"Whereas, by my Proclamation bearing date the 26th day of May, 1832, issued under and by virtue of an Order of the King's Most Excellent Majesty in Council, of the Second day of November, 1831, and prescribing the nature and extent of the Punishments which it might thenceforward be lawful to substitute for the Punishment of whipping in the case of Female Slaves in this Colony, - it was amongst other things provided, That it should be lawful to punish such Female Slaves, under certain circumstances, by confinement in the Pillory for the hands only, with or without a dress of disgrace, for a space not exceeding six hours – such Pillory being fixed at, or near, the Works or principal Buildings, or moveable, so as to be used in the Field or elsewhere on the Plantation, or with confinement in a Pillory for the Hands and Head, with or without such dress as aforesaid, for a space not exceeding two hours; such Pillory being fixed or moveable as aforesaid.*
>
> *And Whereas such Punishments may draw after them most dangerous consequences, unless strict watch be kept over the individual or individuals who may undergo the same. Now, THEREFORE, by virtue of the power in me vested, and authority to me delegated under the said Order in Council of His Majesty, I do hereby expressly Order and Proclaim, that from the date of these Presents, it shall not be lawful to apply any Punishment hereinbefore mentioned to any such Female Slave, unless some one Person of Free condition, or two Slaves, being neither concerned in authorising or in the application of such punishment, but being competent to give evidence thereof in a Court of Justice, be present at, and witnessing the placing of such Female Slave or Slaves in the Pillory; And*

143

*unless such Free Man, or one of such Slaves as aforesaid shall remain to
keep strict watch over such Female Slave or Slaves so punished, during
the whole time that she or they shall be subjected to such punishment.-"*

(CO/255/2/9: 24/4/1833, p.199)

4.7.4.2.2 General reports

A letter of Governor DOUGLASS of St. Lucia dated 16th October 1816
informs of the effects of the abolition of the slave trade in the year 1808
on the treatment of the slaves:

> *"The effects of the abolition of the Slave Trade are certainly favourable to
> the condition of the Black Population, in as much as it is now more than
> ever the interest of every proprietor to preserve the health of his Slaves,
> and particularly to cherish the rising generation which was formerly very
> much neglected upon the sordid principle that it was cheaper to buy slaves
> than to rear them."*

(CO 253/10/2: 16/10/1816)

On the treatment of the slaves in general he wrote:

> *"In general the treatment of this class of the population is just and kind;
> but there are many instances of the reverse according to the disposition of
> their owner, and some of very great cruelty, but these I am happy to say
> are not numerous altho' there appears to me a very strong bias in favour
> of such owners whenever there is an appeal to the Courts of Law for
> Justice, …"*

A further statement gives Mr. JEREMIE in his letter of July 1827:

> *"I should recommend to granting a general amnesty to all slave owners for
> any acts of cruelty of whatever nature committed by them previously to
> the first coming into operation of the Slave Law of 1st June 1826. Instances
> of such conduct are not perhaps so rare in Saint Lucia as at first expected,
> though they are very far from being general."*

(CO 253/24/1: 28/7/1827)

In his book which was published in 1831 JEREMIE referred to the following
ill-treatment of slaves. He mentioned it in connection with the new right of
the slave to complain:

> *"Scarcely was this opinion transmitted, and the new slave law
> promulgated, than a negro came before him with a collar riveted round his
> neck, from which projected three prongs of about ten inches each in
> length, and at the end of either of those prongs were inserted three
> smaller ones about an inch long, and these were attached to a chain,
> reaching to fetters joining round his ankles. His back and limbs were*

wealed from neck to foot, and he declared that this collar was kept on him by day and by night; that he worked with it in the field; and on his return was immured in a solitary cell; and that this course had been practised for some months in order to prevent his running away, the crime with which he was principally charged. This might however be a solitary instance."

(JEREMIE: 1831: 5)

JEREMIE continued:

"A commission stated that there were three other men, at that time, on the estate, with collars of the same description, and that those collars were in use in the country ...

... The report also stated, that there was a women covered with sores, who was found in chains, and who had been so chained for near two years; and yet the commissioners reported that the estate was well managed, and that the arrangements were good! – this was not at a remote period, but in the year 1826."

(JEREMIE 1831: 6)

According to a proclamation of Governor MAINWARING the punishment of slaves with pronged collars was prohibited in St. Lucia up from 1st June 1826 (CO 255/1/1: 1/6/1826)

JEREMIE referred to this proclamation and wrote:

"A proclamation was however issued against these collars. What followed? Scarcely two months afterwards, other reports were spread of discontent and actual mutiny of so serious a nature having broken out on the same estate, that the principal officers of government were directed to investigate the matter anew. The result was, that in lieu of the collar, the following punishment had been used.
The women were hung by the arms to a peg, raised so high above their head that the toes alone touched the ground, the whole weight of the body resting on the wrists of the arms or the tips of the toes. The report of a mutiny was mere invention.

This torture was also stopped, one of the offenders find, and the other imprisoned. But what was the third expedience adopted? The field-stocks, - an invention forwarded from Trinidad, and which was actually legalized by the regulations drawn up by myself ...

(JEREMIE 1831: 7)

Regarding the ill-treatment of slaves in general he wrote:

"- since even those who were shocked at the crimes committed, deemed it prudent to conceal them; ...

... and that slave murder was too common, and might be committed with impunity.

145

In short, the principle, which seems to have been universal, was best expressed by a gentleman, on his sons being arrested on a charge of killing one of his Negroes. His remark was, "What a noise about a brute," (Quel bruit pour un animal!) – and, with this, everything is explained."

(JEREMIE 1831: 16)

The inhabitant of St. Lucia who published a book in 1832 which is an answer to JEREMIE's book, argued against the accusations of the ill-treatment of the slaves with insubordination and unruly conduct of the slaves. On the afore-mentioned case of the runaway slave he wrote:

"This was a species of punishment sanctioned by the former laws of the island. The negro was an incorrigible "runaway" and thief."

(INHABITANT OF ST. LUCIA 1832: 23)

As already mentioned in chapter "4.7.4.2. Treatment of slaves", p. 138, according to the Slave Law of 1826 upon every plantation containing at least two "quarrées" (about 3 acres) of land and to which six slaves of the age of ten years at least were attached a plantation book should be kept. In this book punishments of slaves were to be noted. On the basis of these notes the PROTECTOR OF SLAVES made "Punishment Returns".

In the following table figures of slave punishment are shown. They were reported to the PROTECTOR OF SLAVES:

Punishments in the period from 1/6/1826 to 1/8/1834

Source/Period	Number of carried out punishments	Yearly carried out punishments	Number of registered plantation slaves	Average number of plantation slaves per year	Estimated yearly percentage of punishments
(CO 258/5/1: 1/6/1826-31/12/1826/section A)	879	-	-	-	-
(CO 258/5/2: 1/1/1827-30/6/1827/section A)	801	-	-	-	-
(CO 258/5/3: 1/7/1827-31/12/1827/section A)	606	1.407	-	-	-
(CO 258/5/4: 1/1/1828-30/6/1828/section A)	590	-	-	-	-
(CO 258/5/5: 1/7/1828-31/12/1828/section A)	422	1.012	-	-	-
(CO 258/5/6: 1/1/1829-30/6/1829/section A)	554	-	-	-	-
(CO 258/5/7: 1/7/1829-31/12/1829/section A)	581	1.135	-	-	-
(CO 258/6/1: 1/1/1830-31/3/1830/section A)	296	-	10.769	-	-
(CO 258/6/2: 1/4/1830-30/09/1830/section A)	976	-	10.417	-	-
(CO 258/7/1: 1/10/1830-31/12/1830/section A)	536	1.808	5.417	8.868	20
(CO 258/8/1: 1/1/1831-30/06/1831/section A)	1.143	-	11.063	-	-
(CO 258/9/1: 1/7/1831-05/11/1831/section A)	662	1.805	7.343	9.203	20
(CO 258/11/1: 1/1/1832-30/06/1832/section A)	1.362	-	8.441	-	-
(CO 258/12/1: 1/7/1832-31/12/1832/section A)	1.981	3.343	10.348	9.395	36
(CO 258/13/1: 1/1/1833-30/06/1833/section A)	1.699	-	8.368	-	-
(CO 258/14/1: 1/7/1833-31/12/1833/section A)	1.470	3.169	8.535	8.452	37
(CO 258/15/1: 1/1/1834-01/08/1834/section A)	1.402	-	7.797	-	36

(compiled by Ernestine Kolar by means of reports of the PROTECTOR OF SLAVES of St. Lucia)

According to this table the percentage of registered punishments of slaves in relation to St. Lucia's slave population per year varied from 20% in the year 1830 and 1831 up to 36, 37% in the following years till July 1834.

Regarding the several plantations there might have been great differences concerning the percentage of the punishments. The PROTECTOR OF SLAVES referred in his report for the period from 1st January to 30th June 1831 to three plantations which reported the highest punishment figures:

> "The first is that of Mr. de Marcel, President of the Royal Court, out of 128 slaves 96 had been punished. There is 1 birth only and 2 deaths. The second is the Grand Anse Estate, out of 96 slaves there are 59 punished, 3 births and 1 death. The Marquis-Estate is the third, out of 296 slaves there are 208 punishments of whom 133 are females, 2 births and 2 deaths have occurred."
>
> (CO 258/8/1: 1/1/1831-30/6/1831/section GO)

According to these figures on the plantation of the president of the royal court 75%, on the Grand-Anse-plantation 61% and on the Marquis-plantation 70% of the attached slaves were punished.

A review of the offences for which slaves were punished is shown in the general punishment returns of the PROTECTOR OF SLAVES. For example, the returns for the period from 1st April 1830 to 30th September 1830 (CO 258/6/2: 1/4/1830-30/09/1830/section A) are as follows:

Offences	Number of punishments
"Attempting to strike driver	1
Aiding and abetting	2
Absenting	64
Allowing Stock to eat canes	15
Abusing Driver and others	10
Allowing Stock to trespass in cultivation	6
Abusive language	3
Attempting to commit rape	3
Assaulting	1
Breaking open houses and gardens	3
Breaking open hospital	3
Beating others	19
Breaking locks	2
Breaking stocks	1
Cutting others with Cutlasses, knives, ...	6
Cruelty to animals	18
Conniving at Theft	9
Coming late to work	50
Creating disturbances	4
Causing others	2
Disobedience	54
Disorderly and riotous conduct	4
Drunkenness	19

Dirtiness and Laziness	*1*
Disrespect to parents	*3*
Fighting and Quarrelling	*34*
False Complaints	*11*
Fighting with Cutlasses	*1*
Harbouring Runaways	*8*
Hindering others from working	*1*
Insolence	*37*
Insubordination	*97*
Insubordination and Insolence	*18*
Insolence and Disobedience	*18*
Impertinence	*2*
Insolent to overseer	*12*
Killing stock	*1*
Lying	*3*
Laziness	*19*
Leaving hospital at night	*4*
Mad behaviour	*1*
Misdemeanours	*3*
Marketing on Sunday	*2*
Neglect of duty	*114*
Neglecting Prayers	*10*
Neglecting Children	*2*
Neglecting grounds	*6*
Negligence	*14*
Pretending to be sick	*8*
Refusing to work	*31*
Running away	*77*
Receiving stolen goods	*2*
Instigate the gang	*1*
Working Obeah	*1*
Riding horses at night	*2*
Stealing and eating canes	*21*
Stealing ground provisions	*20*
Striking and abusing driver	*2*
Seditious language	*1*
Striking driver with a cutlass	*1*
Theft	*83*
Throwing stones at others	*2*
Working badly	*3*
	976"

From these 976 persons (698 men and 278 women) 653 were flogged. The total number of lashes stated was 13.831. This is an average punishment of 21 lashes.

The remaining 323 persons were punished as follows:

Means of punishment	Number of punishments
- Confinement	146
- Field-stocks	96
- House-stocks	31
- Confinement and handcuffs	29
- Confinement and stocks	4
- Handcuffs	6
- Chains	6
- Hospital	4
- Treadmill	1

4.7.4.2.3 Complaints of slaves

In the reports of the PROTECTOR OF SLAVES which are available from the year 1826 complaints of slaves before the court are stated. From these documents this writer has chosen some examples of ill-treatment of slaves and disregard of legal stipulations regarding the punishment of slaves. The quotations are from notes of the PROTECTOR OF SLAVES.

In April 1830 the 27 years old slave MANETTE from the Marquis-Estate complained:

> "M. charged the manager with confining her in a cell without just cause.
>
> M. having failed to establish her complaint, the officiating Judge dismissed the charge and found her guilty of insubordination to the manager and in consequence sentenced her to receive 20 stripes and a fortnight's imprisonment."
>
> (CO 258/6/2: 1/4/1830-30/9/1830/section B)

Also in April 1830 the 24 years old slave FANCHINE from the estate of Mr. Grand Cour in Soufrière complained:

> "This slave complained that Mr. Grand Cour had maltreated her in suspending her by the hands tied together and in that position had inflicted stripes on her naked body on account of her 3 days' absence for which she had already received her pardon."
>
> (CO 258/6/2: 1/4/1830-30/9/1930/section B)

Mr. Grand Cour was condemned to pay a certain amount.

The 23 years old EDWARD from the la Pointe-estate complained as follows before the court in November 1830:

"The Slave Edward complained that in the 6th of the month the manager caused so many lashes to be inflicted on the Complainant that he was unable to count them and all without any cause. He complained also of being called to work before the usual time.

Result: The Court dismissed the Complaint against the Manager and declared it to be false and malicious. Thereupon the slave was condemned to 30 lashes."

(CO 258/7/1: 1/10/1830-31/12/1830/section B)

The 30 years old slave SALOMON from the Beau Sejour-estate in the district of Gros Islet complained on December 2nd, 1830:

"S. complained of Mr. Clement Judge for striking and putting him in the Cachot and leaving him 24 hours without food and physic although he was ill.
The Court ... that the charges preferred where by no means proven, admitted off by the defendant's statement and dismissed the complaint – this complaint was malicious, condemned the complainant to 30 lashes in the jail or upon the estate."

(CO 258/7/1: 1/10/1830-31/12/1830/section B)

The 24 years old slave FREDERICK of the Peron-estate complained on October 19th, 1831:

"F. complained against Mr. Miller, the manager and also against Mr. ... of the About d'Or Estate for having on the 18 last month kicked and cuffed him because he asked something to eat on his return from Castries where he had put him on a message. Also with having punished him next day with a Cat, dipped in water to aggravate the punishment."

(CO 258/9/1: 1/7/1931-5/11/1831/section B)

The manager of the Peron-estate was condemned to pay a fine of Pounds Sterling 10,--.

The owner of the Balambouche-estate, Mr. D. Drivon, was accused by five of his slaves on April 16th, 1832, of the following:

"That about a month ago a slave named Petit Joseph was punished with 40 lashes inflicted by Mr. Drivon for taking a little molasses given him by Paul to drink with water. That the cat was soaked in pickle after every third and Petit Joseph after receiving his punishment was immured in a dungeon for the space of one week ...
Pelage states that he was condemned about eight or nine months ago by the Police-Court to 40 lashes and the loss of his Mondays for two months. That Mr. Drivon ordered Manuel, the driver, to inflict upon him 44 lashes and that the cat was soaked in water the whole of the night previous and a tub of rum was placed beside Manuel for the purpose of soaking the cat after every lash."

The main accusation was as follows:

> "That when any of the slaves go to their master to report themselves as sick, he causes them to be placed in a wooden trough 6 feet long and 2 broad in which they are stretched while hot sand, heated for that purpose, is spread all over their body and they are forced to remain therein until the sand becomes quite cold."

The slave BILLY didn't survive this method of treatment:

> "That a short time after Christmas the male slave Billy went to his master to complain of sickness and died two weeks after having been tortured in the above manner."

The witness VICTOIRE gave the following evidence:

> "Victoire: ... frequently the sand is so hot, that the cries of the people are dreadful."

To the last mentioned accusation the PROTECTOR OF SLAVES noted:

> "In the course of the proceedings to the attorney of Mr. Drivon it appeared that the said bath had been recommended for dropsical patients on the Balambouche-Estate by Dr. Drivon, brother of Mr. D. Drivon, a doctor of the faculty of Paris of considerable talent and experience."

(CO 258/11/1: 1/1/1832-30/6/1832/section B)

The last sentence of the PROTECTOR OF SLAVES to this case was:

> "Mr. Drivon having left the Country, the usual slow procedure of continuance or outlawry was instituted against him."

(CO 258/11/1: 1/1/1832-30/6/1832/section H)

On January 22nd, 1833, the planter Du Bocage was condemned to pay a fine of Pound Sterling 10,--:

> "To punish Mr. du Bocage for having compelled Clothilde to pick grass on Sundays and for illegal treatment of her while confined in the Pillory."

(CO 258/13/1: 1/1/1833-30/6/1833/section H)

On June 25th, 1833, the owner of the BELLE-VUE-estate was condemned to pay a fine of Pound Sterling 10,--:

> "To punish the said Théophile D'Yvoley for having assaulted and beaten the slave woman Sabine under his management."

(CO 258/14/1: 1/7/1833-31/12/1833/section H)

Also shortly before the abolition of slavery there were ill-treatments of slaves:

> *"To punish the said Denis for having illegally and immoderately beaten or caused to be beaten the slave Noel under his management.*
> *The said Denis was adjudged to pay a fine of Pound 10 Sterling and Costs Pound 1 Sterling."*
>
> (CO 258/15/1: 1/1/1834-1/8/1834/section H)

4.7.4.2.4 Summary

According to the CODE DE LA MARTINIQUE slaves could be chained and flogged. It was prohibited to put them to torture, to mutilate their limbs and to kill them.

In the Slave Law of 1826 the following amelioration of punishment was made:
-   Prohibition of flogging female slaves
-   Prohibition of the use of the whip in the field
-   Prevention of any domestic punishment whatever until the day following that on which the offence may have been committed
-   Punishments exceeding three lashes were to be noted in a plantation book
-   The maximum of the lashes for an offence of a slave were reduced from 50 to 25

The slave owners protested against these stipulations because they saw therein a limitation of their authority and they also feared a backlash in the working habits of the slaves.

With an ORDER IN COUNCIL of November 2nd, 1831, the maximum number of lashes for punishing men was limited from 25 to 15 lashes, but the period of one day which should elapse between the offence and the punishment was reduced to six hours.

The general means of punishment on the estates were: confinement, field-stocks, house-stocks, handcuffs, chains, the pillory and especially the whip. The punishment of female slaves by the field-stocks was prohibited with an ordinance dated May 26th, 1832. From a report of the PROTECTOR OF SLAVES of March 1833 follows that the field-stocks and the working in chains on the owner's estate were abolished.

Finally it should be noted that the slave owners very often disregarded the legal stipulations. When the slaves complained before the court the result was in several of the cases that the slave was punished because of his complaint and the slave owner or manager was not condemned. This discrimination against the slaves before court is especially seen in the following chapter.

4.7.4.3   The slave's right to complain

4.7.4.3.1 Legal development and treatment of slaves before the courts

The right to complain was fixed in the CODE DE LA MARTINIQUE as follows:

> "Art. XXVI. – Slaves, not clothed and fed by their Masters, as laid down by foregoing clauses, to make their complaint to the Procureur du Roi, who acts in their behalf, and prosecutes the Master ex officio, without expense. Procureur du Roi to act in a similar manner in all cases of improper treatment of Slaves by their Masters."
>
> (BPP/ST/71/2: 16/3/1685, p.185)

In the Slave Law of 1826 these stipulations of the CODE DE LA MARTINIQUE were adopted and specified. The PROCUREUR GENERAL got the title PROTECTOR OF SLAVES:

> 1: "His Majesty's Procureur General is, by virtue of his office, Protector of Slaves. Any Slaves punished illegally or who shall not be clothed and provided with food in the manner enjoined by law, may complain to the Procureur General, and upon such complaint, or even without such complaint, by virtue of his office alone, he shall cause the owner or other offender to be prosecuted. This he is also to do in all cases where the owner, his attorney or manager, or other person placed in authority by the owner, shall be charged with any crime, misdemeanour, or breach of the law, to the prejudice of the slave.
>
> (CO 253/22/4: 1/6/1826)

In a report from the year 1829 Chief Justice JEREMIE noticed that from June 1826 to December 1828 twenty slaves complained before court. Of these complaints 12 were not substantiated:

> "... it appears that in the year 1826 five out of seven complaints from Slaves against their Masters were not substantiated that in the next (which includes the whole of the year) eleven complained and seven did not substantiate and in the last two only complained and they both substantiated. So that in two years and six months twelve Masters have only been brought before the Courts without sufficient proofs by the slaves and in the last year of that period there was not one."
>
> (CO 253/26/5: 30/5/1829)

For the first half of the year 1829 the PROTECTOR OF SLAVES reported five complaints of slaves:

"The complaints of slaves against masters are only five, of which two were founded and three unfounded. Amongst the complaints of masters against slaves there is also a case in which both master and slave were punished. This, if it was necessary, proves convincingly that masters and slaves appeal with equal confidence to the Courts of Justice when they find themselves aggrieved, and that their complaints are patiently heard, duly investigated and impartially decided."

(CO 258/5/6: 1/1/1829-30/6/1829)

The SECRETARY OF STATE in London spoke negatively of the court decisions of St. Lucia. Regarding the period from April 1st, 1830, to September 30th, 1830, he wrote:

In the case of slave MANETTE who was confined by her owner because she wanted to help her aunt MARY ANN who was confined in a cell with hand cuffs and unable to eat:

> *"No inquiry was made into the truth of Manettes statement in regard to Mary Ann and yet the Court sentenced her to receive 40 stripes and to be imprisoned for a fortnight for preferring an unfounded complaint."*

In the case of the slave ROBERT who complained of not being furnished with the clothing required by law and who was sentenced to receive 30 lashes and to receive chains for six months for his complaint:

> *"The Slave Robert brought a charge against his Master, and in his defence the Master accused Robert of theft. This accusation was totally unconnected with the Complaint of the Slave, and it is evident that the Court could not properly take cognizance of it as a part of the matter before them.-The question that they were called upon to decide was, whether Robert had been furnished with the clothing required by Law. If a Complaint of a Slave is to be met by counter charges of misconduct at some former period, it would become impossible for him to obtain redress for any grievance. I must therefore express my opinion that in this case the Court entirely lost sight of their duty in the sentence which they passed."*

In the case of the slave PIERRE who complained that he was beaten with a cutless:

> *"This case affords an example of the want of impartiality which exists in St. Lucia in judging between Slave and his Master.- while the Master was fined in the trifling penalty of livres 200 for striking his Slave with a Cutlass, the Slave was sentenced to receive 40 stripes for disobedience for which he had been already punished by his Master."*

A member of the court, Mr. DU BOCAGE, was accused of whipping two women slaves, for not given them their free Mondays and for breaking their dishes. He was only fined for the first accusation, the second he denied because of not knowing the legal situation and the third he also denied.

"That a plea of ignorance of the law should in any case be received as an apology for its infringement is a circumstance at which I must express my surprise – but that this should have happened in the case of M. Dubocage, who, as a Member of the Royal Court is stated to have been present when the new law was read enregistered and commented on, is matter of deep regret to me. I cannot suppose that in a society so limited as that of St. Lucia, the Judge of the Police could have been ignorant of the fact that M. Dubocage was a Member of the Royal Court, and I must therefore presume that he knowingly admitted a plea, which untenable in any case was entirely at variance with the truth in that of M. Dubocage."

In summary the SECRETARY OF STATE referred to the practice of the court of St. Lucia as follows:

"I cannot but look at the present document as a lamentable commentary on the practice of the Slave Courts in St. Lucia; and as fully demonstrating the necessity of a rigid supervision of their proceedings by the Secretary of State."

He pointed to the general injustice of the court decisions:

"While the faults of Slaves have been visited with a severity as unjust as it was needless, the Offences of the Masters have been passed over with little or no punishment, or have been allowed altogether to escape on the most frivolous pretences."

He criticised the PROTECTOR OF SLAVES:

"The duties of the Protector of Slaves seem to have been entirely misunderstood in St. Lucia. He appears to have considered himself merely as the channel of communication between the Slaves and the Police Court. He does not seem in any instance to have himself made enquiry into the Complaints of the Slaves, but merely to have forwarded them to the officiating Judge and I am unable to discover whether in the proceedings before the Police Court, he was present and assisting the Slaves whose cases were brought forward."

In conclusion the SECRETARY OF STATE noticed:

"... it is not only necessary to protect the Slaves against the violence of his master but also against the severity of the Judicial Tribunals."

(CO 258/6/3: 1/4/1830-30/9/1830)

In a letter of May 3rd, 1832, Governor FARQUHARSON of St. Lucia referred to the court decisions of the months July to October 1831:

"I am disappointed by finding that the Judgements generally pronounced against Slaves by the Judges have still been marked by nearly the same severity as those already commented upon by your Lordship but which I trust and believe will be mitigated for the future – Indeed since the

meeting of the Royal Court on the present occasion a decided change in favour of the Slave has taken place."

(CO 253/39/4: 3/5/1832)

For the months November and December 1832 there was an increase in the complaints made by the slaves. The government in London was satisfied:

"If any opinion may be formed from the brief report now under consideration it would appear that the benefits anticipated from the appointment of Mr. Jurtees have already in some measure been realized. That gentleman appears to have discharged his duties with much zeal and to have made himself intimately acquainted with the Slave Law of the Colony. During the two months comprised in his report 29 applications have been made to him by Slaves or on their behalf; being a larger number than has appeared on any of the reports heretofore received from Saint Lucia. This circumstance is satisfactory as displaying a confidence among the Slaves that their complaints will be received with attention. Some of them appear to have been preferred on sufficient grounds or to have been such as the law could not redress."

(CO 258/10/1: 1832)

It also happened that slaves who complained to the PROTECTOR OF SLAVES were punished.

Some examples from the notes of the PROTECTOR OF SLAVES are:

- Complaint of Rosalie, about 22, female, Bel-Air-Estate, quarter of Castries, field slave:

"That in consequence of her having complained against the master, one of his sons, Mr. Joseph Guesneau, came from another Estate, where he resided, and began to kick and strike her with his fists and afterwards told her to go to complain, ..."

(CO 258/12/1: 1/7/1832-31/12/1832/section B)

- Complaint against Charles de Brettes, Castries, advocate, part proprietor of the Cap estate:

"To punish Mr. de Brettes for confining the slaves Mariette, Leon and Marie-Claire in the Hospital of the Cap Estate, and for having attempted to separate the slaves from their relations and divest them of their property by carrying them away from the said Estate with an intent to punish them for having resorted to the Protector of Slaves to prefer a complaint."

(CO 258/13/1: 1/1/1833-30/6/1833/section H)

156

- Complaint of Marie Louise, about 26, Beauchamp estate, quarter of Micoud, female, field slave:

"On Tuesday before last eleventh inst. I arrived on the said Estate from this office, my master caused me to be immediately confined in the Cachot. I remained 4 days in the Cachot when removed from hence, I was immediately put in the Pillory (head and hands) from 6 a.m. to 12 o'clock and I have suffered the above punishments for no other cause than having preferred my last complaint against my master. When I came out of the Pillory, my neck was swelled and I had the fewer. My master notwithstanding ordered me to go to work, I went to the field but was unable to work so much so that I was placed besides Zo, who did my portion of work. My master told me that he will not have me remain any longer on the Estate and that I must go wherever I pleased. I left the Estate on Tuesday last and arrived at Mabouya and could not proceed further in consequence of the pains I felt from my neck and fever. I left Mabouya yesterday and arrived in town this day."

(CO 258/13/1: 1/1/1833-30/6/1833/section B)

- Complaint against Ernest Revoteau of the Anse Noire estate:

"To punish the said Ernest Revoteau for having endeavoured to prevent the slave Charlotte on his management for resorting to the Assistant Protector of her district to complain and for having punished the said slave for such her resort."

(CO 258/15/1: 1/1/1834-1/8/1834/section H)

4.7.4.3.2 Summary

According to the CODE DE LA MARTINIQUE slaves had the right to complain to the PROCUREUR DU ROI of improper treatment and bad maintenance. This stipulation was adopted in the Slave Law of 1826 and made more specific, whereby the PROCUREUR GENERAL got the title PROTECTOR OF SLAVES.

According to the available sources slaves were discriminated against before the courts. If complaints of slaves were not sufficiently founded, the slaves were punished by whipping or they were imprisoned. The punishments with the whip often reached up to 40 lashes. Imprisonments lasted from 14 days to one month.

The SECRETARY OF STATE in London protested very heavily against this practice at court. He stated that it was not only necessary to protect the slaves against the violence of his master but also against the severity of the judicial tribunals.

From the year 1831 there was a slight improvement of this situation in favour of the slaves.

It happened further that slaves were punished by their owners for making a complaint to the PROTECTOR OF SLAVES. The slaves were flogged, imprisoned or put in the pillory.

Because of this situation it can be assumed that in St. Lucia many slaves voluntarily waived their right to complain.

4.7.4.4   Manumission

4.7.4.4.1 Legal development and discussion

The relevant clause in the CODE DE LA MARTINIQUE was:

> "Art. LIV.-Masters who shall have attained twenty years, can free their Slaves, without being obliged to give an account thereof."

> (BPP/ST/71/2: 16/3/1685, p.188)

For the freed slave the following clause was valid:

> "Art. LVII.- Slaves who have been manumitted, are desired to be singularly respectful to their ancient Masters, their wives, and children, so that any injury done to them will be more severely punished, than if done to other persons; - they are otherwise declared to be free of all other obligations to their former owners."

Whereas a further clause in the CODE DE LA MARTINIQUE (p.188) was:

> "Art. LIX.- Slaves manumitted, to enjoy the same rights, privileges, and immunities as are enjoyed by persons born free."

The freed slaves were discriminated against the whites by legal restrictions, as for example the prohibition of certain professions (cp chapter 4.11. Free non-whites, section 4.11.2. Legal restrictions in contrary to whites and the removal thereof in the years 1826 and 1829, pp. 222-228).

On October 24th, 1713, a new law was passed in which the manumission of slaves depended not only on their owners but also upon the approval of the Governor of the colony (BPP/ST/71/2: 24/10/1713, p.188). This law was confirmed in 1768 (BPP/ST/71/2: 5/2/1768, p.199). In the year 1817 Governor SEYMOUR of St. Lucia proclaimed an ordinance which referred to these French laws:

> "The Ordinances of the King of 24th October, 1713, and 15th June, 1813, and the Ordinance of the Governor of 5th February, 1768, respecting affranchisements to be executed according to their form and tenor. In consequence, all freedoms of Slaves in this island, without the permission

of the Governor, declared null and void. Slaves cannot enjoy the right of freedom unless their affranchisements be approved by the Governor."

(BPP/ST/71/2: 28/8/1817, p.210)

With a circular letter of July 9th, 1823, the SECRETARY OF STATE BATHURST proposed to facilitate the manumission of slaves as well as social measures for disabled freed slaves (BPP/ST/68/1: 9/7/1823, p.282). These proposals were fixed in the Slave Law of 1826 as follows:

Fixation of fees:

> *101: "No fee, tax or impost whatever beyond the said ten shillings with a stamp duty of twenty seven shillings which is not to be increased and the fee to the Notary framing the Act which shall be settled by Order from the Governor and shall not exceed four round dollars, shall be levied or received upon manumissions, by any public officer whatever, either for his own use or for the benefit of the colony, on penalty of refunding thrice the amount of the sum received, and of immediate dismissal from his office."*

An important alteration was the right of the slave to purchase his freedom or the freedom of his family also without the approval of his owner:

> *102: "In case a Slave shall be desirous of purchasing his liberty or that of his Wife or Children, and his Owner shall be unwilling to effect the manumission, the said Slave may apply to the Procureur General, who is hereby required to present a petition to the First President, praying that the Person to be manumitted be valued by Appraisers...*
>
> *The Procureur General shall then obtain Acts of manumission in the usual form; and if the owner should refuse to take the estimated price, it shall be deposited in the Colonial Chest, whence he may, at any time, withdraw it, on obtaining an order to that effect from the First President."*

The paying of respect to the former owners of the slave was adopted from earlier laws:

> *99: "The emancipated Slave is expected to pay the greatest respect to his late Owner, and his Owner's Wife or Widow and Children, an Offence against them shall be more severely visited than if committed against a stranger, but the Slave is entirely exempted from all duties, claims, or services, which his former owner might pretend to, as his Patron, over his person and property."*

Freed slaves had to take a surname:

> *106: "Slaves, when manumitted, shall take a surname, but not their Owner's, except they have his permission, on the penalty of twenty pounds Sterling."*

The other clauses were:

> *107: "Slaves having attained their fiftieth year, or labouring under any permanent or habitual infirmity, shall, if manumitted without a valuable consideration, furnish bail in the usual form, to the amount of two hundred pounds Sterling, that they shall not become hereafter a charge to the Colony."*

> *108: "An Owner or Patron desirous to manumit a Slave under six years of age, shall previously furnish bail to the amount of two hundred pounds Sterling, that the Slave manumitted shall be properly clothed and maintained until the age of fourteen years."*

> (CO 253/22/4: 1/6/1826)

In a petition of "certains Planteurs et Propriétaires de St. Lucie" dated in June 1829, the petitioners protested against the right of the slave to purchase his freedom, and against the will of his owner. They saw therein a limitation of their right of property:

> *"Que ces Lois et les traités ont reconnu les Esclaves comme la propriété absolue du maitre, … Diminuer le nombre des Esclaves, c'est réduire la valeur de la propriété; c'est détruire la base du contrat qui reposait sur les Lois lors existantes, guaranties par les traités et la munificence royale.-Or, on ne peut, d'après les principes de la saine Justice, priver le Propriétaire de la moindre partie de sa propriété; …*

> *Que dans tous les cas, l'affranchisement doit etre entièrement laissé à l'option et à la volonté du maitre. C'est à lui seul que l'Esclave doit avoir obligation, afin que par sa bonne conduit il se fasse un titre à la bienveillance et à la recompense de son maitre."*

> (CO 253/26/3: June 1829)

These laws were adopted in further laws of February 2nd, 1830, (BPP/ST/77/1: 2/2/1830, p.27) and November 2nd, 1831, (BPP/ST/79/1: 2/11/1831, p.93) without essential alterations.

4.7.4.4.2 Trend of slave manumissions

According to a report of the CUSTOM HOUSE of St. Lucia a total of 364 slaves were freed between the years 1808 and 1821 (CO 253/18/3: 12/9/1823). Up from the year 1817 there are the following yearly figures:

Year	Number of manumissions	Source
1817	27	(CO 253/40/3: 4/10/1832)
1818	20	(CO 253/40/3: 4/10/1832)
1819	37	(CO 253/40/3: 4/10/1832)
1820	34	(CO 253/40/3: 4/10/1832)
1821	43	(CO 253/40/3: 4/10/1832)
1821	45	(CO 253/22/2: 1/6/1826)
1822	36	(CO 253/40/3: 4/10/1832)
1822	28	(CO 253/26/7: 30/5/1829)
1822	38	(CO 253/22/2: 1/6/1826)
1823	112	(CO 253/40/3: 4/10/1832)
1823	124	(CO 253/26/7: 30/5/1829)
1823	147	(CO 253/22/2: 1/6/1826)
1824	223	(CO 253/40/3: 4/10/1832)
1824	159	(CO 253/26/7: 30/5/1829)
1824	229	(CO 253/22/2: 1/6/1826)
1825	193	(CO 253/40/3: 4/10/1832)
1825	141	(CO 253/22/2: 1/6/1826)
1826	49	(CO 253/40/3: 4/10/1832)
1827	69	(CO 253/40/3: 4/10/1832)
1827	69	(CO 253/26/7: 30/5/1829)
1828	58	(CO 253/40/3: 4/10/1832)
1829	73	(CO 253/40/3: 4/10/1832)
1829	75	(CO 258/5/6+7: 1829/section F)
1830	78	(CO 253/40/3: 4/10/1832)
1830	75	(CO 258/6/1+2,7/1: 1830/section F)
1831	56	(CO 258/8/1,9/1,10/2: 1831/section F)
1832	38	(CO 258/11/1,12/1: 1832)
1833	30	(CO 258/13/1,14/1: 1833/section F)
1834	21	(CO 258/15/1: 1834/section F)

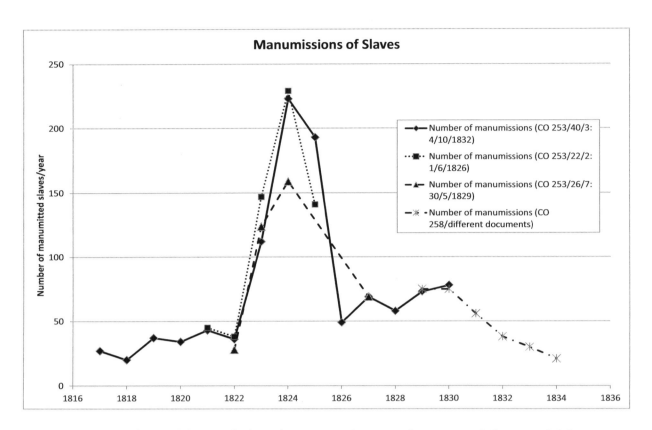

According to the table and the diagram during the period from 1822 to 1826 the number of manumissions was higher. Manumissions reached their highest number in 1824.

Chief Justice JEREMIE reported in May 1829:

> "... it appears that the manumissions which were returned as amounting to 28 in 1822 immediately increased to 120 and 140 in the subsequent years. But that since the law has passed they had fallen to an average of 80, though Slaves were then for the first time allowed purchasing freedom nolente domino. The increase in 1822 is accounted for by the tax on manumission being withdrawn, but the decrease in 1826 when it was expected that Slaves would crowd into free themselves, shows how completely groundless were the alarms which then resounded through the Island. The truth is that the Clause, whereby the Slaves of persons in debt can only be manumitted by appraisement or sold with the Estate, has prevented more Slaves from obtaining freedom than the equitable manumission Clause has obtained freedom for."

(CO 253/26/5: 30/5/1829)

Governor STEWART of St. Lucia mentioned another reason for the decrease in the number of manumissions in his letter of November 1829:

> "I regret much to see that Manumissions are decreasing and regret the circumstance that it proceeds from the new manumission law ...

… that proprietors are beginning to lose the pride they had in giving liberty as a gift to a meritorious slave.

I will not go the length to say that the same indulgence and opportunities to procure the means to purchase the freedom is not given to slaves as was formerly done. But I know that there are several who now repent having so indulged their people, because they have lost or are likely to lose the service of a valuable servant without having the merit of doing a generous act as the recompense for the loss."

(CO 258/5/8: 10/11/1829)

The PROTECTOR OF SLAVES reported in March 1833 of a positive development of the manumissions:

"I have great pleasure in stating generally that the march of enfranchisement becomes more rapid every day."

(CO 253/44/3: 23/3/1833)

In his report of the second half of the year 1833 he wrote:

"Slaves are frequently in the habit of making applications and enquiries respecting the purchasing themselves but the above mentioned are the only one who procured or were supposed to be able to command an adequate sum of money to pay the estimated value and even of the above applicants several have not been able to procure their required sum when called for, …"

(CO 258/14/1: 1/7/1833-31/12/1833/section F)

The number of applicants mentioned above was 14.

Summing up it can be said that the above-mentioned reports confirm the table made on page 161 in general.

4.7.4.4.3 Discharge of apprenticed labourers

In the emancipation period the legal stipulations regarding the manumission of slaves were adopted from the period of slavery unaltered.

Governor DUDLEY HILL of St. Lucia reported in July 1834 to the future APPRENTICES their right of purchasing their freedom as follows:

"You can release yourselves by purchase, at a fair valuation, from the service of your apprenticeship, in like manner as hitherto you had the right of buying your freedom from slavery."

(Z/CO 253/46/1: 30/7/1834)

According to a report of September 1835 in the first year after the abolition of slavery 38 APPRENTICES got their freedom (CO 253/49/4: September 1835).

The reports of the STIPENDIARY MAGISTRATES mentioned that the desire among the APPRENTICES for purchasing their freedom was a very great one. Responding to Governor DUDLEY HILL's question on that matter the STIPENDIARY MAGISTRATES of the several districts answered as follows:

1st district (Castries, Gros Islet, Dauphin and Anse La Raye)

> *"Very general, so much so that if the practice continues at the present rate in less than 2 years the culture of the cane on the Estates must be abandoned."*
>
> (CO 253/52/1: September 1836)

2nd district (Soufrière, Choiseul and Laborie):

> *"The desire of obtaining their discharge is becoming more general."*
>
> (CO 253/52/2: 2/9/1836)

3rd district (Vieux Fort, Micoud, Praslin and Dennery):

> *"The desire amongst the apprentices to purchase their unexpired time is very general."*
>
> (CO 253/52/5: 31/8/1836)

The appraisal of APPRENTICES was in general very high. In December 1836 Governor DUDLEY HILL informed the British travellers STURGE and HARVEY of this situation. In their book published in 1838 they wrote:

> *"He thought the appraisements were in some instances too high. He had endeavoured to dissuade some of them from purchasing their freedom, by telling them, that if they would wait till 1840, they would have their money to commence the world with; but they argued in reply, that wages were now very high, and would fall when all became free."*
>
> (STURGE/HARVEY 1838: 107)

In May 1837 the STIPENDIARY MAGISTRATE of the 2nd district (Soufrière, Choiseul and Laborie) reported:

> *"The desire among the apprentices of obtaining their discharge still continues general, but applications for that purpose have of late been less numerous than usual."*
>
> (CO 253/55/1: 1/5/1837)

This decrease in applications may be due to the high compensation sums which were required. Governor BUNBURY of St. Lucia in his letter of January 1838 also referred to the high compensation sums:

> "... that many of the most respectable of the apprenticed population, especially the Craft are still working for their Masters for the very reason that they have cultivated their abilities, thereby I must admit making themselves more useful, and were on that account prevented from purchasing the unexpired term of their apprenticeship by the exorbitant prices set upon them by the appraisers, ..."
>
> (CO 253/64/14: 31/1/1838)

In March 1838 the STIPENDIARY MAGISTRATES of the 2nd and 4th district [15]reported as follows:

2nd district (Gros Islet, Dauphin):

> "... - the wish for discharge is great, notwithstanding the heavy sum generally paid for the enfranchisement."
>
> (CO 253/64/15: 6/3/1838)

4th district (Vieux Fort, Laborie):

> "... - the estimated value of apprentices coming before the Manumission Court is still very high."
>
> (CO 253/64/16: 1/3/1838)

The hard view of the slave owners regarding the manumission of their APPRENTICES till the last day of the emancipation period is described in a letter of Governor EVERARD of St. Lucia from June 1839:

> "The Gangs throughout the Colony have become factious and unsettled from the heart-burning recollection that they were necessitated to purchase their manumission, even up to the last moment prior to final Emancipation: This consequence might have been prevented, if the Planter at that time, had in the spirit of a more liberal Policy bestowed his freedom as a reward on the most deserving and industrious, instead of forcing the negro (notwithstanding the Planter had already received his full value by compensation) to purchase the unexpired term of his Apprenticeship, with the little means he had accumulated by economy and frugal habits, for his further wants and comforts."
>
> (CO 253/67/2: 20/6/1839)

This view of the slave owners was also described in the afore-mentioned section during the period of slavery and follows from the law of June 1st, 1836, which fixed the right of the slave to purchase his freedom also against the will of his owner.

---

[15] In the year 1837 the division of the districts was altered from three to five (cp. p. 31)

4.7.4.4.4 Summary

According to the CODE DE LA MARTINIQUE masters of slaves in St. Lucia had the right to free their slaves. From the year 1713 manumission also depended upon the approval of the Governor of the colony. Owing to the general movement in Britain to ameliorate the living conditions of the slaves the Slave Law of St. Lucia of the year 1826 provided that slaves could also purchase their freedom against the will of their master. The slave masters protested against this provision. They saw therein a limitation of their right of property. The reaction of the masters was that they lost their pride they had in giving liberty as a gift to a meritorious slave. They saw only a loss of the service of a valuable servant without the merit of doing a generous act as the recompense for the loss. This view of the slave masters lasted till the end of the emancipation period.

According to the available sources approximately 1.370 slaves were freed in the period from 1808 to 1834. Especially between 1822 and 1826 the number of manumissions was high. For the emancipation period no exact numbers could be found. From August 1st, 1834, till August 1st, 1835, 38 APPRENTICES were freed. In the following period till the 1st of August 1838 the desire among the APPRENTICES for purchasing their freedom was a very great one, but the high compensation sums which were required by the colonial government, hindered many APPRENTICES from purchasing their freedom.

4.7.4.5 Sale of Slaves

According to a clause in the CODE DE LA MARTINIQUE members of a slave family had not to be sold separately:

> "Art. XLVII. – Husband and wife, together with their children, under the age of puberty, cannot, if belonging to the same owner, be sold separately; all sales of this description declared to be null and void, whether voluntary or otherwise. Any Slaves so illegally retained, to be adjudged to, and to belong to the purchaser of the other member of the family, without any additional sum being required."

> (BPP/ST/71/2: 16/3/1685, p. 187)

This legal provision was also fixed in the Slave Law of 1826:

> 10: "The Husband, Wife, and Children under the age of Puberty, the Mother and the Children under the age of Puberty, though born out of wedlock, and when the Mother is dead, the reputed Father, and his Children under the age of Puberty, shall not, when they belong to the same owner, be taken under an execution and sold, otherwise than in one and the same lot, all seizures to the contrary are declared illegal and void, neither shall they be separated, when sold or transferred by voluntary

agreement. In the latter case the transfer of part of the Family shall be taken and considered as a transfer of the whole. The vendor or other person transferring shall be deprived of that part of the Family, which he shall have retained, and the same shall, without any increase of price or additional valuable consideration, belong to the Purchaser.

The Slave may claim the enforcement of this Regulation by applying to the Procureur General, to the Procureur du Roi, to his Substitutes, or the Commissary of the Quarter.

If the creditor shall seize the Husband, or Wife, or the Mother, without the remainder of the Family, the owner shall be bound to point out and produce those remaining, that they may be sold in one lot, on pain of forfeiting their value in favour of the Purchaser of the Slave seized, if the seizure be otherwise valid."

(CO 253/22/4: 1/6/1826)

4.7.5 Labour conditions on the plantations

4.7.5.1   Legal development and discussion

The legal labour conditions for slaves valid in St. Lucia at the beginning of the 19th century were fixed in an ordinance of the 15th of October 1786. The relevant clauses were as follows:

> *"Art. I, - Forbidding owners, or others, suffering their Negroes to work on Sundays, or holidays, also in the week days from mid-day until two o'clock, or before daylight in the morning, or after sun-set, under pretext of pressing work, unless it be during the time of crop on sugar estates, or in extraordinary circumstances, or other estates which require a continuation of labour. Governor and Officers charged with the police of the different parishes, to cause these orders to be duly observed, and to direct the Procureur du Roi to prosecute when necessary ..."*

(BPP/ST/7172: 15/10/1786, p. 206)

> *"Art. V, - Forbidding Masters to suffer their female Slaves, in a state of pregnancy, or nursing, to work, unless moderately, and after the rising of the sun, ordering that they shall leave work at eleven o'clock, a.m. and not to return to work until three o'clock in the afternoon, and to leave off work half an hour before the setting of the sun. Under no pretext whatever are they to be allowed to keep watch, or set up at night.*

> *Art. VI. – A female Slave, mother of six children, to be exempt the first year from working in the field, one day in each week, the second year, two days per week, the third year, three days, and so on in succession, until they shall be altogether exempted from working in the field. The said exemption to be claimed by presenting to the Master, or Attorney of the estate, the six children on the first day of each year, and they cannot be debarred of the same, unless it shall be proved, that for want of care, on*

the mother's part, one of the children should have died before having attained ten years."

(BPP/ST/71/2: 15/10/1786, p. 207)

These stipulations were also inserted in the Slave Law of 1826 (CO 253/22/4: 1/6/1826):

Clause regarding the prohibition of working on Sundays:

21: "Masters are expressly enjoined not to work their Slaves from nightfall on Saturday evening till day break on Monday morning."

Exceptions were:

"Nothing herein contained shall be so construed as to prevent Gangs having the care of Cattle, from being employed in bringing Grass or fodder as heretofore on the Sunday evening, or Slaves employed in any domestic occupation, from working in the manner usually required from free domestics, nor to prevent Slaves upon Plantations from being employed on such unforeseen and extraordinary occasions arising upon said Plantations only, as might be otherwise productive of irreparable damage to their masters; but on such extraordinary occasions, the Slaves shall receive three shillings currency per day or the time shall be made good to them, in the course of the ensuing Week at their choice."

Clause regarding the prohibition of working on festivals and the general labour time:

22: "The Slaves shall not be worked on Festivals, nor on working days, from noon till two, nor in the morning before day-break, nor in the evening after nightfall, except when employed at the sugar mills, and in other Manufactories, upon extraordinary occasions of forced Crops absolutely requiring continued labour, and except on such unforeseen and extraordinary occasions as are mentioned in the preceding Section respecting Sundays, but when employed on Festivals they shall not be paid.

The Festivals are New Year's Day, Good Friday, Ascension Day, Fete Dieu, the Assumption, all Saints, and Christmas."

Clause for pregnant and nursing women:

24: "Pregnant women after the fourth month of pregnancy and Mothers nursing for six months from the birth, shall only be required to do light work, they shall commence after Sunrise, have an hour's rest between Sunrise and noon, return to work at three, finally quit it at sunset, and never on any pretence, even when the Gang are employed at the mill or in other extraordinary cases shall they be required to remain up at night."

Exemption of labour for mothers with six children:

25: "Mothers of six Children shall be exempted during the first five years from one day's labour weekly, from two days' the next five years – and when the youngest of the six Children attains its tenth year – they shall be exempted from all labour, except the taking care of their Children, and assisting in providing for their maintenance, and the maintenance of their Families. They shall acquire these exemptions on presenting their six Children on the first day in each year to their Master, and shall only be deprived of them when from ill conduct or the want of care, they shall lose any of their Children before they attain their tenth year."

An additional clause regarding night-work was inserted as follows:

23: "The same Slaves shall not, even when employed at the sugar mills, and upon other extraordinary occasions above mentioned, be worked during two nights consecutively, except when the gang shall have been divided into Watches, and then the Slaves belonging to the same Watch shall not be worked more than half the night."

In April 1827 the following paragraph was added:

"... it is further ordered that when the slaves are employed at night they shall, under any and every circumstances, be entitled to eight hours rest consecutively out of the 24 hours, under the penalty ..."

(CO 255/1/2: 24/4/1827)

In 1827 planters of St. Lucia protested against a law regarding night-work. In their petition they asked if there are really such planters who let their slaves work day and night without interruption and stated that this would not be possible because of physical reasons and that the slaves would die because of exhaustion:

"Qui, donc! y-a-t-il en des maitres non seulement assez durs, mais assez ennemis de leurs propres intérets pour faire travailler jour et nuit sans relache leurs esclaves? Mais la chose est physiquement impossible, dans peu de jours les negres fussent morts de lassitude, où donc a-t-on pu prendre une telle exaggeration? Si ce n'est dans la haine aveugle qu'on porte aux colons? Les Soussignés ne demandent pas la suppression de cet article comme blessant leurs froits, génant inutilement leur administration, mais comme contenant une supposition calomnieuse."

(CO 253/23/1: 28/7/1827)

A letter of Lord BATHURST of August 1st, 1831, contains the proposal that the daily working hours for agricultural or manufacturing labour should be limited generally to nine (CO 253/30/3: 29/10/1831). In the PRIVY COUNCIL of St. Lucia this proposal met with resistance. On September

27th, 1831, three members of the PRIVY COUNCIL of St. Lucia wrote the following:

> "We cannot consecutively sanction the proposed law and are on the contrary of opinion that in the present state of the Slave Population in this Island it is a measure quite unnecessary, …, we are bound to go further and do declare that any further diminution or abridgement of the daily labour of Slaves in this Colony is an interference with the right of private property of His Majesty's Subjects in this Colony which cannot be persisted in with justice towards the proprietors of Estates in this Island, except on the principle of compensation for such diminution or abridgement of the daily labour of the Slaves …
>
> The Undersigned full confident that on the Enquiry it will be fairly established by the Testimony of Medical Men and of the Free Persons who have themselves been Slaves employed in Sugar Plantations, that the present Work required of Slaves both in and out of Crop is far short of what their Physical powers might reasonably be expected to perform even in this Climate, and that the time secured to them by Law for the purpose of raising Ground Provisions for themselves is not only amply sufficient for that purpose, but so ample, - that an industrious Slave may very easily acquire sufficient property to purchase his Freedom in a few Years without any extraordinary exertion."

The mentioned time secured to the slaves by law for the purpose of raising ground provisions themselves comprised one day per week out of crop time and a half day per week in crop time. The last sentence of this quotation points to the aversion of the slave masters to the right of the slaves to purchase their freedom and to do so against the will of their masters (cp. chapter "4.7.4.4.2. Trend of Slave Manumissions", p. 162-163).

In conclusion the three members of the PRIVY COUNCIL wrote:

> "In the present state of things, Sugar Planting barely pay their Annual Expenditure, and if the Labour of the Slaves were farther abridged and things continue in their present state, they must cease to meet even the Annual Expenditure, and consequently the Owners would no longer command the means necessary to pay for those comforts which the present Law secures to the Slave, viz. that of being fed, clothed and being provided with Medical Attendance, and all other convenience during Sickness."
>
> (CO 253/30/2: 27/9/1831)

One month later, on October 31st, 1831, "Proprietors, Planters, Merchants and other Inhabitants of the Island of St. Lucia" protested against the proposed abridgement of the labour time as follows:

> "… the Petitioners now see with the utmost surprise and alarm a proposal from the Right Honourable Secretary of State for the Colonies to enact a

Law for abridging the hours of Labour to 9 hours out of every twenty-four all the year round, which would render the manufacture of Sugar entirely impracticable, destroy all Sugar-Properties and reduce greatly the cultivation of Coffee ...

That the small portion of work now performed by Slaves renders a further abridgement of time unnecessary on the strictest principles of humanity, as sufficient time is already granted them for all the purpose of rest and comfort."

(CO 253/30/1: 31/10/1831)

On November 2nd, 1831, an ORDER IN COUNCIL was passed in London. It was promulgated in St. Lucia on December 24th, 1831, and came into force on January 7th, 1832. This law fixed the labour time as follows (BPP/ST/79/1: 2/11/1831, p. 128-129):

The daily labour time for agricultural or manufacturing labour was from 6 a.m. to 6 p.m. with interruptions from 8 a.m. to 9 a.m. and from 12 a.m. to 2 p.m. It amounted to nine hours daily:

"XC. And it is further ordered, That no Slave shall be compelled or bound to engage in, or perform any agricultural or manufacturing labour in any of the said Colonies, before the hour of six in the morning or after the hour of six in the evening, but that save as is hereinafter otherwise provided, all Slaves in the said Colonies employed in any agricultural or manufacturing labour shall be, and are hereby declared to be entitled to an entire intermission and cessation of every description of work and labour from the hour of six in each evening until the hour of six in the next succeeding morning.

XCI. And it is further ordered, That all Slaves employed in any agricultural or manufacturing labour within any of the said Colonies, shall be allowed, and shall be and are hereby declared to be entitled to an entire intermission and cessation of every description of work and labour from the hour of eight till the hour of nine in the morning, and from the hour of twelve till the hour of two in the afternoon, of each and every day throughout the year; provided nevertheless, that the hours of intermission and cessation of labour in the case of Slaves employed in any manufacturing labour, may be allowed to them at any other period of the day, if an interval of not less than three nor more than six hours intervene between such remissions, and if the same be respectively of such duration as aforesaid."

Night work was regulated as follows:

XCIII. And whereas, at certain periods of the year, it may be necessary occasionally to employ Slaves in and about certain manufacturing processes in the night time; it is therefore ordered and declared, That nothing hereinbefore contained extends, or shall be construed to extent, to render the employment of Slaves in manufacturing processes within the said Colonies in the night time illegal, provided that no such Slave be required or compelled to labour for more than nine hours in the whole, on any one day, the day being for that purpose, understood to commence at the hour of six in the morning, and to terminate at the hour of six in the next succeeding morning."

The labour time for children up to 14 years, slaves up from 60 years and pregnant female slaves was limited to six hours per day. They were also not to work in the night:

"XCII. And it is further ordered, That no Slave, under the age of fourteen or above the age of sixty, and no female Slave known to be in a state of pregnancy, shall be compelled or required to engage in or perform any agricultural work or labour, in any of the said Colonies, during more than six hours in the whole, in any one day, the day being, for that purpose, understood to commence at the hour of six in the morning, and to terminate at the hour of six in the next succeeding morning."

"XCIV. And provided also, That no Slave under the age of fourteen years, or above the age of sixty years, and no female Slave known to be in a state of pregnancy, be ever employed in any agricultural or manufacturing labour in the night time."

The legal stipulations regarding the abridgement of the labour time produced heavy protests in St. Lucia. "Managers and Others having the Administration of Estates" saw the manufacture of their crop endangered. In January 1832 they wrote:

"That the abridgement of the hours of labour by the said Order in Council, deprives your Memorialists of the power of manufacturing the crops of the estates under their charge, inasmuch as that manufacture absolutely requires a continual attendance, with but very short interruptions, during its process, which, according to the said abridgements, cannot be accomplished."

(CO 253/37/5: January 1832)

Merchants residing in Castries also protested:

"The undersigned Merchants residing in the town of Castries beg leave to expose to your Excellency that they cannot supply their planters of this Island with the articles necessary for feeding and clothing the negroes and for taking off the Crops in consequence of the laws promulgated limiting the hours of labour during Crop being persuaded of the utter impossibility of the planters being able to make a sufficient quantity of produce to defray or pay for such expenses, ..."

(CO 253/37/3: 4/1/1832)

A remonstrance also dated in January 1832 refers to the abridgement of the labour time for adults as well as for children:

"... we do most unequivocally declare that with less than twelve hours continuous attendance of the Labourers the manufacturing process of sugar boiling cannot be carried on, but that the Custom is universal of

giving the People so employed due time to eat their food, the work they have to do never requiring the constant attention of all persons so employed – The hours of Field Labour can suffer no difficulty they are those constantly observed in this Island. The Regulation that no Young Slave under fourteen years of age should work more than six hours in the twenty four is an unnecessary restriction – Young male Slaves under that age are perfectly able to do the work required from them – they are employed as Mule or Cart Boys in crop time and out of Crop at work much lighter than that executed in England by the Peasant Boy of the same age.-"

(CO 253/37/2: January 1832)

In a petition of March 27th, 1832, "Proprietors, Merchants, Planters and other Inhabitants of the Island of St. Lucia" demanded an extension of the daily labour time as follows:

"That the restrictions on the hours of labour be modified so as not to prohibit nine hours of agricultural labour out of crop, and ten hours of agricultural and twelve hours of manufacturing labour in crop."

(Z/OPL/LG: 27/3/1832, p. 1219)

Finally these protests were successful and Governor FARQUHARSON of St. Lucia extended with a proclamation dated 3rd January 1833 the daily labour time during crop time regarding manufacturing labour to twelve and fourteen hours respectively:

"Now, therefore, I, JAMES ALEXANDER FARQUHARSON, …, do by this my Proclamation suspend, for the term of one year, the execution of so much of the said Order of the 2nd of November as limits the duration of the labour of Slaves employed in any manufacturing process to nine hours in the whole on any one day, …: And I do hereby Proclaim ad Order that, during the season of crop, no Slave within this said Colony of St. Lucia, engaged wholly in any manufacturing process, shall be required or compelled to labour for more than twelve hours in the whole on any one day; Provided always, that during the said season it shall be lawful to employ any able-bodied Slave in manufacturing labour, during two days in each week, for a period not exceeding fourteen hours in each day, it being hereby expressly declared, that in such case no Slave shall be compelled to labour in any employment whatsoever for a longer space than nine hours in each day, during the remaining days of such week on which such Slave's services may be legally claimed by his Master, and that an interval of not less than twenty-four hours intervene between the days on which such fourteen hours of manufacturing labour shall be exacted from such Slave;"

(CO 255/2/4: 3/1/1833, p. 181)

4.7.5.2   Offences

In a letter of September 1829 Governor STEWART of St. Lucia informed the SECRETARY OF STATE in London of the overworking of the slaves in crop time as follows:

> "I must also take steps to change an objectionable practice (but not a general one) of working a portion of the people in crop time till eight, nine, and later hours: in grinding canes, and boiling sugar. This practice is defended on the plea that it is only done in fine weather, when more than a usual quantity of cane is cut, and that the people, whose turn it is to be thus employed at night, have an indulgence the following day. However plausible this reasoning may appear to them; it is a practice liable to be abused, and ought to be discontinued."
>
> (CO 253/26/6: 29/9/1829)

From the notes of the PROTECTOR OF SLAVES concerning complaints of slaves before court the author chose the following examples:

6th October 1829:

> Mr. Taillason accused of working the slave on Saturdays and during noontime, since crop was over; and also for punishing her without lawful cause.
>
> ... the slave condemned to receive 20 lashes, the complaint being unfounded.
>
> (CO 258/5/7: 1/7/1829-31/12/1929/section B)

Here it should be mentioned that it was common in St. Lucia that slaves had one free day per week (out of crop time) for the cultivation of their provisions. At that time Saturday might have been fixed as that day.

13th February 1832, offence at Fond d'Or estate, quarter of Dennery:

> "That since the beginning of Crop, the Spells work at the Mill from Noon till Midnight without ceasing – that in consequence of the Spells being composed of very few persons, often some of those that left the Mill at Midnight are sent again to the Mill, instead to the Field the next Morning."
>
> (CO 258/11/1: 1/1/1832-30/6/1832/section B)

25th July, 1832, complaint of Lise of the Morne Courbaril estate:

> "... that she is pregnant, that Mr. Prevost put her in the Cachot for five days and only gave her five small potatoes and water every 24 hours. That she has asked Mr. Prevost to give her light work, he however makes her work in the strong gang."
>
> (CO 258/11/1: 1/1/1832-30/6/1832/section B)

The PROTECTOR OF SLAVES sent her to the doctor. After that she didn't announce herself again to the PROTECTOR.

30th July, 1832, complaint of field slave Clothilde of the Fond d'Or estate in the quarter of Dennery:

> *"That she is sick and unfit for field labour in consequence of having been frequently put into the field stocks. On the 25th instant she had fever went to the overseer, Mr. Deville, who sent her to the hospital. But Mr. Du Bocage would not allow her to remain there and compelled her to work for two days in the field with the fever."*

> (CO 258/12/1: 1/7/1832-31/12/1832/section B)

For this case the PROTECTOR OF SLAVES proposed a trial before the royal court.

May 7th, 1833, complaint of slave Charles of the Bois d'Orange estate:

> *"My master has made me work three weeks consecutively from morning to night & I have no time allowed to me for my breakfast and dinner. On Saturday the 27 April I went to my garden at 12 o'clock for the purpose of getting some food and on my returning at 2 o'clock my master ordered me to be confined in the Cachot where I remained for the space of eight days."*

> (CO 258/13/1: 1/1/1833-30/6/1833/section B)

Also in this case the PROTECTOR OF SLAVES proposed a trial before the royal court.

28th October, complaint of Frederic of the Union estate in the quarter of Castries:

> *"I am lame & cannot do my work as fast as the other Negroes having a weakness of the stomach, and sores on the legs. On Saturday last, we were carrying stones to make a path. I did not bring my load at the same time with the rest, but I met them at each time returning to reload.-Mr. Cheesman ordered the driver to tie me up and to inflict fifteen lashes on me which was accordingly done."*

> (CO 258/14/1: 1/7/1833-31/12/1833/section B)

To this complaint the PROTECTOR OF SLAVES noted "for trial before the Royal Court".

10th July, 1833, complaint of Dorothée from the Riche-Fond estate in the quarter of Dennery:

"I am not in a state to work either for myself or for my master as I am in my last month of pregnancy. Mr. De Lobel endeavours to compel me to work by punishing me. On Saturday evening last, the 6th instant, I was shut up in the Cachot until the next morning when I was released on my promising that I would work. I only made that promise to get released and be enabled to come to complain.

On Monday the 18th inst. being ordered to the field, I went with my hoe but I could not work and as I found that Mr. De Lobel had ordered me to be confined again, I left the Estate to prefer this Complaint."

(CO 258/14/1: 1/7/1833-31/12/1833/section B)

Mr. de Lobel was sentenced to pay a fine.

5th March, 1834, offence at the Canelles estate:

"To punish the said Patrick Mc. Cracker for having compelled eight Slaves under his management to manufacture Sugar on Sunday"

(CO 258/15/1: 1/1/1834-1/8/1834/section H)

Mr. Mc. Cracker was also adjudged to pay a fine.

Another case worthy of note is mentioned by the CHIEF JUSTICE of St. Lucia in his "Notes of the Proceedings on the Trial of Donald Shaw, late Manager on the Grand Anse Plantation" dated 29/30th January and 6th February 1833. This estate was located in the district of Dauphin:

"Accused:

1. *of having worked the gang on that Plantation and several times for 24 hours in succession during the year 1829 and of depriving the Slaves of their hours of rest,*

2. *of having committed the same offence in 1830 and*

3. *of having occasioned or accelerated the death of the female Slave Marie-Sainte by ordering her to be flogged with the Cat which he allowed to be carried and used in the field.*

The Trial came on before the Royal Court of Assizes in St. Lucia on the 29th and 30th January and 6th February 1833 ...

The following questions were then submitted for the decision of the Court and Assessors.

1. *Is Donald Shaw guilty of having worked the gang of the Grand Anse-Plantation & on several occasions for twenty-four hours in succession during the Crop of 1829 without allowing them the time to repose prescribed by law?*

The three Assessors noted not guilty. The three Judges noted guilty.

2. Is he guilty of having about the same period caused the female Slave Marie-Sainte to be flogged with a Cat, though she was in bad health?

Guilty by a majority of five votes

3. In consequence of this chastisement is he guilty of having occasioned or accelerated the dissolution of the said Marie-Sainte?

Not guilty by an unanimous vote.

4. Is he guilty of having permitted the Driver Louis Laramie to carry the whip in the field?

Guilty by a majority of four votes

5. Is he guilty of working the same Gang several times at the beginning of the Crop of 1830 during 24 hours without allowing the Slaves the necessary time for rest enjoined by law?

Not guilty by a majority of 4 to 2 votes.

The PROCUREUR GENERAL in his conclusions which were based on the Slave Law of February 1826, Articles 40 and 39 required the infliction of two fines of one thousand Livres each and six weeks' imprisonment.

The Court & Assessors taking in consideration the favourable evidence & testimonies of Donald Shaw as the character sentenced him to pay two fines of one thousand Livres and of two hundred Livres together with the whole costs of the proceedings."

(CO 253/43/6: 6/2/1833)

4.7.5.3 Situation of labour in the emancipation period

According to an Ordinance of Governor DUDLEY HILL dated August 1st, 1834, FIELD APPRENTICES were obliged to work 45 hours per week. When an APPRENTICE had to cultivate his own provisions he had five free hours out of the 45. The maximum labour time per day was for manufacturing labour twelve hours and for agricultural labour nine hours. This Ordinance refers to an ORDER IN COUNCIL passed in London on 5th June 1834 and which carried the abolition act into effect:

"1. That every praedial apprenticed labourer for or in respect of whom any ground shall be appropriated and set apart for his support, shall, out of the annual time during which such praedial apprenticed labourer is by the said recited Act required to labour after the rate of forty-five hours per week, be allowed five hours per week for the cultivation of such ground.

2. That it shall and may be lawful for any person, being an employer of any able-bodied praedial apprenticed labourer, to require and exact from such able-bodied praedial apprenticed labourer, and such apprenticed labourer is hereby bound and obliged to work and labour in the name and for the benefit of his employer, any number of hours not exceeding twelve hours in any one day when employed in manufacturing labour, and any number of hours not exceeding nine hours in any one day when employed in agricultural labour; And Provided Also, That no apprenticed labourer who shall be required to work and labour both in agricultural and manufacturing labour in one and the same day shall be required to work in the whole day more than ten hours; And Provided Always, That the whole number of hours to be exacted from any praedial apprenticed labourer for whom ground shall be set apart shall not exceed forty hours, and for all others shall not exceed forty-five hours per week; And Provided Nevertheless, That all the rules and regulations provided by the said recited Order of His Majesty in Council of the 5th June 1834, and in the first clause of this Order, be duly complied with; And Further, That the day for manufacturing labour shall be held to include twenty-four hours, and the day for agricultural labour to commence at sunrise and terminate at sunset."

(CO 255/2/7: 1/8/1834, p.272)

Before the publication of this Ordinance the Governor had informed the future APPRENTICES of the new labour time in July 1834 as follows:

"As slaves, you had to work for your Masters 9 hours every day or 54 hours every week; - as free apprenticed labourers, you are to work 7 ½ hours per day or 45 hours per week.

As slaves, you were to work these 9 hours every day of every week of your whole lives; - after the 1st next month, you are to work these 7 ½ hours per day for six years, or, if you are domestics, for four years only. The domestics have the shorter term allotted to them because their services are without remission."

(Z/CO 253/46/1: 30/7/1834)

In case of offences he promised punishment:

"As the good things of which I have been before telling you are secured to you and your children, to be sure you in your turn shall receive punishment if you do not honestly and fairly work for your masters the whole time to which by law he is entitled whilst the apprenticeship lasts. Some people tell me, that perhaps you will try not to work at all. I cannot believe you to be such fools, or so ungrateful, or so wicked. Work you must, the moderate time required from you by law. If any of you dare to resist the law, and think that by combining together you can evade or set it at defiance, be assured I shall instantly come amongst you – not as now, to do you good and advice you, but severely to punish the offender."

According to the reports of the STIPENDIARY MAGISTRATES the exact labour time was from 6 a.m. to 8 a.m., from 9 a.m. to 12 a.m. and from 2 p.m. to 5 p.m., totally eight hours (CO 253/52/2: 2/9/1836).
Additional to these labour times APPRENTICES worked in crop time against a compensation of salted fish or molasses; money they got seldom. The respective reports are as follows:

1st district (Castries, Gros Islet, Dauphin and Anse La Raye):

"No apprentices in this district work for money-wages in their own time. The only extra work beyond 40 hours performed by apprenticed labourers is manufacturing labour during Crop time at which period they consent to continue to work in the manufacturing the number of hours necessary to complete the operations of the day. This occupation never exceeds 14 hours in the day and in return for this extra time which on an Estate yielding 100 Hogsheads of Sugar amounts to 140 hours for each apprentice employed, they receive 63 pounds of fish worth on an average 5 ½ Dollars, in some few instances this amount has been in money while on the larger Estates in the district the amount of fish is double. The allowance be continued all year round. Every attempt to induce the apprenticed labourers to work agricultural labour in his own time for money-wages has proved unsuccessful as much as ½ Sterling and ¼ for woman having been offered and refused."

(CO 253/52/1: Sept. 1836)

2nd district (Soufrière, Choiseul and Laborie):

"The apprentices in Crop time are usually engaged at the rate from 8 to 10 Sterling for eight hours extra to labour, sometimes paid in money but oftener by an allowance of salted fish and molasses."

(CO 253/52/2: 2/9/1836)

3rd district (Vieux Fort, Micoud, Praslin and Dennery):

"No instance known of App.Lab. working in their own time for wages."

(CO 253/52/5: 31/8/1836)

Graphic representation of the mentioned districts:

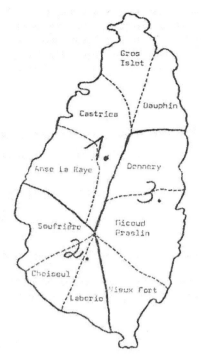

Division of districts extracted from a map of St. Lucia from the Year 1847 (BPP/CG/4/1: 1847, p. 518 as well as from BROCK 1984: 30)

From letters of Governor DUDLEY HILL of August and November 1834 follows that the APPRENTICES behaved according to the wishes of the Colonial government:

> *"I had the pleasure to observe that there were no exceptions to the general good behaviour of the labourers, save those which arising from simple misapprehension of the new rights, which could be remedied gradually and temporarily, and except also those breaches of discipline which amongst a large body of people would occur under any system of compulsory labour and which were not less frequent under that just abolished."*
>
> (CO 253/46/3: 26/8/1834)

> *"... to inform you that the tranquil and orderly conduct of the apprenticed labourers fully justifies my giving you an assurance which cannot fail to be gratifying to His Majesty's Government and that is that the Abolition of Slavery has not up to this period interrupted the industry which was customary previously to that happy event."*
>
> (CO 253/46/4: 3/11/1834)

In another letter to the SECRETARY OF STATE dated 28th November 1834 the Governor wrote:

"I have the pleasure to state that in a very ample opportunity of learning the sentiments of the Manager, I became acquainted with but few complaints against their gangs and was equally gratified on special enquiry from the latter, to find this state of things to be reciprocal."

(CO 253/46/5: 28/11/1834)

This conduct of the APPRENTICES lasted according to the following reports during the whole emancipation period:

The STIPENDIARY MAGISTRATES of the three districts reported in the year 1836:

1st district (Castries, Gros Islet, Dauphin and Anse La Raye):

"We cannot say that we perceive any want of good feeling between them and their employer."

(CO 253/52/1: Sept. 1836)

2nd district (Soufrière, Choiseul and Laborie):

"The general conduct of the apprenticed labourers has uniformly been good …

A good feeling generally subsists between the apprentices and their employer …

Generally they perform their work willingly."

(CO 253/52/2: 2/9/1836)

3rd district (Vieux Fort, Micoud, Praslin and Dennery)

"The conduct of the Apprenticed Labourers has been good in this District …

The labourers throughout this district perform their work willingly and there has been no complaint on the score of idleness for a long period."

(CO 253/52/5: 31/8/1836)

Also Governor DUDLEY HILL referred in November 1836 on the occasion of a tour around the island to the good behaviour of the APPRENTICES:

"I avail myself of this opportunity of acquainting your Lordship that I am at the present moment occupied in visiting the several Estates and nothing can be more gratifying than the general tranquillity and good order which exists amongst the apprenticed population."

(CO 253/52/6: 3/11/1836)

In December 1836 the Governor made a detailed report of his tour for the purpose of visiting the different estates throughout the colony. He wrote:

"… that in every part of the Island which I visited, the utmost tranquillity and good order prevailed, the apprentices appeared to be industrious, contented and happy and from the particular enquiries which I made, there existed a mutual good understanding and friendly feeling between the employer and labourers …

The number of Estates which I visited amounted to One Hundred and Seven, being all of any importance in the Colony. I did not fail in addressing the apprentices on each to make them fully understand the relative duties between their employers and themselves; of the smaller Estates I directed a few of the most intelligent from each to be brought before me in the neighbourhood of their houses, so that I can safely assert I had an opportunity of communicating to the whole of the labouring population and object of my visit; your Lordship will learn with pleasure that I had not any complaints from either party of importance …

My attention was particularly directed to the manner in which the apprentices performed the labour and whether any difficulty existed in hiring themselves during their own time to take off the Crop and it was satisfactory to learn that their employers were satisfied with their industry and that the arrangements for extra labour were entered into with mutual confidence."

(CO 253/52/4: Dec. 1836)

For the year 1837 the reports of the STIPENDIARY MAGISTRATES inform as follows:

1st district (Castries, Gros Islet, Dauphin and Anse La Raye):

"general conduct good"

(CO 253/54/1: 1/2/1837)

2nd district (Soufrière, Choiseul and Laborie):

"The Apprentices work willingly and no complaint has been made of their want of industry …

The conduct of the App. Population has been in general good."

(CO 253/57/1: 1/12/1837)

3rd district (Vieux Fort, Micoud, Praslin and Dennery):

"The conduct of the App. Labourers since last report has been orderly and quiet and there had been very few complaints for a length of time …
The App. Labourers continue to perform their work cheerfully & willingly."

(CO 253/54/2: Feb. 1837)

"The same good conduct and an improved good feeling prevails in this District."

(CO 253/57/2: 1/12/1837)

In the last months of the emancipation period also tranquil and good behaviour of the APPRENTICES was reported in general.

4.7.5.4   Summary

The daily labour time for slaves at the beginning of the 19th century was legally fixed from daylight in the morning to sunset with an interruption from midday to two o'clock. Sundays and holidays were free. For night work, which was especially necessary at crop time, no legal stipulations existed. They were only inserted in the Slave Law of 1826. Special regulations for pregnant and nursing women had also been fixed.

On January 7th, 1832, an ORDER IN COUNCIL came into force in St. Lucia which limited the daily working hours for agricultural or manufacturing labour generally to nine hours. The planters of St. Lucia protested vehemently against this law requesting especially longer daily working hours at crop time. Finally the planters' protests were successful and Governor FARQUHARSON of St. Lucia by a proclamation dated 3rd January 1833 extended the daily working hours during the crop season for manufacturing labour to twelve respectively fourteen hours.

From the year 1826 there are reports of the PROTECTOR OF SLAVES concerning complaints of slaves regarding offences of planters and masters. According to these reports the offences were:

-   Violation of the labour time
-   Working of slaves on their free days
-   Working of slaves when they were ill as well as
-   Overwork of pregnant women and disabled persons.

In the Emancipation Period the FIELD APPRENTICES were – according to an Ordinance of Governor DUDLEY HILL dated August 1st, 1834 – obliged to work 45 hours per week. When an APPRENTICE had to cultivate his own provisions he had five free hours out of th e 45. The maximum labour time per day was for manufacturing labour twelve hours and for agricultural labour nine hours. According to the reports of the STIPENDIARY MAGISTRATES the exact labour time was from 6 a.m. to 8 a.m., from 9 a.m. to 12 a.m. and from 2 p.m. to 5 p.m., totally eight hours per working day.

The reports of the Emancipation Period inform of good behaviour and general good conduct on the part of the apprenticed labourers. Good working relations between the APPRENTICES and their employers are also mentioned.

4.7.6 Subsistence of Slaves and APPRENTICES

4.7.6.1   Period of slavery

The main source of subsistence for the salves was, beside the maintenance of their masters, the purchase of their self-cultivated provisions.

In the year 1829 Governor STEWART of St. Lucia rode round the island and visited and examined the plantations. In his letter to the SECRETARY OF STATE in London dated September 29th, 1829, he reported the following regarding the cultivation of provisions:

> *"The negroes here have another advantage in being allowed a quantity of fertile land for their own cultivation, and are thus enabled to supply themselves with many comforts. The effect of this is seen in the good and often gay dresses (particularly among the females) which they purchase.*

(CO 253/26/6: 29/9/1829)

But not all slaves used this opportunity; many defended only on their master's maintenance:

> *"While the Slaves on estates are, so I have described, well disposed and comfortable, and by the sale of their spare produce from their industry, are comparatively rich, and save what in their circumstances, may be … considerable sums of money, by which many have purchased their own freedom, there are on other Estates people of every different Caste; without industry, badly clothed and without any comfort, except what is served out from the hands and stores of the master. Some of these people would sell their own father or child for a cash of rum."*

Of badly managed estates Governor STEWART noticed:

> *"Few or no pigs or poultry are seen at their doors, with other evident remarks that the proprietors or those who have the plantations in charge are equally neglectful of their own interest, as they are careless about their people."*

From this quotation it follows that on properly managed estates slaves reared pigs and poultry. According to a report of the PROTECTOR OF SLAVES for the year 1830 the slaves of St. Lucia had good possibilities to cultivate provisions:

> *"The extensive tracts of abandoned land throughout the Island, which the negro may occupy and cultivate afford even to the least industrious profitable returns for the produce thereof."*

(CO 258/6/2: 1/4/1830-30/9/1830/section G)

From a protest letter by three members of the PRIVY COUNCIL of St. Lucia dated September 27th, 1831, against the abridgement of the labour time on the estates to nine hours it follows that slaves used their lunch time to cultivate provisions:

> *"... having half an hour for breakfast and two hours for dinner, that is from 12 to 2, the law intended these two hours to be devoted by the Slave to repose himself during the heat of the sun, but what is the manner in which he really does employ these two hours? It is in working and cultivating his own garden, ...*
>
> *That he seriously requires to work in his garden during the Monday which out of Crop is wholly allowed him for that purpose, but spends it together with his Sunday in rest and amusement."*
>
> (CO 253/30/2: 27/9/1831)

They further mentioned the purchase of logwood by the slaves:

> *"In the article of Logwood alone, an occupation exclusively carried on by them, a sum of no less than sixteen thousand Spanish Dollars is annually paid to them in this very limited community."*

In the year 1832 the PROTECTOR OF SLAVES reported as follows:

> *"An industrious slave is able to accumulate money rapidly – more indeed than any other species of property ...*
>
> *Such accumulations are chiefly facilitated:*
>
> 1. *By the extreme fertility of the soil in St. Lucia and the little difficulty in obtaining any quantity which may be wished for cultivation, ..., by the extreme high prices of the markets in the Colony.*
>
> 2. *By the abundance of Fish on the Coast; and the proximity of almost every settled part to the sea.*
>
> 3. *By the great quantity of logwood, growing wild on waste land; which always finds a ready market for Europe, Martinique and America.*
>
> *Hence it will appear that such accumulations are chiefly made by Plantation Slaves."*
>
> (CO 258/11/1: 1/1/1832-30/6/1832/section G)

According to the following reports it was usual in St. Lucia that the slaves maintained themselves mainly by the cultivation of their own provisions:

On the occasion of a meeting of the PRIVY COUNCIL of St. Lucia in August 1832 the opinion of the PROTECTOR OF SLAVES was reported as follows:

"The Protector of Slaves considered that the almost universal practice in this Colony was to allow land and time to the slaves in lieu of provisions."

(CO 253/40/2: 20/8/1832)

From a report of the PROTECTOR OF SLAVES dated March 1833, in which he wrote about the reasons of the augmentation of the population in St. Lucia, it follows that slaves maintained themselves mainly by their own cultivated provisions:

"Yet, unprejudiced reflection based on practical observation induces me to venture to express my conviction that the real foundation of our present augmentation in St. Lucia is to be found in the now shortened hours of labour operating thus on the physical constitution and on the mental energy of the Slaves, improving their food by giving them both time and inclination to cultivate more sedulously their provision gardens from which the Saint Lucia Slaves derive their chief support and enabling them to purchase those luxuries and acquire those comforts which must gradually elevate their moral condition."

(CO 253/44/3: 23/3/1833)

In March 1833 Governor FARQUHARSON of St. Lucia reported:

"On every part which I visited the flourishing state of the negro-gardens convinced me that the Slaves in general were plentifully supplied with food and that few or none of them could have any just cause of complaint, ..."

(CO 253/43/5: 7/3/1833)

Another report of the PROTECTOR OF SLAVES for the year 1833 states:

"That habits of industry are continuing to gain ground rapidly with the great proportion of the slave population. This he would still attribute to the diminution, by law, of the hours in which their labour is dedicated by compulsion to the service of others and to the facility of employing their own time to the best advantage which is afforded them by general fertility of the soil and the abundance of waste land in the immediate neighbourhood of every estate."

(CO 258/14/1: 1/7/1833-31/12/1833/section G)

He further stated:

"In support of this position he advances the notorious fact that within the last three years the articles of negro produce have fallen in price from 1/3 to ½ in the Castries' market."

As articles which were sold by the slaves he mentioned: cassava, charcoal, firewood, forage, fish and vegetables of every description.

Finally he wrote:

> *"The export of logwood to Martinique, America and England affords a sure supply of ready money when required, even to the less steadily industrious negro."*

4.7.6.2   Emancipation period

The good maintenance of the black population of St. Lucia with provisions existed also at the beginning of the Emancipation Period.

From a letter of Governor DUDLEY HILL of November 1835 follows:

> *"…; and articles of produce; and those raised for consumption consist of various descriptions of provisions, most of them indigenous to the soil, and are always in such abundance as to enable the negroes to dispose of great quantities to the small crafts trading to and from the island."*

(CO 253/49/2: 23/11/1835)

In December 1836 the Governor confirmed the abundance of provisions cultivated by the APPRENTICES:

> *"I considered it also of very great importance to look minutely into the state of the negro gardens and as I had lately directed the attention of the Special Magistrates to this important subject, I was happy to observe that they were well cultivated and would yield more than was necessary for their own consumption which would enable them to dispose of a part to purchase such articles as may add to their comforts."*

(CO 253/52/4: Dec. 1836)

According to the following two reports Saturday was made available to the APPRENTICES for the cultivation of their gardens. The British travellers STURGE and HARVEY wrote about a report of a planter of St. Lucia (Mr. Muter) in December 1836 as follows:

> *"He told us, that he found it difficult to induce them to work for him on the Saturday, as they are entirely dependent for support on their labour in their provision grounds. One woman, on his offering her wages for her Saturday, asked him if he did not go to church on the Sunday. Observing, that if she worked on the estate on Saturday, she must cultivate her ground on the Sunday,-reasoning which admitted no reply."*

(STURGE/HARVEY 1838: 107)

A second quotation originates from a report of the STIPENDIARY MAGISTRATE of the 2nd district (Soufrière, Choiseul and Laborie) of May 1837:

"The Apprentices on working days willingly perform extreme labour at the reasonable rate of about 10 s Sterling for eight hours extra. They however are unwilling to work on Saturdays as on these days they cultivate their Gardens for their support during the week;"

(CO 253/55/1: 1/5/1837)

In contrast to the above-mentioned reports is an account of the STIPENDIARY MAGISTRATE of the 1st District (Castries, Anse La Raye) dated September 1837:

"There was a very strong wind which did much damage to the Provision Grounds – which coupled with the characteristic improvidence of the Negro, and his Idleness on Saturday made provisions scarce and very dear."

(CO 253/56/2: 1/9/1837)

On September 4th, 1837, Governor BUNBURY of St. Lucia circulated instructions to the STIPENDIARY MAGISTRATES in which he referred also to the fact that the APPRENTICES neglected their provision gardens:

"The attention of the apprentices to the cultivation of their provision grounds, is a subject of paramount consideration; and you are to impress on the minds of the idle and negligent, the imperious necessity of paying every attention to this important part of their domestic comforts, not only as a means of present support, but holding out, after the expiration of their apprenticeship the prospect of more solid advantages, as by industrious habits they will ensure the continued protection and support of those by whom they are now employed, and the certainty that their labour will be duly rewarded by liberal remuneration."

(CO 253/56/1: 4/9/1837)

By a letter of September 8th, 1837, the Governor informed the SECRETARY OF STATE GLENELG in London of the situation concerning slave refugees from Martinique and the negligence of cultivation provision grounds:

"It having been brought to my notice, that the free labouring population of this Colony is rapidly increasing both by Manumissions, and refugees from the neighbouring Island of Martinique (the latter description of persons amounting to more than five hundred), the majority of whom are out of employment (with the exception of a few squatters, whom charity alone has hitherto prevented the removal of) or decidedly averse either to labour for wages, or to cultivate the soil, as a means of support, and subsistence for themselves, and families; The apprenticed labourers having shown equal disinclination to attend to their provision grounds, for I am informed at this moment there is not five weeks ground provision in the Colony."

(CO 253/56/3: 8/9/1837)

It should be stated that slave refugees from Martinique became free when they reached St. Lucia; compare chapter "4.12. Slave refugees from Martinique", p. 233).

One reason for the negligence of the provision grounds was the possibility of exporting charcoal to Barbados which was more profitable to the APPRENTICES. This follows from a proclamation of Governor BUNBURY of St. Lucia dated December 4th, 1837, and in which the export of charcoal from St. Lucia was declared as unlawful:

> "Whereas it has been represented that the labouring population and more particularly the apprentices of the 1st, 2nd and 3rd Districts of this Colony have of late considerably neglected to cultivate their provision grounds in order to devote themselves to the preparation in sale of charcoal to be exported to Barbados whereby they make a profit apparently easier but which will hereafter prove equally injurious to their interest and to their wellbeing in consequence of the high rate to which ground provisions have risen.
>
> ... that from and after the 1st day of January now next ensuing it shall be unlawful for any person or persons whatever to export from this said Colony of Saint Lucia any quantity of charcoal under any reason or pretext whatsoever and any person or persons offending against the provisions of this proclamation shall upon conviction be subjected to pay a fine of 100 round Dollars for the public uses of this Colony and in default of payment of such fine or penalty the party or parties so offending shall be imprisoned for the space of three calendar months in the Gaol of Castries."

> (CO 255/3/3: 4/12/1837, p. 121)

A report of the STIPENDIARY MAGISTRATE of the 2nd district (Gros Islet and Dauphin) dated January 1838 gives another reason for the negligence of the provision grounds:

> "They frequently work for hire on their Saturdays and neglect their Gardens, - The hire which they get about 15 pence sterling does not compensate for the detriment done to their gardens by the neglect."

> (CO 253/64/17: Jan. 1838)

However, working for hire on Saturdays was not common. A report from the STIPOENDIARY MAGISTRATE of the 4th district (Vieux Fort and Laborie) dated May 1838 states:

> "The apprentices in Crop time work extra for hire on the regular days of labour. The reason that they seldom work for their Employer on a Saturday is that that day is given them to cultivate their Gardens for their Maintenance and besides their market day, when they have an opportunity of disposing of their surplus produce, ..."

> (CO 253/64/18: 1/5/1838)

4.7.6.3   Summary

The main source of subsistence for the slaves beside the maintenance by their masters was the purchase of their self-cultivated provisions. This is especially mentioned in reports of the year 1832:

Because of the good soil and the little difficulty in obtaining any quantity of land – there were extensive tracts of abandoned land throughout the island – the slaves had the possibility to raise a surplus of cassava and vegetables of every description which they could sell on the market.

The slaves also sold fish as well as charcoal, firewood and logwood. The keeping of domestic animals (pigs and poultry) was also usual. At the beginning of the Emancipation Period the black population of St. Lucia was well-supplied with provisions. The APPRENTICES even exported to the neighbouring islands.

From September 1837 reports about the negligence of cultivating provision grounds exists. The main reason was the possibility of exporting charcoal to Barbados which was more profitable to the APPRENTICES. Because of the fear of a lack of provisions Governor BUNBURY of St. Lucia published in December 1837 a proclamation in which the export of charcoal from St. Lucia was declared as unlawful.

4.8 Slave imports and the question of origin

4.8.1 Introduction

4.8.1.1   General remarks to the Atlantic slave trade

According to CURTIN (1972, compare CLAYPOLE/ROBOTTOM 1983: 87) about 9,566.100 African slaves were brought to the coasts of America in the period from 1451 to 1870. The actual victims of the Atlantic slave trade are estimated at about the double, as many Africans died during the slave chase on the way to the coast and during the transfer from Africa to America.

In the 15th and 16th century African slaves were brought to South America – according to WIRZ (1984: 36) 3.1% of the total imports - and Europe. At this time the slave trade had little importance.

"Slaves to the Americas 1451 – 1600"

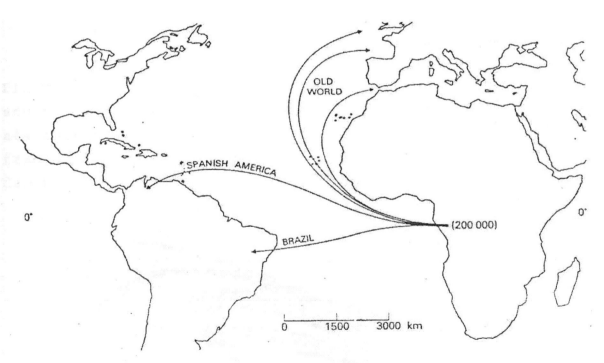

(extracted from ASHDOWN 1983: 16)

In the 17th century about 3.0 million slaves – according to WIRZ (1984: 36) 16% of the total imports – were brought across the Atlantic. Most of them were determined for Brazil (Portuguese colony) and the Spanish colonies in South America.

"Slaves to the Americas 1601 – 1700"

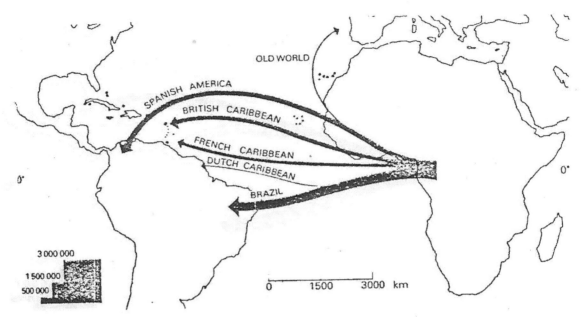

(extracted from ASHDOWN 1983: 17)

The majority of the African slaves was shipped in the 18th century – according to WIRZ (1984: 36) 52.4% of the total imports – as sugar had become the main export produce in the British and French colonies in the Caribbean as well as in Brazil.

"Slaves to the Americas 1701 – 1810"

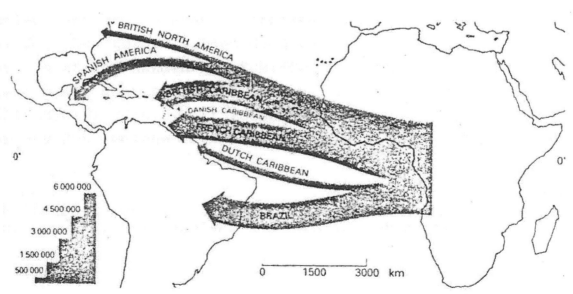

(extracted from ASHDOWN 1983: 17)

The slave trade of the 19th century – according to WIRZ (1984: 36) the slave imports amounted to 28,5% of the total imports – was mainly limited to Cuba and Brazil because there the sugar production was still based on slave work.

"Slaves to the Americas 1811 – 1870"

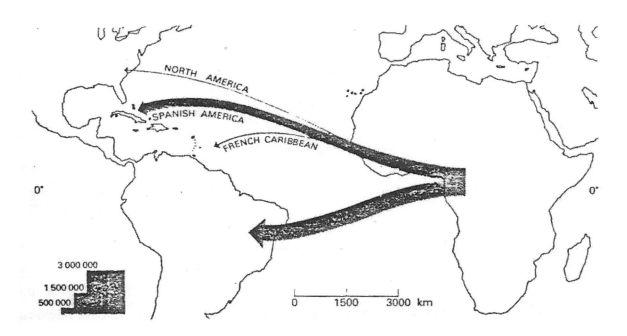

(extracted from ASHDOWN 1983: 18)

It is to mention that England and the USA prohibited the slave trade still in the years 1807/1808. France tolerated the slave trade till 1848 and Brazil declared the slave trade illegal in 1851 and Spain (Cuba) not until the year 1862 (WIRZ 1984: 36).

The Atlantic slave trade was a trilateral trade. From Europe manufactures[16] were brought to Africa. In Africa the empty ships took slaves on board and brought them to America. There they loaded export products of the colonies, like sugar or rum for Europe:

---

[16] According to CLAYPOLE/ROBOTTOM (1983: 89) the following goods were exported: brandy, iron, wine, guns, gunpowder and cloth.

"The Atlantic slave trade – the BLACK TRIANGLE"

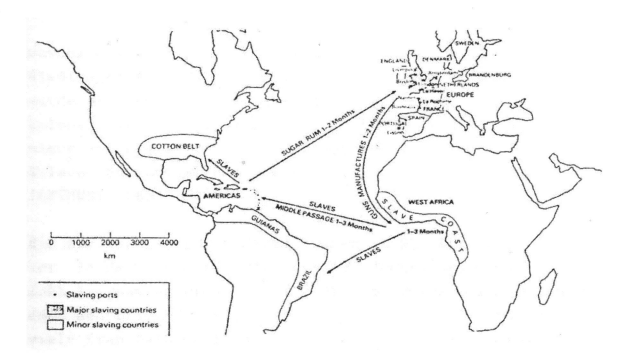

(extracted from ASHDOWN 1983: 16)

The "West African slave coast" where the European ships fetched the slaves, extended from Cap Verde (Senegal) to Benguela (Angola):

"The West African slave coast"

(extracted from ASHDOWN 1983: 15)

4.8.1.2   Slave imports to St. Lucia – general remarks

Although in the 17th and 18th century the British tried to establish settlements in St. Lucia and captured it by force of arms many times it was really colonized by the French. As the French colonized St. Lucia largely from Martinique, it may be presumed that they brought the first slaves to St. Lucia from Martinique (ANTHONY 1965: 74).

Till the middle of the 17th century only few settlers lived in St. Lucia. In the second half of the 17th century their number began to rise. In 1763 Grenada and St. Vincent were ceded to the British. For that reason several respectable French planters emigrated with their families to St. Lucia, the then French colony. By this means also slaves were introduced (BREEN 1844: 275-277).

The population figures of slaves for the 18th century in St. Lucia were estimated by the author as follows (cp. chapter 4.5.2.3. Construction of the development of the slave population, p. 78):

Year	number of slaves/ APPRENTICES
1772	12.795
1789	18.000
1799	13.391
1810	14.397
1825	13.530
1834	13.300
1838	14.000

According to these figures there was a considerable rise in the slave population between the years 1777 and 1789 (approximately 30%). In this period considerable slave imports must have been taken place. Regarding the origin of the slaves imported to St. Lucia in the 17th and 18th century ANTHONY (1965: 75) refers to DU TERTRE (1667)[17] as follows:

> "According to Père du Tertre, writing in 1667, the Negroes then in the French Antilles were all aborigines of Africa, drawn from the coasts of Guinea, Angola, Senegal or Cape Verde." Merchants from France, Spain, Portugal and Holland went to those coasts to engage in the shameful Slave Trade that supplied the markets of the West Indies with human flesh. Du Tertre adds that the French in the Antilles sometimes obtained cargoes of negro slaves by capturing them from the Spanish and Portuguese. He mentions that the French colonists preferred the slaves from Angola to those from Cape Verde."

---

[17] DU TERTRE, Jean Baptiste, Histoire Générale des Isles St. Christopher, Guadeloupe, de la Martinique, et aitres dans l'Amerique

ANTHONY (1965: 75) adds that it is known for certain that, later on, Martinique had hardly enough slaves for itself and that St. Lucia received the surplus of the Barbados slave market.

The following chapter refers to the slave imports to St. Lucia in the period from 1799 to the abolition of slavery on January 1st 1808, as well as to illegal slave imports made afterwards. The last section of this chapter refers to a list of 37 personal slaves and their designation of origin.

4.8.2 Slave imports from 1799 to 1807

In the year 1799 there was a correspondence between the SECRETARY OF STATE PORTLAND in London and the Governor of St. Lucia regarding a planned import of slaves from St. Domingo to St. Lucia and Martinique. With a letter of July 6th, 1799, the SECRETARY OF STATE informed the Governor of St. Lucia as follows:

> "Enclosed I transmit you the Copy of a letter from me to Major General Keppel, relative to the disposal of certain French Negroes who followed the Fortunes of their Masters on our evacuation of the Posts which we held in St. Domingo.
>
> Since writing the above it is considered that a portion of these Negroes may be disposed of in St. Lucia, as well as in Martinico to the advantage of both Islands.
>
> I am therefore to signify to you the King's Pleasure, that you should use your best endeavours to facilitate and promote the sale of them within your Government, for the benefit of the Proprietors."

(CO 253/2/7: 6/7/1799, p. 35)

In September 1799 Governor PREVOST of St. Lucia confirmed the letter of the SECRETARY OF STATE:

> "I have had the honour to receive your Grace's letter dated 6th July, No. 3, relative to the disposal of part of the French Negroes from St. Domingo in this Island, ...
>
> I beg to assure your Grace that every execution on my part shall be made in providing for such as many be sent here, which I have no doubt will prove advantageous to the Colony. The number I think, that this Island is able to receive will be from three to four hundred, ..."

(CO 253/2/8: 4/9/1799, p. 40)

Further correspondence confirming the arrival of the slaves from St. Domingo was not available.

According to the Parliamentary Papers in London St. Lucia received from the Caribbean islands in the years 1799 to 1801 the following slave imports:

Year	Number of imported slaves	place of shipment
1799	80	Grenada
	99	Martinique
1800	10	Martinique
1801	29	Martinique
	20	St. Vincent
	238	

(BPP/ST/61/1: 1799-1801, p. 57-59)

In the table regarding direct slave imports from Africa for the period from 1799 to 1801 only one shipment is mentioned for St. Lucia. On February 8th, 1800, the ship PRINCE JOHN arrived in St. Lucia with 175 slaves on board. A more detailed place of shipment was not mentioned (BPP/ST/61/2: 1799-1801, p. 52).

According to other available Parliamentary Papers St. Lucia didn't receive any slaves from Africa in the period from 1802 to 1804 (BPP/ST/A61/3: 1802-1804, p. 423-428). In the year 1805 two slave ships from Africa arrived in St. Lucia. The notes in the Parliamentary Papers are as follows:

"Date of Entry	at what Island	Vessel's name	from where	No. of Negroes imported
May 3	St. Lucia	Marriott	Africa Part of the Coast not described)	219
July 16	- D -	Backhouse	- D -	153
				372"

(BPP/ST/61/4: 1805, p. 445)

Concerning further slave imports in the period from 1802 to 1805, for example from other Caribbean islands, no further information is available in the Parliamentary Papers. According to a letter of Governor BRERETON of St. Lucia to the SECRETARY OF STATE in London dated in November 1805 it can be assumed that from June 1803 on the yearly slave imports were small. In this letter the Governor referred to a Bill passed by the British Parliament on August 15th, 1805 (BPP/BP/I/1: 1806, p. 273), which prohibited the importation of slaves to colonies shortly conquered by the British. In this Bill a saving clause was included saying:

> *"that it might be expedient to permit the Annual Introduction of a limited Number of Slaves under due Regulations for the Purpose of supplying any Waste that should take place in the Population on particular Estates, from extraordinary or unavoidable Causes, and thereby of keeping up the Cultivation of the Lands already cleared and cultivated, and it was therefore further ordered that any Number of Slaves not exceeding Three for every Hundred of the whole Number of Slaves in the said Settlements, Islands, Colonies, and Plantations respectively (Returns whereof were to be made from time to time in pursuance …) might be imported in each Year (provided Casualities to that extent should appear to have taken place in the preceding Year) under Licences to be previously granted by the Governor …, into the said Settlements …"*

The respective extract of the letter of Governor BRERETON is as follows:

"I can assure your Lordship that St. Lucia cannot with reason complain of this measure as their strength in Slaves being 13.000, it would allow at 3 per cent, an annual importation of 399 Slaves, and the number that have been imported while their ports new opened for that purpose since the last capture of the Island in June 1803 has not been equal on an average to 300 Negroes per annum."

(CO 253/3/5: 20/11/1805)

In March 1807 the British government passed the law regarding the general abolition of the slave trade under British rule. It came into force on January 1st, 1808 (DOOKHAN 1983: 85).

4.8.3 Slave imports of some planters

4.8.3.1   Legal imports

For the years 1817 to 1819 the following notes were made by the slave registrar of the custom house of St. Lucia:

> *1817: "On the 16th May 1817 the following Slaves were imported from Kingstown, Saint Vincent, Sloop Grenada Planter, viz.*
>
> *13 Field Negro Men*
> *13   "   Women*
> * 7 Boys*
> * 1 Male Domestic*
> * 1 Female   "*
> * 3 Girls*
> * 3 Male Children*
> *41 Slaves Total"*

1818: "On the 18th March 1818 there were imported from Saint Johns, Antigua, in the Sloop Samuel Lamb the following Slaves.

Males: *Jack a Sailor*
         Henry a Labourer
         John Thomas a Mason
         George a Child
         Charles a Child
         Sam a Child

Females: *Sally a Washer*
         Cloe a Washer
         Amelie a Washer
         Madelaine Color'd a Drudge
         Diana a Child

         Total: Eleven

On the 1st June 1818 from Saint John, Antigua, Sophie, a Negro Slave"

1819: "12 Antigua	*5 Males*	*7 Females*
5 Barbados	*2 "*	*3 "*
7 Dominica	*3 "*	*4 "*
2 Grenada	*1 Male*	*1 Female*
1 St. Kitts	*1 "*	*-*
14 Saint Vincent	*6 Males*	*8 Females*
2 Trinidad	*1 Male*	*1 Female*
7 Martinique	*4 Males*	*3 Females*
50	*23*	*27"*

(CO 253/18/3: 12/9/1823)

According to these statements a total of 103 slaves were imported to St. Lucia between the years 1817 and 1819. The place of shipment was limited to the Lesser Antilles.

For the period from 1821 to 1825 the following list made by the slave registrar was available:

"Date of import	name and surname	sex	place of shipment
26/11/1821	Francois La Conte	female	Trinidad
8/12/1821	Jacob King	male	Barbados
10/ 5/1821	London King	male	"
"	John Grigg	"	"
14/ 7/1821	Casar	"	"
"	Charlotte Roberts	female	"
"	Henrietta Roberts	"	"
"	Nancy Roberts	"	"
15/11/1822	Fanny Collins	"	St. Vincent
14/ 9/1821	Sarah Brown	"	Barbados
"	Nancy Brown	"	"
1/ 1/1821	Richard	male	"
26/ 6/1822	Tom William	"	"
25/ 2/1822	Susanna Holder	female	"
14/ 1/1822	Mary Ann Wilson	"	"
19/ 3/1822	Joe Rolland	male	Antigua
1/ 4/1822	J'nne Artimise Jaques	female	Grenada
"	George Louis	male	"
"	Anne Louis	female	"
29/ 4/1822	Lucy Ann Mc. Nicol	"	Barbados
10/ 9/1822	Will	male	"
"	Thomas	"	"
18/ 2/1822	Charly Ceoll	"	Antigua
4/10/1823	George & Robert	"	Barbados
"	Charles	"	St. Kitts
22/11/1823	Harriette Bowstick	female	"
16/ 9/1823	Bastian	male	Grenada
11/ 8/1823	Isaac	"	St. Kitts
18/ 1/1823	Lucindah	female	Barbados
"	Beck & Mary	"	"
25/ 1/1823	Lucy & Nancy Ann	"	"
"	Kitty Ann Phillis	"	"
"	Daniel	male	"
10/1823	Bob Dean	"	St. Kitts
25/ 1/1823	Henrietta	female	Barbados
"	James Edward	male	"
"	John & Patterson	"	"
"	Edward & Capt. Dick	"	"
"	John & Tom	"	"
"	Stephen & Greenock	"	"
"	John alias William	"	"
"	Dick Charles & Jack	"	"
"	Rose	female	"
14/ 1/1823	George William	male	"
26/ 8/1823	John Syrus King	"	"
6/ 5/1823	Thomas King	"	"
27/ 2/1823	John King	"	"
22/ 7/1823	Will & Charles	"	St. Kitts
10/1823	Thomas	"	"
18/ 9/1823	Richard	"	"

"Date of import	name and surname	sex	place of shipment
"	Laury	"	"
14/10/1823	Billy Bowman	"	"
11/ 8/1823	Luckey Cane	female	"
"	William Cane	male	"
14/10/1823	Antoine	"	"
11/ 8/1823	Mary Ann	female	"
22/11/1823	John Toby	male	"
18/ 9/1823	Molly	female	"
11/12/1824	Stephen & Thomas	male	Barbados
28/12/1824	Queen	female	"
8/ 1/1824	Lucy Ann Ann	"	"
"	Polly Barney	"	"
"	Thomas Wood	male	"
18/12/1824	Elise	female	St. Kitts
"	Barrington	male	"
21/10/1824	Baza Bazar	female	"
"	Charles Bazar	male	"
"	Kirry Bazar	female	"
28/ 2/1824	Anthony Bazar	male	"
"	George Bazar	"	"
18/ 1/1825	George	"	Barbados
"	Mary Phill	female	"
"	Polly Kitty	"	"

(CO 253/23/2: 1821-1825)

According to this table 82 slaves were imported into St. Lucia between January 1st, 1821, and January 1st, 1825, of whom 50 were men and 32 women. The majority of these slaves (62%) came from Barbados, then follows St. Kitts with a share of 28% of the imports. The rest of the slaves were imported from Grenada (5%), Antigua (3%), St. Vincent and Trinidad (each 1%).

4.8.3.2   Illegal imports

According to a report of the Custom House of St. Lucia dated October 1st, 1822, a slave owner was charged to pay a penalty because of illegal importation of three slaves (CO 253/16/1: 1/10/1822).

In July 1832 a servant of the Custom House of St. Lucia wrote to the Governor:
> "... that I have prosecuted to condemnation since the month of April last year 22 slaves who have been illegally introduced into this Island and that there are three others awaiting a judgement of the Court, making together 25 Slaves in this Island ... and condemned at my instance in the Courts of Vice admiralty and thereby admitting them to the benefit of freedom."

(CO 253/39/5: 4/7/1832)

Also in July 1832 slaves of the Lacaille estate in Dennery reported to have been illegally imported in the year 1815. An extract of the report of the Custom House is as follows:

> "In the year 1815 a Cargo of Africans was imported into this Island, by the late Messrs. Tharelle & Valtou in a Sloop called the "Rose" (which Vessel it appears was only built in 1815) and belonged to the then proprietors of the said Estate, but was registered in the name of Mr. Tharelle only. That the said Sloop was Navigated with Slaves belonging to the said property – That these Africans were purchased at Martinique (then in Possession of the French Government) and had recently been landed there from Africa – That they were disembarked during the Night on the Estate at D'Enery, that several are since dead, some have been sold, and five Males along with three females of that importation still remain there in a state of Slavery, with their increase."
>
> (CO 253/39/6: 30/7/1832)

A further report of the Custom House says:

> "... that the Male Slave Sassal seized from Mdme. Jacob of Castries, and the female Slave Celine seized from Mr. Ruand of Castries, condemned the 22 Inst. and the Male Slaves Louis & Michel Coredaine now in Court awaiting trial were all imported by Messrs. Tharel & Valtou, making a total of Sixteen Slaves (including "John" condemned on the 10th July), Africans with only one exception brought into this Island and placed on the Lacaille Estate since July 1815."
>
> (CO 253/39/7: 25/8/1832)

The Governor of St. Lucia, FARQUHARSON, wrote to the SECRETARY OF STATE in London about this case of

> "... the most nefarious transaction which has come under my notice for many years."
>
> (CO 253/39/8: 25/8/1832)

Another case of illegal importation of slaves became known in December 1832. In the year 1814 slaves were illegally imported from Martinique to St. Lucia. The PROVISIONAL PROCUREUR GENERAL made the following notes:

Mr. Decerelle:

> "... that in the beginning of 1814 Mister La Porte made frequent voyages to Martinique and that he often returned with Negroes who after a short interval were sent to his Estate at Lesly[18] or at Vieux Fort."

---

[18] Lesly (Leslie) was in the vicinity of Castries.

2. Witness:

"... that at the period in question Mr. La Porte has determined to make a Sugar Estate at Vieux Fort, ..., that he was in the constant habit of bringing over Slaves from that Colony to Saint Lucia."

Slaves:

"... that they had often seen Mr. La Porte return from Martinique with Slaves that he had purchased there and that they were brought one after another and as often as Mr. La Porte wanted them for his losses and country house."

Mr. Rocau:

"... that in 1817 he and Mr. La Porte agreed to bring a certain quantity of negroes from Dominique. That Mr. La Porte took ship for that Colony for that purpose and was overtaken by the Hurricane of that year in which he perished."

(CO 253/43/7: 3/12/1832)

4.8.4 Account of 37 personal slaves with designation of origin

The following list dated February 15th, 1819, made by the slave registrar is a correction list of a list made in the year 1816. The original list was not available. The following account is an extract as well as an addition to the original list:

Surname	Name	Age	Designation of origin
Anicette	Jean	22	"Creole"
Maril	Louise	22	"
Marie Hyacinthe	Marie Rose	10	"
Figurdie	Francoise	26	St. Lucia
Anastazie	Fazie	32	"
Joseph	"	5	"
Evelina	"	16	"
Jean	Calotin	21	Guadeloupe
Antoine	Johnston	17	St. Lucia
Angelique	Fatine	27	"African"
Laurette	Laurent	15	St. Lucia
Calisete	Pereau	17	"
Cecile	Belle	36	"
Laurencino	Josephe	45	St. Lucia
Sophie	"	8	"
Felix	Augustin	2	"Creole"
Cecille	Bailiff	43	"Moco"
Honore	"	20	St. Lucia

Surname	Name	Age	Designation of origin
Mathurine	"	12	"
Philip	Mc. Claire	20	"Creole"
Jean	Louis	17	"African"
Auguste	Aimée	5	St. Lucia
Saint John	Theotiste	33	"African"
Rainette	Francois	27	St. Lucia
Marie	Equerre	55	"Ibo"
Pierre Louis	"	18	St. Lucia
Annette	"	15	"
Margueritte	"	12	"
Bernardine	Suivante	27	"
Arsine	"	6	"
Louison	Louis	45	"Congo"
Marie Louise	Lorette	25	St. Lucia
Rosillette	Negress	15	"
Alphonsine	Lapointeuse	12	"
Jean Michel	Judith	2	"
Mathurine	"	4	"
Marie Madelaine	Duchosé	58	"

(CO 253/14/4: 15/2/1819)

In the above mentioned list there are the following designations of origin:

"Creole"	"African"
St. Lucia	"Moco"
Guadeloupe	"Ibo"
	"Congo"

The designation "Moco" is mentioned by KOELLE (1963: 11). He refers to "Móko" –languages which are spoken in West- and East Cameroon, Gabon and Rio Muni. To the designation "Ibo" it is to mention that in Nigeria there exists an ethnic group with this name (compare HIRSCHBERG 1965: 120).

4.9 Slave exports from St. Lucia

4.9.1 Introduction

This chapter examines the export of slaves from St. Lucia from the war period in the last decade of the 18th century until the abolition of slavery. Data was available for the year 1819 and the period from 1821 to January 1825. Illegal slave exports will also be studied.

4.9.2 General situation

The decrease in population in the last decade of the 18th century was due not only to war but also to French slave exports (cp. chapter "4.5.2. Development and structure of population", p. 73). Governor PREVOST of St. Lucia referred in his letter dated June 1799 to these slave exports:

> "... *many having fallen in the field – several having been taken in arms and shipped off the Island and others sent to augment the Republican Forces at St. Vincent, ...*"
>
> (CO 253/2/4: 19/6/1799, p. 24)

From this period onwards there was a shortage of slaves in St. Lucia (cp. chapter "4.6.3.2. General economic development", p. 96).

In the year 1817 Governor SEYMOUR limited the slave exports from St. Lucia to other British colonies by a proclamation. He informed the SECRETARY OF STATE as follows:

> "*I have thought it my Duty for the good of this Colony to issue the enclosed proclamation prohibiting the exportation of Slaves in large numbers from hence to other British Colonies, a Practice which if allowed to continue would depopulate the Island of St. Lucia in a very few years, and consequently render it of no value to His Majesty.-*"
>
> (CO 253/11/1: 20/1/1817)

4.9.3 Special information

For the year 1819 the following export figures were returned:

Number of exported slaves	male	female	place of destination
20	11	9	Trinidad
3	2	1	Tortola
2	1	1	Tobago
1	1	-	France
1	-	1	St. Vincent
1	1	-	Porto Rico
8	5	3	Antigua
1	1	-	Dominica
1	1	-	Martinique
38	23	15	

(CO 253/18/3: 12/9/1823)

According to this table of the CUSTOM HOUSE of St. Lucia in the year 1819 the greatest number of slaves was exported to Trinidad and Antigua.

According to the following list of the slave registrar STEPHENS 26 slaves were exported from St. Lucia between January 1821 and January 1825:

Name	sex	place of destination
Indiana Sadler	female	Barbados
Waterloo Sadler	male	"
John Sadler	"	"
Antoine Sebrieto	"	Trinidad
Magdelaine Pegg	female	"
Francis Lacompe	male	"
John Grigg	"	Barbados
Casar	"	"
Marie Victoire Soupiere	female	Bahamas
Jean Goodsir	male	Trinidad
Antoine Lancandier	"	England
Jean Fameux	"	"unknown"
Aimée Paresseuse	female	"
John Elliot	male	Grenada
Jeffery Hetherington	"	"
Jean Artimise Jaque	female	"
Ann Louis	"	"
Marie Louise	"	St. Vincent
Angelique Ange	"	Martinique
Joseph Ange	male	"
Sabine Banane	female	Trinidad
Eugette Ann	"	"

Name	sex	place of destination
Francis Wood	male	Jamaica
Alexander Danseur	"	St. Vincent
Silvestre Figees	"	"
Richard Mango	"	"

(CO 253/23/2: 1825)

Summarizing the destination of these 26 slaves was as follows:

- Lesser Antilles: Barbados: 5 persons, Trinidad: 6 persons, Grenada: 4 persons, St. Vincent: 4 persons, Martinique: 2 persons
- 1 person each in the Bahamas and in Jamaica
- England: 1 person
- Unknown: 2 persons.

4.9.4 Illegal slave exports

For the year 1832 there are documents confirming an illegal slave export trade from St. Lucia. According to a proclamation of Governor FARQUHARSON in the year 1832 14 slaves embarked on board a ship in the quarter of Soufrière on September 5th, 1832:

> *"Whereas on the Night of the Fifth Instant, FOURTEEN SLAVES belonging to VICTOR GRAENDCOUR, late of Anse-L'Ivronge; in the Quarter of Soufrière, in this Colony, Planter, were embarked on board a Schooner then off the Bay of the said Anse l'Ivroigne; and Whereas, The Honourable STEPHENSON VILLIERS SURTEES, The Honourable CHARLES CHIPCHASE, and THOMAS CLARKE, Esqr., being the Members of the Special Commission in this matter by me appointed, have deemed fit to issue their Warrant for the apprehension of the said VICTOR GRANDCOUR, together with CLERMONT BELMAR, MONJOLI BELMAR, and LAFERRONNAY the Younger, otherwise called BEAUBRUN, the three latter all resident or lately resident at or near Anse l'Ivroigne aforesaid, and of no profession known to the said Commissioners, and who stand charged with having been, in conjunction with others yet unknown, principally concerned as PIRATES, FELONS and ROBBERS upon the High Seas, in the embarkation of the said Slaves. Now, therefore, I, JAMES ALEXANDER FARQUHARSON, Major-General, Commander-in-Chief in and over the said Island of St. Lucia do hereby offer a REWARD OF FOUR THOUSAND LIVRES, to any Person or Persons, whether Free or Slave, who shall arrest or cause to be arrested and lodge or cause to be lodged in the Royal Gaol of Castries, the said Victor Grandcour, Monjoli Belmar, Clermont Belmar, and Laferronnay, the Younger, otherwise called Beaubrun; and I do hereby offer a proportionate part of the said Sum of Four Thousand Livres, to any person who shall arrest or cause to be arrested and lodge, or cause to be lodged, in the said Gaol any one or more of them.*

(CO 253/40/4: 11/9/1832)

4.000 Livres were approximately £ Sterling 200(CO258/30/1:1934,p.131). As the possible place of destination for these slaves the island of Martinique was assumed. This follows from a letter of Governor FARQUHARSON of St. Lucia dated September 11th, 1832, to the Governor of Martinique as follows:

> "Should the Felons have taken refuge in the Colony under your Government, I have the honour of requesting that your Excellency will be pleased to cause them to be delivered up along with the unfortunate Slaves whom they have forcibly carried away with them."

(CO 253/40/5: 11/9/1832)

4.10 Runaway slaves in St. Lucia[19]

4.10.1   Situation within the colony

4.10.1.1   Sources

Punishments for runaway slaves had been already laid down in the Code Noir of 1685:

> "Art. XXXVIII – A slave who shall have absented himself for one month from the day in which his Master shall have denounced him to justice, shall have his ears cut, and be stamped with a fleur-de-lis on one shoulder. If he absents himself a second time for a month, counting also from the day of his being denounced, he shall have his hands cut, and be marked with a fleur-de-lis on the other shoulder, for the third offence, to suffer death.

(BPP/ST/71/2: 16/3/1685, p. 186)

Here it is necessary to mention that laws of the Code Noir and most of the slave laws which were fixed by the French and British colonial government until 1826 were included in the CODE DE LA MARTINIQUE of St. Lucia.

On October 18th, 1763, the French government of St. Lucia commuted the punishment for running away a third time to working in chains in the king's works or in repairs of the high roads. A punishment by the galleys was also possible (BPP/ST/71/2: 18/10/1763, p. 195).

After the taking over of St. Lucia by the British in June 1803 a law was enacted that obliged the slave owners to report their runaway slaves:

---

[19] This chapter had been published in „Wiener Beiträge zur Ethnologie und Anthropologie" (Vienna contributions to ethnology and anthropology), Vol. 3, Horn-Wien, pp. 150-170, by KREMSER/WERNHART 1986.

"Art. I – Proprietors having runaway Slaves to make their declaration eight days after publication on this arret, which declaration to contain the name, age, and sex of the Slaves, also the period of their absence; the declaration to be received by the Civil Commissaries of each quarter gratis, Each Commissary to keep a register signed by the Judge of the district for the purpose. Proprietors ordered in future to make their declarations within the eight days of any slave running away, on pain of confiscation of the Slave to the crown when captured."

(BPP/ST/71/2: 3/10/1803, p. 209)

On January 9th, 1817, five runaway slaves were sentenced by the Court of Sénéchaussée of St. Lucia to the cutting off their ears and branding:

"… les dites Philipe, Gabriel, Jean-Francois, Jean-Baptiste dit Congo et la négresse Marie-Francoise, à avoir chacun les oreilles coupées, et chacun marqué d'une fleur de Lys sur une Epaule, par l'éxécution de la haute justice, conformément à l'article trente huit de l'Edit du Roi de Seize cent quatre vingt cinque."

(CO 253/11/3: 9/1/1817)

Governor SEYMOUR of St. Lucia confirmed this sentence only for two slaves. For the other three slaves the sentence was commuted to whipping. The execution of the original judgement of cutting off the ears and branding led to commotions within the slave population of St. Lucia. The Governor informed the SECRETARY OF STATE in London on Oct. 3rd, 1817, of the situation:

"The circumstances of two Negroes having had part of their Ears cut off (a very small portion of the top which is not even perceptible when the hat is on) & branded, by a sentence of the Court of Sénéchaussée, …, which had been carried into execution on two slaves of the most dangerous Characters, one of whom has absconded since, and is at this moment absent from his owner: They not only ran away frequently, but the last time incited three others to do so, & took with them Cutlasses when they Plundered & Devastated small Plantations of Provisions, …

The Crime for which those Negroes had suffered arose to a most alarming height, large bodies of 30 & 40 having collected together in the woods, and I was obliged in many instances to send Detachments of the Military after them; Your Lordship will perceive that the whole five were condemned to lose their Ears, but I considered, it would only necessary to make an Example of the two most culpable. I consequently remitted the Punishment of the others to twenty nine lashes, a Punishment which any Planter could give to his Slave for the slightest offence, without having recourse to Law."

(CO 253/11/4: 3/10/1817)

Regarding the commotion within the slave population I assume that the mentioned sentence of cutting off the ears and branding was not usually passed or put into execution by the court of St. Lucia.

In 1820 Governor KEANE of St. Lucia proclaimed an ORDER IN COUNCIL with which he augmented the sum to be paid for the capture of runaway slaves. He also mentioned the absence of a vast number of slaves from their owners:

> "Whereas it had been represented to the Governor in Council that the Sum at present allowed for the Capture of runaway Negroes is not an adequate reward for the danger and difficulties attending their apprehension, and that in consequence a vast number of Negroes are permitted to remain absent from their Owners with impunity, His Excellency the Governor hath taken the same into his consideration and judging it necessary to put a stop to an abuse which not only tends to endanger the public tranquillity but is so seriously prejudicial to the wealth and prosperity of the Colony, ..., to order that the sum to be paid in future for the capture of runaway slaves by the Owner thereof shall be four Dollars for every such slave taken in the Towns or Boroughs, eight Dollar for every such slave taken in the immediate vicinity of the same, and sixteen Dollars for every such slave taken elsewhere, ..."

(CO 255/1/3: 8/4/1820, p.22)

There was a discussion of the situation of "maroonage"[20] in the PRIVY COUNCIL of St. Lucia in the year 1822. The following was stated in the minutes of June 7th:

> "System of maroonage which his Excellency was led to believe was carried to a very great extend; members recommend that previous to the adoption of legislative measures that a return shall be ordered from each quarter of the Number of Slaves reported absent."

(CO 256/1/3: 7/5/1822)

In the same year two runaway slaves were captured who had been absent for many years. This information is contained in a petition of June 10th, 1822, in which a certain Mr. Culton sought remuneration for the capture of the two runaway slaves. The content of this petition was mentioned in the minutes of the PRIVY COUNCIL of St. Lucia on July 22nd, 1822, as follows:

> "This Petition stated that under authority of an Order of the Procureur du Roi Petitioner had sent out a Detachment in pursuit of the Runaway Slaves who had established themselves near his Estate in the Valley of Anse de Roseau and had captured two, one a Negro by name Silvester belonging to the Choc Estate, who had been absent thirteen years, and the other a Negro woman by name Magdelaine belonging to Mr. Cuvillier, who had been absent upwards of 7 years."

(CO 256/1/4: 22/7/1822)

---

[20] A „maroon" was a person who escaped from slavery and was not captured again.

According to other accounts it was very favourable for runaway slaves in St. Lucia to hide in the interior of the island at that time. Governor MAINWARING wrote to the SECRETARY OF STATE in London on August 11th, 1823:

> "... that 9/10 of the Island is wholly uncultivated affording almost impenetrable Shelter for the runaways and disaffected."

(CO 253/17/2: 11/8/1823)

Also the communication-system was a very miserable one. In June 1824 Governor BLACKWELL informed the SECRETARY OF STATE in London of problems between the communication of the stationed troops:

> "The roads from the small population, and other causes, are everywhere bad, in some places impracticable excepting during the very few months of the dry season. There is no communication whatever across the Island from East to West, the only road being that which makes the tour of the Island by the Sea cost, making a circuit, as nearly as I can ascertain, of one Hundred Miles and upwards. The Quarters to Windward therefore may be considered as cut off from the seat of Government, and left entirely to their own resources. These are half of Dauphin, Dennery, Praslin and Micoud containing altogether but Thirty Eight Men, ..."

(CO 253/18/1: 15/5/1824)

On February 8th, 1826, a new Slave Law was passed by the Council of St. Lucia. Four months later, on June 1st, it came into force (CO 253/22/4: 1/6/1826). The clause concerning the punishment for runaway slaves was as follows:

> 77: "A fugitive Slave after an absence from his owner's plantation of one month may suffer at the utmost forty lashes & one month's solitary confinement for the first offence, two month's solitary confinement & one hundred lashes for the second, two hundred lashes and three years hard labour in the chain gang for the third, & death for the fourth offence."

For harbouring runaway slaves the following punishment was fixed:

> 78: "Every free person guilty of harbouring or concealing a Slave, shall forfeit and pay two pounds sterling to the Master for every day that the Slave shall have been concealed or harboured by him, ..."

> 79: "Every Slave in whose hut shall be found a fugitive Slave shall suffer corporal punishment for the first offence, which shall not exceed fifty lashes, & his owner shall forfeit five Pounds Sterling. The penalties shall in both cases be doubled upon a second conviction, ..."

There was also a clause through which slave owners were obliged to report their runaway slaves:

211

87: "The owners of fugitive Slaves are required within a fortnight to denounce them to the Commissaries of their Quarters. The denunciation shall contain the presumed cause of the Slave's escape, the Slave's name, age, sex, and the distinguishing marks, if any, on the penalty of forfeiting one hundred livres and losing their eventual claim upon the condemned Slave's Fund."

On the same day as this new Slave Law came into force (June 1st, 1826) a proclamation was issued by Governor MAINWARING (CO 255/1/1: 1/6/1826, p. 164). It offered a free pardon to all runaway slaves who should return to their owners within one month. The Governor mentioned further:

"I have particular cause to know that the crime of desertion has been for the last few years extremely frequent and treated much too lightly, …"

For runaway slaves who would remain absent he announced rigid measures:

"Detachments will be formed in every quarter in the first week in July for the purpose of simultaneously securing the Country and permanent measures will be afterwards taken for fully protecting owners in the just and legal exercise of their right to their slaves' services. And I publicly announce my determination to deliver to the Courts, that they may be punished with becoming rigour all Slaves who shall be hereafter guilty of deserting or who shall not have taken the benefit of this Act of Grace."

Six days after the promulgation of the above mentioned proclamation an ORDER IN COUNCIL was issued which fixed regulations for establishing a permanent detachment for the suppression of maroonage. This order provided that two detachments should be formed each consisting of a sergeant and three men (CO 255/1/4: 7/6/1826, p.166).

In June 1829 "certains Planteurs et Propriétaires de St. Lucie" protested in a petition against certain provisions of the new Slave Law of 1826. They also referred to an augmentation of the number of runaway slaves and their formation into groups:

"… que le marronnage surtout, s'est considérablement multiplié; et, que, ce don't on n'avait point, ou très rarèment, eu d'example autrefois; C'est qu'il s'est fait par bandes, et s'est opéré sur divers points de la Colonie, et si diamétralement opposes les uns des autres, que l'on pourrait supposer quelque plan combine, et à faire craindre les plus funestes effets de la malveillance."

(CO 253/26/3: June 1829)

According to this statement the planters were afraid of the runaway slaves.

With two letters, of April 6th and September 29th, 1829, Governor STEWART of St. Lucia informed the SECRETARY OF STATE in London of a state of alarm in the colony, caused by the conduct of a great number of slaves. He wrote as follows:

"In my letter of 6th April addressed particularly to you, I mentioned the state of alarm of the colony, by the conduct of a great number of slaves. This was occasioned by the injudicious interference of a gentleman, who, in presence of more than one hundred negroes, severely reprimanded the manager of an Estate for permitting a cat in the hands of the driver: … the public interference was construed by the Slaves into an absolute freedom from labour, seeing that the First President had said, that there was to be no more whip, no more punishment. Such was their idea of the subject, and they soon acted upon it. That week, there were only two hogsheads of sugar made by these people, instead of nine, the usual number. Work was nearly at a stand. The news rapidly spread. Slaves not only refused to work, but when compelled, they destroyed their master's property, as manufacturers do at home: and in all parts of the country, numbers left their masters and fled to the woods and mountains."

(CO 253/26/6: 29/9/1829)

After an examination, the Governor explained that *"the poor people were deceived by false reports"* and that they believed *"that the King had made them free, and that they were to work no more to their masters"*. He was then of the opinion that, in such circumstances and as the false reports were generally spread and firmly believed, it would be cruel to punish the *"poor ignorant people"*. Finally the letter of the Governor describes the military actions against the runaway slaves:

"I therefore gave directions to explain to the Slaves in the clearest manner the nature of the new law, and to caution them as to their future conduct. During these proceedings, I ordered out the Militia in all directions into the woods, …, with directions to make a great noise – to fire blank cartridges in every place, where then was an appearance of the runaways being, and to make large fires in short, to frighten & show these misguided people, that the woods were no shelter for them as they had hitherto been (numbers of slaves have been many years in the woods) and that their masters' house was their surest place of safety. All this had the desired effect. The deserters came in, and surrendered themselves in all parts of the Colony. Fifteen people returned to one estate in a body. I gave orders, that none of those who voluntarily surrendered should be punished; and within a fortnight, all had returned to their old habitations and at their usual occupations. One slave came in, who had been 16 years in the mountains; I have reason to believe, that I have prevented the like again, at least for some time, no person was punished; One man who had been out 8 years; - in endeavouring to make his escape down a precipice, when surprised by a party of the militia, fell over a rock, and was so much injured, that he died in a few days. Since then, the slaves have been quiet."

An Ordinance of May 3rd, 1830, fixed new punishment provisions for runaway slaves. The highest extent of the punishment with the whip was reduced from 40 lashes to 30 for the first offence, from 100 lashes to 50 for the second offence and for the third offence from 200 lashes to 100. The periods for solitary confinement of one or two months (first and second offence) as well as the period for working in chains for the third offence remained unaltered. The punishment of death for the fourth offence was commuted to working with chains for the whole life. A new provision was fixed which said that the runaway slaves were obliged to make good the time lost to the slave owner (BPP/ST/77/2: 3/5/1830, p.370).

According to an Ordinance of Governor FARQUHARSON of June 16th, 1832, in which new provisions for the punishment of runaway slaves were stipulated, there were many runaway slaves in St. Lucia at that time. The content of this Ordinance was as follows:

> "And whereas the frequency of a crime of Running away amongst the Slaves of this Island, and the physical Circumstances of the Country rendering it exceedingly difficult, if not impossible, to arrest fugitive Slaves, it is necessary by a rigid penal-enactment to repress this practice.
>
> It is therefore ordered and declared, that any Slave or Slaves who shall have been twice convicted before any local Magistrate, of desertion from his Master's Service, exceeding one week on each occasion, shall for every subsequent offence of this nature, be removed from this jurisdiction and tried before the Assize or Royal Court, and upon a first conviction before the said Court, shall be condemned to receive Corporal punishment (if a Male Slave) of not less than fifty lashes or not more than one Hundred upon a second conviction not less than one Hundred and not more than two Hundred lashes, and upon a third conviction that the Slave shall be condemned to the Chain-Gang for life.
>
> Upon the conviction before said Court of a female Slave for the same Crime as aforesaid, that the said female Slave shall suffer confinement with hard labour, equivalent to the aforesaid corporal punishment and upon a third conviction as the Male Slaves – Chain-Gang for life."

(CO 255/2/6: 16/6/1832, p.133)

Some general information about runaway slaves in St. Lucia is given in a publication by an anonymous inhabitant of St. Lucia. The inhabitant wrote:

> "Since it (St. Lucia) has been in possession of Great Britain, several disasters by fire, hurricane and flood, plunged many of the Inhabitants into the most irretrievable distress; the want of discipline among the negroes, from these accidents or visitations of climate made desertion so common that runaways had their camps in the woods, where they supported themselves by plunder committed on the estates around them. On the

slightest provocation from their master or manager, or even a threat from misbehaviour, the slaves absented themselves for years, and lived either by theft, or were secreted and harboured by other runaways, or free people for whom they worked, sometimes for hire, and often through fear of being surrendered to their owners; and not unfrequently they were taken up and conveyed to jail, for sake of the reward, by the very people for whom they had been working. (This custom was so prevalent, that a gentleman, one of the oldest members of the royal court at that time, was found guilty of hiring and harbouring runaways)."

(INHABITANT OF ST. LUCIA 1832: 16-17)

This passage ends with the words: *"This was the state of things a few years ago."* According to a further section of this publication it was not possible for the colonial government to control the runaway slaves. The slaves even had a certain influence on the planters:

"... it was then and is now the greatest check on industry or improvement, and an evil, for the suppression of which, no efficient remedy has ever been applied: under these circumstances even the negroes, from the extreme points of the island, became known to each other, and any manager, who attempted bring his gang to a proper performance of their duty, was sure to draw upon him the hatred of the whole class, and many were those who are said to have been sacrificed to this resentment; and those managers who were in any degree successful, were only such as might have been said, to have conquered by force the negroes under their charge."

Concerning the situation of harbouring runaway slaves there is a letter of the Chief Justice of St. Lucia, Mr. JEREMIE, to Governor MAINWARING of April 1827. From this document it follows that it was a common practice in St. Lucia that runaway slaves got shelter from the stationed black soldiers. Mr. JEREMIE wrote:

"One of the Police-men having whilst in search of a runaway slave been assaulted and cut in several places by three black soldiers on the road to the Morne. I must beg that they be given up for trial, ... As this is unfortunately not the first time I have had to notice, ..., the misconduct of the military labourers and soldiers of the Corps towards the Police, I am sorry to add, that it has become of late a notorious practice with runaways from town, males and females go to them for protection."

(CO 253/23/3: 17/4/1827)

Another source which refers to the harbouring of runaway slaves is an ordinance from March 1834. From it one can also conclude that the hiding of runaway slaves was very common in St. Lucia:

"Whereas it is expedient to repress the practice of harbouring and concealing slaves who have run away from the plantation and from the service of their owners or managers in this Island and to impose certain penalties on all persons convicted of so doing, ..."

(CO 255/2/10: 3/3/1834, p.257)

The related provisions of punishment were stipulated as follows:

"That if any person or persons in the said Island shall knowingly harbour or conceal or knowingly assist in harbouring or concealing any slave or slaves who may have unlawfully absented and fled from the plantation of the service of their owners or managers with the intention of remaining absent therefrom, such person or persons so knowingly harbouring or concealing or assisting in harbouring or concealing such runaway slave or slaves shall on conviction in a summary manner before any magistrate of this Island be judged to pay a fine which shall not be less than 50 Livres nor exceed 250 Livres Current money for each and every offence, ..."

The last reference to runaway slaves before the abolition of slavery in St. Lucia on the 1st of August, 1834, is a proclamation issued by Governor DUDLEY HILL on July 25th, 1834. It granted an amnesty to all runaway slaves who would return to their masters. This document also confirms the existence of many runaway slaves in St. Lucia at that time. It states in part:

"Whereas it has been represented to me that there are at the present time many Slaves absent without leave from the service of their masters, I have thought it fit to issue this my Proclamation calling upon all such runaways to return forthwith to the duty when an Act of Clemency will be extended towards them, otherwise they will be subjected to the prolonged term of apprenticeship provided for in the 20. Clause of the Act entitled "An Act for the Abolition of Slavery" which takes effect from the first of August next ensuing."

(CO 255/2/11: 25/7/1834, pp.264/266)

4.10.1.2 Summary

At the beginning of the 19th century the following provisions for the punishment of runaway slaves (absence at least for one month) were in force in St. Lucia: for the first offence the slave should have his ears cut and be branded on one shoulder, for the second offence he should have his hands cut and be branded on the other shoulder, for the third offence the slave had to work in chains or on the galleys and he could even be punished by death.

These punishments might not have been passed or put into execution very often by the Court of St. Lucia. The author assumes this because in the year 1817 when two runaway slaves were sentenced to cutting off their ears and branding there was a commotion within the slave population because of the execution of this sentence.

With the slave law of 1826 the mentioned provisions for the punishment of runaway slaves were altered to whipping and solitary confinement. For a fourth offence the slave still had to suffer death. This provision was commuted to working with chains for life by an ordinance of May 1830.

According to accounts of the year 1823 and 1824 it was easy for runaway slaves in St. Lucia to hide in the interior of the island because of the non-development of the densely wooded mountain ranges by the colonial government. Furthermore there was the possibility for runaway slaves to get shelter from free inhabitants. This practice was very common.

Regarding a certain number of runaway slaves in St. Lucia there is no information in the sources. But it follows from it that the running away of slaves was very common and that the colonial government had no control over this situation. Governor STEWART mentioned a slave who had been absent from his owner for 16 years.

Although some planters were afraid of the runaway slaves there was no organized riot in the 19th century. A single slave riot which embraced the whole colony was mentioned by Governor STEWART in the year 1829. But this riot was not organized. It arose from a misunderstanding on the part of the slaves who were believed to have received their freedom, and left the plantations. By a military transaction of the colonial government the runaway slaves were made to return.

4.10.2   Flight of slaves to other colonies

4.10.2.1   Sources

The earliest information about the flight of slaves from St. Lucia to another colony is reported in a letter of Governor BOZON of St. Lucia to the SECRETARY OF STATE GODERICH dated June 28th, 1831. On June 13th, 1831, ten slaves tried to escape to Martinique:

> "I beg leave to state for your Lordship's consideration that in the night of the 13th of this month ten Slaves belonging to two Estates on this Island made their escape. They were picked up as expressed in the Letter of the Governor of Martinique on the following morning and have been since sent back by him to Saint Lucia and I beg leave to forward ... At the request of the Governor of Martinique and in conformity with the opinion of the first President I have received these Slaves pardoned them and have allowed them to return to the Estates from which they escaped. As the case of Slaves belonging to a British Colony making their escape to a foreign Island, and being sent back by that Island does not appear to the first President to be expressly provided for by the consolidated Slave Act of England or that of this Colony, the Owners of the said Slaves have been

217

allowed to take back these fugitives to their Estate upon security that no punishment shall be inflicted and on condition of the part of their Owners of conforming to such orders as His Majesty's Government may be pleased to make on the subject.

The following information was given by the Commander of the French men of war Schooner JOPAZE which brought these fugitives from Martinique and is submitted for your Lordship's information:

1. *that they were picked up about 2 English miles and a half from the coast of Martinique*
2. *that they were in the first instance lodged in the slave prison at Fort Royal,*
3. *that the canoe in which they made their escape is at Fort Royal, ready to be given up when claimed."*

(CO 253/29/3: 28/6/1831)

On October 31st, 1832, there was a discussion in the EXECUTIVE AND LEGISLATIVE COUNCIL of St. Lucia about the flight of slaves. Two letters were mentioned. The first letter from Governor FARQUHARSON to the PROTECTOR OF SLAVES dated October 30th, 1832, referred to a flight of slaves. They were supposed to had embarked in a canoe for Martinique. The answer of the PROTECTOR OF SLAVES was as follows:

"... on my return about 5 this morning I came up with the boat, detached to leeward, which had met with a canoe off the Marigot des Roseaux, with thirteen Slaves on board – twelve belonging to the Perle Estate, and one to the Bois d'Orange Estate."

(CO 256/2/2: 31/10/1832)

On that occasion a proclamation for preventing the flight of slaves to Martinique was published:

"Whereas apprehension have been for some time entertained that some of the Slaves in this Colony are meditating to make their escape with a view of repairing to the adjoining foreign Island of Martinique and such fears having unfortunately been realized by the circumstance of several Slaves belonging to the Perle Estate in the Valley of Roseau, having been detected and apprehended at sea in the act of attempting to escape from this Island to Martinique it becomes urgent and necessary to devise some prompt and efficient means for checking and preventing too criminal and too ruinous a proceeding."

(CO 253/40/6: 31/10/1832)

The stipulations limited the use of boats for slaves:

1st: That in conformity with the 60th Section of the Order in Council of 2nd November 1831 no slave shall in future possess, hold or occupy any canoe of boat in this Island.

2ⁿᵈ: That no slave shall presume or be allowed to enter into or sail in any canoe or boat or craft without a written permission under the hand of his owner, master or manager, except such Slave be in actual attendance of such owner, master or manager."

Additionally it is to mention that the use of boats for slaves without the permission of their masters was already prohibited according to the CODE DE LA MARTINIQUE:

"Art. XVIII.-Forbidding all masters of droghers, pirogues, and canoes, to give Slaves a passage or retreat without a ticket from their Masters or accompanying them, under pain, should it be Slaves who afford such retreat, of being flogged and pilloried; if free, of thirty days' prison and damages."

(BPP/ST/71/2: 25/12/1783, p.202)

A clause regarding the prohibition of possessing boats by slaves – the right of possessing property the slaves got only in 1826 (cp. chapter 4.7.3.1. Prohibition of possessing property, pp. 109-114) – was fixed in an ORDER IN COUNCIL dated February 2ⁿᵈ, 1830, as follows:

"XLIII.-Provided always, That no Slave in any of the said Colonies shall be competent to become the proprietor of, or to hold or retain any boats, or other craft or vessels, or any share or interest therein, or any gunpowder or other ammunition, fire arms or military weapons, of whatever nature or kind so ever."

(BPP/ST/77/1: 2/2/1830, p.35)

On November 1ˢᵗ, 1832, Governor FARQUHARSON of St. Lucia wrote to the SECRETARY OF STATE as follows:

"… that the Governor of Martinique has offered asylum and a peculiar reward of a dabloon each to all Slaves who can escape from hence and reach the Island he governs. This is at present a rumour but I intend to send a person confidentially to Martinique for the purpose of endeavouring to ascertain the truth or falsehood thereof."

(CO 253/40/7: 1/11/1832)

From another letter of the Governor of St. Lucia dated November 3ʳᵈ, 1832, follows that about 21 slaves had escaped to Martinique:

"I regret having to inform your Lordship that from every information I can collect about 21 have effected their escape and landed in that Island, where I understand, they are employed by the Government of that Colony in cutting timber for some public purpose but I cannot ascertain whether as bond or free men."

(CO 253/40/8: 3/11/1832)

In the same month two planters of St. Lucia visited Martinique for informing themselves about the escaped slaves:

The planter Noel reported:

"… that they are caused to work from 6 o'clock in the morning until 6 at night, that they receive 5 dogs per day wages (about 3/2 Sterling) and fed and clothed by the French government. And that the nominal list of them is called every night when they are shut up until the hour of labour the following morning, …, that the Slaves from Mr. Muter's Estate of Roseau declared that they were well used upon that Estate but that nevertheless they preferred their present line of life as to being upon a plantation. They are employed in filling up a swamp."

(CO 253/40/9: 29/11/1832)

The planter James Scott reported about eight slaves of the Roseau estate:

"… they would not return as they were well clothed, fed and lodged, that they had white bread and beef, the same as the soldiers, and some received 12 and the rest 8 sous per day."

(CO 253/40/10: 30/11/1832)

From the mentioned 21 escaped slaves seven returned to St. Lucia. This follows from a letter of Governor FARQUHARSON of January 31st, 1833:

"… 21 Slaves who have absented from this Colony and taken refuge in Martinique, 7 of whom have volunteered to return to their owners in Saint Lucia and have been landed here accordingly."

(CO 253/43/8: 31/1/1833)

For the future preventing of the flight of slaves to Martinique an ordinance was published in November 1833 fixing certain stipulations for boat owners for the regions Roseau and Grande Cul de Sac (CO 255/2/12: 25/11/1833, p.231). According to these stipulations the owners of boats needed special passes. They also had to secure their boats at night with a chain and pad-lock.

The escape of slaves by boats was limited to the areas Roseau and Grande Cul de Sac. In the minutes of the EXECUTIVE AND LEGISLATIVE COUNCIL of St. Lucia dated November 11th, 1833, it was stated:

"As it appears that the disposition manifested by the Slaves to go to Martinique, is confined to the Cantons of Roseau and Grande Cul de Sac, arising no doubt from the facility they have of secreting Boats in the Rivers of these Quarters …".

(CO 256/2/3: 11/11/1833)

Further reports from the flight of slaves from St. Lucia were not available.

4.10.2.2 Summary

Summing up it can be said that the flight of slaves from St. Lucia was limited to the neighbouring island of Martinique. In the year 1831 10 slaves and in the year 1832 21 slaves reached Martinique. An attempt to escape of 13 slaves in the year 1832 failed. The mentioned 10 slaves escaped in the year 1831 were returned to St. Lucia short after their capture in the vicinity of the coast of Martinique. From the 21 escaped slaves seven returned voluntarily to St. Lucia.

A clear reason for the flight of the slaves does not follow from the reports. Some refugees preferred filling up a swamp in Martinique as being upon a plantation in St. Lucia. All refugees were satisfied with the good maintenance and salary in Martinique. Governor FARQUHARSON of St. Lucia mentioned in his letter dated November 1832 that a rumour existed in St. Lucia that the Governor of Martinique had offered asylum and a peculiar reward to all slaves who can escape from St. Lucia. This could have been an impulse for the flight of the slaves.

4.11 FREE NON-WHITES

4.11.1   Introduction

The part of the FREE NON-WHITES (free people of mixed colour and blacks) of the whole population of St. Lucia rose from the year 1772 with 4% to 27% in the year 1835 (cp. chapter "4.5.2. Development and structure of population", table on p. 71). In the available sources for the FREE NON-WHITES the following designations – mostly those with the term "coloured" – were used:

> "Coloured"
> "Free Coloured"
> "Free People of Colour"
> "Free Coloured and Black Population"
> "Free Negroes"
> "Mulattoes, Indians and Negroes"

In the following the legal restrictions of the FREE NON-WHITES in contrary to whites and the actions of the FREE NON-WHITES for the removal of these restrictions are referred to. Then the subsistence and the legal position concerning property of the FREE NON-WHITES are described.

4.11.2   Legal restrictions in contrary to whites and the removal thereof in the years 1826 and 1829

On January 15th, 1824, the FREE NON-WHITES of St. Lucia signed a petition addressed to the then Governor of St. Lucia, MAINWARING, in which they demanded the removal of the legal restrictions of their rights in contrary to whites:

> *"That your Petitioners finding themselves labouring under severe and unmerited restrictions and being deprived of the advantage of laying their situation before a colonial Legislature, none such existing in this Colony, to be their duty to place before Your Excellency an humble exposure of the disabilities under which they labour, with the supplementation that you will be pleased to lay the same before His Majesty's Government at Home ...*
>
> *That your Petitioners in humbly representing their situation to your Excellency remark with feelings of deep regret upon the difference kept up with such unabated rigour, between the White, and free Man of Colour, from the existence of Laws by which this Colony is governed; principally the 'Code Civil de la Martinique' ".*

(CO 253/18/4: 15/1/1824)

Governor MAINWARING forwarded this petition to the SECRETARY OF STATE in London on April 16th, 1824 (CO 253/18/5: 16/4/1824).

As the FREE NON-WHITES didn't get any answer they made a second petition on July 31st, 1824, to the new Governor of St. Lucia, BLACKWELL:

> *"That your Petitioners in the month of January last presented through the Honourable James Muter, Member of His Majesty's Privy Council to His Excellency Major General Mainwaring, then Governor of this Island, the Petition from the Free Coloured Inhabitants of Saint Lucia setting forth certain grievances under which they laboured from the laws in force in this Colony and requesting him to lay the same before His Majesty's Government at home.*
>
> *That several months having elapsed since the said Petition was presented and your Petitioners not hearing any account of the same beg leave most respectfully to submit a copy of your Excellency's Consideration feeling a conviction that from your well known humanity and the ready attention which the unfortunate is always sure to receive from your Excellency, you will be pleased with your … goodness to bestow a favourable regard upon this class of His Majesty's Subjects and take into your consideration the subject of their complaint."*

(CO 253/20/1: 31/7/1824)

In the enclosure to this petition the FREE NON-WHITES prescribed their legal restrictions:

Ordinance of February 1720:
Prohibition of dealing with gold and silver

> *"Art. 4 of this ordinance prohibits all goldsmiths under any pretext from buying any wrought or any unwrought gold or silver from any soldiers or sailors without the permission of the Captains or from any vagrants now residents and free negroes (under this denomination is comprised the whole class of Colour without distinction) …under the penalty of being sent to the galleies and of confiscation of their property."*

Ordinance of June 1720:
Stipulation regarding clothes

> *"Art. 3 of this colonial regulation, …, says that all mulattoes, Indians and negroes manumitted or free may be allowed to wear white linen, check cotton stuff, calicoes or stuff of the same description of little value, with coats of the same, no silk nor anything gilt nor lace, without these be of very inferior value, hats, shoes and stockings of the plainest kind under the penalty of confiscation of their clothes and of losing their freedom."*

Declaration of February 5th, 1726:
Prohibition of receiving from white persons gifts, legacies or donations

> *"In this Declaration of the King of France it is said that in conformity with Art. 52 of the Edict of March 1724 all slaves enfranchised or their children and descendants shall henceforth be incapacitated from receiving from any white person any gift or legacy or any donation of any kind of any*

denomination or under any pretext whatever. Furthermore it is ordained that in the event of any donation or legacy being given or left to any negroes manumitted or free or to their children and descendants, such donations or legacies shall be null and void and shall revert to the nearest hospital."

In January 1820 this declaration was repealed. But another law of the year 1629 saying that all donations made by persons to each other cohabiting together were null and void was in use in St. Lucia. This prohibition referred also to donations from whites to FREE NON-WHITES. For proving the validity of this law in St. Lucia the petitioners gave the following example:

"Mr. Wilson, Merchant of this town, sold several slaves to Mary Jane King. It was proved, she paid for them. Mr. Wilson died and no one thought of contesting the validity of this sale. Sometime after Mary Jane King died and by her last will and testament, left these slaves to her infant daughter and to her sister Betsy Devenish, Mary Jane King being dead, means were taken to have this legacy annulled. The reasons alleged for which were that Jane King had cohabited with Mr. Wilson, that the sale was a simulated gift, that as his concubine this gift was null by the Ordinance of 1629. The sentence of the Court of Sénéchaussée of this Island of the 5th October 1822 was founded upon these motives. The decree of the Court of Appeal, 8th Jan. 1823, confirmed it. Thus the unfortunate Betsy Devenish was obliged to give up the slaves left by her sister."

Ordinance of October 1763:
Assistance of FREE NON-WHITES to government servants when arresting people

"Art. 4: In all cases wherein the Commissaries or the Lieutenants shall stand in need of assistance in order to arrest persons guilty of any public offence or to have such offenders escorted to prison, they shall be at liberty to command the free negroes or mulattoes of their parishes and they are bound to execute any order of the said Commissaries or their Lieutenants."

"Art. 6: When such free negroes or others shall be employed in escorting any persons accused they shall be paid their travelling expenses according to a table of fees which shall be drawn up by the Intendant or the persons named for that purpose."

To article 4 the petitioners noticed:

"In Art. 4 it is positively said that Commissaries can command free people only when they are in need of assistance either to have some offender arrested or escorted to prison. Yet we see every day but more especially in the Country free persons taken from the occupations to carry about letters, sometimes of a private nature."

Regarding the payment of such services the petitioners stated that the mentioned article 6 was completely disregarded in St. Lucia.

Ordinance of April 1764:
Prohibition of the practice of surgery

> "Art. 16 of this Ordinance prohibits all negroes and free people of Colour the practice of Physic or Surgery or to undertake to cure any sick person on any consideration whatever under a penalty of 500 Livres for each offence and corporal punishment as the case may require."

Law (Decree) of May 9th, 1765:
Prohibition of working in public functions

> "This Decree expressly prohibits all registrars, notaries and other lawyers and Huissiers to employ free coloured persons in their offices under a penalty of 500 Livres for the first time and double the sum should the offence be repeated. And the coloured man who might have been employed to be confined one month in prison."

Ordinance of May 1st, 1766:
Penalty for assisting runaway slaves

> "Free people of Colour who shall be convicted of having encouraged or given an asylum to runaway negroes shall be deprived of their freedom and shall be sold for the benefit of the King, ..."

The petitioners mentioned that the above mentioned ordinance had fallen into disuse in St. Lucia and they pointed out that its penalty is in direct opposition to a natural law which always inclines in favour of freedom.

Law (Decree) of September 1769:
Prohibition of working with medicines

> "This Decree prohibits all Surgeons, Apothecaries, Druggists and others to employ slaves and free people of Colour in selling, distributing and composing any kind of medicines, enjoins them when they shall employ slaves or free people of colour to carry medicines to sick persons to paste the labels on the bottles or parcels."

The ordinances of January 1773 and March 1774 prohibited the taking of names similar to those of white persons. To these ordinances the petitioners noted:

> "These two Ordinances are nearly absolute and coloured people generally add to their Christian names the surnames of those to whom they owe their liberty. This proves that they are grateful ... Many lawyers even to this day show a strong disposition in the acts and in other documents to enforce these two ordinances."

<u>Law (Decree) of November 1781:</u>
<u>Prohibition of designation with Mister and Misses</u>

> *"This Decree expressly prohibits all Curées, Notaries, Surveillors and other public Officers to qualify persons of colour with the title of Mister or Miss. It is in rigorous operation in this Island."*

Instead of this designation the term "le nomé" was used:

> *"The coloured man is insulted on seeing his name invariably cut with the contumelious appellation of "le nomé", a term for which we have not a perfect equivalent in the English language but according to the usage of the French courts it is applied only to vagrants or persons not sufficiently known to merit any degree of courtesy."*

<u>Ordinance of December 25th, 1783:</u>
<u>General police regulations</u>

> *"Art. I: That it shall not be lawful for free people of colour to carry any arms either in town or in the country without they be on public duty, neither shall it be lawful for them to assemble together under any pretext of weddings, feasts or dances without the permission from the Commandant of the quarter, signed by the Procureur du roi."*

Finally the petitioners referred to a clause of the CODE NOIR of March 1685:

> *"It is expressly ordered that the enfranchised shall bear himself with a deportment of singular respect to their former masters, their widows and children so that the offence committed against these shall be punished with much more severity than the offence committed against any other person."*

On February 8th, 1826 Governor MAINWARING published an "Ordinance respecting and amending several laws relating to Free Persons of Colour". Introductory it was said:

> *"... that the following laws, ordinances and regulations in as much as they establish distinctions between the free Inhabitants of this Colony prejudicial to the Free Class of Colour shall be and they are hereby repealed."*

Then laws from 1685 to 1787 (laws as mentioned above) were stated. The further clauses of the ordinance were:

> *"And it is further ordered that in all Judicial and Notarial Acts to which Slaves are parties, they shall be named as such, and that all free persons be designated by their rank, profession, occupation, property, family names, birth place or place of residence according to the rules and usages commonly observed in the Courts of England and other European*

Countries without any designation or distinction of Colour or any qualification which may be intended to make or has heretofore served to make a distinction as to Colour.

And it is further ordered that the Mail Fees and Allowances, Fees in Public Offices and bonds of leaving the Island, shall be in every respect the same for free persons of Colour as for Whites.

Nothing herein contained shall be considered as imposing upon free persons of Colour the right of Voting at Parish Meetings or of holding Public Appointments."

(CO 255/1/5: 8/2/1826, p.140)

The last mentioned paragraph contains the remaining restrictions.

In a petition of March 9th, 1826, the FREE NON-WHITES expressed their thanks to Governor MAINWARING for the repealing of the restrictions:

"We His Majesty's dutiful and loyal subjects, the Free Coloured Inhabitants of this Colony impressed with feelings of the most lively gratitude for the benefits lately conferred by the Ordinance of 8th February, beg to approach your Excellency to express our sentiment of profound respect for your Excellency's Person and Administration and to offer to your Excellency and the Members of your Privy Council our most grateful and ... acknowledgements."

At the same time they demanded the repeal of the remaining restrictions:

"And we beg to assure your Excellency that the repeal of those laws will only serve to stimulate us by a proper and ... conduct to merit a continuance of your Excellency's favourable consideration for the removal of the remaining disabilities under which we labour by our gracious and beloved Sovereign."

(CO 253/22/3: 9/3/1826)

These remaining restrictions were repealed with an ORDER IN COUNCIL passed in London on January 15th, 1829:

"Whereas in times past and before the Cession of the Island of St. Lucia to His Majesty, divers Laws, and divers Edicts and Ordinances having effect of Law, were in force within the said Island whereby persons of free condition of African birth and descent were subjected to divers disabilities and restrictions to which other free persons inhabiting the said Island are not subject, and it hath been represented to His Majesty by the Governor and the Council of Government of the said Island, that such Laws, Edicts and Ordinances have fallen into disuse, and that by reason of the ... ally and good conduct of such persons as aforesaid it is unnecessary and inexpedient that the same should be revived or continued in force, His Majesty by and with the advice of His Privy Council is therefore pleased to order and it is hereby ordered that all Laws and all Edicts and Ordinances having the force and effect of Law at any time heretofore made or

promulgated within the said Island of St. Lucia, whereby free persons of African birth or descent are subjected to any disabilities or restrictions to which other free persons inhabiting the said Island are not subject, shall be and the same are hereby repealed and for ever cancelled.

And the Right Honourable Sir George Murray One of His Majesty's Principal Secretaries of State, is to give the necessary directions herein accordingly."

(CO 253/26/8: 15/1/1829)

4.11.3   Subsistence and property

In a petition of January 15th, 1824, regarding the demand for repealing the restrictions in contrary to whites the FREE NON-WHITES stated the following:

> *"The free coloured Inhabitants of the Island of Saint Lucia may on a fair average be calculated to comprise at least two thirds of the free Population and are for the most part landed Proprietors to a considerable extent in the Colony."*

(CO 253/18/4: 15/1/1824)

Governor MAINWARING prescribed the activities of the FRE NON-WHITES in a letter of April 26th, 1824, as follows:

> *"... very few of this class are in possession of any considerable landed property (small sugar Estates, on these they make syrup for retail sale), small coffee, stock and provision Plantations with a few Slaves to work them and Houses, Shops with domestic Slaves."*

(CO 253/18/5: 16/4/1824)

Further he reported of masons, carpenters, sailors, fishermen, tailors and house-servants.

In a report of the year 1829 Mr. JEREMIE wrote:

> *"Yet among the largest proprietors in this town and among the holders of Estates of near a hundred Slaves are men of colour. The most extensive proprietor in Castries is a man of colour."*

(CO 253/26/5: 30/5/1829)

In September 1829 Governor STEWART referred to FREE NON-WHITES who lived independently of the other society of St. Lucia. He was a little bit worried about it:

> *"Now looking to some very important considerations there is an absolute necessity for keeping up in this Colony an efficient Body of Militia, one of the considerations which press on my mind is the propriety of bringing*

forward and keeping under my frequent view and notice the free coloured and black population who inhabit the woods, ravines and hills, where they are seldom seen and from whence they seldom come except when force and necessity calls them."

(CO 253/26/1: 15/9/1829)

A further description of the FREE NON-WHITES is given in JEREMIE's book (1831: 50-51):

"They, the free coloured and free black class, are proved to be about five thousand in number, of whom one eighth, or somewhat more, may be manumitted slaves; and there are eighty discharged negro soldiers. Among the manumitted slaves there are many who possess landed property and slaves."

He further reported that the main part of the militia was FREE NON-WHITES:

"As militia-men, (and they form the bulk of the militia), they are deficient neither in intelligence nor zeal, whether as compared with whites of the same corps, or with persons of their station elsewhere. So much is it otherwise, that there is a company, formed exclusively of them, for the protection of property in town, in case of fire and such other contingencies."

Regarding the above mentioned number of 5.000 FREE NON-WHITES it is to mention that the figures stated in the population tables are lower. For the period from 1825 to 1835 the figures vary from about 2.600 to 4.400 persons (cp. chapter "4.5.2. Development and structure of population", p. 71).

Concerning property JEREMIE wrote:

"As to property, there are two or three sugar planters, and a large number of coffee, cocoa, and provision planters, possessing each from ten to forty slaves. There are two first-rate merchants, and a large number of second-rate merchants and retail dealers, among them; and many of the latter purchase from £ 2000 to £ 3000 currency, or about £ 1000 sterling, of goods, in the course of the year. One third of the trade of the colony is in their hands. The dry-good trade they possess almost exclusively; and they are remarkable for probity in their dealings, and for punctuality in their payments. The generality are retail merchants and small proprietors, nor are they by any means so embarrassed as the whites."

He further mentioned that the FREE NON-WHITES owned about one sixth of the slaves of St. Lucia:

"The coloured class are further proved, by documents collected from the public offices, to possess 2,350 slaves – about one sixth of the whole number in the colony. Of these, 1,202 are plantation and 1,148 personal

slaves; and, as there are but 2,680 personal slaves in the country, they possess nearly half the personal slaves."

Finally he wrote:

"And it is proved that in the town and port of Castries they own more than one half the rental of the town, and full half the registered shipping in number and value.- Such is the proof, such the uncontroverted evidence, adduced."

Regarding the subsistence of APPRENTICES who were freed in the emancipation period the STIPENDIARY MAGISTRATES wrote as follows:

1st district (Castries, Gros Islet, Dauphin and Anse La Raye):

"Squatting on lands unoccupied, or which have been previously illegally occupied by the Martinique refugees where they employ themselves in cutting logwood, burning charcoal and raising a few provisions."

(CO 253/52/1: Sept. 1836)

The refugees from Martinique were formerly slaves who have got their freedom when they have arrived in St. Lucia (cp. the following chapter, p. 233).

2nd district (Soufrière, Choiseul and Laborie):

"Tradesmen and Domestics after obtaining their discharge usually betake themselves to their old occupations and often remain with their Master. As Field Labour is considered here in some degrading, the field labourers who have already obtained their discharge usually become fishermen, grooms, some also who work small patches of land, hired out to them generally by people of colour, themselves too indolent to do so.

They go out to hire but they never go to work with the gang, they think it a disgrace."

(CO 253/52/2: 2/9/1836)

From this quotation follows that APPRENTICES shortly freed worked for FREE NON-WHITES. This also follows from the next report of the STIPENDIARY MAGISTRATE of the 3rd district (Vieux Fort, Micoud, Praslin and Dennery):

"In many instances the freed people get employed by the people of Colour. Some continue to cultivate their grounds and work to effect to purchase off wife, child or some relation but in general labour being higher at Castries."

(CO 253/52/5: 31/8/1836)

The both British travellers STURGE and HARVEY who visited St. Lucia in December 1836 stated the opinion of Governor DUDLEY HILL:

> "The apprentices who bought out their time usually continued to work for wages on the estates."
>
> (STURGE/HARVEY 1838: 107)

Other sources point to a more independent life of the freed APPRENTICES from the estates. The STIPENDIARY MAGISTRATE of the 1st district (Castries, Gros Islet, Dauphin and Anse La Raye) reported:

> "In some instances lately some of the Apprentices freed returned to their former Estates and work for wages."
>
> (CO 253/54/3: 1/3/1837)

Report of the STIPENDIARY MAGISTRATE of the 2nd district (Gros Islet, Dauphin):

> "... those Apprentices who have purchased their freedom generally betake themselves to the same kind of employment they formerly pursued: that is, those who were agriculturists become small settlers upon vacant land and Domestics endeavour to obtain the same employment; ... the negroes appear to have a desire of permanently establishing themselves; but it would seem that those who have been affranchised prefer working upon lands hired or purchased by themselves to returning to the Estates to which they had been attached, they are generally not deficient of industry & endeavour to ameliorate their condition."
>
> (CO 253/64/15: 6/3/1838)

4.11.4   Summary

The FREE NON-WHITES were legally restricted in contrary to whites till the years 1826 respectively 1829. These restrictions generally were as follows:

- They were not to be employed in any public office, nor as attorneys or clerks.
- They could not work in medical professions nor work with medicines.
- They could not deal with gold or silver.
- They could not use names which were similar to those of whites.
- In documents they could not be styled Mister or Misses.
- When they wanted to assemble together they needed the permission of the PROCUREUR DU ROI.
- Their clothes were to be of inferior value.
- On attacking a white person hard punishments were provided.
- When assisting runaway slaves they could be deprived of their freedom.
- For FREE NON-WHITES it was also prohibited to carry arms.

With an ordinance of February 8th, 1826, the most legal restrictions were repealed. The final assimilation in legal status with the whites came with an ORDER IN COUNCIL passed in London on January 15th, 1829.

Regarding the property of the FREE NON-WHITES it is to mention that the most of them were in a relatively good financial situation.

After the abolition of slavery this group made a social rise within the society of St. Lucia. According to BREEN they must have been mainly of mixed colour. He wrote:

> "The coloured population, which may not inaptly be termed the staple population of the Colonies, has rapidly progressed in numbers, wealth, and respectability. Independently of the natural increase amongst themselves, they are constantly receiving fresh accessions of strength through their intercourse with the whites and blacks, and the connexion of these races with each other. Few as yet have become owners of the soil to any considerable extent; but much of the property in houses and land, both in Castries and Soufrière, is possessed by them. Some are opulent merchants; others respectable shopkeepers; and many are industrious tradesmen. The advantages of education, too, begin to be more generally appreciated: not only are the clerkships in the public offices held by persons of colour; but the Medical Profession, the Press, the Bar, the Legislative Council, the offices of Crown Lawyer, Stipendiary Magistrate, Justice of the Peace, Deputy Registrar, Deputy Marshall, and Notary Public, are aspired to by candidates from amongst their ranks, and filled with credit and distinction. Although this result is mainly attributable to the good sense and steady deportment of the coloured classes themselves, it would be unjust to withhold from the whites our need of praise for their liberal encouragement of their coloured brethren."

(BREEN 1844: 166-167)

Also a report of the STIPENDIARY MAGISTRATE of the 1st district (Castries, Anse La Raye) of the year 1844 refers to the social rise of the FREE NON-WHITES. In connection with the description of Christian marriages between the blacks of St. Lucia he mentioned:

> "I am happy to say, that these observations do not apply to what may be considered the middling classes of this Colony.
>
> I mean the anciently free coloured people, who have evinced a vast improvement of late years in this respect. - Some few years ago a coloured girl preferred being the Mistress of a white man, to becoming the legitimate partner of one of her own class; -It is not so now. – Marriages and intermarriages have become the rule, and not the exception, and it is delightful to see, that as the education, wealth, commercial and political importance of this Class of people have augmented, so have their respect for and observance of the best and surest ties of civilized Society increased."

(CO 253/82/1: 10/1/1844)

4.12 Slave refugees from Martinique

4.12.1   Introduction

This chapter refers to the extent of refugees to St. Lucia as well as to their subsistence. As the French abolished slavery only in the year 1848 and the slave refugees from Martinique arrived in St. Lucia till this year, this chapter exceeds the scope of the chapter "4. The period of slavery and emancipation (end of 18th century - 1838)" for 10 years. But the main sources refer to the period from 1830 to 1838.

4.12.2   Extent

According to BREEN (1844: 170, 178) the main part of the refugees from Martinique arrived in St. Lucia between the years 1831 and 1838. As reason he mentioned slave insurrections in Martinique in the year 1831 because of a change in power in France (the "Revolution de Juillet"). The supporters of the revolution pleaded for freedom and equality of all human beings. This had a great influence on the slaves. On February 9th, 1831, eleven sugar plantations and three houses were set on fire in Martinique. The French colonial government put this insurrection down and sentenced 22 persons to death by hanging. These sentences were put into execution on May 19th (BREEN: 171-128; cp. also BERNER 1984: 158).

Slave refugees from Martinique arriving in St. Lucia got their freedom. JEREMIE (1831: 51) wrote:

> "It happened that several slaves took refuge from Martinique, where the salve-trade is avowedly carried on, to St. Lucia, in 1829. This caused a discussion, the effect of which was to make it generally known, that on a foreign slave's reaching a British colony, he, by Dr. Lushington's bill, becomes free; and in consequence of this discussion, several, exceeding 100 in number, came over in the year 1830."

The available figures regarding refugees from Martinique to St. Lucia are:

Source/	date	number of refugees
(CO 253/29/4:	11/7/1831)	204
(CO 253/40/11:	25/9/1832)	301
(CO 253/51/1:	15/3/1836)	400
(CO 253/52/9:	19/9/1836)	466
(STURGE/HARVEY 1838: 113)-Dec. 1836		600
(CO 253/56/3:	8/9/1837)	more than 500
(CO 253/64/19:	2/3/1838)	more than 600
(CO 253/93/1:	28/5/1848)	500

According to these figures there was a rise in refugees in St. Lucia in the period from 1830 to 1838.

The COLONIAL SECRETARY HANLEY of St. Lucia referred in a table regarding immigrants to St. Lucia concerning the period from 1836 to 1842 to the number of refugees from Martinique as follows:

> "During the several periods above mentioned, about 600 or 700 Martinique refugees immigrated into this colony. No office for the registration of immigrants has ever been kept in this colony."
>
> (CO 253/78/7: 1843)

BREEN (1844: 180) mentions that the number of refugees from Martinique never exceeded 800 at any time in St. Lucia. His further remarks (BREEN 1844: 180-181) are:

> "Until 1839 they enjoyed a monopoly of the advantages of free labour, and sedulously did they turn it to account: but on the abolition of slavery, having to compete with the awakened energies of 15,000 labourers, free like themselves, they were literally driven from the field, and many of them have emigrated to Demerara (British Guiana) and Trinidad. Since that period also the arrivals have become less frequent, owing partly to the increased vigilance of the authorities of Martinique, and partly to the prospect of approaching emancipation in the French Colonies."

In the year 1848 the abolition of slavery was promulgated in the French colonies (cp. BERNER 1984: 170). From this time on refugees living in St. Lucia returned to Martinique. But Martinique refugees arrived also in St. Lucia. This follows from reports of the STIPENDIARY MAGISTRATES of the 1st and 2nd district of St. Lucia as follows:

1st district (Castries, Anse La Raye):

> "In consequence of the present unquiet state of the neighbouring Island of Martinique, many families have taken refuge in this Island; whilst on the other hand I have reason to believe that a number of former Slave Refugees have left Saint Lucia, since the promulgation of the Act of Emancipation in the French Islands."
>
> (CO 258/16/14: 1/1/1848-30/6/1848, p.334)

> "Imm. occasional few from the neighbouring Island of Martinique, compensated by the emigration thereto of former residents."
>
> (CO 258/16/15: 1/7/1848-31/12/1848, p.397)

2<u>nd</u> <u>district (Gros Islet, Dauphin)</u>:

> "*Immigrants: 16*
>
> *This considerable increase is attributable to the frequent immigration of the recently emancipated people of Martinique who attracted here by the fertile soil, the cheapness of the price of land, and very often by their family connexions, immigrate to this Island to settle.*"
>
> "*Emigrants: 17*
>
> *Some of the Martinique Refugees formerly settled here, have returned to their native land, there to enjoy that freedom, which they have formerly sought in a British Colony, the privation of which had first induced them to abandon their native land.*"

(CO 258/16/16: 177/1848-31/12/1848, p.406)

> "*People come and go as they please; and although an ordinance has been recently enacted by the Colonial legislature, for preventing the irregular landing of goods or persons arriving from foreign parts in this Island, yet since the abolition of Slavery in Martinique, frequent excursions from one Island to the other take place amongst the numerous refugees of Martinique, settled in this district.*"

(CO 258/17/6: 1/1/1849-30/6/1849, p.11)

To the extent of the refugees from Martinique it is also to mention that many refugees died during their flight. BREEN wrote as follows:

> "*And truly, when we consider the difficulties of escape – the vigilance of the authorities of Martinique – the system of espionage employed by the planters to check desertion amongst their slaves – the strict surveillance of the "guarda-costas" and the distance and dangers of the passage between the two islands, it is matter of surprise that so many of them should have succeeded in accomplishing their object. The distance from the place of embarkation in Martinique is in some instances upwards of forty miles, and the means of conveyance, the first boat or canoe that comes in their way. Still, it is no unusual occurrence to see twelve or fifteen men and women land on the coast of St. Lucia, from a canoe in which five persons could not sit at their ease. We know that numbers perish in the attempt, either from the roughness of the weather or the wretched condition of their boats; and that many, upon being closely pursued by the guarda-costas, plunge into the deep, never to rise again, preferring death and a watery grave to the life and labour of bondage.*"

(BREEN 1844: 169-170)

Slave refugees from Martinique are also described in the thesis of BERNER (1984: 159-160). She confirms in general the above mentioned.

4.12.3   Subsistence

JEREMIE (1831: 51-52) reported in his published book that when he left St. Lucia in April 1831 the refugees from Martinique worked as masons and carpenters or domestics, others in cleaning land or as labourers on estates. Further he mentioned the erection of a pottery by the refugees; according to him the first in St. Lucia:

> "... whilst about twenty-six had clubbed together and placed themselves under the direction of a free coloured man, an African – one of the persons deported from Martinique in 1824. These last had erected a pottery at a short distance from Castries: they took a piece of land, three or four cleared it, others fished up coral and burnt lime, five or six quarried and got the stones and performed the mason-work, the remainder felled the timber and worked it in; and the little money that was requisite was supplied, in advance, by the contractor for the church, on the tiles to be furnished for the building. This pottery was completed, a plain structure but of great solidity, and surprising neatness. Thus had they actually introduced a new manufacture into the country, for which it was previously indebted to our foreign neighbours, or to the home market.

Further information of this pottery contains a book which was published in the year 1832 by an anonymous inhabitant of St. Lucia as comment to the book of JEREMIE published in 1831. The information is as follows:

> "The pottery scheme so eulogized, turned out to be a complete failure; the tiles for the church (the only one they fabricated) took several quite unsuccessful trials; the manufacture of them was at last abandoned; and some few pots, for negro utensils, is now all they endeavour to complete;"

(INHABITANT OF ST. LUCIA 1832: 86)

Governor DUDLEY HILL informed the SECRETARY OF STATE in London in a letter dated November 1834 about the refugees as follows:

> "... and I have the satisfaction of informing you that the whole band present for the most part a most gratifying appearance of comfort and content, are generally well clothed and gain their subsistence as Domestics, Tradesmen or Cultivators of land, peaceably and without the least inconvenience to the Government."

(CO 253/46/6: 4/11/1834)

Special information about the subsistence of the refugees from Martinique contains the reports of the STIPENDIARY MAGISTRATES which were made short before the end of the emancipation period by order of Governor MEIN.

1st district (Castries, Anse La Raye):

"All Refugees in this Island form, with few exceptions an indolent Class, whose ambition is only and general to be usurpers of small tracts of Land in the interior, where they grow provisions and burn charcoal for the market. The greater number constantly launching about the Streets in Castries satisfying their natural wants with the small stipends occasionally bestowed upon them by persons employing them ..."

(CO 253/62/6: 8/6/1838)

2nd district (Gros Islet, Dauphin):

"... there are from 50 to 60 Refugees, (with the exception of 5) – located upon lands either hired by them or have been abandoned (and of the latter are believed as a considerable quantity) where they are chiefly occupied in planting Provisions and burning Charcoal.

The five Individuals, before alluded to, are employed on the Grand Anse Estate as field labourers and receive a monthly allowance of 16/8 Stlg., with sufficient ground for gardens;"

(CO 253/62/7: 7/6/1838)

3rd district (Soufrière, Choiseul):

"Martinique Refugees, ... I have the honour to state that in the 3rd District there are not more than from twelve to fourteen of them resident and all of them are industrious and I can add sober in their habits – Three are employed in the Pirogues, two or three have made permanent engagements as agriculturists on some of the neighbouring Estates. The only female Refugee in this Quarter is an industrious washer-woman – and one Man is the head-workman in the newly established Pottery of Mr. Tesné. This last individual deserves much grace as he has introduced the manufacture of tiles, bricks &c., which promises much benefit to this Colony."

(CO 253/62/8: 18/6/1838)

4th district (Vieux Fort, Laborie):

"They are Logwood-Cutters, Charcoal-Burners, Squatters, Jobbers, Fishermen and Boatmen by terms as suits their convenience. They are anything and everything but field labourers, and prefer any mode of livelihood to that gained by steady industry;"

(CO 253/62/9: 14/6/1838)

5th district (Micoud, Praslin, Dennery):

"... that I have never entertained a favourable opinion of the Martinique Refugees, many acts said to have been committed by the Apprenticed Labourers, may with much more justice be attributed to these people – formerly this District was entirely free from them – within a year they have

spread over the Country without being under the slightest degree of surveillance – one day a party of them may be found at one point, the next gone; ... the monthly muster at Castries kept them near the Town, since this has fallen into disuse, they straggle where they please leading a wandering life – The greater part of their time passed in listless idleness – by night they traverse the Country after the Women, spreading the most absurd reports, at dances they perform a prominent part, keeping up intelligence with the runaway Apprentices, and informing them of all the movements of the Police &c."

(CO 253/62/10: 2/6/1838)

Graphic representation of the mentioned districts:

Division of districts extracted from a map of St. Lucia of the Year 1847 – BPP/CG/4/1: 1847, p.518)

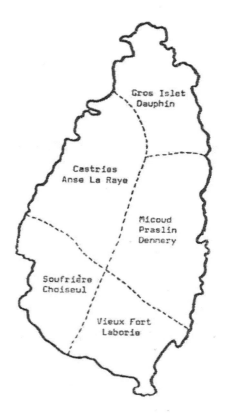

According to the mentioned reports only few refugees worked steadily on estates. The most of the refugees preferred a way of life independent from the estates. This might also be the reason why in some reports of the STIPENDIARY MAGISTRATES an antipathy against the refugees in general is shown.

To this independent way of life of the refugees pointed also the STIPENDIARY MAGISTRATE of the 5th district (Micoud, Praslin, Dennery) in the year 1843. From his report further follows that the refugees from Martinique were already partly integrated in the local black population of St. Lucia:

"Another Class which may be comprised amongst the Immigrants into this place are the fugitives from Slavery in the French Island of Martinique; and who are dispersed all over this Colony, they are restless wandering people now inhabiting one quarter of the Island, than flying to another, so that it would be a hopeless attempt to fix their number.

They carry their labour generally where Jobs are offered by the piece, such as in cleaning away lands preparatory to planting, or in weeding canes; those who located themselves for anything like a permanency on the plantation, or in the towns, or villages are so mixed up & cofounded with the Creoles of the place, that it becomes impossible to distinguish one from the other."

(CO 253/79/5: 7/8/1843)

4.12.4   Summary

According to the sources of the British colonial government the stream of slave refugees from Martinique to St. Lucia began in the years 1829 and 1830 and increased till the end of the emancipation period in the year 1838. The reason for their flight was the chance of getting their freedom when they arrived in St. Lucia. Another reason was slave insurrections in Martinique in the year 1831 which occurred because of a change in power in France (the "Revolution de Juillet"). The supporters of the revolution pleaded for freedom and equality of all human beings and they had a great influence on the slaves. The French government put these insurrections down and sentenced 22 persons to death by hanging. This caused the start of the essential stream of refugees to St. Lucia.

As no office for the registration of immigrants has been kept in St. Lucia till the emancipation period no exact figures are available. In the year 1831 about 200 refugees might have been in St. Lucia. Till the end of the emancipation period this figure raised to about 700 (the estimates vary from 600 to 800). After the end of the emancipation period when the refugees had to compete with 15.000 freed APPRENTICES on the labour market many of the refugees from Martinique emigrated to British Guiana and Trinidad. Since that period also the arrivals of refugees from Martinique to St. Lucia had become less frequent, owing partly to the increased vigilance of the authorities of Martinique, and partly to the prospect of approaching emancipation in the French colonies. When in the year 1848 the abolition of slavery was promulgated in the French colonies refugees living in St. Lucia returned to Martinique. But the arrival of refugees in St. Lucia still continued. In St. Lucia the refugees preferred a way of life independent from the estates. They cultivated provisions and burned charcoal for the market, worked as logwood-cutters, boatmen, fishers, masons, carpenters or domestics. Some also worked as labourers on estates. It is also said that they introduced the manufacture of pottery from Martinique to St. Lucia.
According to a report of the year 1843 a part of the refugees were already integrated in the local black population of St. Lucia.

5 The period after the emancipation (1838 –end of 19th century)

5.1 Population

5.1.1 Development and structure of population and distribution of the sexes

For showing the development of the population after the end of the period of slavery a review of the population figures from 1838 to 1871 will be given in the following by means of a table and a diagram. For the period from 1838 to 1850 the figures are stated yearly, and for the period from 1850 to 1871 only for the first, fifth and tenth year of a decade. In the first year of the respective decades a census was always made in St. Lucia.

In the report of the BLUE BOOKS the population of St. Lucia was divided into whites and "Coloured". BREEN and MARTIN adhered to the division into whites, "Coloured" and "Blacks" as in the period of slavery. Owing to the preponderance of the figures of the BLUE BOOKS as well as to the better possibility of comparison of the sources the division into whites and blacks is used in the following.

As mentioned in chapter "4.5.2. Development and structure of population", p. 71, in the tables of the BLUE BOOKS additional errors had been made sometimes which were not adopted by the author of this book. In some cases therefore the shown total diverges slightly from that of the BLUE BOOK. The relevant totals of the BUE BOOKS are shown in brackets (see footnotes) for information.

Year	WHITES Male Figure	%	Female Figure	%	TOTAL Figure	%	BLACKS Male Figure	%	Female Figure	%	TOTAL Figure	%	TOTAL POPULATION		SOURCE
1838	561	51	548	49	1.109	7	6.859	46	8.037	54	14.896	93	16.005	(16.017)	(CO 258/34/1: 1838/"Population"
1839	533	54	450	46	983	8	-	-	-	-	11.062	92	12.045		(CO 258/35/1: 1839/ "
1840	982	54	820	46	1.802	8	9.629	46	11.226	54	20.855	92	22.657		(CO 258/36/1: 1840/
1841	971	54	819	46	1.790	7	10.647	46	12.386	54	23.033	93	24.823		(CO 258/37/1: 1841/
1842	920	53	821	47	1.741	6	11.593	46	13.496	54	25.089	94	26.830	(26.630)	(CO 258/38/1: 1842/
1843	539	53	487	47	1.026	5	9.177	47	10.478	53	19.655	95	20.681	(20.694)	(CO 258/39/1: 1843/
1843	-	-	-	-	1.039	5	-	-	-	-	19.655	95	20.694		(BREEN 1844: 165)
1844	580	55	471	45	1.051	5	9.394	47	10.715	53	20.109	95	21.160	(21.180)	(CO 258/40/1: 1844/"Population"
1845	590	54	505	46	1.095	5	9.509	47	10.853	53	20.362	95	21.457		(CO 258/41/1: 1845/
1846	598	48	635	52	1.233	6	9.726	47	11.124	53	20.850	94	22.083		(CO 258/42/1: 1846/
1847	600	53	540	47	1.140	5	10.008	47	11.399	53	21.407	95	22.547	(22.545)	(CO 258/43/1: 1847/
1848	604	52	555	48	1.159	5	10.225	47	11.661	53	21.886	95	23.045		(CO 258/44/1: 1848/
1849	600	52	553	48	1.153	5	10.566	47	11.936	53	22.502	95	23.655		(CO 258/45/1: 1849/
1850	600	52	556	48	1.156	5	11.073	47	12.289	53	23.362	95	24.518	(24.516)	(CO 258/46/1: 1850/
1851	468	47	522	53	990	4	11.295	48	12.005	52	23.300	96	24.290		(CO 258/47/1: 1851/
1851	-	-	-	-	984	4	-	-	-	-	23.201	96	24.185		(MARTIN 1851-1857: IV, 125)
1855	430	46	513	54	943	4	11.501	47	12.786	53	24.287	96	25.230		(CO 258/51/1: 1855/"Population"
1860	320	44	400	56	720	3	12.435	48	13.490	52	25.925	97	26.645 *)		(CO 258/56/1: 1860/
1861	482	51	454	49	936	4	11.901	48	12.884	52	24.785	96	25.721 **)		(CO 258/57/1: 1861/
1865	440	49	452	51	892	3	14.095	49	14.457	51	28.552	97	29.444		(CO 258/61/1: 1865/
1870	394	48	433	52	827	3	15.486	48	16.683	52	32.169	97	32.996		(CO 258/66/1: 1870/
1871	-	-	-	-	837	3	-	-	-	-	30.773	97	31.610		(CO 258/67/1: 1871/

*) For the year 1860 496 Indian immigrants were stated in addition (Total population: 27.141)

**) For the year 1861 984 Indian immigrants were stated in addition (Total population: 26.705)

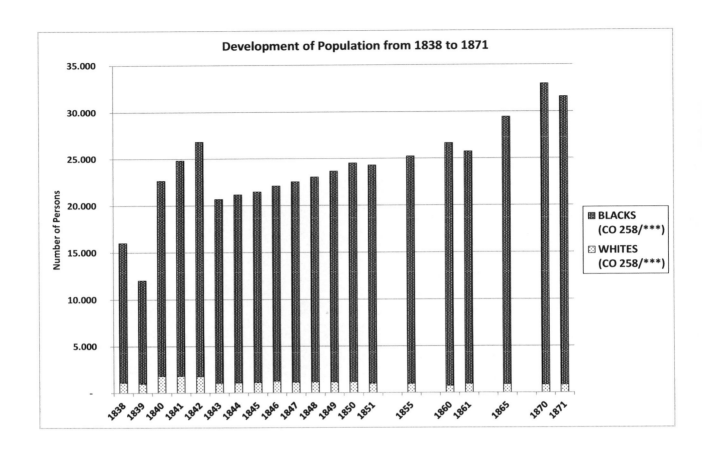

Development of Population from 1838 to 1871

According to the stated figures the share of the blacks varies between 92% and 97% whereas in general a rise of the black population can be shown. The share of the whites declined slightly.

Regarding the distribution of the sexes of the blacks there is a surplus of women. The share of the black women varies between 54% in the period after the emancipation till the year 1842 and 51% in the year 1865.

The strong deviations of the population of the blacks in the period from 1838 to 1843 are not explained in the sources. They probably follow from rough estimates. Regarding the difficulty of the British officials to receive correct population figures there are the following reports:

Report of the STIPENDIARY MAGISTRATE of the 1st district (Castries, Anse La Raye):

> *"There can be no doubt now as to the steady natural increase in the population; for altho' the present work of registration is very imperfect, it amply proves that the births exceed the deaths considerably."*

> (CO 253/79/1: 27/7/1843)

Additionally it is to mention that the figures of the BLUE BOOKS are based on censuses which were made in the 19th century in general every ten years (1851, 1861, 1871, …) and corrected every year on the bases of the births and deaths reported by the STIPENDIARY MAGISTRATES (CO 253/114/1: 20/6/1854).

The STIPENDIARY MAGISTRATE of the 2nd district (Gros Islet, Dauphin) reported in August 1843:

> *"The want of a compulsory measure and proper Officer to oblige parties to report Births and Deaths, when they do not obtain the rites of baptisms, …, makes it almost impossible to furnish a correct report on these heads."*

> (CO 253/79/2: 1/8/1843)

Owing to the incorrect population figures Governor CLARKE of St. Lucia ordered a census in August 1843:

> *"Conceiving that the Return of the Population in the Blue Book for 1842 was exceedingly incorrect and being informed that no means had been adopted since emancipation for ascertaining the number of inhabitants; in the month of August last, I issued a proclamation, for the taking off a Census, this was accordingly done and I have every reason to believe that the return of the Population exhibited in the Blue Book for 1843, is near the truth."*

> (CO 253/81/1: 30/3/1844)

A fact which rendered the registration of births and deaths difficult was the geographic situation of the island itself. Governor TORRENS of St. Lucia described this situation in a letter to the Governor of Barbados in March 1845 as follows:

> *"I have had an opportunity of visiting every quarter of the island, and I have convinced myself of the great difficulty of establishing an efficient system, in consequence of the inaccessible nature of many parts of the country, and the widely scattered manner in which the population is therein diffused. The present registry is certainly not to be depended on, especially with respect to deaths; many persons dying, and being buried in distant and wild localities, unknown to the magistrate or the cure. I am, however, considering this subject."*

> (CO 253/83/1: 3/3/1845)

In January 1846 Governor TORRENS referred to a population report of 1844 which he doubted as follows:

> *"The present population of St. Lucia is officially computed at 21.457. The census of 1844 gave 21.001 as the total, probably, however, far below the real amount. The difficulty may be imagined with slight administrative means of enumerating a population, which, though scanty, occupies an extent of mountainous and wooded country of 150 miles in circumference; a difficulty then further aggravated by the apprehension of the negroes that the measure was preparatory to the reimposition of a poll-tax, with*

which former experience rendered them already familiar. Hence many evasions and inevitable inaccuracy. This will account for the uncertainty with which I report the present numbers of the people.

(CO 253/85/1: 4/1/1846)

In the year 1850 Governor DARLING of St. Lucia mentioned the uncertainty of the stated population figures:

"The population of the island is estimated at 23.688 souls, being an increase of 643 upon the return of the previous year. The arrival of 362 liberated Africans accounts for the larger proportion of this increase; and I have little doubt that the remainder (281) is far from representing the actual augmentation of the Creole population, although the ravages of the small-pox which, having been introduced into the island in the month of October 1848, has now taken root amongst us, have much increased the ordinary rate of mortality."

(CO 253/103/1: 29/4/1850)

From his letter further follows that many persons died by the bite of the snake "Fer-de-Lance":

"The mortality from small-pox accounts for a large portion of the increase under the latter head, and I am concerned to add that no less than 19 persons are reported in one small parish of the island alone to have been destroyed by the bites of the venomous serpent, known as the "Fer de Lance", or "craspedocephalus lanceolatus", with which this island and the neighbouring colony of Martinique is abound."

Also Governor GRANT of St. Lucia doubted the figures of the censuses. This follows from his letter dated June 1862 as follows:

"According to the Census taken in 1843, the population of the Island amounted to 20.694; in 1851, ..., it amounted to 24.185; showing an increase in eight years of 3.491; whereas, comparing the population of 1851 with that shown by the Census of 1861, after throwing in the number of persons supposed to have died from cholera, the increase in ten years was only 3.536.

The conclusion then seems inevitable that the Census was badly taken, and such is the prevailing opinion. The sum allowed for the purpose was, in a country like St. Lucia, insufficient, and so consequently was the machinery employed."

(CO 253/130/1: 30/6/1862)

5.1.2 Distribution of population

For showing the development of the population in St. Lucia after the emancipation period three detailed population tables from the BLUE BOOKS were used. Both population reports of the years 1838 (CO 258/34/1: 1838/"Population") and 1845 (CO 258/41/1: 1845/"Population") could be compared because of the same division of the districts. The population table in the BLUE BOOK of 1861 (CO 258/57/1: 1861/"Population") was chosen because of the detailed statements – In this year a census had been made.

The following tables and diagrams were made:

District	WHITES				BLACKS				TOTAL			
	1838		1845		1838		1845		1838		1845	
	figure	%	figure	%	figure	%	figure	%	figure	%	figure	%
1st district:												
Castries, Anse la Raye	405	37	368	34	4.111	28	6.866	34	4.516	28	7.234	34
2nd district												
Gros Islet, Dauphin	76	7	46	4	1.803	12	2.402	12	1.879	12	2.448	11
3rd district												
Soufrière, Choiseul	406	37	517	47	3.352	23	5.460	27	3.758	23	5.977	28
4th district												
Vieux Fort, Laborie	180	16	130	12	3.750	25	3.352	16	3.930	25	3.482	16
5th district												
Micoud, Praslin, Dennery	42	4	34	3	1.880	13	2.282	11	1.922	12	2.316	11
TOTAL	1.109	100	1.095	100	14.896	100	20.362	100	16.005	100	21.457	100

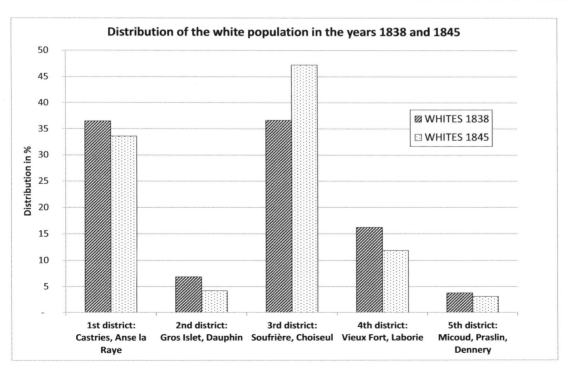

245

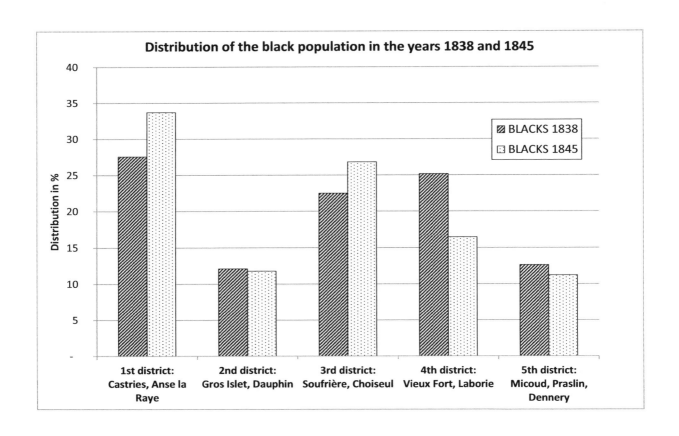

Distribution of the black population in the years 1838 and 1845

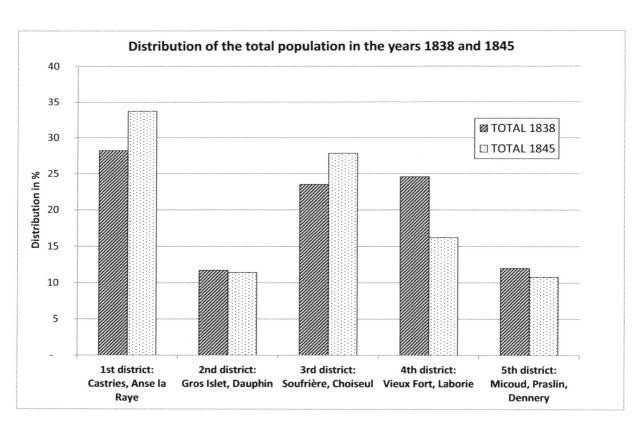

Distribution of the total population in the years 1838 and 1845

District	WHITES		BLACKS		INDIANS *)		TOTAL	
	figure	%	figure	%	figure	%	figure	%
1st. district								
Town Castries	288	31	3.191	13	35	4	3.514	13
Area Castries, Anse La Raye	206	22	3.932	16	135	14	4.273	16
Total	**494**	**53**	**7.123**	**29**	**170**	**17**	**7.787**	**29**
							-	
2nd district							-	
Town Gros Islet	5	1	581	2		-	586	2
Area Gros Islet, Dauphin, Dennery	36	4	3.631	15	137	14	3.804	14
Total	**41**	**4**	**4.212**	**17**	**137**	**14**	**4.390**	**16**
							-	
3rd district							-	
Town Soufrière	145	15	1.646	7	2	0	1.793	7
Area Soufrière, Choiseul, part of Laborie	173	18	7.153	29	453	46	7.779	29
Total	**318**	**34**	**8.799**	**36**	**455**	**46**	**9.572**	**36**
							-	
4th district							-	
Town Vieux Fort	23	2	851	3		-	874	3
Area of Vieux Fort, Micoud, Praslin, part of Laborie	60	6	3.800	15	222	23	4.082	15
Total	**83**	**9**	**4.651**	**19**	**222**	**23**	**4.956**	**19**
Total all districts	**936**	**100**	**24.785**	**100**	**984**	**100**	**26.705**	**100**

(compiled by means of the source CO 258/57/1: 1861/"Population")

*) From the year 1859 Indian immigrants were imported to St. Lucia as contract workers; cp. p. 344-345.

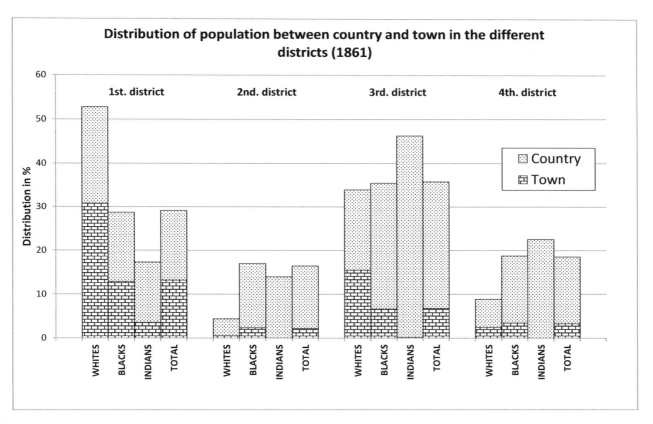

Distribution of population between country and town in the different districts (1861)

Explanations to the diagram Town/Country:

1st District:
Town CASTRIES   Country: Area Castries, Anse La Raye

2nd district:
Town Gros Islet   Country: Area Gros Islet, Dauphin, Dennery

3rd district:
Town Soufrière   Country: Area Soufrière, Choiseul, part of Laborie

4th district:
Town Vieux Fort   Country: Area of Vieux Fort, Micoud, Praslin, part
                                              of Laborie

According to these tables and diagrams the following can be stated:

Total population

In the year 1838 the area Castries/Anse La Raye had with 28% the highest portion of the population of St. Lucia. The areas Vieux Fort/Laborie with a portion of 25% and Soufrière/Choiseul with 23% followed. The most sparsely populated areas were Gros Islet/Dauphin and Micoud/Praslin/Dennery with a portion of 12% each.

In the year 1845 the portion of the population had raised in the area Castries/Anse La Raye from 28% to 34% and in the area Soufrière/Choiseul from 23% to 28%. The area Vieux Fort/Laborie had a decline in population from 25% to 16%. The most sparsely populated areas Gros Islet/Dauphin and Micoud/Praslin/Dennery showed a decline in population of 1% absolute each.

According to the population figures of the year 1861 Soufrière/Choiseul/Part of Laborie was with a share of 37% the most populated area. The area of Castries/Anse La Raye with 29% followed. The remaining areas showed portions of population of 16% and 18%.

Black Population

In accordance to the high portion of the blacks in the total population of St. Lucia (92% - 97%) follows a similar distribution as the total population. In the first both years of comparison Castries/Anse La Raye had the highest portion of black population: in the year 1838 with 28% and in the year 1845 with 34%. The portions of the other areas in the year 1838 were as follows:

-   Vieux Fort, Laborie: 25%
-   Soufrière, Choiseul: 22%

- Micoud, Praslin, Dennery: 13%
- Gros Islet, Dauphin: 12%

In the year 1845 the second highest portion of population (27%) had moved from Vieux Fort/Laborie to Soufrière/Choiseul. The area Vieux Fort/Laborie showed a decline in population of 9% absolute. Also the area Micoud/Praslin/Dennery had a decline in population of 2% absolute. The portion of the area Gros Islet/Dauphin was unchanged.

In the year 1861 the area Soufrière/Choiseul/Part of Laborie had with 36% the highest portion of the black population. The area Castries/Anse La Raye with a portion of 29% followed. The remaining areas showed portions of 17% and 18%.

White population

In the year 1838 the white population was concentrated in the areas Castries/Anse La Raye and Soufrière/Choiseul with a portion of 36,5% each. In the area Vieux Fort/Laborie settled 16% of all whites. The lowest portions showed the areas Gros Islet/Dauphin with 7% and Micoud/Praslin/Dennery with 4%.

In the year 1845 the area Soufrière/Choiseul had with 47% the highest portion of the white population. Castries/Anse La Raye with a portion of 34% followed. The other areas showed in general slight declines in population. The portion of the population of Gros Islet/Dauphin declined from 7% to 4%, of Vieux Fort/Laborie from 16% to 12% and of Micoud/Praslin/Dennery from 4% to 3%.

According to the figures of the year 1861 Castries/Anse La Raye was with a portion of 53% the main settlement area of the whites. The area Soufrière/Choiseul/Part of Laborie with a portion of 34% followed. The other areas showed together a portion of 13%.

Indians

With the ship PALMYRA the first Indian labourers came to St. Lucia in 1859. They were 318 persons (COMINS 1893: 3). According to the population table of the year 1861 their number had risen already to 984 persons. The portion of Indians in the several districts was as follows:

- Soufrière, Choiseul, Part of Laborie: 46,2%
- Vieux Fort, Micoud, Praslin, Part of Laborie: 22,6%
- Castries, Anse La Raye: 17,3%
- Gros Islet, Dauphin, Dennery: 13,9%

Distribution of population "Town[21] - Country"

According to the population figures of the year 1861 49,5% of the whites, 25% of the blacks and 3,8% of the Indians lived in the following towns: Castries, Gros Islet, Soufrière and Vieux Fort. The percentages regarding the several towns were as follows:

	WHITES	BLACKS	INDIANS
CASTRIES	31 %	13%	3,6%
GROS ISLET	0,5%	2%	-
SOUFRIÈRE	15,5%	7%	0,2%
VIEUX FORT	2,5%	3%	-
TOTAL	49,5%	25%	3,8%

Concerning the total population there were the following percentages of town inhabitants:

CASTRIES	13%
GROS ISLET	2%
SOUFRIÈRE	8%
VIEUX FORT	3%
TOTAL	26%

---

[21] The population of the towns/villages Anse La Raye, Choiseul, Laborie, Micoud, Praslin, Dennery and Dauphin were counted in the sources to the country population.

5.2 Economy

5.2.1 Economic development

5.2.1.1   Development of the export produces

For showing a review of the exports of St. Lucia after the end of the emancipation period the following three tables (A, B, and C) were made.

Table A comprises the period from 1838 to 1870 and was made by means of the yearly reports in the BLUE BOOKS. Regarding the reliability of the figures of the BLUE BOOKS the author refers to the quotation from the BLUE BOOK dated in the year 1839 in which a British official wrote of the impossibility to get accurate returns because of the ignorance of the police men and wilful misrepresentations made by many of the proprietors (cp. chapter "4.6.3.1. Tabular review and diagrams of the exports", p.88).

Table B was extracted from the book publication of BREEN (1844: 319). It covers the period from 1836 to 1843.

A further source was a statement of HER MAJESTY'S TREASURER M'HUGH (table C) which was published for the British parliament in London. It refers to the period from 1839 to 1856.

After a graphical representation of the development of the export produces by means of tables and diagrams a comparison of this development with general reports was made.

Table A

Year	Sugar lbs. 1)	Coffee lbs.	Cocoa lbs.	Cotton lbs.	Rum galls 1)	Molasses galls.	Source
1838	5.822.000	82.012	38.550	300	82.064	136.360	(CO 258/34/1: 1838/"Agricul.")
1839	4.050.003	325.275	72.250	-	72.510	111.660	(CO 258/35/1: 1839/"Agricul.")
1840	4.453.033	48.002	35.133	750	67.820	69.794	(CO 258/36/1: 1840/"Agricul.")
1841	6.036.290	35.787	48.400	-	91.925	120073	(CO 258/37/1: 1841/"Agricul.")
1842	6.844.210	144.625	6.950	1.000	113.146	216.826	(CO 258/38/1: 1842/"Agricul.")
1843	5.090.130	77.788	6.200	482	70.955	131.576	(CO 258/39/1: 1843/"Agricul.")
1844	7.294.770	50.593	26.700	538	112.689	185.510	(CO 258/40/1: 1844/"Agricul.")
1845	7.780.270	65.475	11.440	300	108.864	183.073	(CO 258/41/1: 1845/"Agricul.")
1846	6.148.540	46.227	18.524	280	83.524	138.533	(CO 258/42/1: 1846/"Agricul.")
1847	8.684.265	36.695	19.912	50	106.048	121.759	(CO 258/43/1: 1847/"Agricul.")
1848	6.221.500	25.140	29.420	-	58.104	136.525	(CO 258/44/1: 1848/"Agricul.")
1849	6.157.352	25.000	27.000	200	46.932	192.980	(CO 258/45/1: 1849/"Agricul.")
1850	5.527.912	4.600	14.650	300	104.000	140.280	(CO 258/46/1: 1850/"Agricul.")
1851	6.691.800	18.620	15.143	-	45.058	159.540	(CO 258/47/1: 1851/"Agricul.")
1852	7.130.560	25.938	40.350	-	66.929	206.540	(CO 258/48/1: 1852/"Agricul.")
1853	6.782.700	6.051	21.600	-	58.348	214.712	(CO 258/49/1: 1853/"Agricul.")
1854	7.414.100	10.250	17.480	-	77.751	208.625	(CO 258/50/1: 1854/"Agricul.")
1855	6.683.867	7.732	60.880	-	75.373	176.151	(CO 258/51/1: 1855/"Agricul.")
1856	6.285.660	8.236	42.106	-	86.052	183.721	(CO 258/52/1: 1856/"Agricul.")
1857	6.262.095	6.866	101.696	-	49.957	173.435	(CO 258/53/1: 1857/"Agricul.")
1858	7.240.668	45.050	79.902	-	80.866	166.442	(CO 258/54/1: 1858/"Agricul.")
1859	7.202.937	6.093	80.350	-	63.533	207.839	(CO 258/55/1: 1859/"Agricul.")
1860	7.788.051	16.358	120.213	540	54.801	284.404	(CO 258/56/1: 1860/"Agricul.")
1861	8.715.928	4.290	76.840	-	46.043	162.700	(CO 258/57/1: 1861/"Agricul.")
1862	8.770.174	2.820	15.108	980	42.101	148.868	(CO 258/58/1: 1862/"Agricul.")
1863	9.527.768	2.897	156.338	3.400	61.066	114.456	(CO 258/59/1: 1863/"Agricul.")
1864	8.342.761	680	62.040	7.200	40.308	191.948	(CO 258/60/1: 1864/"Agricul.")
1865	9.191.401	9.887	161.557	8.236	58.602	192.843	(CO 258/61/1: 1865/"Agricul.")
1866	10.627.422	1.105	168.116	3.520	55.011	437.774	(CO 258/62/1: 1866/"Agricul.")
1867	8.776.512	200	151.194	-	36.495	420.810	(CO 258/63/1: 1867/"Agricul.")
1868	10.402.898	250	129.625	-	35.395	434.950	(CO 258/64/1: 1868/"Agricul.")
1869	10.766.590	11.692	54.155	700	51.127	144.058	(CO 258/65/1: 1869/"Agricul.")
1870	12.444.136	441	258.000	100	56.724	153.088	(CO 258/66/1: 1870/"Agricul.")

1) 1 Pound (lb.) = 453,59 grams, 1 Gallone (gall.) = 4.5459 litres; cp. Chapter "2.3 List of used British measuring and weight units", p. 23)

(compiled by means of the BLUE BOOKS)

Table B

Year	Sugar	Coffee	Cocoa	Rum	Molasses	Logwood
	lbs. 1)	lbs.	lbs.	galls 1)	galls.	tons 1)
1938	5.533.320	135.008	38.590	6.930	110.002	109
1939	5.151.108	145.832	54.639	11.340	119.300	218
1940	3.683.820	303.820	82.293	9.900	73.200	206
1941	4.677.350	67.251	78.225	10.900	103.800	132
1942	6.384.365	144.791	55.175	9.910	124.900	102
1943	5.065.195	35.320	48.279	180	112.340	40

1) 1 Pound (lb.) = 453,59 grams, 1 Gallone (gall.) = 4.5459 litres, 1 long ton = 1.016,05 kilograms; cp. Chapter "2.3 List of used British measuring and weight units", p. 23)

(extracted from BREEN 1844: 319)

Table C

Year	Sugar	Coffee	Molasses	Rum	Firewood	Logwood	Cocoa	Manioc
	lbs. 1)	lbs.	galls. 1)	galls	"Cords" 1)	tons 1)	lbs	brls
1839	3.487.000	448.650	122.800	1.200	55	195	91.280	-
1840	3.625.500	411.000	67.000	13.200	115	197	105.450	-
1841	4.782.400	82.704	101.300	13.300	175	130	68.656	-
1842	6.461.000	59.100	127.200	9.200	158	131	55.650	-
1843	7.283.360	48.379	136.310	236	179	56	80.961	-
1844	6.983.300	25.312	111.800	11.200	168	51	44.800	-
1845	7.041.100	67.078	99.700	17.000	287	69	130.592	-
1846	5.224.800	65.856	197.420	3.559	351	82	123.456	-
1847	10.512.422	48.363	166.021	43.468	167	167	105.476	-
1848	6.533.968	19.722	120.822	13.921	399	180	107.512	-
1849	7.874.832	31.471	104.042	5.391	467	97	104.912	-
1850	6.530.608	11.722	105.774	840	452	148	89.635	-
1851	7.560.224	25.979	122.158	958	300	156	122.875	-
1852	7.113.904	30.520	151.130	3.400	474	93	134.721	1.437
1853	6.883.072	16.068	166.850	2.890	310	365	186.782	463
1854	6.635.045	145	106.200	12.500	325	1.154	161.216	24
1855	6.356.821	745	102.035	38.848	200	1.294	137.931	-
1856	5.693.435	-	91.220	28.572	56	1.519	209.729	-

1) 1 Pound (lb.) = 453,59 grams, 1 Gallone (gall.) = 4.5459 litres, 1 cord = 1.120 pounds or 3,62 m³, 1 ton (long ton) = 1016,05kg, 1 "barrel" (brl.) = 163,656 l; cp. Chapter "2.3 List of used British measuring and weight units", p. 23)

(extracted from the table made by His Mayesty's Treasurer M'HUGH)

Diagrams:

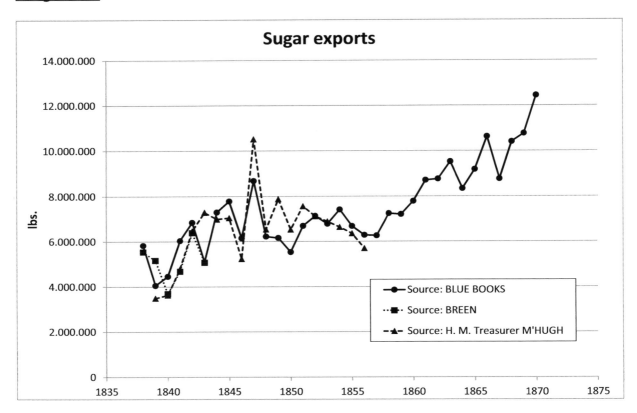

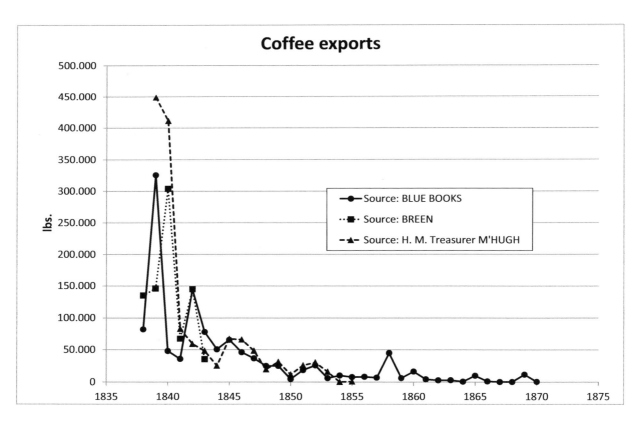

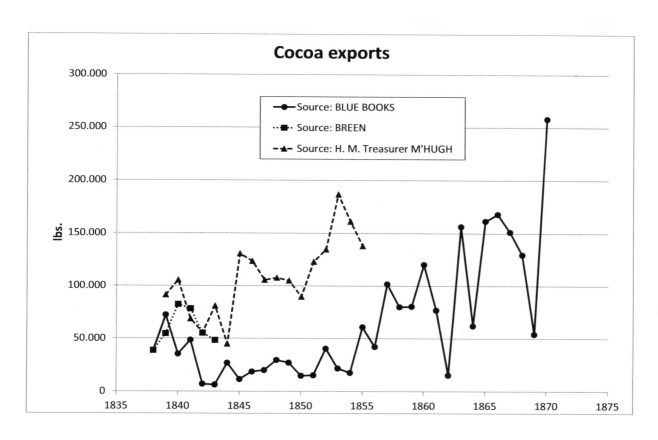

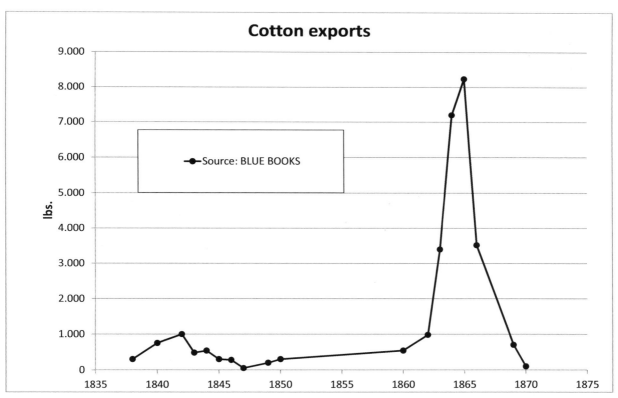

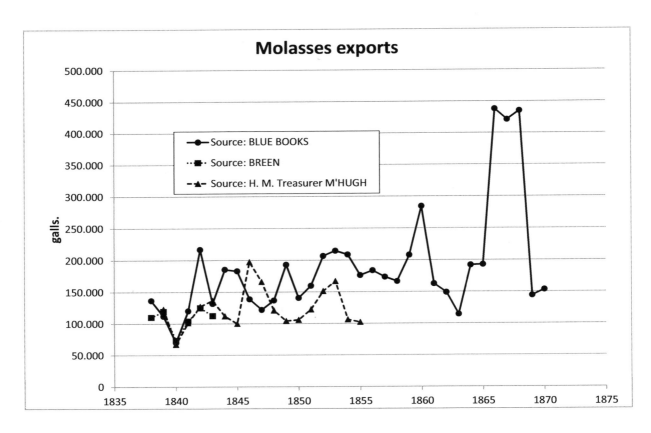

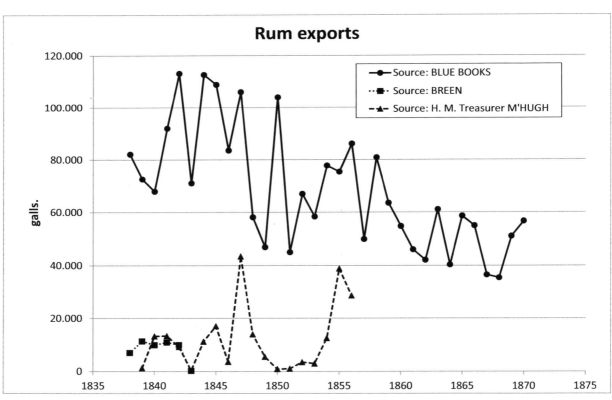

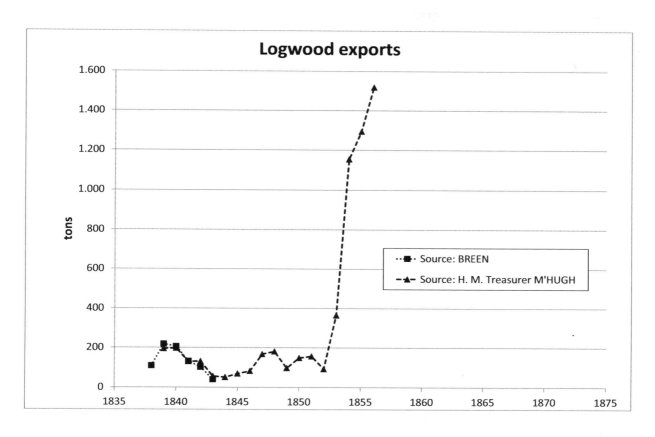

According to the available export figures at the end of the emancipation period sugar, coffee, cocoa, molasses and rum were the main export produces of St. Lucia. Further fire- and logwood was exported. The export of cotton had very little significance.

The export figures of sugar show from 1838 to 1860 a steady trend although there were also considerable variations. Up from 1860 there was a general raise in the export of sugar.

Whereas coffee lost in significance the produce of cocoa gained in significance.

BREEN (1844: 294-295) refers to St. Lucia's export products as follows:

> "The chief exports at the present day are sugar, coffee, cocoa, rum, molasses and logwood."

He further mentions the insignificance of cotton:

> "Cotton, once a staple production, has been totally discontinued, although it still grows wild in many parts of the island."

Regarding the commercial relations of St. Lucia he points to the United Kingdom, "British North America" (= Canada and the remaining areas of the British colonies in North America), Barbados, Martinique and the United States (BREEN 1844: 311).

A petition of 225 inhabitants of St. Lucia from the year 1847 refers to the significance of sugar production and the abandonment of the cultivation of coffee and cotton:

> "That the maintenance of the social position of your Petitioners, and that of all the other Inhabitants of Saint Lucia, depends on the profitable cultivation of the Cane and the Manufacture of Sugar.
>
> That your Petitioners ever since the Emancipation of the Slaves by the Imperial Parliament have continued the cultivation of the soil; struggling under great and increased difficulties.
>
> That these difficulties arise from excessive, and increasing local taxation, imposed by an irresponsible body, selected solely by the Crown; and from the high rate of the wages of labour – which have already caused the Cotton and Coffee cultivation to be abandoned in this Island; being driven out of the Market by the same articles produced by Slave-labour."

(CO 253/91/1: 21/10/1847)

The significance of sugar especially up from the year 1860 as well as the general lost in significance of coffee is confirmed by a letter of Governor BREEN dated in May 1861 as follows:

"Sugar is now the only staple exported from St. Lucia. Some years ago coffee was cultivated to a considerable extent, but owing, on the one hand, to the blight which injured the plant in many places, and, on the other, to the more certain prospect of gain held out by cane cultivation, the principal coffee plantations have been abandoned or converted into sugar estates."

(CO 253/128/1: 25/5/1861)

Further he mentioned the doubling of sugar estates within a short period:

"Till within a comparatively recent period the number of sugar estates in St. Lucia was only 80. To these may now be added upwards of 80 others, some of them of considerable extent, which had been established within the last few years, and which owe their existence mainly to the stimulating influence of the sugar market."

Finally he informed of two gentlemen who attempted to export sulphur:

"Among the minor articles of export in 1860 I may mention that of sulphur. Some years ago two enterprising gentlemen from Antigua commenced working the sulphur beds of St. Lucia. Their plan was to dig out the sulphur, together with the earth in which it is embedded, and ship it in that condition. This process was soon found to be anything but remunerative, and after some further experiments the undertaking was abandoned."

By the rise of the export figures of sugar up from approximately 1860 a general economic progress of St. Lucia is shown. In 1870 Governor DES VOEUX referred in a letter to this development:

"In the present year there has been the largest crop of sugar ever produced in the Island ...

On the whole the Island appears to be advancing towards prosperity, slowly indeed but steadily. The exports of produce are, as I have said, greater now than in the days of slavery, and greater even then when the largest number of Indian Immigrants was present. This is partly no doubt owing to the natural increase of population, but partly, I hope, to increasing industry on the part of the labourers, and a greater disposition to conciliate them on the part of planters."

(CO 253/145/1: 18/11/1870)

5.2.1.2 Labour situation and effects of the free labour market after the end of the emancipation period (1838-1846)

In the period from August 1st, 1838, till the end of this year many planters mainly complained because of the lack of labourers; many former APPRENTICES refused to work on the estates. Further complaints of the planters referred to the high wages they had to pay to the labourers as well as to unsatisfactory execution of the work. This information follows from some articles of the newspaper PALLADIUM:

> "The labourers of a few estates are at work at high wages, the planters having determined upon risking everything on the out-set, in the hope of time bringing on some favourable change. Various arrangements have been entered into by masters and labourers. The latter obtain from $ 2 to $ 8 monthly wages, being so much extra upon all the ancient indulgences granted them; and for this, they give from 6 to 9 hours' daily labour. Unfortunately, however, this is not the extent generally to be desired. There is not one plantation in the island that has succeeded in obtaining a full complement of working hands. Even on some estates, where proprietors have admitted the labourers to the enjoyment of one-third of the proceeds, numbers have declined to work."

(N/CO 258/1/1: 15/9/1838, p.2)

> "Two-thirds of the labouring population refuse to work, whilst the working portion are with difficulty retained with exorbitant wages and unheard of indulgences."

(N/CO 258/1/2: 22/9/1838, p.3)

> "The labourers are becoming a little better disposed. Although there remain many estates that are almost completely depopulated, yet, there are some working tolerably well; so that, it may hence be concluded that the newly-freed people begin to comprehend the nature of their obligations."

(N/CO 258/1/3: 4/10/1838, p.6)

> "Now that the labourers are all free, and have the encouragement of high wages to induce the exercise of industrious habits; though we hear occasionally of a whole gang refusing to fulfil its engagement with its employer; or, that those who do turn out upon estates, are perfectly careless whether the quantity of labour they give be satisfactory or not5; we are not worse than many of our neighbours. It is a fact that high wages hold out no inducement to the newly freed people to put aside their idle habits. Still, however, work is not totally abandoned."

(N/CO 258/1/4: 15/12/1838, p.20)

Two reports of the STIPENDIARY MAGISTRATES of April 1839 refer to a bad working morale of the labourers:

Report of the STIPENDIARY MAGISTRATE of the 2nd district (Gros Islet, Dauphin):

"... that the Labouring Population in the district under my charge are orderly and well behaved, but at the same time I regret to say that they do not anything like perform, the terms of their Contracts; in the first place by not turning out to work at proper hour whereby they do not give a full day's work, and secondly by their totally absenting themselves from their Employer's service for several days together; in consequence, as far as I have been able to ascertain, a considerable portion of the Crop on some Estates must remain uncut."

(CO 253/67/3: 5/4/1839)

Report of the STIPENDIARY MAGISTRATE of the 4th district (Vieux Fort, Laborie):

"Generally speaking the Labourers do not honestly fulfil the conditions of the Contracts entered into by them; - that is to say generally speaking they don't work steadily and continuously, the slightest cause suffices to excuse their absence from labour, and when actually working I regret to say that they labour with a nonchalance which must be very detrimental to their Employer."

(CO 253/67/4: 9/4/1839)

Governor EVERARD of St. Lucia substantiated in his letter to the Governor of Barbados of June 1839 the bad relationship of the labourers to the work on the estates as follows:

"- Original ill-treatment on the part of the Master towards his Slave, so long as servitude existed; and no attempt subsequently made during Apprenticeship, to break down the great barrier of distinction which separated the one from the other, or to prepare their minds for the great change then in contemplation, the result is therefore, safe evident that on final Emancipation, the Negro, having no kindly feeling to bind him to his late Master, naturally looked out for a settlement of his own; And from the many persons who possess large tracts of land uncultivated, they easily obtained, and still obtain as much as they require, and become settled thereon, and instead of paying Money as rent, the Proprietor is ready and willing to receive, in lieu thereof, a portion of the product of the Soil ...

The Gangs throughout the Colony have become factious and unsettled from the heart-burning recollection that they were necessitated to purchase their manumission, even up to the last moment prior to final Emancipation: This consequence might have been prevented, if the Planter at that time, had in the spirit of a more liberal Policy bestowed his freedom as a reward on the most deserving and industrious, instead of forcing the negro (notwithstanding the Planter had already received his full value by compensation) to purchase the unexpired term of his Apprenticeship, with the little means he had accumulated by economy and frugal habits, for his further wants and comforts.

It is not therefore, singular that on the attainment of his Liberty, he quitted the employ of his Master and settled in the above mentioned lands."

This opinion of the planters follows from the introduction of the right of the slave to purchase his freedom also against the will of his master (cp. chapter "4.7.4.4. Manumission", pp. 159-160).

Further the Governor mentioned the different wages which were offered by the planters:

> *"The Proprietary Body have never come to any fixed or settled management with regard to the amount of wages to be paid to the Labourers, these (wages) therefore vary according to the exigencies of the moment and the Labourer roams from one Estate to another wherever the highest price is offered for his labour, instead of being fixed and permanent."*

(CO 253/67/2: 20/6/1839)

According to an article of the newspaper PALLADIUM of October 1839 the crop yields of the year 1839 were lower than that of the year 1838. The exports of both years were compared as follows:

	Sugar	Coffee
1838	3.635 Hogshead	1.831 Bags
1839	3.146 "	1.565 "
Decline	489 Hogshead	266 Bags

(N/CO 258/1/5: 5/10/1839, p.73)

As reason for this decline in exports it was mentioned that labour could not have been obtained to the extent required.

Additionally it is to point out that according to the export figures stated in the before mentioned chapter on pp. 252-254 in the export of sugar there was also a decline but in the export of coffee a slight rise was shown.

On September 4th, 1839, the INDEPENDENT PRESS of St. Lucia published an article which described the labour situation on the estates as follows:

> *"The injudicious anxiety evinced by the generality of the Proprietors in this Colony, encouraged as it was by the ready assistance afforded them by the Special Magistrates, led most of them, immediately after the first of August, 1838, to bind their labourers by contracts, stipulating a very low rate of wages but like all undue attempts to impose restraint upon an equitable adjustment of the labour market, they have so signally failed in their attempts to enforce the fulfilment of the bond (even the penal enactments imposing imprisonment and hard labour for breach of a civil contract; sanctioned by a Royal Order in Council, and rigorously enforced by the Special Magistrates, having been found insufficient) that the opinion*

seems to be now pretty generally established, that it is more advantageous, to both parties to have a free labour market. Many of the contracts entered into by the labourers have now expired, but many more have been cancelled by mutual consent. Since the commencement of this second year of liberty, we have visited most of the districts of the Island, and we have found the labourers quite disposed to enter into arrangements with the proprietors for the cultivation of the Estates. – it is true they will not again enter into yearly contracts at the rate of two or three dollars' wages per month, but they are willing to pay rent for their houses and gardens and to perform contract work upon terms which we consider highly advantageous to the Proprietor. It must not however be concealed, that in this Colony, as well as elsewhere, we hear bitter complaints from certain quarters, of the utter impossibility of cultivating estates under the new system."

Regarding the working morale of the labourers the following was written:

"- at present we can only say, that where our labourers have been dealt with frankly and honestly, and let us add , civilly, they have evinced corresponding virtues, they have been steady and industrious in the performance of their labours, and respectful in their bearing towards their employers."

(N/BL/ND/C.misc.425 (2): 4/9/1839)

In the second half of the year 1839 there was a general amelioration of the labour situation on the estates. Extracts of the reports of the STIPENDIARY MAGISTRATES of the several districts are as follows:

1st district (Castries, Anse La Raye):

"With the exception of those Estates where a Contract still exists very few complaints are brought against the Labouring Population by their employers, and the Planters generally are satisfied; I find that on the Estates where a Contract is still in force the work is by far more irregular and also no increase in the number of Labourers."

(CO 253/68/1: 5/11/1839)

2nd district (Gros Islet, Dauphin):

"The monthly Report of this District for October is highly satisfactory, in as much as it presents the cultivation of the several Estates, in an advanced state, as regards the Crop about to be reaped, as also that planted for 1841."

(CO 253/68/2: 1/11/1839)

3rd district (Soufrière, Choiseul):

"I should certainly say, that there is on all sites a much greater feeling of confidence generally than last August."

(CO 253/68/3: August 1839)

"The number of Labourers on the respective Properties remains the same as in the last month and on the Coffee Estates they are busily engaged in gathering in the Crop which promises to be very abundant."

(CO 253/68/4: 4/11/1839)

4th district (Vieux Fort, Laborie):

"I should say that a good feeling exists between Master and Servant;"

(CO 253/68/5: 3/9/1839)

5th district (Micoud, Praslin, Dennery):

"I have the honour to report that during past month not one case of Complaint either from Employer or Labourer has been preferred to me in the 5th District during that period – I am sorry to observe that the Labourers altho' tranquil still show little inclination to work like honest men for their wages:"

(CO 253/68/6: 3/8/1839)

Graphic representation of the mentioned districts:

(Division of districts extracted from a map of St. Lucia from the year 1847 –BPP/CG/4/1: 1847, p.518)

In the newspaper PALLADIUM the bad financial situation of the planters was mentioned:

"From the unwillingness of the peasantry to enter upon contract or task-work – the slovenly and imperfect manner in which that work, when undertaken, is performed by them – and the exorbitant wages which proprietors are at all times obliged to give, - the crop cannot pay the expense of its production … Many estates are hastening to ruin. Amongst these may be mentioned the Roseau and the River Doré – two of the most productive estates of former days."

(N/CO 258/1/6: 21/12/1839, p.89)

In the year 1841 there was a further amelioration in the relationship planter – labourer. This had its favourable effect on the agriculture of St. Lucia. Extracts of reports of the STIOPENDIARY MAGISTRATES of the several districts are as follows:

1st district (Castries, Anse La Raye):

"Generally speaking, the best possible understanding exists between the peasantry and their employers; …

The crop, which is nearly now terminated, has been more abundant than last year's, and a considerable augmentation has been made to the plantations for next crop, and which, from present appearance, is expected to be still more fruitful than the present. The weather latterly has been very favourable."

(CO 253/74/1: 1/10/1841)

2nd district (Gros Islet, Dauphin):

"… that the proprietor has not suffered greatly by the measure of emancipation, for it appears that cultivation of the staple product of the island, instead of receding, has advanced, …

That the cultivation of the cane has not diminished is evident on the face of every estate, some of them having augmented considerably their cane-fields, as in the case of the Union, Corinthe, and Choc estates of this district, where from 40 to 60 acres have been added to the cultivated land since the abolition of slavery."

(CO 253/73/1: 2/4/1841)

"A decided and general improvement has taken place both in the character and condition of the labourer."

(CO 253/74/2: 20/9/1841)

3rd district (Soufrière, Choiseul):

"The labourers continue to work pretty steadily and the sugar crop is now far advanced, and although the season has been excessively dry, will prove an average one."

(CO 253/73/2: 10/5/1841)

"As to the state and prospects of cultivation in this district, they are better than at any period since the abolition of apprenticeship. The rains have not, as during the last two, failed this year; and although late, have ensured a superb sugar crop for the coming year. The coffee planters have commenced gathering, perhaps, the most abundant harvest which has cheered the planter during the last ten years. The only fear is that the trees will not be able to ripen the immense load with which they are covered."

(CO 253/74/3: Sept. 1841)

4th district (Vieux Fort, Laborie):

"The sugar crop in the Fourth District, under my superintendence, is for this year at an end; and if increased produce, as compared with other years, is to be considered as indicative of corresponding increase of industry in the labouring population, and satisfaction on the part of their employers, I have the satisfaction to inform you that, in the Fourth District, this has been fully realized."

(CO 253/74/4: 15/9/1841)

The STIPENDIARY MAGISTRATE of the 5th district (Micoud, Praslin, Dennery) mentioned the return of the labourers to the estates:

"After the dissolution of the apprenticeship, the labourers were irregular and unsettled in their habits and fond of roving from one estate to another, not so much in search of employment, as with a view to ascertain how far they were really free; and some time elapsed before they could be convinced that their fears were groundless; the feeling originated from their having been liberated during the French Revolution, and afterwards relapsed into a state of slavery; With the delusion, however, vanished also their fears, and most, if not all of them, returned to the estates to which they had been formerly attached, where they still remain."

He also mentioned the good crop yields:

"By returns received from the proprietors in the district, the last year's crop yielded 697.000 pounds of sugar, 11.700 gallons of rum, and 19.600 of molasses; and for the present year it will not be under a million of pounds of sugar, with rum and molasses in proportion.

... the prospect for the next year's crop are very encouraging, and should no untoward circumstances intervene, will greatly exceed that for the present year."

(CO 253/74/5: 17/9/1841)

In connection with the illegal settlement of labourers on crown land also BREEN (1844: 309) mentions the return of the labourers to the estates:

> *"During the early period of Emancipation the practice of "squatting" prevailed to an injurious extent, ... and if it has now almost entirely disappeared, we owe that circumstance to the harmonising influence of exorbitant wages, whereby the squatters were enticed from their precarious seclusion in the woods to the more profitable occupations of the filed."*

The good crop yields for the year 1841 as mentioned above by the STIPENDIARY MAGISTRATES as well as the favourable prospects for the next year regarding sugar exports are confirmed by the figures shown in the tables on pp. 252-254 in the before mentioned chapter. According to these figures a slight rise in sugar exports is shown. Only the report of the STIPENDIARY MAGISTRATE of the 3rd district regarding the very good coffee crop in the year 1841 cannot be confirmed with the available export figures.

Another factor which contributed to the good economic situation of St. Lucia and the good satiated labour market in the early forties was the run of former non-filed labourers to the estates. The labourers were attracted by the high wages which were paid on the estates. The respective reports of the STIPENDIARY MAGISTRATES are as follows:

4th district (Vieux Fort, Laborie):

> *"There are two villages and one hamlet in this district, each of the former may contain about 400, the latter 50 inhabitants. During the existence of slavery and the apprenticeship system, none of this population could be induced by the most extravagant offers to labour in the cultivation of canes. The contrast now is striking; one third of the sugar produced in this district is the fruit of their industry."*
>
> (CO 253/74/4: 15/9/1841)

3rd district (Soufrière, Choiseul):

> *"Many coloured and black persons, free from birth, have turned their attention since emancipation to cane cultivation. It is no longer reckoned "mauvais ton" to be seen in the cane-field, how in hand. These people, however, prefer raising canes in halves with some estate, rather than hire labour at a daily wage[22]. It was expected that household servants would have become plentiful after emancipation. The contrary has turned out to be the case, for, strange to say, the best domestic servants, who, previous to emancipation, would have thought themselves degraded if even threatened to be sent to the field, have gone regularly to field labour; and*

---

[22] The cultivation of canes in halves was termed the „Métairie system" a tenancy between proprietor and labourer whereby the labourer received a portion of the produce (cp. chapter "5.2.2. The METAIRIE-System", pp. 269-274).

several, whom I knew very well during their household servitude, have become the steadiest jobbers of task-work, and are really valuable members of the agricultural part of the community."

(CO 253/74/3: Sept. 1841)

2nd district (Gros Islet, Dauphin):

"... labour is abundant in proportion to the population and I consider the number of agricultural labourers has increased since the emancipation in consequence of a large number of persons who were formerly domestic Servants, then induced by the rate of wages "one shilling three pence to two shillings per diem." To abandon their former employ and work on the plantations, both males & females; and even those, who were born free."

(CO 253/79/2: 1/8/1843)

1st district (Castries, Anse La Raye):

"... the scarcity of domestic servants has increased surprisingly; many who were formerly domestic servants, and have been so all their lives, have abandoned the town altogether, and established themselves as agricultural labourers on the estates; and I have no doubt they find it, in a pecuniary point of view, much to their advantage, for, in most instances, they earn higher wages."

(CO 253/83/8: 17/1/1845)

A confirmation of these reports can be found in BREEN'S book published in the year 1844. BREEN refers to the little extent of immigration to St. Lucia because of the good satiated labour market on the estates:

"Immigration, the universal topic of the day - ... - has received as yet but little encouragement in St. Lucia. Too prudent or too poor to embark in those bold schemes which have proved all but ruinous to some of the more independent Colonies, she has devoted her energies and her resources, such as they are, to the training and improvement of her own offspring and the encouragement of her native industry. In this she has so far succeeded that, although money wages continue at a higher rate than in some of the other islands, there is no lack of labourers for the field; while many of the freemen and artisans, who in the days of slavery would have regarded manual labour as degrading, are now seen in the foremost ranks, setting an example of patient toil and assiduity to their more indolent neighbours amongst the newly-emancipated classes."

(BREEN 1844: 303-304)

In the year 1846 Governor TORRENS of St. Lucia reported of a successful change in the labour system from slavery to free labour:

"The cultivation improves from year to year in good hands, and with sufficient capital, it appears to realize to the planter an ample return. In few islands, perhaps, has the experiment of free labour been more successful, in spite of an insufficient population, a lack of capital, much raised land, and plentiful and cheap food."

(CO 253/85/1: 4/1/1846)

5.2.2 The METAIRIE-System

The term METAIRIE originates from the French and means estate, leasehold farm (LANGENSCHEIDTS GROSSWÖRTERBUCH 1972: I, 581). It is further referred to the term "métayage".

In the GRAND LAROUSSE encyclopaedia (1962: VII) the term "métayage" is defined as follows:

"Contrat par lequel le propriétaire ou l'usufruitier d'un bien rural le remet, pour un certain temps, à un preneur que s'engage à le cultivar et à partager – en nature – les fruits et récoltes avec le bailleur."

In the ENCYCLOPAEDIA BRITANNICA (1768: 331) for "métayage" the following is explained:

"The cultivation of land for a proprietor by one who receives a proportion of the produce"

According to these sources the METAIRIE-system is a special kind of a tenancy whereby instead of paying a rent the crop yield is divided in a certain proportion between proprietor and leaseholder.

In the sources used by the author for this work this tenancy was termed METAIRIE-system respectively "cultivation in halves". BREEN for example wrote (1844: 300):

"The cultivation of canes in halves, commonly termed the Métairie system"

In the following description of this tenancy in St. Lucia the term METAIRIE-system was used.

The STIPENDIARY MAGISTRATE of the 5th district (Micoud, Praslin, Dennery) described in his report of April 1842 the application of the METAIRIE-system in St. Lucia as follows:

"The arrangement is generally to this effect, that the Labourer shall clear, hoe and plant the land himself – shall cultivate it properly, until the canes arrive at maturity. – Then the Proprietors become responsible for one half of the expenses occurring subsequently; that is to say the expense of cutting and carrying the canes, and manufacturing them into sugar is equally divided between the Proprietor of the soil & the Cultivator, the

Molasses' drainage of the Sugar being allowed to the former for use of stock, and tear and wear of Machinery – the same agreement continues in force during subsequent Years, so long as the Canes continue to reproduce, and give remunerative returns for the labour expended."

(CO 253/76/1: 2/4/1842)

This system was applied by planters who had little money. They could get a crop yield, scanty however, without spending much money. Also the price for the labourer was a favourable one. BREEN (1844: 301) writes thereto:

"The planter who owns an estate, but is destitute of the requisite capital to enable him successfully to compete with his wealthier neighbour, is glad to avail himself of the services of a few industrious cultivators, on condition of dividing the profits of the crop. In this way he derives a return, however scanty, from his land and the estate's machinery, which must otherwise have remained idle and unproductive; while the cultivator receives a price for his labour, which he might have sought for in vain in the market. The advocates of this system are all those who participate in its benefits, from the sinking planter to the aspiring peasant: in their estimate it is the only measure of salvation for the Colonies."

He points to the opponents of this system as follows:

"Its opponents are to be found amongst the capitalists and independent proprietors, supported by the mercantile and shipping interests both in the Colonies and the mother-country: by these it is regarded as a ruinous speculation."

According to BREEN (1844: 300) the METAIRIE-system was the first time applied in St. Lucia in the year 1840. DOOKHAN (1981: 13) writes that St. Lucia was the first colony in which this system was applied. Montserrat, Tobago, Grenada and St. Kitts followed later.[23]

The first reports of this system in St. Lucia are available for the year 1841. The STIPENDIARY MAGISTRATES of the 1st and 2nd district reported as follows:

1st district (Castries, Anse La Raye)
"... many of the planters have given pieces of canes to cultivate at half profit with their labourers: at first the latter entered into those contracts with suspicion, being obliged to wait till the end of the crop to ascertain their earnings during the year, but finding now that it is to their interest, they are desirous of obtaining them."

(CO 253/74/1: 1/10/1841)

---

[23] According to the ENCYCLOPAEDIA BRITANNICA (1768: 331) the METAIRIE-system has never existed in England and has no English name, but in certain provinces of Italy and France it was once almost universal. It was also practised in the United States, in Portugal and Greece, and in the countries bordering on the Danube.

<u>2nd district (Gros Islet, Dauphin):</u>

"Many proprietors also to encourage good labourers, and induce them to settle in their neighbourhood, have adopted the expedient of working considerable fields of canes in shares with one or more such labourers, the labourer undertaking to cultivate in canes and keep in proper cultivation a certain quantity of land at his own individual cost, the proprietor receiving as his free share from one-half to two-thirds of the sugar made, as the case may be."

(CO 253/73/1: 2/4/1841)

From the report of the STIPENDIARY MAGISTRATE of the 3rd district (Soufrière, Choiseul) follows that also former free non-whites worked on the basis of the METAIRIE-system:

"Many coloured and black persons, free from birth, have turned their attention since emancipation to cane cultivation. It is no longer reckoned "mauvais ton" to be seen in the cane field, hoe in hand. These people, however, prefer raising canes in halves with some estate, rather than hire their labour at a daily wage."

(CO 253/74/3: Sept. 1841)

He pointed further to the fact that the majority of the 3rd district applied the METAIRIE-system:

"... of the 22 sugar estates in this district, 14 or 15 have some portion of their canes cultivated in shares by the labourers. Two estates are entirely cultivated on these conditions, and one, a very pretty little property, has been partly purchased by a family of the newly emancipated, and is most admirably managed by the head of the family, a man named Firmin."

From another report concerning the 3rd district of January 1845 follows that the METAIRIE-system was also applied on coffee and cocoa estates. The STIPENDIARY MAGISTRATE wrote as follows:

"..., they divide and separate their coffee or cocoa estates in small establishments, and construct, at distances, cottages, some of which are very neat, built of stone and covered with trash, in which they locate families, to whom they abandon a certain portion of coffee plantations, which the latter are obliged to cultivate and reap for a certain proportion of the produce. These cottages are generally surrounded with enclosures, which allow the tenants to feed, in the inside, pigs and poultry, and it is also left to themselves to plant on their own account so much vegetables and ground provisions as they can cultivate, provided that such cultivation does not prove injurious to the coffee and cocoa plantations under their charge. In payment of the rent of the farm, and of the lands appropriated thereto, for the cultivation of their own gardens, the proprietors are in the habit of exacting two days' labour per week from one member of each family."

(CO 253/83/5: 13/1/1845)

Also in the 4th and 5th district the STIPENDIARY MAGISTRATES reported of the application of the METAIRIE-system:

4th district (Vieux Fort, Laborie):

"An excellent practice prevails here, worthy of adoption, in my opinion, not only in other districts of this Colony, but also in other islands, - I allude to the cultivation of canes in halves between proprietors and labourers, the expense of manufacture being deducted from the gross proceeds, and the remaining balance equally divided between the contracting parties."

(CO 253/73/3: 1/3/1841)

5th district (Micoud, Praslin, Dennery):

The peasantry are allowed to cultivate as much ground as they please for garden, but many prefer planting canes with the proprietors for half the produce as being more profitable."

(CO 253/74/5: 17/9/1841)

From a further report of the STIPENDIARY MAGISTRATE of the 5th district of April 1842 follows that the cultivation of sugar cane on the basis of the METAIRIE-system meant only an extra income for the labourers:

"The canes they plant are to be cultivated only on Saturdays, and during extra hours; and they can only do all this but attend to their own ground provisions, besides."

(CO 253/76/1: 2/4/1842)

This statement is confirmed by a report of the STIPENDIARY MAGISTRATE of the 4th district (Vieux Fort, Laborie):

"On an estate in this district there resides a labourer who, cultivating canes in halves, planted during 1840 canes which will this year yield from four to five hogsheads of sugar. Taking, however, the lowest estimate – four hogsheads – at the present prices of produce, each hogshead cannot clear less, after the deduction of all expenses, then 30£sterling; so here is a labourer earning by his industry 60£sterling per annum. Be it remembered in addition, that these canes have been cultivated on Saturdays, holidays, and during his spare hours only, whilst all the rest of his time he has been working and receiving daily wages as a general labourer on the property, with free tenancy of house and provision-grounds. His young children also, instead of running about idle and useless, would be acquiring habits of industry and knowledge, whilst assisting their parents by carrying plants and manure to his cane piece."

(CO 253/73/4: 1/5/1841)

According to the report of the STIPENDIARY MAGISTRATE of the 4th district of May 1842 the METAIRIE-system had a favourable influence on the economic development of St. Lucia:

> "The System of cultivating the soil to which the attention of Government has been directed and ..., is one which has been, years after year, growing into more general adoption in this island, and which already forms an important and distinguished feature in the history of agricultural progress in St. Lucia."
>
> (CO 253/76/2: 10/5/1842)

Also Governor GRAYDON of St. Lucia referred in his letter of December 1842 to the Governor of Barbados to this influence of the METAIRIE-system:

> "The most important of the changes in agriculture appears to be the great increase of the Sugar Crop, since the cultivation of the Canes for the halves, though the favourable season has in some degree contributed to this increase, yet it seems mainly attributable to this new stimulus to industry."
>
> (CO 253/78/1: 20/12/1842)

According to a letter of Governor TORRENS of St. Lucia of March 1845 the METAIRIE-system was mainly applied in the 4th district (Vieux Fort, Laborie):

> "Fourth District: ... The métairie system is said to increase in this district; it is already more extensively diffused here than elsewhere."
>
> (CO 253/83/1: 3/3/1845)

The enclosed report of the STIPENDIARY MAGISTRATE of the 4th district is as follows:

> "The métairie, or half-and-half system is still progressing, and there is no likelihood, as far as can be judged from circumstances, of its retrogression.
>
> During the last crop 228 acres of land were cultivated in canes under the half-and-half system, from the production of which the quantity of sugar arising to the labourers exclusively, amounted to 3907,759 lbs., which, calculated at the market price of produce, amounted to the sum of 2,313£14s. 5d. sterling.
>
> There are about 280 acres now under cultivation under the métairie system, for the ensuing crop, and should no unforeseen casualties intervene, it is expected that the quantity of sugar which will fall to the share of the labourers will not fall short, but rather exceed that of last crop."
>
> (CO 253/83/2: 10/1/1845)

In the late forties the significance of the METAIRIE-system further increase, Governor DARLING of St. Lucia informed Governor COLEBROOKE of Barbados in June 1849 as follows:

> *"The métairie system, or cultivation of estates for shares (always, I believe, the half) under various modifications, is carried on to an extent of at least one-fourth of the whole cane cultivation, and is undoubtedly upon the increase notwithstanding that the state of the law is highly unfavourable to the metayer in the case of mortgaged properties."*

(CO 253/99/1: 15/6/1849)

Governor POWER of St. Lucia reported in the year 1855:

> *"... and the working of Estates on the Metairie system has lately increased."*

(CO 253/116/1: 4/6/1855)

In the second half of the fifties the METAIRIE-system became more and more uneconomic. Governor BREEN of St. Lucia reported in May 1861:

> *"The métairie system, introduced into St. Lucia, as into some of the neighbouring islands, on the abolition of slavery, continued for some years to be extensively adopted on many estates. The system, however, is gradually disappearing; and the few estates on which it is still found to linger are among the least prosperous in the Colony. Richfond is the only one which is now wholly conducted on that plan.*
>
> *This reaction is chiefly to be ascribed to the healthy state of the home market. So long as the price of sugar continued unsatisfactory, the planter and the labourer were drawn towards each other for mutual co-operation and assistance; each possessed what the other wanted; and a union of means and a division of profit were the natural result. With the rise, however, in the price of sugar, this state of things could not last. The planter and the labourer, influenced by the same motive, were now led to a separation of interests; the planter soon found that it was more easy and less expensive to pay for labour, and the labourer that it was less difficult and more profitable to purchase land and cultivate it for himself."*

(CO 253/128/1: 25/5/1861)

5.2.3 The adoption of the plough

At about 1841 the plough was only sporadically used in St. Lucia. The general implement was the hoe.

The STIPENDIARY MAGISTRATES of the several districts reported in September respectively October 1841 as follows:

<u>1st district (Castries, Anse La Raye):</u>

"... three estates only make use of the plough, and it has been found to considerably decrease manual labour."

(CO 253/74/1: 1/10/1841)

<u>2nd district (Gros Islet, Dauphin):</u>

"The plough is not in general use, but I feel confident will be adopted when its advantageous application is made manifest by experience. The nature of the soil, and generally flat or even ground of this district, is favourable for its use in preparing cane land."

(CO 253/74/2: 20/9/1841)

<u>3rd distrct (Soufrière, Choiseul):</u>

"Not even a single plough brought into use."

(CO 253/74/3: Sept. 1841)

<u>4th district (Vieux Fort, Laborie):</u>

"I regret that I cannot, on this occasion, report to the Right Hon. Secretary of State for the Colonies, any new "improvements or discoveries" either concerning agriculture or machinery in the Fourth District."

(CO 253/74/4: 15/9/1841)

<u>5th district (Micoud, Praslin, Dennery):</u>

"In consequence of the uneven nature of the soil, the hoe is principally in use. On two estates in the district, where the ground is sufficiently level, the plough has lately been brought into operation with advantage, and will no doubt get into more general use, where practicable."

(CO 253/74/5: 17/9/1841)

This situation didn't change very much till the year 1845, although the use of the plough became more common. The STIPENDIARY MAGISTRATES of the several districts reported as follows:

<u>1st district (Castries, Anse La Raye):</u>

"The plough has been used but partially."

(CO 253/78/2: 24/12/1842)

"Not even one plough made use of in the District although so many favourable reports respecting its use reach us from the neighbouring Colonies –"

(CO 253/79/1: 27/7/1843)

2nd district (Gros Islet, Dauphin):

"The Plough, sometimes since introduced, continues in use wherever the evenness of the soil admits of its practicability."

(CO 253/78/3: 21/12/1842)

"The Plough is occasionally used and which would be more in practice, were it not for the difficulty in obtaining people capable to work it."

(CO 253/79/2: 1/8/1843)

"The adoption of the plough is, I am happy to say, extending in this district. With the view of encouraging so desirable an improvement, I have attempted to form an agricultural society in the district, which, though as yet unformed, I trust may, before long, be established, Ploughmen are much wanted.

A few refugees are the only persons employed at the plough in this district, except on the Union estate, where Mr. Todd, the proprietor, has very wisely placed a competent hand, brought out from Scotland in February last."

(CO 253/83/3: 5/7/1845)

3rd district (Soufrière, Choiseul):

"There is not even one plough in the District although many of the Estates are admirable adapted for its use."

(CO 253/78/4: Dec. 1842)

"The Plough is not in use in the District, the mountainous nature of the Country being inimical to it."

(CO 253/79/3: 1/8/1843)

4th district (Vieux Fort, Laborie):

"I have not seen the Plough made use of, although there is no quarter of the Island so well adapted from the lightness of soil and the level state of the lands, for the effective application of this powerful aid to husbandry."

(CO 253/79/4: 5/8/1843)

"The plough has been occasionally resorted to, but it appears to me, in an exceedingly inefficient manner, owing to the inexperience of the conductors, or deficient training of the cattle employed."

(CO 253/82/2: 10/1/1844)

<u>5th district (Micoud, Praslin, Dennery):</u>

"The hoe is chiefly used in preparing the soil for planting of all descriptions, on some Estates the plough is used, and as well in this District as in the others of the island has invariably been proved to be highly beneficial to the cultivation, and a diminution in the expense of manual labour, and it continues to increase in getting more into general use."

(CO 253/78/5: 30/12/1842)

Up from the year 1845 the use of the plough progressed generally: The STIPENDIARY MAGISTRATES reported:

"The plough and common Hoe are generally used;"

(CO 258/16/1: 1/7/1847-31/12/1847, p.266)

"more general use of the Plough"

(CO 258/16/2: 1/7/1848-31/12/1848, p. 390)

"Ploughing, where practicable, is generally in progress."

(CO 258/17/1: 1/7/1850-31/12/1850, p. 168)

A description of the plough was not available but the author assumes that the plough in St. Lucia was the French turning plough "tourney-oreilles" which was introduced in the Antilles by French colonists in the middle of the 17th century. The introduction of its use was very slow (cp. BERNER 1984: 287, CHAULEAU 1979: 153).[24]

<u>Plough "tourne-oreilles"</u>

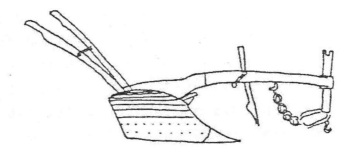

The above mentioned assumption that the plough "tourne-oreilles" was used in St. Lucia is mainly substantiated on the report of the STIPENDIARY MAGISTRATE of the 2nd district from the year 1845 in which he mentioned that the refugees from Martinique were the only persons employed at the plough (cp. p. 276)

---

[24] CHAULEAU, L.: „La vie quotidienne aux Antilles francaises au temps de Victor SCHOELCHER, XIX. siècle, Paris, 1979.

5.2.4 Summary

The main export products of St. Lucia at the end of the emancipation period were sugar, coffee, cocoa, molasses, rum as well as fire- and logwood, whereby sugar was the most important product. Whereas coffee lost in significance the produce of cocoa gained in significance. The export product cotton totally lost its significance after the emancipation period.

After the end of the emancipation period many former APPRENTICES didn't continue to work on the estates. This led to a lack of labourers on the estates. Further complaints of the planters referred to unsatisfactory execution of the work as well as to the high wages they had to pay to the labourers. This situation had a negative effect on the agriculture of St. Lucia and there was a decline in sugar exports. But already in the second half of the year 1839 there was a general amelioration of the labour situation on the estates. The STIPENDIARY MAGISTRATES mainly reported of a better labour situation. In the year 1841 there was a further amelioration in the relationship planter – labourer. The STIPENDIARY MAGISTRATES wrote of a decided and general improvement which had taken place in the character and condition of the labourers. There was no lack of labourers because the most of the former APPRENTICES had returned to the estates to which they had been formerly attached. Owing to this situation there were good crop yields and a rise in sugar exports. Another factor which contributed to the good economic situation of St. Lucia and the good satiated labour market was the run of former non-field labourers to the estates. These labourers were attracted by the high wages which were paid on the estates.

In the year 1846 Governor TORRENS of St. Lucia reported of a successful change in the labour system from slavery to free labour.

Approximately up from the year 1860 there was a rise in the exports of sugar. In the year 1870 Governor DES VOEUX wrote of the largest crop of sugar ever produced in St. Lucia and also of the island's appearance advancing towards prosperity.

At the beginning of the forties the METAIRIE-system was the first time applied in St. Lucia. This system is a special kind of a tenancy whereby instead of paying a rent the crop yield is divided in a certain portion between proprietor and leaseholder. Up from the late forties till about 1855 its significance increased. In the second half of the fifties the METAIRIE-system became more and more uneconomic because of the economic situation of the island and at the beginning of the sixties it was only found on few estates in St. Lucia.

To the use of the plough in St. Lucia it is to mention that till about 1845 the plough was not used very much. The general implement was the hoe. But up from the year 1845 the use of the plough progressed generally.

5.3 Way of life of St. Lucia's black population

5.3.1 The situation after the end of the emancipation period as well as illegal land appropriations

After the end of the emancipation period many labourers left the estates and settled on small pieces of land. As mentioned in chapter "5.2.1.2. Labour situation and effects of the free labour market after the end of the emancipation period (1838-1846)", pp. 261-262 Governor EVERARD of St. Lucia informed the Governor of Barbados, Mac GREGOR, with his letter of June 1839 of the bad relationship of the labourers to the work on the estates and the therefrom resulting desire for independence of the labour on the estates. From this letter follows on the one hand that the labourers rented pieces of land:

> "... the result is therefore, safe evident that on final Emancipation, the Negro, having no kindly feeling to bind him to his late Master, naturally looked out for a settlement on his own; And from the many persons who possess large tracts of land, uncultivated, they easily obtained, and still obtain as much as they require, and become settled thereon, and instead of paying Money as rent, the Proprietor is ready and willing to receive, in lieu thereof, a portion of the product of the Soil."

On the other hand the labourers settled on crown lands:

> "The Crown lands have also afforded them "ample room and scope enough" to squat in all directions, the island being so extensive and mountainous that there is no possibility, with the present small police force, of dislodging them or of ascertaining to what extent in point of number they have taken up their abodes in the heights and ravines of the Country."

(CO 253/67/2: 20/6/1839)

As already mentioned in the before quoted chapter "5.2.1.2.", p. 256 BREEN (1844: 309) refers to the illegal method of land appropriations and states that "during the early period of Emancipation the practice of "squatting" prevailed to an injurious extent". Further it follows from his statements that in the early forties the number of the illegal settlers had reduced to a large extent. As reason BREEN mentions "the harmonising influence of exorbitant wages, whereby the squatters were enticed from their precarious seclusion in the woods to the more profitable occupations of the field".

The large extent of illegal settlements at the time of the emancipation period is confirmed by a letter extract of Governor MEIN of St. Lucia in August 1838:

"It is essentially necessary, that some Law should be enacted to suppress the practice which exists to a very considerable extent amongst the free persons of squatting on land belonging to the Crown and Vacant Successions."

(CO 253/62/5: 4/8/1838)

The reduction of the number of the illegal settlers in the early forties mentioned by BREEN is confirmed by a letter extract of Governor CLARKE of March 1844:

"I have ascertained that the Squatters on Crown lands are not numerous; from various causes some difficulty will attend their removal, these I hope will be able to overcome."

(CO 253/81/1: 30/3/1844)

5.3.2 Representation of the way of life of St. Lucia's labour population by means of reports of the STIOPENDIARY MAGISTRATES in the period from 1841 to 1845

5.3.2.1 Selection of place of residence

According to the following reports among the labourers there was generally the tendency to reside on small pieces of land which were hired or bought from the planters. The labourers preferred living independently. Other labourers stayed at their former residence on the estate. The STIPENDIARY MAGISTRATES of the 1st, 2nd and 3rd districts reported thereto as follows:

1st district (Castries, Anse La Raye):

"The labouring population, since the dissolution of the apprenticeship, study to conduct themselves in such a manner as to show they know how to appreciate the great boon which has been conferred on them; and, finding themselves now more independent than they were during the apprenticeship, they employ their means in establishing themselves and their families in a manner suitable to their altered condition. Their great ambition is to have their own private residence; and, in order to do this, notwithstanding the generality of the planters in this district allow them a house and provision-grounds on their estates, without exacting any payment; still they prefer to hire from those same planters, at a fixed annual rent, and sometimes even to purchase portions of land, where they establish their domicile and provision grounds;"

(CO 253/74/1: 1/10/1841)

2nd district (Gros Islet, Dauphin):

"A good understanding and friendly feeling exists between the labourer and his employer. No rent for house or provision-grounds is required of such labourers as are located on the estate benefited by their labour. The labourers are generally desirous of being totally independent, and many of them have become proprietors of small allotments of land, and a very large number hold several acres of land by annual lease."

(CO 253/74/2: 20/9/1841)

3rd district (Soufrière, Choiseul):

As to the progress which the labourers have made in establishing themselves as freeholders, about 60, so far as I can yet learn, have purchased lands in this district: the price differs, according to position and quality, from 10 to 100 dollars the acre. Three new hamlets have arisen. 1st Mr. Tisnés, owner of the Morne Belair estate, an abandoned coffee property, in the Fond St. Jacques, has leased out this property in lots, varying from 3 acres to 10; and there are at present about 26 houses seated in the midst of their grounds, which are generally well cultivated in provisions and young coffee, where, before emancipation, scarcely a dwelling was to be seen. 2dly The Hon. H. King has in the same way leased out a long abandoned coffee estate, called St. Jour; 22 men, 21 women, and 24 children are now living in houses built by themselves on this property, and seem to enjoy peace and plenty. The third hamlet which has newly sprung up is situated on the Hermitage estate, which was purchased at public sale about three years ago by Mr. Boucher, of the Rabot estate. This gentleman has now sold in portions the fee simple of the whole of this property: the first portions, which were the best situated and most fertile, brought about 30 dollars the acre; the price has gradually augmented, and the latter sales have brought more than 100 dollars per acre.
About a dozen families are here established, some of whom, however, are of a better grade than mere labourers; nearly all the labourers on the coffee estates are leaseholders of portions of coffee in full bearing;"

(CO 253/74/3: Sept. 1841)

The above mentioned division of the estates into lots had been already mentioned in chapter "5.2.2. The METAIRIE-system", p. 271, where according to a report of the STIPOENDIARY MAGISTRATE of the 3rd district from the year 1845 coffee and cocoa estates were divided into small pieces of land and abandoned to the labourers who were obliged to cultivate and reap it for a certain proportion of the produce. For these labourers the planters had erected small cottages at some distance of the coffee and cocoa fields which were generally surrounded with enclosures which allowed the tenants to feed in the inside pigs and poultry. The labourers could also plant ground provisions. In payment of the rent of the house and of the lands appropriated thereto for the cultivation of ground provisions the proprietors were in the habit of exacting two days' labour per week from one member of each family. In this report the STIPENDIARY MAGISTRATE described these cottages as follows:

> "The formation of these small establishments, situated at equal distance from each other, represents the delightful aspect of a hamlet, surrounded by luxuriant vegetation, an abundance and variety of provisions of every description."
>
> (CO 253/83/5: 13/1/1845)

According to a report of January 1844 in the 3rd district it was more usual than in other districts to live in the former residences on the estates because of the difficulty of obtaining lands to purchase or lease:

> "... the labourers are more accustomed to reside on the Estates, than in other districts with which I have been charged: this may be caused by the difficulty of obtaining lands to purchase or lease, particularly in the valley of Soufrière, where many of the Sugar Estates are situated and the distance would be too great, if living off the Estate, to be able to attend work at a proper hour."
>
> (CO 253/82/3: 10/1/1844)

In July 1845 the STIPENDIARY MAGISTRATE of the 3rd district reported of an erection of a new village in the vicinity of Choiseul which was named "Victoria":

> "The only new remark which arises to notice under this division of my six-monthly report, refers to the establishment of a new village or hamlet of some considerable extent in the heights of Soufrière on the confines of Choiseul.
>
> This settlement, composed of about 40 houses, surrounded with luxuriant gardens, producing an abundance of every description of edibles, has been named "Victoria"; a compliment which, according to their manner of considering things, has been conceived to be due by them to Her Most Gracious Majesty.
>
> This, I believe, is the first inland settlement of the kind that has been known in the whole colony, and considering the natural advantages of the locality, its soil in the highest degree rich and productive, environed by forest woods equally available for fuel, building materials, and for the supply of grain, not only for local consumption, but likewise as profitable commodities, in the neighbouring seaport markets of Soufrière and Choiseul. The infant village of Victoria seems to hold forth the strongest promise of rapid advance in numbers and extent, nor is it likely to be unimportant as a nursery of agricultural labourers, to be afterwards available for the general resources of the colony.

The preliminary work of erecting houses and opening lands on the above settlement tended in some measure to abstract some labour from the large plantations in the neighbourhood; yet this was only temporary, for no sooner had they provided suitable habitations for their families, and opened up a sufficient extent of ground for the employment of their youths and women, than most of the male settlers of Victoria turned their attention to the profitable employ of the sugar estates, their earnings upon which enhancing the comfortable enjoyment of their new home."

(CO 253/83/4: 1/7/1845)

From reports of the STIPENDIARY MAGISTRATE of the 4th district (Vieux Fort, Laborie) follows that the labourers also resided in already existing villages:

"Several amongst the labourers had built small houses in the villages, but still continue to reside permanently on the Estates, where they work. These town houses are intended for the use of their families, when occasion calls them to the village either for business or devotion."

(CO 253/82/2: 10/1/1844)

"The labourers continue to increase the number of the houses in the villages, and on independent lots of land, but insofar as my observation and enquiry extent, such location of the labourers has not been attended with any serious diminution of labour for the Estates. Many thus provide an independent lodging for an aged mother or a wife with a numerous family; but I have remarked that a great proportion of the houses in the villages are made use of only on Sundays or holidays, when the Owners have occasion to come to town.

(CO 253/82/4: 2/7/1844)

Extracts of the reports of the 5th district (Micoud, Praslin, Dennery) are as follows:

"The labourers are in general allowed free use of their former houses, and grounds, and in no instance is rent either in specie or kind exacted for the same. Many Labourers hire a piece of land for cultivating provisions: this however is entirely independent of their connection as Labourers with any particular Estate."

(CO 253/70/1: 7/3/1840)

"About 25 labourers in the district have purchased, and 40 leased, lands for a longer or shorter period, varying from three to ten acres, upon which provisions are chiefly planted and huts erected. The greatest part, if not the whole of them are, however, still employed as labourers on the sugar estates."

(CO 253/74/5: 17/9/1841)

Also in this district the labourers settled in villages:

> "… many little settlements of families are to be seen studied over the environs, this new sprung emulation of uniting together in the small villages, and to live in Societies, I am induced to attribute to the lively desire of the labouring class to be located within a convenient distance of their Churches & Chapels in order to be the better enabled to attend Divine Worship and assist in the Ceremonies of the Church, as well as to facilitate their procuring of their Domestic Comforts at the cheapest rate possible, …"

(CO 253/79/5: 7/8/1843)

From this report follows further that in the villages Micoud and Dennery the population had increased three times since the end of the emancipation period:

> "The Towns of Micoud and Dennery, which prior to the general change in Society were composed of nothing better than a rude and … mass of huts, serving chiefly as a temporary refuge and shelter to the fishermen of the Quarter, have now increased in population to three times its former number, and though the houses, it is true, continue to be fetched yet order, cleanliness, and comfort characterize the whole."

Graphical representation of the mentioned districts:

(Division of districts extracted from a map of St. Lucia from the year 1847 – BPP/CG/4/1: 1847, p.518)

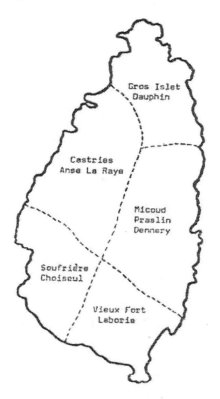

5.3.2.2   Subsistence

Beside the work on the estates the labourers cultivated provisions as plantains, yams, potatoes or cassava, raised horn-cattle, pigs, goats and poultry or were fishers. Extracts of the reports of the STIPENDIARY MAGISTRATES are as follows:

1st district (Castries, Anse La Raye):

"The profits of the sale of provisions grown by the labourers are very considerable. Plantains, Yams, Potatoes and Cassava are brought into town in large quantities, and find a ready Market. Poultry of all descriptions are raised by the labourers, and the number of horn-cattle now raised by those settlers who have hired or purchased lands, has become a source of great profit to the Cottager and means of supplying the market with Butcher-meat far superior in quality to any that is imported and surpassed by none to be had in the other islands."

(CO 253/78/2: 24/12/1842)

2nd district (Gros Islet, Dauphin):

"... and though the disposition of the negro of one Estate be found to differ widely from that of another, notwithstanding their frequently working together, yet the force of good example is seldom lost upon him. Some will be satisfied to live entirely upon their earnings in the employ of a master, while others will add to such wages the fruits of their own well cultivated provision grounds, an abundantly stocked yard of pigs, goats and poultry; and not frequently combining with these advantages is the possession of a canoe and fishing baskets, which they will visit and give all necessary attention to, early in the morning, before repairing to the Estates' work."

(CO 253/83/6: 12/1/1845)

3rd district (Soufrière, Choiseul):

"Generally, I can hardly conceive it possible for any peasantry to be more happy, prosperous and contented than the black population of Soufrière and other parts of the district. Naturally a strong-limbed race, and living in a quarter of the island remarkable for the purity of its air, and the advantages which it presents to the agricultural labourer of abundant lands available for agricultural purpose, the peasantry of this district have been in a great measure the instruments of their own contentment, by devoting a great portion of their time to the cultivation of the staples upon the large established plantations, where good wages are invariably given and by carefully husbanding the not inconsiderable perquisite presented in their provision grounds."

(CO 253/83/4: 1/7/1845)

4th district (Vieux Fort, Laborie):

"It is rare to find a labourer, ... Many of them possess milk cows, and pigs and poultry are raised by all of them. – Their provision grounds are extensive and well cultivated, giving abundant Crops of ground provisions for their own consumption, and for the supply of the Market."

(CO 253/82/2: 10/1/1844)

In another report of the STIPENDIARY MAGISTRATE of the 4th district it was mentioned that the sale of logwood had been abandoned. In the period of slavery the sale of logwood was very important for the blacks. (cp. chapter "4.7.6. Subsistence of slaves and APPRENTICES", p.158) The STIPENDIARY MAGISTRATE also mentioned the burning of charcoal:

"Formerly the Negroes cut and sold quantities of Logwood, but of late years this traffic has been abandoned for the more lucrative employment in cane cultivation, growing of ground provisions and raising live stock. The burning of Charcoal for which a good price is obtained, is practised to a considerable extent in some localities, but is only resorted to as a casual employment."

(CO 253/82/4: 2/7/1844)

From the report of the STIPENDIARY MAGISTRATE of the 5th district (Micoud, Praslin, Dennery) dated July 1845 follows that the labourers also reared horses:

"The condition of the laborers resident on the estates remains unchanged; they still continue to enjoy possession of their houses and provision grounds, free of rent or charge. They possess, as hitherto, the privilege of rearing live stock, and many of them have both horses and cows in pasture on the properties whereon they reside."

(CO 253/83/7: 2/7/1845)

The possession of horses by the labourers is also mentioned in reports of other districts:

2nd district (Gros Islet, Dauphin):

"The labourers are generally desirous of being totally independent, and many of them have become proprietors of small allotments of land, ..., and it is no uncommon thing for a proprietor to ride his own horse to church, or to the estate on which he bestows his extra labour."

(CO 253/74/2: 20/9/1841)

3rd district (Soufrière, Choiseul):

"Marriage is always of frequent occurrence, and I have remarked that after the ceremony the married couple as well as the assistants, …, on returning to their domiciles in the Country are invariably provided with Horses, the only mode of conveyance here."

(CO 253/79/3: 1/8/1843)

4th district (Vieux Fort, Laborie):

"It is rare to find a labourer who cannot sport his … and Beaver, and such as are moderately industrious, are often to be seen riding their own horses, when travelling or going to Church."

(CO 253/82/2: 10/1/1844)

Another kind of occupation of the labourers was the production of sugar syrup. The STIPENDIARY MAGISTRATE of the 1st district (Castries, Anse La Raye) wrote as follows:

"- petty independent plantations of canes are numerous far beyond any of the other districts, …, a labourer will keep possession for purchase or lease of a Carrèe or two of land within a few miles of the Town of Castries, will plant an acre or so of this land in canes, will erect two small hard wood-rollers turned by hand like a windlass, set up small iron-boilers, and will then with infinite pains and labour in a small way manufacture syrup, he cannot with such apparatus make sugar, which he will convey in Demi-johns to Castries and dispose of it by retail."

(CO 253/79/1: 27/7/1843)

The STIPENDIARY MAGISTRATE of the 2nd district (Gros Islet, Dauphin) reported also of these small sugar establishments:

"I have already had occasion to notice the fondness of home, causing many of the negroes to establish themselves on small lots of land in the vicinity of the estates on which they had formerly been slaves or choose to work. These settlements augment every day, and many of them are assuming the character of small sugar estates. There are not less than 40 small establishments of this kind whereon canes are grown by the negroes, to be afterwards manufactured in halves on the nearest estate, and more than 10 of 40 have erected small wooden hand-mills and manufacture their own produce, while others, by means of an ingenious contrivance, forming a sort of lever attached to some strong tree, squeeze out the juice of their canes, which they boil down to coarse syrup, and for which they find a ready sale in the town."

(CO 253/83/3: 5/7/1845)

An extract of a report of the STIPENDIARY MAGISTRATE of the 4th district (Vieux Fort, Laborie) is as follows:

"There are some few of the small proprietors who, perhaps, may cultivate a quarter of half an acre of land in canes, and by use of a pressing machine, of rude construction, extract the juice, which they boil into syrup, but the quantity is so inconsiderable as scarcely to be worth noticing."

(CO 253/83/2: 10/1/1845)

According to a report of the agriculture of St. Lucia as well as of the prevalent lack of labourers published in the newspaper PALLADIUM in May 1846 the above mentioned small sugar-mills made by the labourers themselves were found especially in St. Lucia and Grenada:

"- the quantity of waste land encourages a daily increase of settlements, which lead to a daily and irregular secession from the field, and the hand and other small sugar-mills of the negroes (which are almost peculiar to St. Lucia and Grenada) absorb more people, who thus become permanent absentees from estates.

(N/CO 258/1/7: 9/5/1846, p.408)

The STIPENDIARY MAGISTRATE of the 1st district (Castries, Anse La Raye) referred in his report to former non-field slaves:

"… the females employ themselves generally as washer-women and domestics to the higher classes, whilst the males under the appellation of Jobbers, pursue a trade of speculation, in which I am sorry to say, they pay no regard to the honesty of means by which their object is to be gained."

(CO 253/82/5: 3/7/1844)

As mentioned in chapter "5.2.1.2. Labour situation and effects of the free labour market after the end of the emancipation period (1838-1846", p. 258) many former non-field slaves worked on the sugar plantations because of the high wages paid to them.

5.3.2.3   Situation of the children

The STIPENDIARY MAGISTRATE of the 1st district (Castries, Anse La Raye) reported in December 1842 as follows:

"There are many descriptions of works on a Sugar Estate, adopted to the strange and capacity of children and young people, and for the performance of which they are indeed peculiarly fitted, in particular, children can be advantageously employed in assisting a responsible Stock-Keeper, in watching and herding the cattle at pasture, in collecting stray sheep, and in procuring … and other food for rabbits, swine &c. In the distribution of manure throughout the cane fields and other similar light work, young people can be employed with advantage, where it would be a sacrifice of labour to bestow the time of an able-bodied man. Many

labourers have withdrawn their children from the work of the Estates. Some employ them in assisting in the cultivation of their own provision grounds, and not a few have been withdrawn to obtain the benefits of education, which can only be attained by removal to the neighbouring towns or villages."

(CO 253/78/2: 24/12/1842)

In another report dated January 1845 the STIPENDIARY MAGISTRATE of the 1st district wrote:

"Many have withdrawn their children from agricultural occupations to place them in town, apprenticed to learn different trades; such as cabinet makers, carpenters, shoemakers, tailors, &c. &c.

(CO 253/83/8: 17/1/1845)

5.3.2.4   General supply position

According to the following reports there were three kinds of supply possibilities for the labourers: shops on the estates, shops in towns and villages as well as hucksters.
After the end of the emancipation period many planters established shops upon their estates. BREEN (1844: 312) wrote as follows:

"... on the abolition of slavery almost every planter was induced to establish a shop upon his estate, with the two-fold object of attaching the labourers to the property, and of drawing back in exorbitant profits a portion of the exorbitant wages he was compelled to give them in that early stage of the experiment of free labour."

From reports of the STIPENDIARY MAGISTRATES of the 2nd and 4th district follows that credits were granted to the labourers on goods bought by them in the shops on the estates:

2nd district (Gros Islet, Dauphin):

"During the past year, cases of complaint against employers by their Labourers have been comparatively few, and these consist chiefly of some supposed or real injury in the settlement on paying of wages. Many difficulties in such cases arise from the very reprehensible practice of encouraging the labourers to contract debts by purchasing goods or provisions from the shop or store of the estate, and then on paying his wages, exacting or requiring of him the liquidation of this debt. The labourer, finding his weekly earnings so diminished and exhausted by his improvident extravagance, (encouraged as I have stated,) feels dissatisfied, and considers himself injured or imposed upon by his employer; then seeks redress before the magistrate, or quits his employ with disgust, and wanders somewhere else, to become a second time victim to the same pernicious system."

(CO 253/74/6: 2/8/1841)

<u>4th district (Vieux Fort, Laborie):</u>

> *"Some of the Planters opened Shops upon their estates for furnishing articles of the above description to the negroes; whilst, on the one hand, this system extends a mutual advantage to the Planter and Labourer, in the time saved by bringing the articles so close to their homes; on the other, it is attended with a prejudicial circumstance that I cannot avoid pointing out: - viz: in order to enlarge their sales as much as possible, the planters frequently give credit to the labourers, and thus make considerable advance of future wages to them. Thus the labourer soon becomes discouraged, no longer seeing before him the prospect of any tangible gain, the fruits of this future labour having been forestalled and absorbed by the expenses already made, often very idle, ..., he relaxes in his labour, and not unfrequently to procure himself cash for his present wants, absconds from his creditor, and carries his labour to a neighbouring Estate on which he is unencumbered by any debts. In this manner many planters have been victims to the system of exceeding by the advances the actual wants of the labourer."*
>
> (CO 253/78/6: Dec. 1842)

BREEN (1844: 312) writes also of positive examples regarding the credit system:

> *"In some cases the speculation has proved a losing affair; but wherever the person in charge of the shop has been found trustworthy, and careful in not extending the credit system beyond the resources of the labourers, it has answered well."*

According to a report of the STIPENDIARY MAGISTRATE of the 1st district (Castries, Anse La Raye) the labourers in this district supplied themselves mainly in the shops of the town Castries:

"There is no other internal traffic than a few hucksters, who go upon the estates with a few dry goods and comestibles. On some estates shops were established, but they have all been abandoned with the exception of one; the labourers being paid their wages in money, prefer coming to town with their provisions and poultry, and purchasing what they may require: Saturday is the day fixed throughout the colony for the market day."

(CO 253/74/1: 1/10/1841)

In the 2nd district (Gros Islet, Dauphin) there was the same situation:

"The labourers in this district are enabled, by their proximity to the town of Castries, to supply themselves with such necessaries, provisions, and articles of dress, as they may require; consequently there is little affected by sale on the estates, or by travelling hucksters."

(CO 253/74/2: 20/9/1841)

From reports of the year 1845 follows that in the town Gros Islet shops had also been established, although however according to the following report the goods were very expensive there:

> *"There is not at all installed a good store in the town of Gros Islet, and the articles above described are to be procured at exorbitant prices from small retail shops, eight or ten of which exist there at present. Finding that he must pay so high at Gros Islet for these things, the negro in general proceeds to Castries, over a road of 12 miles to procure them. He goes on the Saturday morning loaded with plantains, yams, and other production of his garden, and returns in the evening with his purchase."*

> (CO 253/83/6: 12/1/1845)

In July 1845 the STIPENDIARY MAGISTRATE of the 2nd district reported of the establishment of a new shop:

> *"There are several shops in the town of Gros Islet, and the firm of MacFarlane & Co. have recently established a branch store there, which will save to the labourers much of the time they were obliged to lose before, in proceeding to Castries (a distance of 12 miles) for what they wanted from the stores."*

> (CO 253/83/3: 5/7/1845)

The situation in the 3rd district (Soufrière, Choiseul) was described by the STIPENDIARY MAGISTRATE of this district as follows:

> *"Here a great change has taken place. Immediately after August, 1838, almost every proprietor started a retail shop on his estate, and in this attempted to get back the money which he had distributed in wages. Fortunately, from the competition of the many retail shops in the town of Soufrière, which is luckily in the centre of the district, this modification of the truck system did not long thrive; and in the Third District, estate-shops are now few in number. The town of Soufrière contains 228 houses, and nearly every third house is a shop, where something or other is sold. Six or seven are respectable enough to merit the name of "stores" where the usual assortment of a West India store can readily be obtained. Most of the second-rate shopkeepers employ "marchands", who travel from estate to estate with trays on their heads, containing Madras handkerchiefs, prints, and so forth, which they retail at an enormous rate of profit."*

> (CO 253/74/3: Sept. 1841)

In 1844 the STIPENDIARY MAGISTRATE of this district mentioned:

> *"There is a brisk traffic kept up between Castries, the principal town, and the districts of Soufrière and Vieux Fort."*

> (CO 253/82/3: 10/1/1844)

The STIPENDIARY MAGISTRATE of the 4th district (Vieux Fort, Laborie) reported:

> "The internal traffic of the District is confined to the trade carried on by the licensed hucksters and small shop keepers in the villages, on a few Estates, there are also shops from which the labourers often purchase their supplies, ..."
>
> (CO 253/82/4: 2/7/1844)

In December 1842 the STIPENDIARY MAGISTRATE of the 5th district (Micoud, Praslin, Dennery) reported:

> "On most of the Estates there were Shops for retailing provisions, clothing, wines, spirits, and so on to the labourers, but the difficulty of obtaining regularly supplies from Castries, has induced the proprietors generally to give them up;"
>
> (CO 253/78/5: 30/12/1842)

In the year 1845 the situation in this district was as as follows:

> "The traffic of this District is carried on through the Hucksters and small shops in the villages. On some of the Estates there are shops for the greater convenience of the resident labourers."
>
> (CO 253/83/9: 10/1/1845)

5.3.2.5   Nourishing

According to the reports of the STIPENDIARY MAGISTRATES the nourishing of the labourers was based on the one hand on provisions cultivated by themselves, as cassava, yams, plantains or potatoes and on the other hand on salted meat and fish. Other provisions were lard, butter, olive oil, rice or tea. On special occasions also fresh meat as mutton, turkeys or poultry as well as ham was eaten. For alcoholic beverages liquors, wine and beer was mentioned:

Extracts from the reports of the STIPENDIARY MAGAISTRATES of the several districts are as follows:

1st district (Castries, Anse La Raye):

> Although the labourer still manifests a strong and decided partiality for salt provision, especially salt cod fish, still he is not averse to an occasional indulgence in more substantial food, and on the occasion of a marriage feast, or the celebration of a festival, the display of mutton, turkeys, capons, and hams is in perfect keeping with the supply of good French liquors, claret vine and porter. The profits of the sale of provisions grown by the labourers are very considerable. Plantains, yams, potatoes and cassavas are brought into town in large quantities, and find a ready market."
>
> (CO 253/78/2: 24/12/1842)

"The sort of merchandize chiefly in demand amongst the labouring population may be classified under the two general heads of cured provisions and dry goods. The former comprehends beef, pork, mackerel, cod, herrings, lard, butter, sweet oil and meal, which are the necessaries of common consumption chiefly purchased by the peasantry."

(CO 253/82/5: 3/7/1844)

2nd district (Gros Islet, Dauphin):

"Except on days of festivals and holidays (when they show themselves as … epicurean as any other class of persons) the food of the peasantry consists principally of salted beef, pork, cod, mackerel &c. so that the abundance of poultry, pigs, &c. reared about their houses, are sent to market for sale, and the proceeds converted principally, to the acquisition of personal decorations, and salt provisions."

(CO 253/78/3: 21/12/1842)

3rd district (Soufrière, Choiseul):

"The tastes of the peasantry differ little from those of other classes of the inhabitants and depend entirely upon the means of gratifying them. On extraordinary occasions, hams, fresh meet, and all descriptions of poultry are liberally used, and their dresses and decorations are generally of the most costly materials, claret vine (en de Cote) is in great requisition and easily obtained, from the price being so very moderate; seldom more than six pence the bottle.

On ordinary occasions Salted Beef and Pork, Cod, Mackerels &c. are the principal articles of food, with ground provisions abundantly supplied from their Gardens, and an industrious labourer has always a sufficient quantity, as well as poultry, beyond his wants, to dispose of, to procure necessaries for domestic purposes."

(CO 253/82/3: 10/1/1844)

4th district (Vieux Fort, Laborie):

"In the quarter of Vieux Fort and Laborie Shops are established for the vending of various of domestic necessaries, not the produce of the country. The principal commodities kept on sale at these Shops are salted cod-fish, salt beef, salt pork, rice, tea, and grocery in general."

(CO 253/78/6: Dec. 1842)

5th district (Micoud, Praslin, Dennery):

"The principle articles of food are salt fish, and manioc farina, the produce of their provision grounds and manufactured by themselves; since the emancipation the consumption of butter and oil is considerably augmented."

(CO 253/78/5: 30/12/1842)

5.3.3 Leisure-time activities

In September 1835 Governor DUDLEY HILL of St. Lucia referred in his letter to the SECRETARY OF STATE GLENELG in London to new established police regulations which he refused regarding the point that no negro drums should be allowed to be beaten in the town of Castries. On this topic he wrote:

> "I know of no amusement to which the negro of both sexes looks forward with more delight than that of dancing to the beating of the drum, (not unlike the English kettle-drum), …"
>
> (CO 253/49/5: 2/9/1835)

The mentioned prohibition of beating the drum was cancelled by a letter of the SECRETARY OF STATE GLENELG on February 15th, 1836 (CO 253/49/6: 2/9/1835).

General reports of the leisure-time activities of the black population are available for the period from 1841 to 1845.

In September 1841 the STIPENDIARY MAGISTRATE of the 3rd district (Soufrière, Choiseul) mentioned as main leisure-time activities dancing and narrating:

> "It may not be, perhaps, irrelevant to say a word upon the amusements of the negro labourer, inasmuch as, by the amusements of a people, we can often guess pretty fairly as to their character and condition. Well, then, the only amusements worthy of the name which the negro possesses is the dance and narrative relation. The dance he is passionately fond of, and I am happy to say that this amusement is now conducted with more decorum and decency than formerly. So fond are they of the dance that frequently parties who meet at set periods do not break up until three or four days have been wasted; and I have known many a fatal catarrh and pleurisy caused by their devotion to this amusement. Sometimes, on moonlight nights, a party will assemble at the door of their house, and will remain the whole of the night attentively listening to some wild narrative of African origin, which some few amongst them have the talent to relate. The negro, like his betters, is fond of chit chat and scandal, and is delighted when he can pick up a piece of news of this description, especially if it relates to his superiors in rank. The gout and embellishment with which he will relate at these evening circles, and the shouts of laughter with which his auditors listen to it, show their enjoyment."
>
> (CO 253/74/3: Sept. 1841)

According to a report of the STIPENDIARY MAGISTRATE of the 1st district (Castries, Anse La Raye) of December 1842 the black population loved to celebrate feasts:

"The negroes are fond of holidays, and their taste in this respect is fully gratified by the frequent recurrence of the feast days observed in the Roman Catholic Church, … They have also certain festivals of their own, which they celebrate with much pomp and extravagance, …"

(CO 253/78/2: 24/12/1842)

The STIPENDIARY MAGISTRATE of the 2nd district (Gros Islet, Dauphin) reported:

"The tastes of the peasantry may be stated to assimilate, according to the means of gratifying them, with those of the other classes of inhabitants. The same love of showy dresses, dancing, and every description of gaiety, prevails amongst them."

(CO 253/78/3: 21/12/1842)

Also BREEN referred in his book published in 1844 to the passion of the blacks to celebrate feasts, to dance and to wear extravagant clothes:

"Not satisfied with aping those above them in finery and dress, the Negroes carry their love of dancing to the most extravagant pitch – much too extravagant perhaps for their means …

The spoiled children of artificial enjoyment, French Negroes, like their betters, will have their feasts and festivals, their dressing and dancing."

(BREEN 1844: 190-191)

Whereas the STIPENDIARY MAGISTRATE of the 1st district reported of a decline in the frequency of public dances in January 1845 the STIPENDIARY MAGISTRATE of the 2nd district mentioned their continuance:

1st district (Castries, Anse la Raye):

"The frequency of the public negro dances, and the displays of finery on those occasions, are very much diminished in some districts, particularly in the First District; this I consider in a great measure attributable to the extraordinary influence exercised by the alien Roman-catholic priests over nearly all classes, who always find some excuse for obtaining contributions from their followers."

(CO 253/83/8: 17/1/1845)

2nd district (Gros Islet, Dauphin):

"Their taste for dancing continues unabated amongst the peasantry, and the sobriety which generally characterizes the negro may in a great measure be ascribed to their devotedness to that amusement."

(CO 253/83/3: 5/7/1845)

5.3.4 The development of an independent peasantry

The black peasantry of St. Lucia cultivated provisions, in some cases also sugar cane, and reared cattle. The surplus was sold at the market (cp. chapter "5.3.2.2. Subsistence", pp 285-288).

From a letter of Governor TORRENS of St. Lucia of January 4th, 1846, follows that at that time an independent peasantry had been already developed:

> "The rise of a class of small proprietors and farmers is apparent among the emancipated population. This class of the negroes, the most industrious, has established settlements in many parts of the country hitherto covered with forests. These lots, whether bought or hired, are usually within reach of the neighbouring sugar establishments, permitting the negro to resort at crop time to the cane fields."

(CO 253/85/1: 4/1/1846)

According to reports of the STIPENDIARY MAGISTRATES the number of the proprietors of small pieces of land rose in the period from 1845 to 1850 as follows:

Source/Period of time	number of proprietors
(CO 258/16/3: 1/7/1845-31/12/1845, p.3)	1.345
(CO 258/16/4: 1/1/1846-30/6/1846, p.68)	1.388
(CO 258/16/5: 1/7/1846-31/12/1846, p.134)	1.390
(CO 258/16/6: 1/1/1847-30/6/1847, p.195)	1.329
(CO 258/16/1: 1/7/1847-31/12/1847, p.259)	1.333
(CO 258/16/7: 1/1/1848-30/6/1848, p.320)	1.848
(CO 258/16/2: 1/7/1848-31/12/1848, p.388)	1.868
(CO 258/17/2: 1/7/1849-31/12/1849, p.41)	1.920
(CO 258/17/3: 1/1/1850-30/6/1850, p.101)	2.180

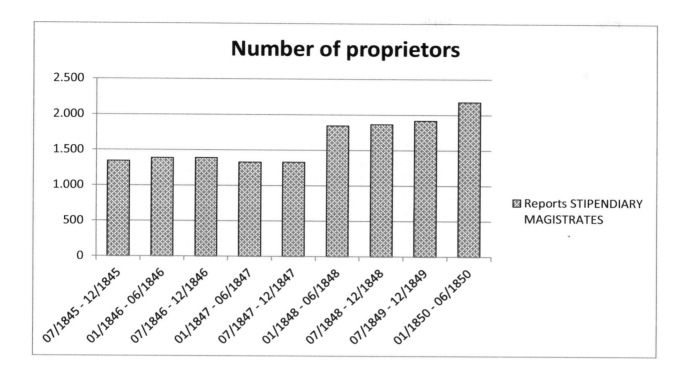

Number of proprietors

Regarding the trustworthiness of these figures a statement of the STIPENDIARY MAGISTRATE of the 1st district concerning the rise of the figures from 1847 to 1848 must be considered:

> *"The great increase which appears on the present Return may be accounted for by the correction of former miscalculation, together with the fact of an increasing number of small freeholders from amongst the labouring population."*
>
> (CO 258/16/7: 1/1/1848-30/6/1848, p.320)

Also in the report regarding the second half of the year 1848 he refers to the incorrectness of the stated figures:

> *"Many purchases of land are made without the deeds of sale being registered, or made known, therefore the number of freeholders stated in the several District returns, cannot be said to be altogether exact; unquestionably a great increase has taken place over the number returned in 1846."*
>
> (CO 258/16/2: 1/7/1848-31/12/1848, p.388)

The general rise of the peasantry is also mentioned by the STIPENDIARY MAGISTRATE of the 1st district in the year 1850:

> *"The increase here is attributed to the great progress of the rural Population in establishing themselves in small freehold-lots, which from the great extent of uncultivated abandoned land they can purchase very cheap, thus forming a rising middle class of industrious Settlers."*
>
> (CO 258/17/3: 1/1/1850-30/6/1850, p.101)

From a letter of Governor DARLING of St. Lucia of March 1850 follows that also townspeople took part in agriculture:

> *"There can be no doubt that the usual labourer has hitherto preferred to invest his savings in the soil, and in cattle; and even the lower classes who reside in the Towns are possessors of cows to a considerable extent. These animals are sent to graze on the Lands of their Country-Friends, upon condition of the produce, both in calves and milk, being divided between the Owner & the Grazier."*
>
> (CO 253/102/1: 30/3/1850)

5.3.5 Fear of re-enslavement

On May 16th, 1839, Governor EVERARD of St. Lucia published the following proclamation:

> *"Whereas information has been received by me, that certain evil-disposed Persons, with a view to excite the minds of the labouring population within this Island, and to interrupt the good feeling and understanding between Employers and Labourers, have spread a certain rumour to the effect, "That all the Labourers who shall be found residing on the Estates on the first of August next, shall be again reduced to a state of Slavery," and other reports of a similar tendency;*
>
> *And whereas it is expedient and necessary, that the minds of the labouring population should be disabused with regard to such rumours and reports, and that sentiments of mutual confidence and good faith be re-established amongst all the Inhabitants of this Colony:*
>
> *NOW, THEREFORE, I, MATTHIAS EVERARD, C.B. & K.K., Lieutenant Colonel of the 14th Regiment, and Administering the Civil Government of this Colony of Saint Lucia, do issue this my Proclamation to all the Inhabitants of this said Island, for the purpose of assuring all such Persons as may have given credence to such rumours and reports, that the same are utterly false and groundless; and that, on the contrary, all Labourers employed on Estates, or otherwise, who shall faithfully and diligently fulfil and perform the several contracts entered into by them, shall be entitled to the special protection of Her Majesty's Government.*
>
> *And I do hereby caution all Persons against circulating reports calculated to excite or mislead, in any manner whatsoever, the minds of the labouring population, or the Public generally, under the severest penalty provided for by the LAWS of this Island."*
>
> (CO 253/67/5: 16/5/1839)

According to the reports of the STIPENDIARY MAGISTRATES this rumour was limited to the 1st and 2nd district.

On June 3rd, 1839, the STIPENDIARY MAGISTRATE of the 1st district (Castries, Anse La Raye) reported of a restless situation on the estates:

> *"I regret to observe that the Labourers generally on the respective Estates are in a very unsettled state, partly owing to the report in circulation that they are to be made Slaves of again on the 1st of August next, many of them employing it as a pretext to absent themselves from the Estates, partly to the general disinclination of their having anyone placed over them to superintend and examine their work, and to their great desire to hire and cultivate land for themselves."*

(CO 253/67/6: 3/6/1839)

He further noticed:

> *"I have reason to believe that those reports have been purposely circulated by persons, who are endeavouring to persuade the Labourers to emigrate to Trinidad, doubtless with the hope of making a Traffic of it, as has been the case in the other islands."*

On July 31st, 1839, he mentioned effects of this rumour:

> *"Vide Bouteille Estate"*
>
> *The whole of the Labourers have abandoned this Property, leaving a considerable portion of the Crop unfinished. I can only attribute this to the same cause as on the majority of Estates, the idea that if found on the Properties on the 1st August they will be made Slaves again."*
>
> *"Entrepot Estate:*
>
> *The whole of the Labourers have abandoned this property. The Crop is unfinished: no contract existed."*
>
> *"La Pointe Estate:*
>
> *The Crop on this property is not yet finished owing to the irregular conduct of the Labourers; on this Estate many of the people have absented themselves at the end of the month in consequence of the approaching 1st August, but I have no doubt they will return to their regular avocations in a few days."*

(CO 253/68/7: 31/7/1839)

These mentioned estates were situated in the vicinity of the town of Castries.

The STIPENDIARY MAGISTRATE mentioned further:

> *"I have been given to understand that the Labourers generally, have been induced to leave the Estates, under the pretext that they will be made Slaves of again on the 1st August by the free persons who occupy small provision grounds in the neighbourhood of the Estates with the object of*

offering them refuge, and so get them to work their Grounds for them for little or nothing, but I have no doubt they will soon find out their mistake and be glad to return to their usual employ.-"

From the both last quotations follows that the STIPENDIARY MAGISTRATE of the 2nd district didn't attach much importance to the whole situation.

In August 1839 also the STIPENDIARY MAGISTRATE of the 2nd district (Gros Islet, Dauphin) reported of a rumour concerning re-enslavement:

> *"Notwithstanding the various rumours to the contrary it may be safely asserted of the 2nd district that they have gradually settled to their work – nothing has been more beneficial than allowing them a few days after the first of August, - they have become convinced of the absurdity of the reports circulated by interested individuals. Many of the Labourers in the first instance quitted their Estates – most of these have returned and are now at their labour."*

(CO 253/68/7: 17/8/1839)

Two years later the STIPENDIARY MAGISTRATES reported again of the rumour of re-enslavement. This rumour was especially mentioned by the STIPENDIARY MAGISTRATE of the 4th district (Vieux Fort, Laborie):

> *"I regret to add that a ridiculous rumour, originating, as I am informed, in the districts contiguous to Castries, has been, by the malice of a few, and the credulity of many, converted into a cause of considerable misunderstanding. The rumour I allude to was one, which sought to endanger the staple cultivation of the colony, by impressing the labourers with the idea that all persons found engaged in planting the cane would be once more subjected to bondage."*

(CO 253/74/7: 1/6/1841)

The STIPENDIARY MAGISTRATE of the 1st district (Castries, Anse La Raye) reported of the unfoundedness of this rumour:

> *"... that, notwithstanding the report that was in circulation in the beginning of last month, that the labourers had abandoned their work on the different estates, I have much satisfaction in informing his Excellency that such report was unfounded, ..."*

(CO 253/74/8: 2/6/1841)

The STIPENDIARY MAGISTRATE of the 5th district (Micoud, Praslin, Dennery) referred to interruptions of the work on the estates owing to another rumour:

> *"The tranquillity of the district was likely to have been disturbed, in consequence of some idle rumours which had been afloat in the quarter of Micoud.*

It would appear, from what I have been able to ascertain, that a report has been circulated, that the Queen had expressed her disapprobation at the labourers continuing to be employed in the cultivation of the cane; that Her Majesty had directed the scale of wages to be reduced, and that all persons following that occupation should be compelled to wear a red cap or bonnet, by way of distinguishing them from those otherwise employed. I lost no time in repairing to the quarter, and actually found that some of the labourers had already left, and others were preparing to retire into the heights with their effects. I assembled such as I could get together on the emergency (and fortunately there were some of the most intelligent amongst them), and after having pointed out the folly of their conduct, I ridiculed their fears. The effect was such as I had anticipated; they appeared to be ashamed of their behaviour, and promised to act more wisely in future."

(CO 253/74/9: 2/6/1841)

The rumour of re-enslavement was mentioned the last time in the year 1844. On the occasion of a report of a riot in the town of Castries in October 1844 owing to the conviction of a boy to 15 lashes with the whip because of perjury. Governor TORRENS of St. Lucia informed the Governor of Barbados, GREY, as follows:

"I yesterday informed His Honour the Chief Justice, that I will never again sanction the infliction of any Corporal punishment in the Island whatever description: for observation has convinced me that the people associate the idea of whipping with Slavery; and already yesterday mischievous persons had not failed to publish in various parts of the Island the rumour that Slavery was to be re-established. Of these mischievous persons (by whose Agency I have reason to believe much of this excitement has arisen) there exist several in different parts of the Island: - chiefly immigrants and refugees from Martinique, being free persons who have fled here from the laws of their own Colony.

It would give me great satisfaction to be able to fix on these persons the guilt of their sedition, and I shall neglect no means of doing so. I am told that it was this class of persons who in Dominica took advantage of a similar ebullition of popular feeling to raise wickedly the same false and dangerous impression on the minds of the lately enfranchised negro population.

So short a time has elapsed since that enfranchisement that the Negroes, who in Castries on this occasion, contrary to their wont fraternised cordially with the Coloured part of the population, seem to be easily excited by any proceeding which recalls to them the yoke from which they have been so lately liberated: and many were yesterday heard to say: Puis qu'on nous a faits libres, fallait pas nous battie.

Another circumstance which is fresh in the recollection of the oldest negroes (and they being of African origin are the most barbarous) viz: that the English in their conquest of the Island after the French Revolution reduced the black population which by that revolution had been freed, once more to a state of Slavery – this circumstance handed down as it has

301

been from Sire to Son, may perhaps aid in creating that peculiar susceptibility which has been made manifest on the present occasion, and which apparently … them to dread that their present happy state of freedom and prosperity may prove evanescent as the liberty enjoyed and misused by their Grand Sires in the last Century."

(CO 253/81/2: 15/10/1844)

The Governor further mentioned:

"… that the work has never been interrupted on the Estates, and that the best feelings continue to exist among the black Population."

On this occasion Governor TORRENS published a proclamation in which he explicitly confirmed the freedom of the black population:

"Whereas it has come to my knowledge that certain wicked and evil disposed Persons who have no attachment to Our Gracious Queen VICTORIA or to Her Government, have laboured and are yet labouring to raise among the lately enfranchised Population of this Island, the false idea that it is intended again to re-establish among them that SLAVERY, which on the 1st of August 1838, was by the Blessing of Almighty GOD, so happily and irrevocably abolished FOR EVER throughout ST. LUCIA.

I now call on you, as good and faithful subjects to the Queen to attend to these words addressed to you by me YOUR GOVERNOR and sincere and hearty Friend.

My dear Friends, and fellow Subjects,

I have in the first place to thank you for your loyalty and excellent conduct in refraining from any participation in the Riot which took place in Castries, on Monday the 14th day of the month: -- I have to thank you for the kind and joyful welcome which I everywhere received from you when I lately visited the Island.

That kind and joyful welcome, your happy and free condition, the prosperity and industry I everywhere saw, will never be banished from my recollection.

I thank you for your addresses of attachment to our Gracious Queen, and of respect for me her humble Representative.

I now beg of you, not to listen to the wicked tales you may hear respecting Slavery – YOU ARE FOR EVER FREE – no person can ever make you slaves again.

You are as free as I am, or any Englishman under the Government of QUEEN VICTORIA.

Trust in HER, trust in your GOVERNOR, believe nothing that does not come through him, or your MAGISTRATES, who you know are your best Friends;

-- And of this be assured that your present happy and free condition, will endure as long as this World will endure; in your persons and in those of your free and happy Children.

And now Farewell, and may the GOD of all mercy, that GOD under whose Almighty Protection you became Free, for ever bless you and watch over you, and preserve you from the base and wicked lies of those who are seeking to deceive you!"

(CO 253/81/3: Oct. 1844)

5.3.6 Summary

After the end of the emancipation period many labourers left the estates and settled on small pieces of land. Especially during the emancipation period and short thereafter freed APPRENTICES frequently settled illegally on crown lands. In the early forties the number of these illegal settlers reduced to a large extent. This decline is to be seen in connection with the return of the labourers to the estates.

According to the reports of the STIPENDIARY MAGISTRATES in the period from 1841 to 1845 follows the following picture of the way of life of St. Lucia's black labour population:

Selection of place of residence

Among the labourers there was generally the tendency to reside on small pieces of land which were hired or bought from the planters because the labourers preferred living independently. Other labourers stayed at their former residence on the estate. In this case the planters generally didn't exact any payment.

From reports of the 4th and 5th district follows that the labourers built small houses in the villages for their families. The labourers themselves still continued to reside on the estate and used these houses only on Sundays or holidays or when occasion called them to the village. The STIPENDIARY MAGISTRATE of the 3rd district reported of village formations as on the Morne Belair estate in Fond St. Jacques, on the St. Jour as well as on the Hermitage estate, which were divided into lots by their owners and rented or sold to the labourers. In the year 1845 the erection of the village Victoria in the vicinity of Choiseul was mentioned.

Subsistence

On the one hand the labourers continued to work on the estates and on the other hand they cultivated provisions as plantains, yams, potatoes or cassava, raised horn-cattle, pigs, goats and poultry or were fishers. The sale of logwood which was very important for the blacks in the period of slavery was discontinued because of uneconomical aspects.

The labourers also burned charcoal and they reared horses. Another occupation was the cultivation of sugar cane from which they made sugar syrup by themselves or they let them make on the estate. This syrup they sold on the market.

Many of the former non-field slaves worked on the sugar plantations because of the high wages paid to them.

Situation of the children

Either the children worked on the estates where they were employed in "light work" as herding cattle or distributing manure, or they assisted their families in the cultivation of their provision grounds. Some were sent to the villages or towns where they learned different trades.

General supply position

There were three kinds of supply possibilities for the labourers: shops on the estates, shops in towns and villages as well as hucksters. According to the geographical situation on the island the focus varied between these three supply possibilities.

The running of shops on estates which was very common shortly after the end of the emancipation period, lost in significance in the early forties because of bad business practices as well as difficulties in competition. The main supply function had the shops in the towns and villages as in Castries, Soufrière, Vieux Fort, Laborie, Micoud, Dennery and Gros Islet. As an additional supply possibility there were the hucksters which mainly could be met in the 3rd, 4th and 5th district.

Nourishing

The nourishing of the labourers was based on the one hand on provisions cultivated by themselves, as cassava, yams, plantains or potatoes and on the other hand on salted meat and fish. Other provisions were lard, butter, olive oil, rice or tea. On special occasions also fresh meat as mutton, turkeys or poultry as well as ham was eaten. For alcoholic beverages liquors, wine and beer was mentioned.

Leisure-time activities

According to a report of the STIPENDIARY MAGISTRATE of the 3rd district the main leisure-time activities of the black population of St. Lucia were dancing and narrating. They also loved to celebrate feasts with much pomp and extravagance.

Development of an independent peasantry

Further it is to mention that about the middle of the forties an independent peasantry had been already developed in St. Lucia which rose in the second half of the forties.

Fear of re-enslavement

Another point was the fear of re-enslavement. This rumour occurred among the black population of St. Lucia three times: in the years 1839, 1841 and 1844. Especially in the year 1839 there were concrete effects of this rumour where for fear of re-enslavement estates in the 1st and 2nd district were left. In the years 1841 and 1844 no concrete effects were mentioned. An uniform reason for the origin of this rumour couldn't be found in the sources. As reasons there were stated: inducing the labourers to emigrate to Trinidad, engaging the labourers on small pieces of land and influence of immigrants and refugees from Martinique.

5.4 Immigration

5.4.1 Introduction

This chapter gives a review of the immigration to St. Lucia in the 19th century, whereby regarding the thematic of this work the immigration of Africans was mainly handled. Immigrants came also from Europe and India.

Generally to the immigration to St. Lucia it is to mention that it started not before the middle of the forties in the 19th century as in the early forties there was a good satiated labour market in the colony (cp. chapter "5.2.1.2. Labour situation and effects of the free labour market after the end of the emancipation period (1838-1846), pp.260-269). The first complaints of a lack of labourers appear in reports of the STIPENDIARY MAGISTRATES of the year 1845. The STIPENDIARY MAGISTRATE of the 2nd district (Gros Islet, Dauphin) reported:

> "The want of hands has been much felt in this district during the whole of the last six months; one of the consequences of this is that upon none of the estates has the crop been yet completed, and upon many it will be impossible to take off all that is in the ground. I am very much afraid that, without the intervention of considerable emigration, this want will but increase from year to year."
>
> (CO 253/83/3: 577/1845)

Also the STIPENDIARY MAGISTRATE of the 4th district (Vieux Fort, Laborie) mentioned a lack of labourers:

> "By returns received from the proprietors of sugar estates in the district (there are no coffee or cocoa estates), it appears that the greatest number of labourers, male and female, employed at any one time during the year, amounted to 714, and that the additional number required, according to their own statement, would be 646, making altogether the number of labourers at present required for agricultural purposes to amount to 1,360, being little more than double the number now employed on the sugar estates in the district."
>
> (CO 253/83/2: 10/1/1845)

5.4.2 European Immigration

In a "return of the number of immigrants into the island of St. Lucia, from the 1st day of August, 1834, to the 30th April, 1843,..." the following European immigrants are stated:

Year of immigration	Country of origin	M	F	Ch	T[25]	Remarks
1836	Ireland	5	4	8	17	"Brought out by Mr. Muter
"	France	1	-	-	1	-
"	England	1	-	-	1	-
1837	Scotland	6	5	7	18	"Imported by Mr. Muter"
1838	France	1	-	-	1	-
1839	England	1	-	-	1	-
1840	France	6	-	-	6	"Imported from France to the Canelle estate, the property of Mr Muter"
"	Scotland	6	6	5	17	"Imported by Mr. Muter"
"	Germany	12	10	7	29	"These Germans were imported by Mr. King, via England; three men have since died; one man, two women, with one child, returned to England; and three men, two women, and three children have left the colony."
1842	France	16	4	3	23	"Imported in this island By Mr. Beaucé; eight of These immigrants died; Seven left the colony for Martinique."
TOTAL		55	29	30	114	

(CO 253/78/7: 1843)

---

[25] M=male, F=female, Ch=Children, T=Total

Regarding these immigrants BREEN (1844:304-306) gives the following information. At first he referred to five Irish families who were imported by Mr. Muter in 1836 and established in the "notoriously insalubrious district of Roseau". Further he wrote:

> "The consequence was that the immigrants fell off one by one, victims to the insidious fevers of that humid locality. In 1837 the same gentleman made another essay of a similar nature. This time, however, the stream of immigration was made to flow from Scotland; but, as in the former case, the immigrants, numbering eighteen persons, were located in the valley of Roseau; and notwithstanding the most lavish expenditure in food, clothing, nursing, and medical attendance, the experiment met with no better success. In 1840 Mr. Muter made another importation, consisting of seventeen persons, from the same quarter, and with the like unfortunate results."

Regarding the German immigrants BREEN mentioned that they were located in the district of Soufrière on the coffee estate of Mr. King. In this area there was a more favourable climate than in the before mentioned area of Roseau. He further wrote:

> "The result has been highly favourable: of twenty-nine German labourers, imported in 1840 and 1841, only two have fallen victims to disease. The others continue in excellent health, and by their industry and sobriety contribute to exalt the character of the free cultivator amongst the commonalty of St. Lucia. Their gardens, the only ones in the island that deserve the name, abound in every description of European vegetable and tropical fruit, with which they supply the Soufrière market, and sometimes even that of Castries, a distance of twenty miles from the estate."

When comparing this quotation with the before mentioned return of the COLONIAL SECRETARY HANLEY regarding the German immigrants the following is to be stated:

- BREEN mentions a German immigration also in the year 1841; but the total number of German immigrants is stated in both sources with 29
- According to the statement of the COLONIAL SECRETARY in the year 1843 out of the 29 Germans three were dead, four had returned to England and further eight persons had also left the colony. BREEN mentions only two deaths. From this information follows that BREEN's source is dated earlier than 1843.

The statement of BREEN that also in the year 1841 German immigrants arrived in St. Lucia is confirmed by a report of the STIPENDIARY MAGISTRATE of the 3rd district (Soufrière, Choiseul) of July 1841 as follows:

> "I am happy to report the arrival of another German family upon the Belle Plaine estate. I mention this, as it is a very good proof of the prosperity of

this interesting settlement, inasmuch as the new comers (husband, wife, and three children) are intimately related to one of the earlier emigrants, and induced to come out by their happy representatives."

According to a letter of Mr. King of October 1840 the first German immigrants arrived in St. Lucia on April 1st, 1840. Their names and ages were stated therein as follows:

"Conrad Wessler	50 years of age
Elizabeth (his wife)	44 "
Mary (daughter)	18 ½ "
Effa "	15 ½ "
Josepha "	13 "
Jacob Habel	43 "
Mary his wife	38 "
Frederick de Boss	23 "
Charles Kraft	20 "
Alexander Heid	18 " "

(CO 253/71/1: 1/10/1840)

The successful settlement of the German immigrants stated by BREEN is also mentioned by the STIPENDIARY MAGISTRATE of the 3rd district (Soufrière, Choiseul) from the years 1840 and 1841:

"His Excellency will no doubt be glad to hear that the German Immigrants brought out by Captain King are doing well – a more contented, sober, or industrious little settlement cannot I am sure be found in the West Indies – the houses and gardens are now completed and the experiment has so far completely succeeded – the Emigrants have materially bettered their condition and Captain King is well satisfied with the results –"

(CO 253/71/2: 16/8/1840)

"The German emigrants on the Belle Plaine estate continue in excellent health and spirits, and there can now be no doubt but that these people have greatly bettered their condition in life. From my own positive knowledge, many of them, besides the comforts which they daily enjoy, have amassed considerable sums of money, two of the members of this interesting settlement were married last month, and I believe that other matrimonial engagements amongst them are now in contemplation."

(CO 253/74/11: 7/6/1841)

To the French immigrants mentioned in the return of the COLONIAL SECRETARY who arrived in the year 1842 BREEN (1844: 306-307) reported that they were established on an estate in Dennery and that they either died or left the area because of the unfavourable climate.

From the reports of the STIPENDIARY MAGISTRATES of the 5th district (Micoud, Praslin, Dennery) follow this information:

> "A body of twenty one European Labourers, natives of France, of both sexes and all ages has recently been established on Anse Canot Estate, in this District, ...
>
> They consist of Artisans, Field and House Labourers;"

(CO 253/76/3: 1/2/1842)

> "I regret, so soon after my last Report, to have to report the painful circumstance that five deaths have occurred amongst the twenty-one French and Sovyard Labourers, recently introduced into this District. When in my report of January, I mentioned their introduction, I was not aware that the Estate selected for their location was one of the most sickly in the Colony."

(CO 253/76/4: 1/3/1842)

Summing up it can be said that the attempt to establish European labourers in St. Lucia failed with the exception of the German settlers. The period of European immigration to St. Lucia is restricted from 1836 to 1842.

5.4.3 Caribbean Immigrants

5.4.3.1   Sources

The Caribbean immigrants mainly originate from Barbados. Sporadically there are also reports of immigrants from St. Kitts. In the already mentioned return of the COLONIAL SECRETARY HANLEY of St. Lucia (CO 253/78/7: 1843) for the year 1840 one immigrant from St. Kitts was stated. The arrival of further eleven immigrants (nine men, two boys) were reported by the STIPENDIARY MAGISTRATE of the 2nd district (Gros Islet, Dauphin) for August 1852 (CO 258/17/4: 1/7/1852-31/12/1852), p.313)

The first immigrants from Barbados arrived according to BREEN (1844: 307-308) in the year 1841. He mentions the figure of 110:

"The only other immigrants are one hundred and ten Barbadian Negroes introduced in 1841. Seventy-five of these are indented to Mr. Goodman of Union Vale, twenty-seven to Mr. Todd of Union, and eight to M. Lacorbiniere of Corinth. They appear to afford satisfaction to their employers; but the outlay attending their removal and location has far exceeded the original estimate, and neither of these gentlemen has been tempted to repeat the experiment."

According to the return of the COLONIAL SECRETARY HANLEY (CO 253/78/7: 1843) the first labourers from Barbados immigrated already in the year 1840. Totally 77 persons were mentioned.

Regarding the reports of the STIPENDIARY MAGISTRATES of the Barbadian immigrants the first were from the 3rd district (Soufrière, Choiseul):

> "One of the wealthiest proprietors of this district (Mr. Goodman) has brought down a party of emigrants from Barbados. The wages which this gentleman gives to these people are eighty livres per month, together with house, provision-grounds, medical attendance, and rations, until their grounds are in full bearing; and it is but justice to add, that these people and their employer seem much pleased with each other."
>
> (CO 253/74/11: 7/6/1841)

> "Since I last had the honour to report to His Excellency Colonel Graydon, 72 Barbadians, immigrant labourers, have arrived in the district; viz., 43 men, 14 females, and 15 children. They are all of them, without exception, most respectable agricultural labourers from the rural districts of Barbados; eight men and their families have located themselves on the Morne Courbaril estate, and the others have made engagements with the proprietor of the Union Vale and Black Bay estates. The wages given to these people are eight dollars per mensem, with rations, until the provision-grounds allotted to them shall be in full bearing. They appear delighted with their prospects in this country, and I need hardly say that the parties who have engaged their services seem well pleased at such an acquisition.
>
> (CO 253/74/12: 7/8/1841)

> "Mr. John Goodman, the other capitalist alluded to, has brought from Barbados a body of nearly 100 immigrants, including children; and at present all parties seem pleased with the result. The wages given by Mr. Goodman are high, comparatively speaking; but the labour performed by the Barbadians is equivalent, for it is no less strange than true, that the Barbadian labourer will, with ease to himself, do in the week at least twice as much work as the Lucian."
>
> (CO 253/74/3: Sept. 1841)

Later also the STIPENDIARY MAGISTRATES of the 2nd and 4th district reported of the arrival of immigrants from Barbados:

2nd district (Gros Islet, Dauphin)

> "A few more Immigrants from Barbados have arrived this month. They are located on the "Corinthe estate" of this district, a fine Sugar Property and in eligible situation."
>
> (CO 253/74/13: Nov. 1841)

<u>4th district (Vieux Fort, Laborie)</u>:

>*"A few Barbadian Labourers, recently brought to this Colony, have been located on one Estate in the District. I fear, however, that in truth the experiment has proved unsuccessful. There has been mortality amongst them, brought on, I believe, in a great measure by their own imprudence; and, on the slightest symptoms of sickness they appear to yield themselves to despondency."*
>
> (CO 253/76/5: 1/1/1842)

From this last quotation follows that among the immigrants deaths already had occurred. In December 1842 the STIPENDIARY MAGISTRATE of the 1st district (Castries, Anse La Raye) also pointed to this fact:

>*"The Barbadians have been distributed on several Sugar Properties, situated on the leeward side of the island, the mortality amongst them has been considerable; many have left the colony and few are now to be seen on the Estates where they were first located. I do not consider the Creole negro of Barbados to be an eligible immigrant as an agricultural labourer in this island: coming from dry uniform climate to take up his abode in a place where the atmosphere is peculiarly variable and humid and the soil wet and marshy, the native of Barbados is eminently predisposed to the influence of Malaria."*
>
> (CO 253/78/2: 24/12/1842)

Only the STIPENDIARY MAGISTRATE of the 3td district (Soufrière, Choiseul) reported of no sickness among the immigrants which can be referred to the favourable climate in this district as already mentioned in connection with the German immigrants (cp. p. 308):

>*"The Barbadian Immigrants are likewise, I am glad to say, doing pretty well just now."*
>
> (CO 253/76/6: 12/3/1842)

>*"..., all natives of Barbados, appear to be contented and happy."*
>
> (CO 253/82/3: 10/1/1844)

From the year 1842 to the middle of the year 1845 no new arrivals of Barbadian immigrants were reported by the STIPENDIARY MAGISTRATES. Also the newspaper PALLADIUM reported of the end of Barbadian immigration in January 1843:

>*"The immigration of Labourers from Barbados has ceased for some time past; and, with the exception of an occasional arrival of Refugees from Martinique; there has been no addition to our agricultural population."*
>
> (N/CO 258/1/8: 5/1/1843, p.272)

The next reports of the arrival of immigrants from Barbados were made in July 1845. The STIPENDIARY MAGISTRATE of the 1st district (Castries, Anse La Raye) wrote:

> *"In this district there has been no immigration, but numerous labourers having arrived from Barbados recently for other districts in the island, ..."*

(CO 253/83/10: 14/7/1845)

The STIPENDIARY MAGISTRATE of the 4th district (Vieux Fort, Laborie) mentioned the arrival of 28 immigrants:

> *"Within the last fortnight, and for the first time in the district, 28 immigrants, of whom 17 were adults and 11 children, have been imported from the neighbouring island of Barbados; but as their arrival has been of such recent date, I am unable to offer remarks at present;"*

(CO 253/83/11: 1/7/1845)

Regarding the number of immigrated labourers from Barbados from the year 1845 onward according to the reports of the STIPENDIARY MAGISTRATES there are the following figures:

Source/time period	Number of immigrants	District
(CO 258/16/8: 1/7/1845-31/12/1845, p. 28)	33	2.
(CO 258/16/9: 1/7/1845-31/12/1845, p. 39)	49	3.
(CO 258/16/10: 1/7/1845-31/12/1845, p. 50)	28	4.
(CO 258/16/11: 1/1/1846-30/6/1846, p.105)	23	3.
(CO 258/16/12: 1/7/1847-31/12/1847, p.294)	26	3.
	159	

From the beginning of the year 1848 onward no arrivals of Barbadian immigrants were reported in the available reports of the STIPENDIARY MAGISTRATES:

Concerning the exactness of the stated figures by the STIPENDIARY MAGISTRATES the STIPENDIARY MAGISTRATE of the 1st district mentioned in the year 1848 as follows:

> *"There are no means of ascertaining with accuracy the number of persons coming to or leaving the Island."*

(CO 258/16/7: 1/1/1848-30/6/1848, p.320)

<u>2nd district (Gros Islet, Dauphin):</u>

"The labourers introduced into this district from Barbados are working cheerfully, and all are in good health."

(CO 258/16/13: 1/1/1846-30/6/1846, p.94)

<u>3rd district (Soufrière, Choiseul):</u>

"I am sorry to say that the behaviour of Barbadian Immigrants is such as not to make their coming very desirable. Mostly given up to hard drinking and quarrelling, they add to these the horrible habit of carrying with them knives and even razors, which, in fighting, they make use of and with which they inflict most fearful wounds. Their cunning at Court and trifling with truth, is a pernicious example to the natives of this Island. I may add that out of twenty complaints adjudicated upon by myself, there are, at least, four concerning Barbadians, though their number is not greater than 150 or 200 in all this district."

(CO 258/16/12: 1/7/1847-31/12/1847, p.294)

5.4.3.2 Summary

Owing to the incompletely available sources no definitive statement is possible regarding the number as well as the exact arrival of the immigrants of Barbados. But it can be assumed that the main part of the immigrants who arrived in St. Lucia at the beginning of the forties of the 19th century, came in the year 1841. The figure of 110 immigrants mentioned by BREEN seems to be the most nearest to the truth. The main part of these immigrants was established in the 3rd district (Soufrière, Choiseul).

Regarding the second immigration period starting in the year 1845 and ending in 1848 an import of approximately 160 immigrants can be assumed according to the reports of the STIPENDIARY MAGISTRATES. The main part settled also in the 3rd district.

Concerning the labourers immigrated at the beginning of the forties the STIPENDIARY MAGISTRATES reported of a good and satisfactory execution of their work but many dies because of malaria or left the colony. Owing to a favourable climate in the 3rd district the immigrants there were wealthy.

The two available reports from the year 1845 onwards diverge from each other. While the STIPENDIARY MAGISTRATE of the 2nd district (Gros Islet, Dauphin) reported positively the STIPENDIARY MAGISTRATE of the 3rd district complained of their bad moral.

According to a report of the STIPENDIARY MAGISTRATE of the 1st district (Castries, Anse La Raye) it was generally difficult to obtain labourers from Barbados:

> "-doubtless also there would be a considerable augmentation to the population here by immigration were it not for obstruction & formalities offered by the authorities of Barbados to prevent their labouring population from emigrating."
>
> (CO 258/16/3: 1/7/1845-31/12/1845, p.3)

5.4.4 African Immigrants

5.4.4.1   Introduction

As source for the following remarks DOOKHAN (1981: 48-49) was used:

The lack of labourers in the British colonies in the Caribbean forced the British government to search for labourers in other parts of the world and in that situation also Africa was considered. Under pressure from colonial planters and governors, approval was granted by the British government in December 1840 to a colonial bounty on immigration from Sierra Leone. The first batch of immigrants to Guyana, Trinidad and Jamaica arrived in 1841 in merchant ships chartered by private individuals, but two years later the British government assumed direct control. The cost, however, was borne by the colonies.

Immigration from Sierra Leone was opposed by European timber merchants there who were fearful of losing their best labourers, and by the Christian missionaries who did not want to lose prospective converts and evangelists. Besides, Africans showed little interest in emigration despite the considerable effort to induce them by offers of high wages and free return passages.

Emigrations from Gambia, the Kru coast as well as from Liberia were insignificant.

The greatest number of Africans was obtained from seizures made from foreign slave ships captured by British naval patrols in the Atlantic. Africans liberated in the western Atlantic were landed directly in the British West Indies; others intercepted off the African coast were condemned to the British by the International Courts of Mixed Commission at Sierra Leone and at St. Helena, and later transferred to the West Indies. By 1867 Trinidad had received 8.854 liberated Africans, Guyana 14.060, and Jamaica 11.391, while 5.027 others had been distributed among Grenada, St. Vincent, St. Lucia, Dominica and St. Kitts.

5.4.4.2   Sources

On February 6th, 1849, the ship UNA arrived with the first African immigrants in St. Lucia. According to the report of the GOVERNMENT IMMIGRATION AGENT they were 365 persons from Sierra Leone. Originally 367 persons were embarked. One man and one boy died during the voyage. The ship had left Sierra Leone on January 16th, 1849, and reached St. Lucia on February 6th, 1849, after a 20 days' voyage. Exact figures follow from the report of the GOVERNMENT IMMIGRATION AGENT as follows:

	Adults		Children under 14		Total
	Male	Female	Male	Female	
Immigrants embarked	180	109	38	40	367
Deaths on the voyage	1	-	1	-	2
Immigrants landed	179	109	37	40	365

(CO 253/97/1: 16/2/1849)

On February 7th, 1849, Governor DARLING of St. Lucia informed the Governor of Barbados of the arrival of the ship UNA with "Liberated Africans":

> "I have the honour to report to your Excellency that the Ship "Una", Canszar Master, and Dr. J Udny, Surgeon Superindendant, arrived here yesterday morning the 6th instant from Sierra Leone having on board 365 Liberated Africans."

(CO 253/97/2: 7/2/1849)

In contrast to the report of the GOVERNMENT IMMIGRATION AGENT which was made 10 days after the arrival of the ship and in which the immigrants were divided into 179 men, 109 women, 67 boys and 40 girls, Governor DARLING stated another classification of the immigrants: 164 men, 101 women, 52 boys and 48 girls. The statements regarding the two deaths during the voyage also diverge. While the report of the GOVERNMENT IMMIGRATION AGENT states the death of one man and one boy, the Governor mentioned the death of two boys:

> "Two Deaths only, both of boys, occurred during the passage and those on the last two days of the voyage. The rest are in good health with the exception of two cases, one of inflammation of the eyes, and the other of ulcer."

To the Governor of St. Lucia a letter of Governor PINZ from Sierra Leone dated January 12th, 1849, was handed over. Extracts therefrom are as follows:

> "I have the honour to inform your Excellency that I have deemed it proper to permit the ship "Una" though without a Licence for that purpose from

316

the Secretary of State to take her complement of 367 Emigrants equal to 328 statute adults from our Liberated African Yard and to proceed with them to St. Lucia.

The following circumstances have induced me to take this step.

The "Una" left England for the purpose of proceeding hither with a charge of merchandise and hence to St. Helena with the view of there procuring Emigrants for St. Lucia, and I am informed by the master that just before he sailed from Liverpool, a telegraphic despatch announced that a Licence for that purpose had been promised and would be forwarded to him.

After discharging that portion of this cargo intended for this place, finding a large number of Liberated Africans in the Yard, and being apprehensive that he might not be successful in procuring Emigrants at St. Helena, the master applied to me, to be permitted to take his complement of Emigrants from hence to any island in the West Indies to which I might think proper to send him.

With this request I have deemed it advisable to comply because a large number of Africans have been for some time past in the yard, whom in the absence of emigrant vessels, I should be compelled to discharge, as independently of the great expense to which their maintenance puts the government, it has been found by experience that the longer such persons remain in the yard, the greater is the difficulty of inducing them to emigrate.

On the other hand there is no doubt that the discharging large numbers of persons from the yard into the body of the population is prejudicial to the general interests of emigration by affording a matter of ... encouragement to this community in the constant struggle which in they believe that emigration is opposed to the welfare of the Colony, it maintains with the local government upon the subject."

(CO 253/97/3: 12/1/1849)

According to the before mentioned letter of Governor DARLING dated February 7th, 1849 (CO 253/97/2: 7/2/1849) he was surprised of the arrival of the immigrants. He expected them only in the middle of March:

"Your Excellency will be aware that I was informed by Earl Grey's despatch general no. 4 of the 17th November last, (transmitted with your Excellency's Circular no. 68 of the 9th January 1849) that the "Una" was at that date about to leave England immediately for St. Helena; there to receive her quota of liberated Africans, and that I had therefore no reason to expect her arrival before the middle of next month ...

In a Colony in which Immigration at a Public Expense has never yet taken place, and no organization of any kind for the proper conduct of it, had been established, we were of course wholly unprepared for the reception of these people."

The labour terms of the immigrants were published in a "Government Notice" on February 6th, 1849, as follows:

"The following are the TERMS upon which it is proposed to allot the Immigrants under Written Contracts of Service: -

1. *Contracts will be limited to One Year's duration, as enacted by the Royal Order in Council of the 7th day of September 1838.*

2. *Dry, wholesome, and comfortable Lodging, to be previously inspected and reported upon by the Stipendiary Magistrate and approved of by the Lieutenant-Governor, must be provided for the Immigrants.*

3. *To each Male and Female Immigrant must be allotted not less than Half an Acre of Land suitable to the production of the Ground Provisions of the Island.*

4. *Medical Attendance, by a duly qualified Practitioner, and Medicines, to be supplied to each Immigrant of all ages at the cost of the Employer.*

5. *The following RATIONS and WAGES to be assigned to the Immigrants during the first Six Months of their Contract:-*

   To each Immigrant above 14 years of age, a weekly Ration of 3lbs Salt-fish, or 2 lbs. of Beef or Pork or a proportion each of Beef and Pork equal to 2 lbs of Meat in all.

   7 lbs Bread; or

   2 ½ pots = 5 quarts of Farina Manioc; or 3 pots = 6 quarts of Corn-Meal; or 2 pots = 4 quarts of Rice, or 21 lbs of Yams, or 28 lbs Sweet Potatoes, or 21 lbs Eddoes[26], or 25 lbs Plantains – or equivalent proportions, if it is found convenient to comprise more than one of the above enumerated Grain and Vegetables in the weekly Ration.

   Two-pence a day Wages for each day on which the Immigrant works – the Employer being bound to find work for the number of days per week specified in the Contract.

6. *During the Second Six Months, Half the above Ration only to be issued, and the Wages to be increased to Five-pence a day.*
   Children under 14 to receive Half Rations, but those between 10 and 14 to receive in addition Two-pence per diem Wages during the Second Six Months.

7. *The Immigrants will be bound to labour for Nine Hours on Six Days in the Week, or Five Days only if so specified in the Contract, between Sunrise and Sunset, at least one break of an hour being allowed for rest."*

(CO 253/97/6: 6/2/1849)

---

[26] „Eddoes" = Taro (The Oxford English Dictionary 1969, Vol. III, p.38)

According to a table of the STIPENDIARY MAGISTRATE of the 1st district out of the 365 immigrants 362 were allotted to the following estates:

Name of the estate	male	female	total	district
Anse Galet	7	13	20	1.
Anse Latoque	1	-	1	1.
Beauchamp	4	10	14	5.
Beausejour	10	10	20	4.
Beausejour	6	1	7	2.
Belle Plaine	8	-	8	3.
Bonneterre	10	5	15	2.
Chateau Belair	15	-	15	3.
Cocoa Nuts	5	-	5	1.
Corinth	7	4	11	2.
Entrepot	9	8	17	1.
Fonds Estate	13	9	22	5.
Grand Anse	9	9	18	2.
La Redoute	8	2	10	1.
Marquis	17	15	32	2.
Morne Courbaril	11	1	12	3.
Pointe Sable	6	-	6	4.
Two friends	9	4	13	3.
Troumassée	15	24	39	5.
Union	14	10	24	2.
Union Vale	20	20	40	3.
Total	216	146	362	

(CO 253/100/1: February 1849)

The allotment of the immigrants to the several districts in percentages is as follows:

Districts	number of allotted Immigrants	share in percent
1. (Castries, Anse La Raye)	66	18
2. (Gros Islet, Dauphin)	107	30
3. (Soufrière, Choiseul)	88	24
4. (Vieux Fort, Laborie)	26	7
5. (Micoud, Praslin, Dennery)	75	21
Total	362	100

Graphic representation of the mentioned districts:

(Division of districts extracted
from a map of St. Lucia from
the year 1847 –
BPP/CG/4/1: 1847, p.518)

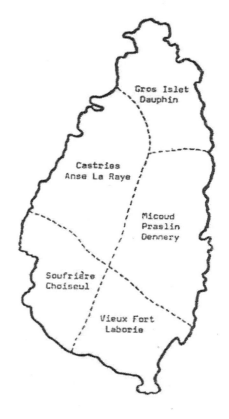

These first immigrants from Africa were asked by the STIPENDIARY
MAGISTRATES of their origin. A table with the title:

*"Return of African Immigrants per "Una" specifying their Tribes and Sexes,
compiled from the Special Magistrates Reports.-"*[27]

(CO 253/100/2: 1849)

was made by the STIPENDIARY MAGISTRATE of the 1st district,
DRYSDALE; and signed with "Act. Col. Secretary".

In the following the terms specified as "tribes" and the mentioned
number of persons is listed below. Owing to the difficult readability
sometimes the author used two styles.

Terms	Number of persons
Ganomerly/Gammerly + Yeroba	44
Yarriba	20
Akoo	17
Ogirila/Oguila	7
Yoriba	18

---

[27] The original reports of the „Special Magistrates" were not available in the PUBLIC RECORD OFFICE,
Kew/London.

Terms	Number of persons
Akoo; Adgo. + D'Issa	22
Housa	54
Adamoura	2
Egba	13
Ifes	2
Onda	8
Oror	4
Sakatou/Jakatou	40
Gabon	2
Not identified persons by the STIPENDIARY MAGISTRATES	79
	332

When interpreting these terms there is the following picture:

Ganomerly/Gammerly:	no information was available
Yeroba:	= Yoruba; they mainly live in the south of Nigeria. Their whole settlement area extends from the north of Nigeria to the coast inclusive of Ibadan, Igbolo, Igbona, Ilorin and Oyo (cp. HIRSCHBERG 1965: 120-121)
Yarriba:	= Yoruba; CUST (1883) designates the Yoruba as Yariba in his book "A Sketch of the Modern Languages of Africa".
Akoo:	= Aku = Yoruba; in Freetown, the capital of Sierra Leone, the Yoruba were termed as Aku (WESTERMANN/ BRYAN 1970: 84, ISICHEI 1977: 130)
Ogirila/Oguila:	no information was available
Yoriba:	= Yoruba
Adgo:	This term could have a connection with the language ADJOLO which is a KASENA language and belongs to the GRU languages. The ADJOLO-speakers settle in the hinterland of the Gold Coast (WESTERMANN/BRYAN 1970: 61)

D'Issa:

This term could have a connection with the following languages:
SISALA (HISSALA, ISSALA, SISAI); they designate themselves al LA-ISA or SISALA and belong to the GRU languages. Today they settle in the area from Cuagadougou (Uppervolta) to the western hinterland of the Gold Coast (WESTERMANN/BRYAN 1970: 63). IDSESA is according to CUST (1883: 260) a Yoruba language.

Housa:

= Hausa; the centres of the HAUSA-speakers are Kano, Sokoto, Zaria, Bautschi inclusively the former inhabitants of Daura, Gobir, Kano, Katsina, Kebbi, Zamfara and Zaria (cp. HIRSCHBERG 1965: 70)

Adamoura:

Adamawa/Adamaoua; geographic designation in North-Caneroon (WORLD TRAVEL MAP)

Egba:

= Yoruba-dialect: is spoken in Dahomey and French-Togo (WESTERMANN/BRYAN 1970: 85)

Ifes:

= Ife; IFE is according to WESTERMANN/ BRYAN 1970: 85) a Yoruba-dialect. The IFE-speakers settle near the town IFE in Nigeria (cp. HIRSCHBERG 1965: 121)

Onda:

probably the Yoruba-dialect ONDO is concerned, which is spoken in the Ondo-province in the south of the settlement-area of the Ekiti (cp. WESTERMANN/BRYAN 1970: 85)

Oror:

no information was available

Sakatou/Jakatou:

probably it can be referred to the town Sokoto in the north-west of Nigeria

Gabon:

political designation of an African state

According to this interpretation the following persons can be identified as Yoruba-speakers:

Yarriba:	20
Akoo:	17
Yoriba:	18
Egba:	13
Ifes:	2
Total	70

In comparison to the total number of arrived immigrants of 365 this is a percentage of 19.

Further Yoruba-speakers are contained in the group "Ganomerly/Gammerly + Yeroba" as well as in the group "Akoo; Adgo + D'Issa" which totally comprise 66 persons. A separation of the Yoruba-speakers out of these groups is not possible owing to a lack of information.

The eight persons stated under "Onda" could also be Yoruba-speakers. A clear identification is not possible.

The share of the Hausa-speakers was calculated with 15%.

In a letter of Governor DARLING dated February 21st, 1849, a list of the immigrants was mentioned, but this list was incorrect:

> "In conclusion I beg to point out that much inconvenience has been experienced from the want of a proper list of the Immigrants embarked. A list was certainly forwarded containing 367 Numbers and Names: but, in allotting the Immigrants, the greatest difficulty and delay were occasioned by the endeavour to find persons who acknowledged their names in the list; and in very few instances was this accomplished.- The Surgeon states that they were not mustered by names and numbers when handed to him, but merely the total number counted and given over; and the interpreter alleges that the List does not apply to this body of Immigrants at all, or at any rate was never altered; although a large proportion of the Immigrants were substituted for a number originally intended for the ship, and included in the List, but who were otherwise disposed of."

(CO 253/97/4: 21/2/1849)

This list was not transferred to London and therefore not available in the PUBLIC RECORD OFFICE.

Governor COLEBROOKE from Barbados visited St. Lucia in February 1849 and reported of the immigrants as follows:

"From personal observation of the condition of those who are located in the neighbourhood of the Town of Castries, they appear to be well contented with the arrangements made for them, and the attention shewn to their comfort.- Their employers being equally satisfied with the cheerful and willing performance of their allotted work."

(CO 253/97/5: 26/2/1849)

Already by the end of March 1849 the "principal Landed Proprietors and Merchants" of St. Lucia requested the SECRETARY OF STATE in a petition for further immigrants:

"... by sending us a further supply of freed Africans, who are the most efficient labourers who can be sent to these Colonies. Those received by the "Una", have been promptly distributed on about twenty of the Estates of the Colony, have now commenced labour, and are happy and contented;"

(CO 253/98/1: 30/3/1849)

From the reports of the STIPENDIARY MAGISTRATES for the first half year of 1849 follows that the immigrants were healthy and laborious:

1st district (Castries, Anse La Raye):

"Of a number of 365 African Immigrants which evinced here in February last, fifty three have been allotted to Estates in this District. They are doing remarkably well, are healthy and laborious, and have proved of the greatest advantage to the properties on which they are located."

(CO 258/17/5: 1/1/1849-30/6/1849, p.2)

2nd district (Gros Islet, Dauphin):

"The Africans composing the Cargo of the "Una" are a remarkable fine race of people, and have already proved an excellent addition to the labouring force of our plantations. I am glad to report that they have generally enjoyed excellent health since their arrival; and have received every kind of good treatment at the hands of their employers."

(CO 258/17/6: 1/1/1849-30/6/1849, p.11)

4th district (Vieux Fort, Laborie):

"26 Africans of whom 14 are males & four females, Adults, & 2 boys & 6 girls

They have enjoyed good health since their arrival, & the Provisions of the Contract have been fulfilled; they appear to be happy & contented with their situation, & perform with alacrity & cheerfulness what they are ordered to do, & on more than one occasion when the native labourers have been dogged by obstinate or refused to work, the readily came forward to the Assistance of their Employer.

At the commencement some bad feeling was manifested towards them by the resident peasantry, who assaulted & wounded slightly two of them, but a little legal coercion seasonably applied, soon restored them to their senses, they have since come to a better understanding, & live upon more friendly terms."

(CO 258/17/7: 1/1/1849-30/6/1849, p.31)

In August 1849 the newspaper PALLADIUM published an article about the African immigrants:

"As agricultural labourers, these people are generally acknowledged to have proved of the greatest benefit of the estates on which they have been located; they are good-natured and cheerful, and work willingly under the stimulus of the reward of money-payment, of the value of which they already evince a keen appreciation. They have established fine provision grounds for their own use, have begun to employ a portion of their leisure time in cultivating the sugar-cane on the Metairie system and are most comfortably housed."

(N/CO 28/171/1: 17/8/1849)

For the second half of the year 1849 the STIPENDIARY MAGISTRATE of the 4th district (Vieux Fort, Laborie) confirmed the good health of the immigrants as well as their will to labour:

"The African immigrants have invariably enjoyed good health, are steady & industrious, & afford universal satisfaction; they really may be considered an acquisition to the agricultural interest, & it is to be hoped they will continue so. No better proof can be offered in support of any assertion than the fact that applications are pouring upon the Government for a supply whenever more should arrive & I say the more the merrier."

(CO 258/17/8: 1/7/1849-31/12/1849), p.85)

The STIPENDIARY MAGISTRATE of the 2nd district (Gros Islet, Dauphin) referred in his report of March 1850 to the ability of the immigrants to speak with the local labourers. He also mentioned tattoo marks on the faces of the immigrants:

"The immigrants generally are very intelligent; those on the ... Estate speak the Creole Language remarkably well, in fact one would hardly know some of them to be Africans, were it not for the Tattoo Marks on their faces. The Immigrants on the other Estates, with the exception for those allotted to the ... Estate, who can neither speak nor understand English or Creole, generally can speak Creole enough to make themselves comprehended."

(CO 253/102/2: 7/3/1850)

In April 1850 Governor DARLING of St. Lucia reported to the Governor of Barbados:

> "..., that out of 355 who were alive at the expiration of their first year's contract, 303 remained in the service of their former employers; the remainder seeking employment elsewhere. But in no case has the labourer consented again to place himself under the compulsion of a contract.

(CO 253/103/1: 29/4/1850)

He further informed of seven deaths and four births.

To the remaining of the immigrants in the service of their employers the STIPENDIARY MAGISTRATE of the 4th district (Vieux Fort, Laborie) wrote:

> "The Africans mentioned in my last report, are still employed on the Estates, on which they were located, altho' their contract of Service expired since the month of February last; they have fine Gardens, which are considered to be a leading cause for their remaining on the properties, they continue steady & industrious & I feel pleasure in repeating that they are really an acquisition to the agricultural interest."

(CO 258/17/9: 1/1/1850-30/6/1850, p.145)

Already on January 4th, 1850, a further ship with immigrants from Sierra Leone arrived in St. Lucia. The report of the GOVERNMENT IMMIGRATION AGENT contains the following information: the ship's name was TROPIC and had 186 Africans on board. The ship had left Sierra Leone on December 7th, 1849 and reached St. Lucia after a 27 days' voyage. Detailed figures are:

	Adults		Children under 14		Total
	Male	Female	Male	Female	
Immigrants embarked	107	29	34	19	189
Deaths on the voyage	2	-	-	1	3
Immigrants landed	179	109	37	40	186

(CO 253/102/3: 9/1/1850)

The health of the immigrants was in general good:

> "The Immigrants were disembarked in general good health and appeared to have been properly attended to and taken care of on board of the ship. Two cases of sleight dysentery and of a wound in the thigh through accident were the only cases of illness at the time of arrival they were however all distributed and none sent to hospital."

The Governor of St. Lucia, DARLING, informed the Governor of Barbados on January 19th, 1850, of the arrival of the immigrants as follows:

"I have the honour to report the arrival on the 4th inst., of the Barque "Tropic" having on board 186 African Immigrants from Sierra Leone; three having died upon the passage."

(CO 253/102/4: 19/1/1850)

Four months later, on May 11th, 1850, the next immigrants arrived from Africa. According to the report of the GOVERNMENT IMMIGRATION AGENT the ship TUSKAR came from Sierra Leone to St. Helena where it left on April 12th, 1850. The duration of the total voyage from Sierra Leone to St. Lucia was 72 days. Totally 568 immigrants arrived in St. Lucia. In Sierra Leone 92 immigrants and in St. Helena 520 immigrants had been embarked. From the original 612 embarked persons 41 died during the voyage and three others before the distribution in St. Lucia. Exact figures are as follows:

	Adults		Children under 14		Total
	Male	Female	Male	Female	
Immigrants embarked	175	154	153	130	612
Deaths on the voyage	19	8	12	5	44
Immigrants landed	156	146	141	125	568

(CO 253/103/2: 20/5/1850)

Worth to mention is the high part of the children under 14 as well as the great number of deaths.

The surgeon of the ship wrote the following report:

"The Immigrants were shipped at Sierra Leone, numbering ninety-two,…, were generally in good state of health although considerably emaciated and enjoyed pretty good health till we reached St. Helena, with the exception of Coughs, and chest complaints, due to the change of temperature. The thermometer varying from 85 to 69, and one death from Pneumonia. After shipping 520 Immigrants at St. Helena, the Sierra Leone Immigrants did not enjoy such good health, Diarrhoea being more prevalent amongst them, this was I believe partly owing to the more crowded state of the vessel, and in some measure due to some heavy showers when passing the equator, where some of them unavoidably might get wet from the suddenness of the rain. In reference to the St. Helena Emigrants, I found that the majority were labouring under Catarrh or Bronchitis in addition to the almost universal prevalence of Dysentery & severe Diarrhoea, the former it is supposed arising from the variableness of the Climate compared with their own & not having been checked a sufficient length of time at St. Helena to recruit."

(CO 253/103/3: May 1850)

On May 23rd, 1850, Governor MENDS of St. Lucia informed the Governor of Barbados about the arrival of the immigrants as follows:

"I have the honour to report to your Excellency, that the Ship "Tuskar" Chapman Master, arrived at this Island on the 11th Instant, with 568 African Immigrants from Sierra Leone and Saint Helena."

(CO 253/103/4: 23/5/1850)

The distribution of the immigrants was according to the reports of the STIPENDIARY MAGISTRATES as follows:

District	Number of immigrants per TROPIC	per TUSKAR	Total	%
1. (Castries, Anse La Raye)	60	155	215	30
2. (Gros Islet, Dauphin)	41	105	146	20
3. (Soufrière, Choiseul)	-	-	104	14
4. (Vieux Fort, Laborie)	52	118	170	23
5. (Micoud, Praslin, Dennery)	-	-	95	13
			730	100

(CO 258/17/3: 1/1/1850-30/6/1850, p.41)

Further it is to mention that according to the reports of the GOVERNMENT IMMIGRATION AGENT totally 754 immigrants (186 with the ship TROPIC and 568 with the ship TUSKAR) arrived in the year 1850 in St. Lucia. The difference of 24 persons in comparison to the above cannot be explained by means of the available sources.

The STIPENDIARY MAGISTRATE of the 1st district (Castries, Anse La Raye) reported as follows:

"Sixty arrived ex on board the "Tropic" in February last, out of which number Fifty-one have been located as Agricultural Labourers, on the different Estates of this District, and Nine have been distributed in town as domestics, owing to their state of infancy.

155 were landed from on board the Barque "Tuskar" in May last and were distributed as follows:

125 have been allotted to the Proprietors of the different Sugar Estates in this District to be employed in agricultural pursuits and thirty children of both sexes have been distributed to respectable persons in Castries to be employed in a light domestic service proportionate to their age and bodily constitution. These people have proved to be a great acquisition to the

Estates, and their steady labour tends to increase the cultivation of the Staple Produce of the Colony."

(CO 258/17/10: 1/1/1850-30/6/1850, p.115)

The STIPENDIARY MAGISTRATE of the 2nd district (Gros Islet, Dauphin) referred to the immigrants as follows:

"Those per the Tropic are of a very wandering nature, almost the whole of them, having left their Employers for days, together roaming about in the woods and so on. The Immigrants by the Tuskar are a quite tractable set of people, but unfortunately, many of them arrived in a sickly state from dysentery, a few have fallen victims to the disease & others are still so very weak, as to be of little use to their employers."

(CO 258/17/11: 1/1/1850-30/6/1850), p.125)

The STIPENDIARY MAGISTRATE of the 4th district (Vieux Fort, Laborie) reported of the immigrants arrived with the ship TROPIC as follows:

"The Immigrants by the "Tropic" are of different tribes, & very dissimilar in character, they are generally indolent & appear to be fond of a roving & unsettled life; several of them absconded from Estates where they were employed under Contract, & were settling themselves in the woods, in another district, when they were arrested; they had already commenced erecting thatched huts, for the purpose no doubt for enjoying life without the trouble of working, & at the expense of the community at large, …, they were well supplied with provisions which they had obtained by pillaging; they have been punished for their delinquencies."

(CO 258/17/9: 1/1/1850-30/6/1850, p.145)

Regarding the immigrants of the ship TUSKAR he wrote:

"The Immigrants by the ship "Tuskar" are a miserable lucky set of beings, & fitter subjects for a Hospital than manual labour; the greater part of them were in such an emaciated state when they arrived that nine of the number died soon & will be unable, as far as I can judge, to perform any ordinary quantity of work for some time yet to come, they have all had medical attendance,-"

To the immigrants in general he wrote:

"The Immigrants in question are tractable & obedient, & those that are able, willingly attend to any kind of work pointed out to them, they are undoubtedly superior in every respect (except health) to those of the "Tropic", …"

A half year later the STIPENDIARY MAGISTRATE of the 4th district reported of an essential amelioration of the health of the immigrants who arrived with the ship TUSKAR:

> *The immigrants mentioned in my former report as being in a sickly state, have latterly much improved in health, & are with a few exceptions able to attend to their work."*
>
> (CO 258/17/12: 1/7/1850-31/12/1850, p.191)

Further reports of the African immigrants were made by the STIPENDIARY MAGISTRATES in October 1850.

1st district (Castries, Anse La Raye)

> *"It is my pleasant duty to report that the Africans under contract in this District are generally kindly treated, and well taken care of, particularly upon the Anse Galet, Mont Pleasant, Roseau, La Pointe, Marigot and Entrepot Estates. The Planters are unanimous as to their general good behaviour and their Value as labourers. They appear also quite happy, and satisfied with their Employers."*
>
> (CO 253/105/1: 11/10/1850)

It was further stated:

> *"Whilst on the Plantations under the Superintendence of the Proprietors themselves, the Africans look healthy, clean, able-bodied, and well clothed, those placed on the Estates under charge of the Managers, exhibit quite a different appearance with the exception, however, of those located on the Roseau Estate, who seemed to be well treated and kindly attended too. On the Soucis Estate, the property of Mr. Muter for instance, they look wretched, and filthy, they wear tattered and dirty clothes;"*

To the general state of health it was noted:

> *"But generally they have enjoyed excellent health since their location on the different Estates in this District, Medicines are liberally supplied, but – Hospital accommodation is generally wanting."*

Remarks about children labour:

> *"The Children have been found exceedingly useful in cleaning young canes, carrying manure into the cane fields, or as stock-keepers."*

Way of life:

> *"... that there is not one Estate in this District, where the Africans do not enjoy the quite possession of a fixed habitation and flourishing Provision Gardens. (Thirteen of them have embarked in the cultivation of canes under the Métairie-System, upon verbal agreements,) and there is no*

doubt, that the profit the Metayers will derive from such cultivation will be a great allurement to others to engage in similar undertakings."

Marriages and baptisms:

"Eight Marriages have taken place amongst the First-comers, which indicates a tendency towards morality and better life. The number of Baptisms is of an encouraging increase, ..."

2nd district (Gros Islet, Dauphin)

"The Immigrants in the 2nd District, with the exception of those on the Reduit-Estate are a contented and happy set of people working to the satisfaction of their Employers: Most of those per the "Una" in February 1849 possess either Cattle, Pigs or Poultry with large Gardens of Provisions. Those on the Grand Anse and Marquis Estate in particular may be said to be rich in stock."

(CO 253/105/2: 26/10/1850)

Remarks regarding the immigrants on the Reduit estate:

"With regard to the Immigrants on the Reduit-Estate, I am sorry to say that they are not, and never have been either happy or contented, I have heard various complaints or reports of neglect and want of food, ..."

5th district (Micoud, Praslin, Dennery)

"I found them generally healthy, well treated, well behaved, and constantly at work during the time engaged for in the contract. I ascertained that their wages and allowances were regularly paid and given to them. Those who possess gardens invariably work at them, and these gardens are in a perfect state of cultivation. Generally speaking the planters seemed to be quite satisfied with them. This is evident by the fact that many of them, who have a supply of Immigrants desire an increase of their number."

(CO 253/105/3: 3/10/1850)

The reports of the STIPENDIARY MAGISTRATES for the second half of the year 1851 confirm the contentment with the African immigrants:

2nd district (Gros Islet, Dauphin, Dennery):

"The African Immigrants introduced into the Colony in 1849 & 1850 are giving general satisfaction in this District."

(CO 258/17/13: 1/7/1851-31/12/1851, p.274)

<u>3rd district (Soufrière, Choiseul, part of Laborie):</u>

"The Immigrants generally enjoy good health, are steady & industrious in their habits & afford general satisfaction to their Employers: - Many of them receive as high a rate of wages as any other Cultivator of the soil in the Colony."

(CO 258/17/14: 1/7/1851-31/12/1851, p.284)

<u>4th district (part of Laborie, Vieux Fort, Micoud, Praslin):</u>

"All the African Immigrants are apparently happy and contented, and are a great acquisition to the Colony."

(CO 258/17/15: 1/7/1851-31/12/1851, p.294)

Regarding the division of the districts it is to mention that according to the available sourced the districts were reduced from five to four in the year 1851.

By the end of June 1853 the actual population figure of the African immigrants were stated by the STIPENDIARY MAGISTRATES as follows:

District	Adults		Children under 15 years		Total	%
	male	female	male	female		
1. (Castries, Anse La Raye)	108	74	59	32	273	27
2. (Gros Islet, Dauphin, Dennery)	105	59	48	42	254	26
3. (Soufrière, Choiseul, part of Laborie)	118	46	52	57	273	27
4. (Part of Laborie, Vieux Fort, Micoud, Praslin)	82	65	22	26	195	20
TOTAL	413	244	181	157	995	100

(CO 253/112/1: 1853)

The sums and the percentages were calculated by the author. In the 1st, 2nd and 3rd district the part of the immigrants is similar whereas the 4th district shows a lower part.

According to the mentioned reports of the GOVERNMENT IMMIGRATION AGENT the number of immigrants arrived in St. Lucia till the year 1853 can be summarized as follows:

Date of arrival of the ship	Name of the ship	Number of the arrived immigrants
6th February 1849	UNA	365
4th January 1850	TROPIC	186
11th May 1850	TUSKAR	568
TOTAL		1119

When comparing this figure with that of the before mentioned table (1.119 : 995) there is a difference of 124 persons. The difference could concern deaths, emigrations or incorrect stated figures in the table of the year 1853. A complete explanation is not possible by a lack of sources.

Further figures in the mentioned table of 1853 concern the attendance of churches and schools as well as the number of immigrants on the estates. They are as follows:

District	Church-goers	School-goers	Number of immigrants on the estates
1. (Castries, Anse La Raye)	127	-	142
2. (Gros Islet, Dauphin, Dennery)	122	3	122
3. (Soufrière, Choiseul, part of Laborie)	227	23	246
4. (Part of Laborie, Vieux Fort, Micoud, Praslin)	107	-	107
TOTAL	583	26	617

According to these figures 59% of the immigrants attended the churches, 7% the schools and 62% lived or worked on the estates.

Referring to this table the STIPENDIARY MAGISTRATE of the 2nd district pointed to the tendency of the immigrants to be independent of the estate which shows a harmonisation to the local black population who prefer an independent way of life:

> "It appears by the return that there is now something less than half the number of Immigrants originally allotted to the Estates in this district, at present working or located on them, this may be accounted for as follows:

Several of them have hired small portions of land which they till and feel satisfied if they can reap a sufficiency of provisions for their own consumption and the procuring of a little salt-fish and a few clothes, and they seldom trouble the Estates with their presence for the purpose of working – others again are employed by Creole labourers to assist them in the cultivation of their provision gardens, which employment the Immigrants appear to prefer to working in the Cane fields."

(CO 253/112/2: 10/8/1853)

The STIPENDIARY MAGISTRATE reported also of the emigration of some immigrants:

"I am sorry to have to report that several of the best of the Immigrants have left and others purpose leaving the Colony for Barbados en route as they say for their native land – which however I much question whether they will ever see again several of those who have left, industrious & good labourers – stated that they were only stimulated to work as they did by the hope that they would be able to realize the means of returning to their own Country."

These emigrations could be only some exceptions because according to "An Ordinance Promoting African Immigration into the Colony of Saint Lucia and the Industry of the Immigrants" the immigrants had to stay five years in the colony:

"3. And be it enacted, that to every such registered immigrant desiring to leave this Colony, and who may be entitled to a free passage back to the port or place whence he came, and who shall have completed an industrial residence of five years within this Colony, a license or passport in writing signed by the Colonial Secretary or other person duly appointed by the Lieutenant-Governor for that purpose, shall be delivered by such Colonial Secretary or other person, free of charge, on the application of such immigrant …

4.Provided always, and be it enacted, That when any such registered immigrant shall be desirous to commute his right to a free passage, for a piece or parcel of land, and the Government shall see fit to grant to such registered immigrant, out of the Crown or other lands of the Colony, such piece or parcel of land, then such immigrant shall have the same in lieu of his right to a free passage, …"

(CO 253/104/1: 2/5/1850)

Also the STIPENDIARY MAGISTRATE of the 1st district (Castries, Anse La Raye) referred to emigrations:

"A few African Immigrants have been induced to go lately to Barbados, saying they were going to Sierra Leone, I rather suspect they have been kidnapped."

(CO 258/17/16: 1/1/1853-30/6/1853, p.373)

334

"African Immigrants have left different Estates in this District for the sisters' Colonies, particularly for Trinidad."

(CO 258/17/17: 1/7/1853-31/12/1853, p.423)

"Thirty six of the African Immigrants brought into the Colony in 1849 and 1850 are reported to have left the Island, and proceeded to Trinidad, whether they have been induced to go under the expectation of a higher rate of wages."

(CO 258/17/18: 1/7/1853-31/12/1853, p.413)

In December 1853 Governor POWER of St. Lucia informed the Governor of Barbados of the emigrations to Trinidad as follows:

"... that there is a constant drain of Africans from this Island to Trinidad. They invariably come to me, a day or two before the arrival of a Steamer, to obtain permission to leave, which I have always refused to grant them on the ground, that by leaving this Island, they would expose themselves to the danger of being carried into slavery. But they meet this argument by saying that they avoid all such risks, by going in the steamer."

(CO 253/113/1: 4/12/1853)

He further mentioned:

"... that they were desirous of joining their friends in Trinidad who had given them encouragement, to proceed thither.

To satisfy me that what they had stated was the fact, one of them drew from his pocket a letter, which he said he had received from his sister in Trinidad, in which she advised him to lose no time in coming to that place, as he would be much better off there than in St. Lucia."

In February 1862 two further ships arrived in St. Lucia with African immigrants.

On February 15th, 1862, the ship ULYSSES arrived in St. Lucia with 320 Indian and 63 African immigrants. It came from Calcutta via St. Helena. The IMMIGRATION AGENT reported of the arrival of the ship as follows:

"... that the Ship "Ulysses", ..., arrived in Port Castries this morning after a passage of 89 days from Calcutta and 22 from St. Helena. The "Ulysses" took on board at Calcutta 255 male and 56 female adults, 11 male and 8 female children, and 2 male and 4 female infants in all 336 souls. Of the number 16 adult males died on the passage, 10 from diarrhea, 3 from dysentery, 2 from fever and 1 from debility. The "Ulysses" took in at St. Helena 63 male adult Africans among whom no mortality has occurred."

(CO 253/130/2: 15/2/1862)

The health of the immigrants was good:

> *"I visited the "Ulysses" immediately after her arrival, and I have much pleasure in stating that the Immigrants appear to have been well treated during the voyage. They are in good health with the exception of 5, 4, ..."*

One day after the arrival of the ship ULYSSES the ship DAMIETTA arrived on February 16th, 1862, in the port of Castries. She came from St. Helena with 116 African immigrants on board:

> *"... that the Barque "Damietta", ..., arrived in Port Castries, yesterday from St. Helena with African Immigrants for this Colony. This Vessel left St. Helena on the 25th ultimo and has consequently been 22 days at sea. She took on board 60 male and 57 female adult Africans; and of that number only one of the former is dead. These Immigrants are in good health; and after a personal inspection of them I am glad to be able to state that they appear to have been well-treated during the voyage."*

(CO 253/130/3: 17/2/1862)

The 63 African immigrants of the ship ULYSSES were distributed to the following estates according to the report of the IMMIGRATION AGENT:

Name of the estate	Number of the immigrants
Grand Anse	4
Black Bay	10
Pointe Sable	10
Tourny	8
Beauchamp	6
Cap	5
Delcer	5
Diamond	4
Union Vale	6
Terre Blanche	2
"Died after landing"	1
"In Hospital"	2
TOTAL	63

(CO 253/130/4: 3/3/1862)

The distribution of the immigrants of the ship DAMIETTA was as follows:

Name of the estate	Number of the immigrants
Cap	3
Reunion	9
Beauséjour	11
Delcer	2
Diamond	3
Troumasse	6
Canelle	7
Volet	6
St. Urban	8
Pensée	5
Belle Plaine	3
Pointe	7
Anse Galet	11
Bellevue	4
Jalousie	5
Pearl	3
Morne Courbaril	5
Fonds Doux	3
Beauséjour	8
Anse Mahaut	5
"Died on the voyage"	1
"In Hospital"	2
TOTAL	117

(CO 253/130/5: 3/3/1862)

In both mentioned reports of the IMMIGRATION AGENT the immigrants were designated as "Liberated Africans".

According to an ordinance of July 1858 African immigrants who, on their arrival in St. Lucia, had attained the age of eighteen years were obliged to make a working agreement for three years. African immigrants under eighteen years should make a working agreement till their attainment of the eighteenth year (OPL/C.S./F 246/1: 21/7/1858).

An ordinance of March 31st, 1862, altered this regulation for the immigrants under 18:

> "That every agreement with an African Immigrant, who, on his arrival in this Colony, shall not have attained the age of eighteen years, shall be for a term not less than three years, any law to the contrary notwithstanding."

(OPL/C.S/F 246/2: 31/3/1862)

In this ordinance also the salary as well as the maintenance of the African immigrants was fixed:

"And be it enacted, That every person in possession of the Estate in respect of which the services of any African Immigrant shall be assigned, shall be bound to supply such Immigrant during the first six months after his arrival in this Colony, with such wages and daily food as are specified in the Schedule B, to this Ordinance annexed. And at the end of the said term of six months, every such African Immigrant (in the absence of an express agreement to the contrary) shall be entitled, in lieu of such wages and food, to wages at and after the same daily rate as is paid to labourers, not under indenture or agreement, working on the said Estate ..."

"Schedule B ...

NONEY WAGES

Two pence a day for each day the Immigrant works, the Employer being bound to find work for the number of days per week specified in the Contract.

FOOD

To each Immigrant a weekly Ration of 3 lbs. Salt-Fish; or 2 lbs. Beef, Pork or other Meat; 7 lbs. Bread; or 5 quarts Farina Manioc; or 6 quarts Corn-Meal; or 4 quarts Rice; or 21 lbs. Yams; or 28 lbs. Sweet Potatoes; or 21 lbs. Eddoes; or 24 lbs. Plantains, or equivalent proportions if it is found convenient to comprise more than one of the above enumerated articles of grain and vegetables in the weekly Rations.

Children above 10 and under 14 years of age, to receive half the above Wages and Rations, Children of 10 years and under to receive sufficient food and clothing"

These regulations are in general the same as those of the year 1849 (cp. p. 318)

The IMMIGRATION AGENT McLeod reported in September 1862:

"I have indentured these Immigrants for a period of three years from February last. The employers speak highly of them, and appear to appreciate their services. They are now on the same footing as the Creoles in regard to their wages.

... the estates on which Immigrants are located and with few exceptions I have been satisfied with the accommodation afforded them; the payment of their wages and their treatment generally."

(CO 253/131/1: 16/9/1862)

In his report of March 1863 he mentioned:

"The money wages paid to the Africans during the first six months were spent in buying clothing. Some employers supplied clothing to the Immigrants to an amount exceeding the wages earned and gave them besides small sums of money."

(CO 253/132/1: 31/3/1863)

"The Africans although considered "adults" are for the most part young people. They are docile, industrious and sober and make excellent agricultural labourers."

One year later his opinion of the immigrants had not changed:

"I have much pleasure in being able to state that the African Immigrants continue to give satisfaction to their employers. They are industrious, sober and docile."

(CO 253/134/1: 3/2/1864)

"A considerable number of them have been baptised by the Roman Catholic Clergy."

Further reports of IMMIGRATION AGENTS confirm the good health as well as the good labour morale of the immigrants:

Report of the IMMIGRATION AGENT Jennings of August 1864:

*"On the 31st Dec. 1863, there were 182 African Immigrants in the Colony ...
In my recent visit to the Estates, I inspected these Immigrants and found them looking strong and healthy ...*

The employers of these Immigrants speak of them as steady able bodied Labourers, and very industrious employing the time where their Services are not required by them in cultivating provision grounds."

(CO 253/135/1: 13/8/1864)

Report of the IMMIGRATION AGENT Chadwick of January 1865:

"On the 30th June there were 185 of these Immigrants in the Island; (adults: 174) ...

I have visited all the Estates upon which African Immigrants are located twice during the six months and found them comfortably lodged and looking strong and healthy, they are regularly employed and receive their wages fortnightly, their Employers speak of them in the highest terms and are anxious to get more of them."

(CO 253/136/1: 30/1/1865)

With a letter of April 1865 Governor GRANT of St. Lucia informed the Governor of Barbados:

> "The Africans continue to give great satisfaction. They are much better suited for these Colonies than Indians for they can perform more work and are less affected by change of weather."

From his letter further follows that the immigrants arrived in the year 1849 and probably also in the year 1850 had already merged with the black population of St. Lucia:

> "The number of Immigrants in the Colony at that period was 1515, namely 1325 Coolies and 190 Africans. This does not include the liberated Africans brought here in 1849 who have long merged in the general population."

(CO 253/136/2: 29/4/1865)

From further reports of the IMMIGRATION AGENT Chadwick from the year 1866 till the year 1868 regarding the African immigrants arrived in St. Lucia in the year 1862 follows that those immigrants also settled and merged with the local black population. The following settlement areas were mentioned:

> Gros Islet
> Castries
> Anse La Raye
> Soufrière
> Choiseul
> Vieux Fort
> Dennery

In general he confirmed the good health and the good labour morale of the immigrants. The respective extracts of the reports ("Return of African Immigrants") are as follows:

> "The African Immigrants with some exception of desertion, are working satisfactorily; 43 of them are indentured to different Estates from that number 27 will have completed their time of service on the 21st of this month, and 16 who are under age will have another year of industrial residence, …
>
> It is difficult to render any correct account of those who have been liberated, as they are constantly wandering from one Estate to another, and above all have taken their abode with old resident Africans of whom a large number are located in the Valley of Dennery, where they are owners or lessees of parcels of land upon which they have built their houses."

(CO 253/136/3: 10/2/1866)

"I have visited all the Estates on which these Immigrants are located during the past quarter and found them without one exception in good health, they are strong and effective labourers and are highly spoken of by their employers, they are very industrious and have large provision grounds on the several Estates.

Those who left the Estate since they were liberated have joined their Countrymen old resident Africans, and are residing principally in the quarters of Gros Islet, Anse Laraye and Dennery, where they employ their time in raising stock and growing provisions."

(CO 253/138/1: 28/1/1867)

"These Immigrants since they were released from Contract have nearly all left the Estates and settled in the heights in the 1ˢᵗ and 3ʳᵈ districts where they have leased land on which they have built houses and cultivate provisions and are in fact quite independent of the Estates only working on them when it suits their purpose and they doing contract work …

I am glad to be able to report that the condition of these Immigrants is most satisfactory, all those whom I have seen on recent tour of inspection both resident on Estates and non-resident being strong and in good health and are spoken of generally in their respective Districts as being orderly and industrious people."

(CO 253/139/1: 2/8/1867)

"These Immigrants have nearly all left the Estates, have built houses and settled in considerable numbers in the quarters of "Anse Laraye" and "Dennery" and "Vieux Fort", they are very industrious and have large provision grounds and at times work on the Estates by Contract."

(CO 253/140/1: 25/2/1868)

These Immigrants as I have already reported, are fast making themselves independent of the Estates and have settled in different parts of the Island, many of them have houses of their own and large provision grounds and when it suits them they work on the Estates by contract and many of them have intermarried with the Creoles."

(CO 253/140/2: 14/8/1868)

5.4.4.3   Summary

5.4.4.3.1 Tabular review

After the end of the of the emancipation period totally 1.298 African immigrants arrived in St. Lucia. A detailed table is as follows:

Arrival of ship	Name of ship	Port of shipment	Number of embarked immigrants		Deaths during the voyage	Arrived immigrants
6. February 1849	UNA	Sierra Leone	367		2	365
4. January 1850	TROPIC	Sierra Leone	189		3	186
11. May 1850	TUSKAR	Sierra Leone	92	612	44	568
		St. Helena	520			
15. February 1862	ULYSSES	St. Helena	63		-	63
16. February 1862	DAMIETTA	St. Helena	117		1	116
TOTAL			1.348		50	1.298

(compiled by the author)

5.4.4.3.2 Miscellaneous

All in St. Lucia arrived African immigrants except those 189 persons arrived with the ship TROPIC on January 4th, 1850, were designated in the sources as from slave ships liberated Africans. Regarding the above mentioned 189 immigrants it is also assumed that they were liberated Africans.

The investigation of the origin of the Africans was only possible of the 365 immigrants arrived in St. Lucia with the ship UNA on February 6th, 1849; but here only partially. An analysis of the respecting sources showed a definitive share of 19% Yoruba-speakers (70 persons) and 15% Hausa-speakers (54 persons). Further Yoruba-speakers were contained in other groups as for example in the group "Ganomerly/Gammerly + Yoruba", but a separation of the Yoruba-speakers out of these groups was not possible owing to a lack of information. The respecting groups totally comprise 56 persons. It can be noted that the above mentioned share of the Yoruba-speakers of 19% was certainly higher.

In general the immigrants had a good labour morale and were healthy. The planters were satisfied with them. Exceptions were:

1. The immigrants who arrived on January 4th, 1850, (186 persons with the ship TROPIC): After their arrival they were designated by the STIPENDIARY MAGISTRATES of the 2nd and 4th district as lazy and *"of a very wandering nature"*. But later there were no more complaints.
2. The immigrants who arrived on May 11th, 1850 (568 persons with the ship TUSKAR): They already arrived in a bad health condition. 41 persons had died during the voyage and three at their arrival in the port. But within a few months after their arrival their health condition had improved essentially.

The immigrants from the year 1849 and 1850 had to make one year labour contracts and had to stay five years in St. Lucia. The immigrants from the year 1862 got three years' labour contracts. Besides the labour on the estates the immigrants cultivated provisions. Sporadically they also cultivated sugar cane according to the METAIRIE-system and raised cattle, pigs and poultry. After the expiration of the contractual labour time on the estates the immigrants preferred to be independent as well as the local blacks. In general they merged with the local black population.

For the year 1853 there are some reports regarding the emigration of immigrants to Barbados and Trinidad. But the share of these immigrants was very low. In further reports the emigration of immigrants was no more mentioned.

5.4.5 Indian immigrants

This chapter shall only give a short review.

COMINS published in the year 1893 notes given to him by the PROTECTOR OF IMMIGRANTS of St. Lucia as follows:

Year of arrival	Name of the ship	Adults		Infants		Children	Total
		M	F	M	F		
1859	PALMYRA	240	58	4	11	5	318
1859	FRANCIS RIDLEY	146	63	23	20	9	261
1860	VICTOR EMMANUEL	294	67	18	7	7	393
1860	ZEMINDAR	213	66	15	16	6	316
1862	ULYSSES	239	56	11	8	6	320
1878	LEONIDAS	286	158	50	32	54	580
1879	CHETAH	116	75	13	10	7	221
1880	FOYLE	40	17	3	4	3	67
1881	BANN	202	80	22	8	4	316
1884	BRACADAILE	336	127	14	7	135	619
1885	POONAH	163	76	4	5	58	306
1891	ROUMANIA	309	126	10	8	101	554
TOTAL		2.584	969	187	136	395	4.271

(COMINS 1893: 3-4)

According to ANTHONY (1975: 5) and DOOKHAN (1981: 59) the immigration period of the Indians in St. Lucia ended only in the year 1893. Both state also total figures of Indian immigrants. ANTHONY mentions the figure of 4.427 and DOOKHAN the figure of 4.354.

Till the year 1890, according to COMINS (1893: 4), already 1.486 immigrants had left St. Lucia for their homeland. He gives the following review:

Year of leaving	Name of the ship	Adults		Infants		Children	Total
		M	F	M	F		
1867	GANGES	263	103	36	33	16	451
1868	LINCELLES	180	56	23	12	27	298
1871	HARKAWAY	87	27	25	10	13	162
1883	JUMMA	35	24	7	3	26	95
1888	MOY	130	70	11	13	103	327
1889	RHONE	51	31	4	3	43	132
1890	HEREFORD	12	3	-	2	4	21
TOTAL		758	314	106	76	232	1.486

Four years later according to ANTHONY (1975: 5) this figure was risen to 2.075. He further mentions that in the year 1901 the total population figure of St. Lucia was 49.883 and that 2.28% of them were Indians. Shown in persons this is 1.137 Indians.

According to these figures most of the Indian immigrants had left St. Lucia after the expiration of their contract labour.

5.4.6 African immigration refugees from Martinique

5.4.6.1   Sources

The STIPENDIARY MAGISTRATE of the 2nd district (Gros Islet, Dauphin, Dennery) informed Governor BREEN of St. Lucia of the arrival of seven refugees from Martinique in April 1858:

> "I have the honour to report to your information that seven male African Immigrants arrived in a small Canoe from the neighbouring Island of Martinique, on Saturday night the 3rd April Instant."

> (CO 253/123/1: 13/4/1858)

Their names were stated as follows:

> "Tom Nimble, Jim Crash, Jack Will, Africa, George, Tom Toly, Tom Peter."

On May 4th, 1858, Governor BREEN of St. Lucia informed the Governor of Barbados, HINCKS, as follows:

> "The Country they came from is called "Grandees" and is situated a short distance from Sierra Leone. The English call them "Kroomen" and their particular names they received from the English Sailors by whom they were employed as Porters or Boatmen."

> (CO 253/123/2: 4/5/1858)

It is evident that KRU-speakers are meant here. They settle mainly in the Ivory Coast and in the interior of Liberia (cp. HIRSCHBERG 1965: 125-127).

According to the before mentioned report of the STIPENDIARY MAGISTRATE these immigrants were imported about a year ago into the island of Martinique. They escaped from this island to St. Lucia because their master designated them as slaves and prohibited them to leave Martinique. After their arrival in St. Lucia they expressed their desire to return to "their Country" after one year's residence in St. Lucia.

On July 10th, 1858, the newspaper PALLADIUM reported of the flight of further "Kroomen" from Martinique. Of their arrival in St. Lucia there was nothing known:

> *"On Tuesday last, at about 6 o'clock, P.M. the French man-of-war Steamer Lucifer, entered the Port of Castries in search of some Kroomen who had affected their escape from Martinique. It appears that during the preceding night twenty-three of these unfortunate beings, employed on the estate of Mr. Sempé, in that Island, had embarked in a canoe, and had directed their course towards the northern point of St. Lucia... Up to the date of our going to press no news has been received of the arrival of the Kroomen, and the likelihood is either that they have been recaptured by the Lucifer, or that they have perished at sea. The latter alternative seems the more probable when it is considered that they were twenty-three in one canoe and had to struggle against a rough sea."*
>
> (N/CO/253/123/1: 10/7/1858)

From a letter of Governor BREEN to Governor HINCKS of Barbados dated August 23rd, 1858, follows that these refugees didn't arrive in St. Lucia. It was assumed that they were all drowned (CO 253/123/3: 23/8/1858). Governor BREEN reported further that a French war steamer had arrived for searching eight refugees from Martinique who had left that island on August 21st.

On September 1st, 1858, Governor BREEN informed the Governor of Barbados of the arrival of five "Kroomen" from Martinique. These refugees had been working in Martinique for one year. At their arrival in St. Lucia they were prepared to work on an estate in St. Lucia (CO 253/123/5: 16/9/1858).

Also for the year 1859 there are reports of the arrival of refugees from Martinique.

According to a report of the STIPENDIARY MAGISTRATE of the 3rd district (Soufrière, Choiseul, Part of Laborie) six refugees arrived in St. Lucia at the bay Anse Mahaut. Their names as well as their place of origin were stated by the STIPENDIARY MAGISTRATE as follows:

> *"Their names are Richard, Blackwell, Freeman, Murcey, Tom Mimlen, Joe. They appear to me to be boys of about 19 to 24 years of age. They declare being natives of Chissalmas near Sierra Leone, and came out two years and a half ago to Martinique, ..."*
>
> (CO 253/125/1: 12/10/1859)

As reason for their escape they stated a bad treatment on the part of their masters.

In November 1859 the STIPENDIARY MAGISTRATE of the 3rd district reported again of an arrival of refugees from Martinique. They were four refugees who reached the bay Anse Mamin. Their names, place of origin as well as their reason of their flight were stated by the STIPENDIARY MAGISTRATE as follows:

> "*Their names are Bergley, Guisseau, Antoine, and Quamie, and understand the Creole language. They informed me they are not Kroomen, but natives of Kiplaon in Africa; ... and in consequence of ill treatment, and not being paid of their wages, they deserted.*"

(CO 253/125/2: 22/11/1859)

According to the further statements of the STIPENDIARY MAGISTRATE the refugees agreed to work on the Anse Mamin estate.

5.4.6.2 Summary

According to the mentioned reports totally 25 African immigrants escaped from Martinique to St. Lucia in the years 1858 and 1859. A review is as follows:

Date of arrival	Number	Designation	Place of origin	Stay in Martinique
3rd April 1858	7	KRU	"Grandees" (next to Sierra Leone)	1 year
August 1858	5	KRU	-	-
12th September 1858	3	KRU	-	1 year
11th Octobre 1859	6	-	"Chissalmas" (next to Sierra Leone)	2 1/2 years
November 1859	4	no KRU	"Kiplaon"	-
TOTAL	25			

The reason for their flight from Martinique was ill treatment on the part of their masters. Reports of the further fate of the immigrants were not available.

6 Special subjects

6.1 OBEAH: Sources in the 19th century (1800-1873)

6.1.1 Introduction (What is OBEAH?)

ANTHONY (1970: 3) defines OBEAH as follows:

> *"In St. Lucia obeah has two functions: it is medicinal (GUARDESE OR GUARDEUR) on the one hand, and on the other, it is a source of sorcery (Quimbois or Chembois)."*

He further writes:

> *"If someone is seriously ill and a physician is unable to help, the patient is normally referred to the obeah man "or local astrologist to teway chapetre." On the other hand, the obeah man is also invoked to poison or hurt an enemy. The obeah man is supposed to be in contact with the spirit-world, and his remedies are reputedly attained from spirits. When an obeah man is dying, he too confesses his misdeeds (deparler)."*

BREEN (1844: 249) writes as follows:

> *"In nothing is the want of religious instruction so conspicuous as in the addiction of the peasantry to the practice of sorcery. This popular infatuation, known in St. Lucia by the name of Kembois, still prevails to an incredible extent amongst the uneducated classes. "Kembois" is another name for Obeah, with certain Caribbean diableries and incongruities engrafted upon it."*

Then he refers to the practice of OBEAH:

> *"Indeed, of late years it appears to have assumed a more formidable character; and while its operations extend to the common dealings of life, there is no species of maléfice that is not put in requisition by the dabbler in spells and potions. So long as the art was limited to the conferring of invulnerability upon a duellist, or enthralling of a reluctant lover; and it was sought to accomplish such ends by means of broken bottles and bits of bone, the professors of Kembois might have been laughed at as hypochondriacs, or pitied as fools; but now they have extended their speculations to the mutilation of male children and other revolting practices: ..."*
>
> (BREEN 1844: 250-251)

In the following chapter a review of the available sources of the 19th century (especially from 1800 to 1873) is given:

6.1.2 Sources of the 19th century

The best known source is BREEN who writes in his book published in 1844 generally of OBEAH (pp.249-251) as well as of a special OBEAH-case of the year 1841 (pp.251-255). The special OBEAH-case will be mentioned in this chapter in chronological order of the sources.

The earliest source in the 19th century is a proclamation of Governor BRERETON of St. Lucia from the year 1804, which declares the practice of OBEAH as punishable. The clauses were fixed as follows:

> *"Art. I.-Slaves accused of poisoning, witchcraft, or sorcery, to be immediately arrested, and a report made to Government by the Civil Commissary, who will name at the same time four disinterested inhabitants to Government, to form a special commission which he will preside over.*
>
> *Art. II.-So soon as the Civil Commissary shall have received authority from Government to that effect, he is to assemble the four inhabitants so named, and to proceed to the trial of the Slaves; the sentence, however, not to be put into execution until the proceedings shall have been submitted to and sanctioned by Government."*

> (BPP/ST/71/2: 17/4/1804, p.210)

The next source is an ordinance of Governor FARQUHARSON of June 1832, in which the punishment for practicing OBEAH was fixed more detailed: At the first or second offence a punishment till 39 lashes with the whip or imprisonment in a goal till two months was fixed. At the third offence a trial was ordered. The punishable practices were defined as follows:

> *"43: Practising Obeah or pretending to be Obeah People, or pretending to administer, or educe to be administered pounded Glass, or other deleterious substance or matter."*
>
> (CO 255/2/6: 16/6/1832, p.133)

For the years 1841 to 1842 there are reports referring to four OBEAH-cases.

On April 3rd, 1841, the STIPENDIARY MAGISTRATE of the 1st district (Castries, Anse La Raye) reported of a murder of a child:

> *"I have also the honour to state, for His Excellency's information, that during the past month I have held two coroner's inquests; the first on a male child of about two years old, on which the jury found a verdict of wilful murder against some person or persons unknown."*

> (CO 253/73/5: 3/4/1841)

He further informed:

"I immediately forwarded the depositions to the attorney-general; and, since then, four persons have been arrested and lodged in gaol, suspected of being parties concerned in the murder. It is generally supposed that this unfortunate infant has been murdered for the purpose of the abominable and superstitious practice of sorcery, his private and other parts of his persons having been removed."

To this case was also referred in the newspaper PALLADIUM and in the INDEPENDENT PRESS. Already on March 20th, 1841, the newspaper PALLADIUM reported of the death of the child:

"The other was held before the Coroner of the 1st District, Mr. Special Justice Laffitte, on the body of a young male child, found dead in the neighbourhood of Incommode Estate. The body of the child was most barbarously mutilated, and no doubt could be entertained as to death in this case having been caused by violence of a most savage nature. The Jury gave a verdict of "Murder, by some person or persons unknown". We understand, the Police are endeavouring to trace the inhuman perpetrator of the crime."

(N/CO 258/1/18: 20/3/1841, p.182)

From this article as well as from a further article, published in the newspaper PALLADIUM on April 3rd, follows that the boy was murdered in the "Grand-Cul-de-Sac" valley. In that last mentioned article the murder was brought into connection with OBEAH:

"Three men have been apprehended and committed for examination, on suspicion of having been concerned in the murder of a child at the Grand-Cul-de-Sac Valley lately mentioned by us as the subject of a Coroner's Inquest. From the mutilation of the body, as shewn on the Inquest, there is no doubt of the murder having been committed by some of those monsters in human shape – unfortunately, too numerous in this Island – who profess the power of charming bullets, rendering the human body invulnerable, etc. by witchcraft, or, as it is called here, quembois-"

(N/CO 258/1/9: 3/4/1841, p.186)

On Wednesday, April 15th, 1841, in the newspaper INDEPENDENT PRESS also an article of the murder of the child was published. The same article was also published in the PALLADIUM on April 17th, 1841, and interpreted with another article (N/CO 258/1/10: 17/4/1841, p.190). Here it is to mention that the author of the article in the INDEPENDENT PRESS didn't take OBEAH serious in contrast to the author of the article published in the PALLADIUM. The author of the newspaper INDEPENDENT PRESS wrote as follows:

"Without some past experience of the capacity of Mr. Attorney-General Agostini's power of belief in such necessaries, we would never have

brought ourselves to believe, that in this age of intellectual advancement –
a Magistrate could be found seriously to play the part of a witch finder; -
but such has really been the employment of the above mentioned
functionaries, and all the disposable Police Force of the district, during ten
or twelve days."

Further extracts of the mentioned articles are as follows:

The disappearance of the child as well as the discovering of the dead child
was mentioned in the INDEPENDENT PRESS as follows:

"It appears that some two or three weeks ago, a young child, between two
or three years of age, which had been placed by its mother, at nurse, in
the care of a woman residing in a cottage, situated in an uncultivated part
of this parish, lying between the Soucis Estate in Grand Cul-de-Sac and
the Pointe Estate, wandered away from the Cottage on a Monday
afternoon, in the absence of the woman; apparently, from the evidence
produced at the Coroner's Inquest, in search of food. On the return of the
woman, late in the day, the child was discovered to be absent; and it is
stated, that search was immediately made after it – but without success.
On the following morning, the woman came into Castries to inform the
mother of the loss of her child, and make known the circumstances to the
Magistrate. The mother and the nurse then returned and as they state,
continued to search for the child, without discovering or being able to
obtain any tidings of it. On the Sunday following, a Labourer who has a
plantain walk, about half a mile from the Cottage whence the child had
wandered; having gone there for the purpose of cutting a bunch of
plantains, had his attention attracted by the bussing of a great quantity of
flies, and proceeding to examine the cause, he discovered the body of a
child, in a state of advanced decomposition. Knowing the circumstance of a
child having been lost by a woman in the neighbourhood, this man
immediately proceeded to inform the woman of his having found the child
– and the mother and the nurse having visited the body, recognized it as
that of the missing child."

Further it was noted:

"At this time all the parties seem to have come to the natural conclusion
that the child had lost itself in the bushes, and had perished of hunger and
exposure; and the woman in consequence made application to Mr.
Doussard, the nearest Magistrate, (who having satisfied himself by inquiry,
of the identity of the child) gave permission for the interment. The body
was found to be in that state of decomposition that a hole was dug on the
spot, and the body without any further ceremony dragged into it, and
covered up. Three days later however, one of the newly appointed
Coroners hearing of the circumstances, summoned a jury, and had the
body disinterred, and Dr. A. Clavier, was requested to be present. The
Doctor examined the body, but declared that the state of putrefaction was
such as to render it impossible to pronounce any opinion as to the cause of
death, and that the body appeared to be perfect, except in so far as was
caused by natural decay of the soft parts, and the destruction occasioned
by the enormous mass of worms, generated by the flies, during the time

the body had remained exposed; but the jury were novices, in this sort of investigation, and they, led away by a love of the marvellous, found a verdict of "WILFUL MURDER, against some person or persons unknown."!!!"

The author of the article in the PALLADIUM was of another opinion:

"The body of a child being found in the woods, and recognized, a Coroner's inquest was held upon it, when it was considered impossible that the child could have wandered of itself over the ravines and other impediments which lay in the distance between the hut of its nurse and the spot where the body was found; and Dr. A. Clavier, who was called to examine the body, stated to the Coroner's Jury (as he also since informed the writer of this article) that he found marks of strangulation upon the corpse, and that certain parts of it had been cut off; upon which, the Jury, very properly found a verdict of "Wilful murder against some person or persons unknown."

Regarding the investigations of the police the author of the article in the INDEPENDENT PRESS reported as follows:

"The result of these "zealous efforts" has been but small. The woman to whose negligence, (to use the mildest terms applicable to her conduct), the death of this child is attributable – to relieve herself from the blame justly attachable to her; upon afterthought, insinuated to the zealous functionaries that she had a neighbour, who was a sorcier, a dealer in witch-craft, &c., and as this woman had an old quarrel to score off against her neighbour, she charitably supposed that Malalou MIGHT have killed her nurse-child, for the use of his unholy incantations; on this hint, the Chief Commissary of Police, with the aid of Mr. Public Prosecutor Agostini, commenced an enquiry which led to the arrest and committal of various persons, as "suspected of being accomplices in a wilful murder" – in the first instance, and subsequently after many days "zealous" but fruitless "endeavours" to discover the murderers – Mr. Attorney-General Agostini commits to prison three individuals as "suspected of attempting to poison balls to fight a duel" – (we quote from the legal documents). The Royal Court has since applied to and the parties have been liberated from the imprisonment in the condemned cells to which they had been consigned, without bail or main-prize, by Mr. Attorney-General Agostini."

The author of the article in the newspaper PALLADIUM informed concerning the police investigations as follows:

"The Commissary of Police then received information, that Mr. Servé Cornau, had been seen on a white horse, in the neighbourhood, about the time that the child was probably murdered, and that he was heard to inquire for "Mr. Malalou", famed, as the "Independent Press" admits, as "a sorcier, a dealer in witchcraft, &c.". This Mr. Cornau, too, it was discovered, was about the same time to prepare the balls with which a duel was to have been fought by Mr. Barnes and Mr. Charlery. These circumstances, added to a general outcry raised by Cornau's neighbours

against the nuisance of his "unholy incantations" – in which, it was said, use was made of human flesh – led to the adoption of those steps by the Attorney General and the Commissary of Police, which have drawn upon them the mighty displeasure of the Reddie faction."

From another article of the PALLADIUM follows that if a duel had to be fought the principals visited an OBEAH-man and procured a charmed ball, warranted never to miss its object, or got themselves immersed in a cauldron and made invulnerable to pistol shots, and in this "hell-broth" the members of a murdered human being had to be the chief ingredients (Z/CO 258/1/11: 10/4/1841)

The before mentioned article in the PALLADIUM was continued as follows:

"The inquiry instituted into the circumstances, has been productive already of proof, that, besides other strong circumstantial evidence, Cornau and Adelson, two of the parties committed for examination, had been seen in the performance of their "unholy incantations" – had been engaged in disinterring bodies in the burial ground – that one of them had been heard to say human flesh was an indispensable ingredient in the composition of the "quembois" or charm, by which the invulnerability of their dupe was to be effected! Their dwellings were searched, and in them were found phials of unaccountable decoctions, and oils, and rams' horns stuffed with we know not what. These individuals were committed, in the very words of "the legal documents", as "suspected of having poisoned balls to fight a duel" – not as the hypercritical Editors of the Independent Press have it, "suspected of attempting to poison", &c. They were examined and recommitted for further examination, agreeably to the provisions of the Ordinance:-"

In the article published in the newspaper PALLADIUM it was further mentioned that both persons "Cornau" and "Adelson" who had been committed to goal were released on April 13th because it was stated "that it was no crime to poison balls to be used in a duel." The author of the article protested against this decision. Finally he wrote:

"No less than four instances have occurred in different parts of the Island, during the last two or three months, of the mysterious disappearance of children. And it is, at least, generally believed, that they have been sacrificed to the occult purposes of the professors of obi."

On the occasion of the before mentioned OBEAH-case the PALLADIUM published already before the becoming known of the legal decision regarding the committed persons on April 10th, 1841, an article which referred generally to OBEAH as well as to the difficulty to give evidence before court (N/CO 258/1/11: 10/4/1841, p.188). At first the author answered the question "What is Quembois":

"It is a new name for witchcraft, or sorcery, or obeah; it is an imposture practised but too successfully by impious wretches upon the credulity of the ignorant; and all the finer impulses of humanity, are abandoned for a devotion to its incantations."

Then he continued:

"Formerly, we are told, the professors of Obeah, or Quembois, were the natives of Africa; and these oracles were resorted to, by the Creoles, with the most implicit faith, whether for the cure of disorders, the obtaining revenge for injuries or insults, the conciliating of favour, the discovery and punishment of the thief or the adulterer, the prediction of future events, or the rendering themselves invulnerable. Blood, feathers, parrots' beaks, dogs' teeth, alligators' teeth, broken bottles, grave-dirt, rum, and egg-shells, were the materials used in the composition of the Obi. But in our day, these trumperies are deemed insufficient, and the shedding of innocent blood is resorted to, as a primary step to the consummation of the supposed charm."

He referred to a special magic potion:

"If a quarrel occurs, a duel must be fought – the principals immediately fly to the Obeahman, and, according to the price given, procure a charmed ball, warranted never to miss its object, or get themselves immersed in a cauldron, and made invulnerable to pistol shot – and, in this "hell-broth", the members of a murdered human being must be the chief ingredients. For this, about five years ago, Maitre Jacques committed a murder a few miles from this town – and for this again, an infant has recently been murdered in the Valley of Grand-Cul-de-Sac."

Regarding this mentioned murder in the vicinity of Castries no further details could be found in the available sources.

The second part of the article refers to the difficulty to give evidence before court:

"Will the monsters, authors of a dead so repugnant to nature, be brought to justice, and made an example to deter others from similar pursuits? We very much fear, that, notwithstanding the very zealous efforts which, to our knowledge, have been employed by the Commissary of Police, in endeavouring to trace out the perpetrators of this crime – and however strong the suspicion engendered from the evidence of circumstances – the fact will be but imperfectly brought to legal proof. "The secret and insidious manner", as it was observed to the Lords of the Privy Council some years back, in which this crime is generally perpetrated, makes the legal proof of it extremely difficult; suspicion, therefore have been frequent, but detections rare; and so it is still."

Another case refers to the murder of a young woman with the name Eucharisse which is described by BREEN (1844: 251-255) as follows:

"In the wild and thinly inhabited district of Mabouya, there resided in 1841 a coloured female, named Eucharisse, who followed the business of a huckster. Being a stranger in that part of the island, which had long been noted for the lawless character of its inhabitants, Eucharisse placed herself under the protection of a Negro, named Louis Elie, in whose house she hired a room. This house was divided into two apartments, separated by a wattled partition, six feet high: Elie occupied the one and Eucharisse the other. There were a door and a window to each, but the only communication between them was over the wattled partition. Soon after the arrival of Eucharisse in Mabouya, a young man of colour, named Aurelien Martelly, conceived a violent love for her, and tried all the arts of seduction to gain her over to his desires, but his overtures were contemptuously rejected. He then had recourse to her protector, and with the assistance of another coloured man, named Alphonse Guis, a notorious professor of sorcery, he obtained the consent of Elie to be allowed access to her room. The night of the 29th December 1841 was fixed for the execution of this nefarious scheme; and Elie, in the delusive hope of impunity through the incantations of Guis, assisted Martelly over the wattled partition, while Guis himself stood outside to keep watch. Martelly having thus taken the girl by surprise, as she lay fast asleep, succeeded after a violent struggle in effecting his purpose. He was then about to retire, when Eucharisse stood up, and, upbraiding him in an accent of despair, threatened to denounce his brutal conduct to the public prosecutor. At this Martelly became exasperated, and to wreak his vengeance upon her, he repeated the assault with such savage violence, that the poor girl, struggling in the defence of her honour, was actually strangled in the ruffian's grasp, and fell a corpse on the floor."

About the further investigations he reported:

"On the first news of the murder of Eucharisse, suspicion naturally attached to Louis Elie, who, although assured by Guis that he was perfectly safe, was arrested and committed to gaol. A preliminary investigation then took place; but sufficient evidence could not be elicited to bring the charge home to him, and he was accordingly released – a circumstance which had to untoward effect of strengthening his belief in the efficacy of Guis' incantations. After a lapse of some months a clue was at length obtained to the guilty parties, and Martelly, Elie, and Guis were committed to take their trial on a charge of murder. Still the only evidence that could be adduced was of a circumstantial nature; for, although the particulars were well known to every inhabitant of Mabouya, such was the prevailing dread of sorcery, wound up as it was with the whole affair, that no one had the moral courage to come forward and substantiate the charge.

The Attorney-General was compelled to proceed with the trial, his main chance of success resting on the hope that Elie might be induced to turn evidence on behalf of the Crown; but the latter persevered in his design to save the other prisoners. At the trial little was elicited beyond what had transpired at the preliminary inquiry; and it ended in a verdict of acquittal in favour of Guis and Martelly, and of guilty against Elie.

When Elie heard the verdict of the Court he became dreadfully agitated, and appeared as if anxious to make some disclosure; but at that moment Martelly, who stood near him in the dock, whispered in his ear: "don't be afraid; they can do you no harm;" and the miserable dupe suffered sentence of death to be recorded against him with apparent unconcern.

From the intense interest that pervaded the public mind, and which this case was so eminently calculated to excite, I was induced to watch the convict through every stage of the proceedings. His delusions, unbroken by the sifting ordeal of the judicial investigation, accompanied him back from the crowd of the Court House to the solitude of his prison cell. On the following day, however, haunted by a vague misgiving of his impending fate, he sent for his counsel and disclosed the different circumstances of the murder – still pertinaciously clinging to a hope of deliverance through the interposition of Guis; nor was the spell wholly dissolved until he beheld the formidable array for his execution. On the 22nd October 1842 he was led forth amidst the wailing and lamentations of the populace, and though his firmness and assurance remained unaltered to the last moment, "the big round tears" that glistened in his eye, as he approached the fatal gibbet, plainly showed that all confidence in the protecting power of Kembois had now vanished, exhibiting to the gaze of the sympathising multitude nothing but the wretched victim of sorcery and superstition."

This case was also described in the PALLADIUM of January 6th, 1842, but only regarding the discovering of the dead woman as well as of the first testimony of the house owner, Louis Elie. At the time of the publication it was not clear if it was really a murder. The author wanted to point the public's attention to this case and to his opinion that it was a crime. His introduction was:

"We feel it our duty to bring before the public, the following case, in the hope that it will not be deemed too late for the institution of such an investigation as may at least be partially productive of results to which public justice have a rightful claim."

Then the author described the further circumstances and reported of the death of the young woman Eucharisse on the Riche-Fond-estate, who – according to the public opinion – had been murdered:

"The circumstances of the case are as follows:- A young woman, named Eucharisse, who earned her livelihood by selling dry goods about the country, lodged in a room of one of the labourers' houses of the Riche-Fond Estate (Mr. Delobel's). She was in good health and spirits, and had been dancing in the neighbourhood on Christmas night. She left the dance at a late hour, accompanied by several young men, who escorted her to her own residence; - the man from whom she hired the room, himself occupied an adjoining room, and was there when she came home; he has stated that he heard when she entered – that she placed refreshments before the persons who accompanied her – that they talked for a considerable time – that one of the parties had something which displeased Eucharisse, and she thereupon requested they would leave the

house, adding that in the morning she would make a proper answer to the person who had offended her – that the party went away, and she retired to bed – that he also went to bed, heard nothing during the rest of the night, and started for Castries early in the morning. The man who made this statement, is, we believe, named Elie. Another man, who had been employed by Eucharisse in building a house, came to her lodging at about 7 or 8 o'clock on the same morning, for the purpose of taking his tools, which had been deposited in her room; he found the door closed – called Eucharisse several times, but received no answer – he then looked in through a crevice over the door and saw her lifeless corps lying on the ground. The door was then forced open – Mr. Delobel was called to the spot – he saw the state of the body – with tables and other articles of furniture, broken cups &c. strewn about the room in confusion, and yet the Coroner of the District was never apprised of the circumstance; Mr. Delobel merely imposed his seal upon the effects of the deceased, and ordered that the body should not be touched until the arrival of La Justice; and, it was eventually buried, without any Medical Man or the Coroner having been called to a view of the body.

The public now guess that there were marks of strangulation about the neck of the deceased – and the conjecture is, she may have been murdered for the sake of the money which, as a huckster, she was known to have in her possession. Some ascribe her death to some extraordinary paroxysm. But this is all matter of opinion - …"

(N/CO 258/1/12: 6/1/1842, p.227)

A further case which was brought in connection with OBEAH was reported by the STIOENDIARY MAGISTRATE of the 1st district (Castries, Anse La Raye) on June 3rd, 1842):

"A Coroner's Inquest was held before me, on the 27th ultimo at Anse La Raye Village, on view of the body of a Labourer named "Jean Pierre", whose death was supposed to have been caused by the administration of poison. The jury returned a Verdict of "natural death", accelerated by the injudicious "administration of improper medicines". The suspicion of the cause of death of this individual existed in the mind of the brother of the deceased, and had its origin in the deep rooted belief of the agency of "Obeah". It is painful indeed to observe with what tenacity even our most enlightened negroes, still cling to believe in this superstitious practice, inconvertible by argument or reasons, and unmoved by ridicule or division. In this instance the deceased had some month previously been present at a dance on a neighbouring Estate, where a quarrel and fight ensued, and he had then been threatened by his opponent, to the effect that he would not have long to live. He died several months after this occurrence, of extensive disease of the liver, as was proved on the Inquest, his friends and relations had not forgotten the threat, and nothing could divest them of the impression that "Jean Pierre" had become a victim to the influence of "Obeah" upon him by his enemies."

(CO 253/76/7: 3/6/1842)

Another case was described in an article of the newspaper PALLADIUM in November 1842. It referred to the death of a young man with the name Louis:

> "The Coroner of the 2nd district was called out, on Tuesday last, to hold an inquest on view of the body of a young man, named Louis, found hanging to a door frame in his lodging on the lands of the Union Estate. The deceased had been for about a year suffering from painful malady, and was generally dejected in spirits, fancying himself the victim of poison, or "obi". He had been recently removed from his own residence, in the valley of Grand-Cul-de-Sac, to the place where he was found dead, for the purpose of undergoing the usual treatment of cases similar to his. From the evidence of the inmates of the house, it appeared that death was caused by the act of the deceased man's own hand; and a verdict to that effect was accordingly returned by the Jury."

> (N/CO 258/1/13: 24/11/1842, p.264)

Two further reports of the years 1844 and 1845 refer to OBEAH in general:

In July 1844the STIPENDIARY MAGISTRATE of the 1st district (Castries, Anse La Raye) reported:

> "The black man is growing more and more diffident as to the powers he was wanted to attribute to the impostor known by the name of Obea-man. Witchcraft is now known by many to mean nothing more than knowledge of poisonous herbs; and when threatened with the pretended horrors of the occult art of Obeah, instead of being awe-struck as formerly, they but bring the matter in shape of complaint before the magistrate. In the absence of sufficient proof to punish the processing Obea-man, I have found it a salutary method to warn him, that should any of the complainant's family, or cattle suffer from poison, the law would look to him as the suspected author of the mischief."

> (CO 253/82/5: 3/7/1844)

On January 12th, 1845, the STIPENDIARY MAGISTRATE of the 2nd district (Gros Islet, Dauphin) reported of a wide spreading of OBEAH in St. Lucia:

> "The delusions of witchcraft (Obeah) are wide spread amongst the peasantry, and present the greatest impediment to their advancement in civilization. If an offender is cunning and expert in evading justice for any time by concealment, he is immediately attributed by his fellows with the supposed knowledge of Obeah; whilst he, on the other hand, is equally ready when captured to ascribe it to the working of Obeah by his enemies."

> (CO 253/83/6: 12/1/1845)

Also at the beginning of the seventies OBEAH was wide spread in St. Lucia. On December 6th, 1871, Governor DES VOEUX published an ordinance "For the repression of Obeah and other kindred practices" 8CO 253/148/1: 6/12/1871). The preamble was as follows:

> "Whereas the profession of obeah as tending to deceive and intimidate the ignorant has been productive of Serious Evils and it is expedient to provide for its more effectual repression.
>
> Be it enacted ..."

The terms OBEAH, OBEAH man and Instrument of OBEAH were defined as follows:

> "... the word "Obeah" means the profession or practice of witchcraft, palmistry or any occult art as well as what is commonly termed Kembois or Obeah or any act or profession which according to the testimony of two credible witnesses is intended as the practice or profession of Obeah; the term "Obeah man" means any person, whether man or woman, who professes a knowledge of "Obeah" and any person who professes by means of such knowledge or by the manipulation or use of cards or by instruments of Obeah as hereinafter described or by any supernatural devices to cure or impart as the case may be disease, love, or any other good or evil affection or to influence a Court of Justice or to tell fortunes or future or past events or to discover lost or stolen property or in any way to benefit or injure another either in person or property. The term "Instrument of Obeah" means any philtre, phial, blood, bone, image or other article or thing which according to the testimony of two credible witnesses is intended for the practice of obeah."

The punishments for the practice of OBEAH were imprisonment and hard-labour as well as whipping for men and solitary confinement and cutting the hairs for women. The respecting clauses were as follows:

> "3. Any Obeah man who shall in respect or by virtue of his profession receive or endeavour to obtain from any person either money or other property, whether belonging to such person or otherwise, or who shall promise, undertake or threaten to put his profession into practice, or any person who having Instruments of Obeah in his possession or on his premises shall do any act or use any Expression which shall be declared on oath to be intended as the practice of Obeah or peculiar to such practice shall be liable on Conviction of a Magistrate to be imprisoned and kept to hard-labour in the Royal Gaol for any period not exceeding six months.
>
> 4. Any person who shall be imprisoned on a conviction under the last preceding Section shall during such imprisonment be liable, if a male, to be whipped in such place as shall be appointed by the Governor, if a female to Solitary Confinement for any period not exceeding one month and to have her hair cut close to her head at the beginning and towards the termination of such imprisonment.

5.Any person who shall consult an Obeah man with the view of procuring the practice of Obeah, any person who shall in the belief that another person is an Obeah man endeavour to induce such other person to practice Obeah, any person who by threatening recourse to Obeah, poisoning or other means or pretended means of injury or by any mysterious and indefinite threat shall intimidate or endeavour to intimidate any other person, or any person who while in lawful confinement upon any charge shall have on his person any Instrument of Obeah shall be liable on conviction to be imprisoned with or without hard-labour for any period not exceeding four months.

6.Any person who shall be convicted a second time under the third Section of this Ordinance or having been previously convicted under the fifth Section shall be liable to be imprisoned with or without hard-labour for any period not exceeding one year and during such imprisonment shall be further liable if a male to be once or twice whipped as prescribed in the fourth Section, if a female to Solitary Confinement for one or two separate periods each not exceeding one month."

Already with the letter of November 16th, 1871, Governor DES VOEUX had transferred a draft of the above mentioned ordinance to the Governor of Barbados. In this connection he informed generally of OBEAH in St. Lucia:

"The Ordinance numbered 4 is for the suppression of "Obeah", the system of pretended sorcery and real intimidation called by this name is exceedingly prevalent in St. Lucia. I doubt indeed whether there is any other English island, except perhaps Trinidad, where the fear of it is so general or where the belief in it exists among persons so high in the social scale."

(CO 253/148/2: 16/11/1871)

Then he mentioned an example:

"I have heard from those who should be well informed, that there are among the professors of this deception persons whose means at least entitle them to be considered among the upper classes; and as an illustration of the superstition that exists, I may mention that only a few years ago a planter, in a letter to the administrator, charged two others of leading position with holding an interview with the devil."

Concluding the Governor referred to the general practice of OBEAH and the necessity for its legal repression:

"It is generally believed, and I think in this case with some foundation, that the practice of Obeah is not unusually poisoning under another name. Mysterious threats of death, which I am informed almost invariably refer to Obeah, are of everyday occurrence; and the joy manifested and expressed at a mere mention of a proposed law for repressing the practice is a proof of how much such a measure is needed."

Finally the two volume book of DES VOEUX published in 1903 is worth mentioning: Therein he refers to a man with the name "Adolphe la Croix" as a dangerous Obeah man. This man was hanged in the year 1876 because of murdering a child and the practice of OBEAH. DES VOEUX (1903: I,273) wrote as follows:

> "Notwithstanding rumours to the contrary, I had up to this time been inclined to think that terror was the only evil caused by Obeah; but an event occurred early in 1876 which rudely undeceived me. One who had long been reputed to be a dangerous Obeah man was convicted before the Supreme Court on the clearest evidence of murdering a little child with the object of using the body for some of his abominable rites. The principal witnesses against him were his own children, examined separately, and the body of the victim was mutilated in a peculiar way, which was sworn to be the method employed for Obeah purposes."

He further mentioned that after the death of Adolphe La Croix that man was accused of further child murders:

> "It came out subsequently, when after the man's death people were no longer afraid to speak out, that this wretch, Adolphe la Croix by name, had previously disposed on one of his own children in the same horrible manner. Further, it appeared that it was in the immediate neighbourhood of this man's house that a child had disappeared, for the discovery of whom I had some years before offered a large reward without success."

To this case there is another publication from the year 1933. It was written by DIZ, Jabetz, with the title "Adolphe – one of the most terrible of Obeah-men"

6.1.3 Summary

According to the available sources OBEAH was wide spread in St. Lucia in the 19th century. Beside general OBEAH-practices as for example poisoning, oracles for the cure of disorders or for obtaining revenge for injuries or insults, also special OBEAH-cases were mentioned.

In April 1841 a dead boy, approximately two years old, was found mutilated in the Grand-Cul-de-Sac-valley in the south of the capital of Castries. Another case referred to the murder of a young woman with the name Eucharisse at the beginning of the year 1842, for which a co-perpetrator who didn't disclose the truth because of his belief that OBEAH will protect him against the conviction, was convicted to death. In May 1842 the labourer Jean Pierre died. His relatives and friends had the suspicion that he had been poisoned. A further case was mentioned in November 1842 in the newspaper PALLADIUM, where a young man with the name Louis committed suicide. He was sick and thought this was in connection with OBEAH. A last report refers to Adolphe la Croix who was hanged in 1876 because of a murder of a child and the practice of OBEAH.

The general practice of OBEAH in St. Lucia in the 19th century was prohibited by several proclamations and ordinances. Punishments were confinement and hard labour and whipping for men and solitary confinement for women.

Also in 1985 – when I wrote my thesis - the practice of OBEAH was punishable in St. Lucia, although some attempts had been made to legalize it. Literature (Newspaper articles) is as follows: BRANFORD (1973: 19), JESSE (1973) and HUGHES (1973).

6.2 The flower festivals LA ROSE and LA MARGUERITE: Sources of the 19th century

6.2.1 Introduction

A good description of the flower festivals LA ROSE and LA MARGUERITE gives CROWLY with his article "La Rose and La Marguerite Societies in St. Lucia" published in the Journal of American Folklore 71 (Oct-Dec., 1958). He writes of singing societies dedicated to praising the rose or the marguerite flower and that they form important segments of the island's social structure. A further feature is the hierarchical organization of the societies which represents a kingdom. Each of the societies holds an annual "Grande Fete" whereas the participants are beautifully dressed:

> "... the queen wears a ball gown copied in every detail from a court photograph of the British Royal Family, varied or elaborated according to the taste and finances of the queen. She wears a gold paper crown and carries a gilded wooden sceptre. A long velvet cloak is thrown over her shoulders, and a wide sash runs across her breast. Her costume is in the society colour, whether red or blue."

Red is the colour of the society LA ROSE and blue of the society LA MARGUERITE.

The origin of these festivals could not be explained till today (1985). BREEN (1844: 191-192) assumed a political connection:

> "In order to gratify their propensity for dancing the Negroes have formed themselves into two divisions, or "societies", under the somewhat fantastic style of "Roses" and "Marguerites". These "societies" exist by immemorial usage in the French colonies, and are still to be found in more or less activity in St. Lucia, Dominica, and Trinidad. The history of the Antilles is involved in such total obscurity in all that concerns the black population, that it would be impossible at the present time to trace the origin of the Roses and Marguerites. It appears that at one period they were invested with a political character; and their occasional allusions to English and French, Republicans and Bonapartists would seem to confirm this impression. Their connexion with politics must have ceased at the termination of the struggle between England and France, from which period their rivalry has been confined to dancing and other diversions."

> (BREEN 1844: 191-192)

Both SIMMONS (1953) and CROWLEY (1958: 551) doubt the original political connection of these societies but have no alternative proposal.

According to an assumption of Prof. Dr. Karl R. WERNHART (Institute of Social and Cultural Anthropology, Vienna) the LA ROSE and LA MARGUERITE festivals could be, because of their hierarchical organization, in connection with former African sacral kingdoms which reached in the last nine centuries from Niger to the Nil as well as from Ethiopia across the lake areas to the South-Congo and Rhodesia (cp. HIRSCHBERG 1974: 86-87). To this assumption Dr. WERNHART came during his stay in St. Lucia in the years 1982 and 1983.

Similar memories of the blacks in America to the sacral kingdom in Africa shows also KUBIK (1981: 6-10) in his article "Extensionen afrikanischer Kulturen in Brasilien" (Extensions of African cultures in Brazil). He mentions the dance "Congada" which is held in the south of Brazil and which he refers to the old kingdom of Kongo:

> *"Unter den aus dem Kongo-Gebiet und seiner Umgebung stammenden und ursprünglich Kikoongo-sprechenden Bevölkerungsteilen im Süden Brasiliens wurden Aspekte der politischen Organisation des alten Königreiches Kongo in Form eines Tanzdramas erhalten, das bis heute tradiert wird: der C o n g a d a. Dieses gipfelt in der Wahl eines „Königs von Kongo" und umfaßt eine Reihe zeremonieller Akte eines fiktiven Staatsapparates mit einem „Botschafter" (e m b a i x a d o r), „Kriegssekretär" (s e c r e t á r i o   d e   g u e r r a) usw., in denen viele Reminiszenzen aus der Zeit reger diplomatischer Beziehungen zwischen Portugal und dem unabhängigen Königreich Kongo eine dramatische Auferstehung finden. Die C o n g a d a war zunächst eine interne Angelegenheit vor allem der aus Nordangola und dem südwestlichen Zaire verschleppten Sklaven, und eine Farce, ohne wirklichen politischen Machtgehalt. Aber das jährlich wiederkehrende Fest der C o n g a d a hatte einen starken Einfluß auf das Zusammengehörigkeitsgefühl der Kongo-Gruppen in Brasilien und wurde zu einer Art politischem Symbol."*

BREEN (1844: 192) wrote that during the period of slavery the practice of the LA ROSE and LA MARGUERITE festivals was restricted but that after the end of the emancipation period their significance rose.

Between the years 1840 and 1860 there was according to GACHET (1975: 137) a strong relationship between the LA ROSE and LA MARGUERITE societies and the church. But he also mentions quarrels between the societies and that therefore the good relationship to the church became strained. Finally in the year 1860 Bishop Ethelridge of St. Lucia condemned both societies and forbade Catholics to join them, remain in them and take part in there "fetes".

Not before the second half of the 20th century the festivals of LA ROSE and LA MARGUERITE had been revived in a big way (ANTHONY 1970: 8).

In the following a review of the sources of the 19th century is given, whereby on the one hand the already known sources are mentioned – stated in an article of ANTHONY published in June 1979 in Castries – and on the other hand unknown sources are quoted.

6.2.2 Sources

6.2.2.1   Known sources of the 19th century

ANTHONY (1979: 7-14) refers in his articles to the following sources:

<u>Book publications</u>

BREEN, Henry, H.
  1844   St. Lucia: Historical, Statistical and Descriptive, London
                (p. 192-205, 512, 522-523)

<u>Newspaper articles</u>

ANONYMOUS

  1841   The "Roses" and the "Marguerites"
                In: Palladium and St. Lucia Free Press,
                Vol. IV, No. 162, 11th September
                (CO 258/1, p.209)

  1865   "editoral"
                In: The St. Lucian, Vol. 2, No. 85, 15th July
                This newspaper is available in the newspaper
                department of the BRITISH LIBRARY in Colindale/London
                under C. 506

  1880   "The roses" and "Marguerites"
                In: The VOICE of St. Lucia, Vol. 3, No. 3, 24th July

  1892   Three articles regarding the opinion of a catholic priest
                to the flower festivals
                In: the VOICE of St. Lucia, Vol. 8, No. 383, 25th June,
                no. 385, 9th July, no. 386, 16th July

<u>Archive material</u>

"Travel Journal" of an Anglican priest from the middle of the 19th century
kept in the National Library of Scotland under MS. 14194, Catalogue of
MSS. Vol. X MSS. 13494 -, CH 10634.

6.2.2.2   Not known sources

The first source originates from the year 1819. From the letter of the PROCUREUR DU ROI of St. Lucia dated January 29th, 1819, follows that on January 25th, 1819, three free non-whites where convicted to money fines and three slaves to whipping before the police court in Castries. As offence meetings between these people under the name of "Roses Marguerites" were stated. This letter is an answer to Governor KEANE of St. Lucia, who asked the SENECHAL and the PROCUREUR DUD ROI to comment the above mentioned conviction. This letter is as follows:

> *"C'est avec un sentiment bien vif de regret, et de chagrin; que Monsieur le Sénéchal et moi; nous nous voyons encore obliges, de nous justifier de l'acte de sévérité prononcé contre 3 personnes libres de couleur et 3 esclaves par la sentence rendue à l'audience de Police du 25 courant, à ma requete et sur mes conclusions; acte commandé par le bien public, et qu'exigeait la sureté des personnes et des propriétés singulièrement compromises, si au mépris des lois, ordonnances et réglements de Police les attroupements des esclaves aidés des gens libres eussent été plus longtems tolérés...*
>
> *Prévenu depuis longtemps qu'en contravention aux ordonnances de Police de tous les temps il existait des rassemblements clandestins d'esclaves ou présidait un luxe effrayant par ses consequences et une débauche excessive don't les frais ne pouvaient etre faits qu'aux dépens des maitres ... je m'empressai de réprimer un abus aussi dangereux ..., je me bornai dès le principe à rappeller les contrevenants à leurs devoirs et à leur infliger pour toute punition pour tells rassemblements de ne point laisser les Esclaves dancer les dimanches; ce qui eut lieu pendant près d'un anj. Mais dans ces derniers tems, et lors des fetes de la Noel, du Jour de l'an, des Rois, et suivantes sur la promesse qu'ils me firent de ne plus donner lieu à aucunes plaints pour raison de ces rassemblements, je leur accordai permissions de danser toutes le fois qu'ils me le demanderont, mais toujours à la condition expresse et de rigueur de ne former aucune espèce d'association sous les titres de Roses Marguerites &c. (couleurs qui désignent leurs companies) et de ne point s'attrouper comme ils le faisaient par le passé. Ce qu'ils promirent, mais je fus bientot averti que loin de tenir à leur promesse et de se conformer aux ordonnances de police à cet égard, ils s'assemblaient tous le dimanches sous le titre de clubs qui étaient presides par des Rois, et où ils se choisissaient d'autres officiers, sous les titres de Sénéchal, Procureur du Roi, Procureur Général &c.*
>
> *En effet un témoin auriculaire de l'invitation faite le 17 du courant par le nommé Jean-Marie, esclave de M.P. Muter, et Pierre-Louis, celui de M.M.J.P. Alexandre aux autres esclaves assembles dans le lieu ordinaire de leur reunion, voisin de celui de ce témoin d'avoir à se trouver le dimanche 24 suivant à la collation qui devait lieu et pour les frais de laquelle le Messieurs payeraient une gourde et les dames deux mocos."*

(CO 253/14/5: 29/1/1819)

The answer of Governor KEANE by means of a letter signed by the COLONIAL SECRETARY of St. Lucia, SHAW, was as follows:

"Son Excellence ne peut regarder avec méfiance le titre de Roi &c. &c. &c. dans un moment de l'année où les coutumes de tous les pays permettent de s'entre donner des noms et des titres ..."

(CO 253/14/6: 1/2/1819)

The above mentioned extracts confirm that at least during the time of the mentioned correspondence the slaves were allowed, although with restrictions, to meet as LA ROSE and LA MARGUERITE societies.

Further reports originate already from the time period after the end of the emancipation.

In July 1840 the STIPENDIARY MAGISTRATE of the 5th district (Micoud, Praslin, Dennery) reported of his opinion that at the Riche-Fond-estate a LA ROSE society had been established. He also mentioned the rivalry between the LA ROSE and the MARGUERITE societies:

"No sooner had I commenced to flatter myself that the Labourers throughout the District had become more settled on the several Estates and had in a great measure desisted from that restless change of Employer and dwelling, which had hitherto being but too prevalent, than I have been most grievously disappointed by the conduct of the Labourers in the quarter of Dennery. – on one Estate (the Fond d'Or) the greater portion of the Labourers constantly employed and located on that property abruptly quitted their employ and repaired to the neighbouring Estate of "Riche Fond". Many of the Labourers located on the "Anse Canot" Estate adopted the same sudden and unexpected step.- I have endeavoured to ascertain the cause of this conduct, and I fear that other arguments than those of fair competition in wages, have made use of as the means of seduction.

It would appear that the minds of the Labourers have been excited and unsettled by the revival of an ancient spirit of party and rivalry, existing under the denomination of "St. Roses" and "St. Marguerites".

On the present occasion I have reason to believe that those Labourers who have thus left their dwellings and abandoned their former habits of industry, have been induced so to act under the persuasion that they are performing an act of religion, by enrolling themselves, as it were, under the banner of their adopted Saint, "St. Rose", and working for, or in the course of that worthy Saint's representative, in this Quarter of the Island. Independently of the injury thus caused to the employer as well as to the Labourer himself, I respectfully submit to the consideration of His Excellency the Lieut.-Governor my apprehension that the creation and fostering of such rivalry and jealousy amongst the labouring population may ultimately if not indeed soon lead to some serious disturbance of the public peace."

(CO 253/71/3: 3/7/1840)

According to the opinion of the author also BREEN refers to this case:

"Thus in 1840, an attempt was made by an unscrupulous planter to set one society in opposition to the other, by pandering to the worst passions of undisciplined humanity, and exciting their emulation beyond its legitimate sphere. The object was to allure the labourers to his estates and get them to work on his own terms: for this purpose he took one of the societies under his special protection; had himself elected their king; purchased superb dresses for the queens; and got up splendid fetes for their entertainment. Attracted by these dazzling frivolities hundreds of the labourers hastened to range themselves under the banner of the "white king". For some time all went on well, and the planter had every cause to exult in the success of his scheme; but when the day of reckoning came, and the labourers discovered that all their wages had been frittered away in gilded extravagance, the prestige of the white king's popularity speedily vanished, and his estates were deserted."

(BREEN 1844: 198-199)

A report of Governor EVERARD of St. Lucia of October 1840 refers to a LA ROSE meeting which was disturbed by inhabitants of Soufrière:

"… that on the evening of Saturday the 11th September certain Labourers and other Persons, composing the Society of the roses, had a meeting in a house in the Town of Vieux Fort, and that they were disturbed by certain Individuals from Soufrière who had just arrived in the Town. The Police interfered and prevented any serious disturbance for that night. On the following day (Sunday) during the Celebration of Mass, and the persons from Soufrière, having met at a friend's house, in the vicinity of the Church, commenced singing aloud, so as to disturb the service, and require the interference both of the Priest and of the local authorities – It further appears that in consequence of these proceedings, the report became current that the young men from Soufrière intended to assault the Clergyman; and a great many Laborers from the neighbouring Estates assembled in the Streets of Vieux Fort with the intention of protecting their Pastor: - the subsequent rioters' behaviour of the assembly and the violent proceedings which commenced, where checked by the Police, and order was with some difficulty resorted –"

(CO 253/71/4: 9/10/1840)

According to the opinion of the author the mentioned inhabitants of Soufrière could have been members of the LA MARGUERITE society.

In the year 1842 the newspaper PALLADIUM published two articles of the festivals of both societies. On August 4th an article with the name "Les Marquerites" was published as follows:

"The association so called made their grand sortie for the year on Thursday last, to celebrate their annual fete. – It was a brilliant gala, and we are glad to say, went off with perfect order and decorum."

(N/CO 258/1/15: 4/8/1842, p.251)

Regarding the festival LA ROSE the newspaper reported on September 19th:

> "There has been, during the week, a good deal of hilarity amongst the party of "The Roses" in celebrating the anniversary fete. The turn-out was certainly magnificent in the extreme, far surpassing any former effort of the rival parties. With standards of the most costly silks, and various other attractive decorations, these humble votaries of the "Bonnie English Rose" have been deservedly the objects of general admiration. The dresses of their cavaliers (of Fenelon's best cut), could only be excelled in brilliance by the tasteful display of the female train."

(N/CO 258/1/16: 29/9/1842, p.257)

According to a report of the STIPENDIARY MAGISTRATE of the 1st district (Castries, Anse La Raye) the meetings of the societies were not as frequent as in earlier days:

> "Those idle and meaningless displays of extravagant finery, feasting, and uproarious merriment, the party dances of the Roses and Marguerites, are not so frequent as during the earlier days of emancipation;…"

(CO 253/82/1: 10/1/1844)

In January 1845 the STIPENDIARY MAGISTRATE of the 4th district (Vieux Fort, Laborie) reported:

> "There are in the district, as throughout the island, two rival societies called "Roses" and "Marguerites", …, and of one or the other of these societies all the labourers in the island are members."

(CO 253/83/2: 10/1/1845)

Further he referred to the strong relationship of these societies to the church:

> "The church in the village of Vieux Fort being much too small to afford accommodation for all who attend at Divine worship, both societies have voluntarily come forward and offered, at their own expense, to augment the edifice; the society of Marguerites having undertaken to add another aisle to the church, whilst that of the Roses have engaged to erect a steeple; when completed it is calculated the work will be worth about 1,200£sterling, and from the zeal manifested by both parties, it is expected that it will not remain long unfinished. It is no uncommon thing to see after sunset from 150 to 200 persons (chiefly labourers) employed in carrying stone, sand, and other materials for the building. It is to be observed, however, that as each society furnishes the labour and materials from among themselves, the cost in money will by no means be as much as otherwise would be the case, and it is only to be hoped that priest craft

might not intervene to mar the good work, as the proprietors commence
already to complain that the labourers give too much time to the church,
and too little to the estates; having, however, had no complaint made to
me as yet, it is not my province to anticipate evil before it arrives."

The last source to be mentioned is a newspaper article in the PALLADIUM of August 1845 which informs of the 7th anniversary of the emancipation of St. Lucia as well as of the speech of the queen of the LA MARGUERITE society before Governor TORRENS of St. Lucia. The article starts as follows:

"On Monday last, as soon as it was known that His Excellency Colonel
Torrens would be accessible to them at the Government Office,
deputations, composed of the leading members of the associations known
as the "Roses" and the "Marguerites" waited upon His Excellency with
complimentary addresses occasional of the anniversary of emancipation.
Handsome banners, gaudy dresses, and massive jewellery, dazzled the
sight as the "Queen of the Marguerites" was ushered into the presence of
Queen Victoria's Representative to present the following Address-"

(N/CO 258/1/17: 7/8/1845, p.365)

An extract of the speech is as follows:

"We, the Association of the "Marguerites", comprising a large number of
the population of this Island, who, on this anniversary of the day on which
ourselves and the whole of our race incurred a debt of imperishable
gratitude to Her Most Gracious Majesty Queen Victoria and the British
Nation for that great blessing of universal freedom conferred on the
African race throughout the British Dominions, now approach Your
Excellency with feelings of the most profound respect to renew the
expressions of our acknowledgement of this unbounded gratitude for the
great boon conferred on us …"

6.2.3 Summary

The new sources found correspond in generally with the already known sources.

The correspondence between the PROCUREUR DU ROI and the Governor of St. Lucia from the year 1819 confirms that at least during the time of the mentioned correspondence the slaves were allowed, although with restrictions, to meet as LA ROSE and LA MARGUERITE societies. From this correspondence also follows that the societies were supported by free inhabitants.

Further reports originate already from the time period after the end of the emancipation (1840-1845). These sources confirm the rise in significance of the LA ROSE and LA MARGUERITE societies after the abolition of slavery. For example in January 1845 a STIPENDIARY MAGISTRATE reported that all labourers of St. Lucia are members of these societies. Further the rivalry between the LA ROSE and LA MARGUERITE societies as well as the strong relationship to the church was mentioned.

6.3 Clothes

During the period of slavery the slave owners were legally obliged to maintain the salves with clothes. The men got shirts and trousers, the women "shifts" and "petticoats" and the children got shirts (cp. chapter "4.7.4.1. Maintenance of slaves", pp 121-133).

Some remarks of the clothes of the slaves are contained in a letter of Governor STEWART of St. Lucia of September 1829. The Governor reported of his tour through the island:

> "The negroes here have another advantage in being allowed a quantity of fertile land for their own cultivation, and are thus enabled to supply themselves with many comforts. The effect of this is seen in the good and often gay dresses (particularly among the females) which they purchase. To an European newly arrived in the country, whose feelings are affected by the view of so many human beings held in slavery, nothing is more striking than seeing forty, fifty, or a greater number of women working in a field with hoes or other implement, and dressed in white or printed Calico jackets and Petticoats."
>
> (CO 253/26/6: 29/9/1829)

Another source is a circular letter of Governor DUDLEY HILL of St. Lucia addressed to the STIPENDIARY MAGISTRATES of July 1834. An extract therefrom is as follows:

> "Although the climate will not permit much clothing to be worn, nor is it so habitual amongst the negroes, especially by the working labourer in the field, still I should much wish you would impress on their minds the actual necessity of some covering being used, particularly by the females, to prevent the exposure of their persons so indecently (through, perhaps, innocently) as they do. In some of the estates in the 3rd district the women were mostly naked from the waist up. A handkerchief, or some slight covering, should be introduced, and a sense of decency ought to be instilled in their minds, which would soon expand; ..."
>
> (CO 253/49/3: 28/7/1834)

A further informative source – especially of Sunday and feast clothing – are the reports of the STIPENDIARY MAGISTRATES from the early forties. According to these reports the black population of St. Lucia set a high value on clothes. A special women cloth was the "Jupe". BREEN (1844: 196) describes it as follows:

"The Jupe is a species of gown worn by the Negresses and some of the coloured women in the French Antilles. Having neither sleeves nor bodice, it presents the exact dimensions of a petticoat – hence the name."

The material of the clothes often was very expensive. They bought fine cotton textiles, Indian textiles (Madras) or imitations of silk material. The labour clothing still consisted of coarse linen or cotton textiles. As jewellery the women wore "necklaces and ear-rings of massive gold and precious stones". Also to mention are silk parasols which were preferred by the women.

Extracts of the reports of the STIPENDIARY MAGISTRATES are as follows:

1st district (Castries, Anse La Raye):

"I have made inquiries of the Shopkeepers, and at the Dry goods' Stores in town, and I find that the coarse stuffs formerly in demand for clothing can no longer be disposed of, the universal choice of the labourers being confined to the selection of superior fancy goods; even a cotton parasol cannot obtain a purchaser in the person of a labourer, and the highest prices are paid for every article of dress."

(CO 253/78/2: 24/12/1842)

2nd district (Gros Islet, Dauphin):

"Their taste for dress and luxury has wonderfully increased. The coarse stuff for clothing, as formerly worn by the slave, has been driven from the market, and fine calicoes, silks, Madras head kerchiefs substituted"

(CO 253/74/2: 20/9/1841)

"On festivals and holidays, the labourers, male or females, are to be seen attired and decorated in Style and material, inferior to none in use amongst the politer classes; the only difference being that of the female peasant adopting a "Jupe", an external petticoat, generally of the finest textured chintz or Callico, - instead of the Robe or Gown used in higher society, with a costly madras Kerchief as a turban or head dress."

(CO 253/78/3: 21/12/1842)

3rd district (Soufrière, Choiseul):

"There are likewise, particularly in the larger town of Soufrière, other shops, supplied chiefly with large assortments of dry goods, of such qualities as are frequently purchased by the labourers; such as ready-made clothes, fancy stuffs, boots, shoes, shifts of every kind and colour, checks, Osnaburghs, imitation and Madras head kerchiefs, and variegated patterns for the external petticoats (jupes) generally worn by the females,"

(CO 253/83/5: 13/1/1845)

4th district (Vieux Fort, Laborie):

"The negro owns an inflexible propensity to pleasure, and delights in decorating his person with all finery that can possibly be procured. In this regard, there has occurred no change in the bent of his taste from what it was heretofore, though he may be enable to gratify that taste more fully now, than under any former system. Thus, in the years of the apprenticeship system; a few of them might be seen here and there, on occasions of any extraordinary holiday, or fete, to wear their Shoes and Stockings, round Jackets, or coat of coarse stuff; to procure which it required most uncommon exertion and industry during the hours left over, from that claimed by their masters; and not unfrequently were dishonest practices resorted to, for the acquisition. But now their whole time being their own, and so much may be gained by honest industry, that there remains no longer, either a necessity for plunder, or any inordinate exertion, in order to enable him upon high days, to sport the best of everything; and it would be difficult to find a labourer, who does not possess a trunk or press, abundantly garnished with coats, and pantaloons of superfine broad cloth, or with whom a cotton parasol would not be, so to speak, an object of disdain, whilst there is a silk one to be had at any of the stores of the merchants. As for the women, nothing can surpass the sumptuousness of their Dress, which generally consists of "jupes" or petticoats, made up of the finest chintz, with richly worked cambric chemises shown from the neck, to the waist, and madras head kerchiefs, all of the most radiates colours and most costly description. Necklaces and ear-rings of massive gold and precious stones, invariably form a prominent part of their personal decorations."

(CO 253/78/6: Dec. 1842)

5th district (Micoud, Praslin, Dennery):

"The negroes generally are exceedingly fond of dress and show, and will spend any sum within (and often exceed) their means, to procure costly dresses and decorations; perhaps in 99 cases out of 100 a female will be seen with none other than gold earrings, costing from 2£ to 3£ sterling; and 15s. to 20s. are commonly paid for working a chemise, to be worn on some particular occasion, and the stuff always of the finest texture. It is to be observed that the costume of the female labourers in the French islands (and those here still follow the same mode), is entirely different from that of the English colonies; here they use petticoats (jupes) made of fancy coloured prints, sometimes of silk, gowns not being in use. A labourer must be idle or worthless, indeed, if he has not his coat, value about 3 £, or at least a jacket of half the worth, with a hat of good quality, and it is seldom that either male or female is seen on Sundays or holidays, without their shoes and stockings and silk parasols, cotton ones being little in fashion among them."

(CO 253/74/5: 17/9/1841)

"... and for clothing for the females showy patterns of printed calicos, madras and other Indian and imitation kerchiefs, silk foulards, and for the men drill, calicos and fancy trousers, stuffs of all descriptions, also coats, shoes, hats."

(CO 253/78/5: 30/12/1842)

>*"... upon working days, common osnaburghs, cheques, ginghams penistone
>and other coarse stuffs are resorted to."*
>
>(CO 253/82/8: 3/7/1844)

BREEN refers also to the clothing (1844: 195-196). In connection with the
LA ROSE and LA MARGUERITE societies he wrote:

>*"The costume of the men differs little from that commonly worn by
>gentlemen in England or France. The silk or beaver hat, the cloth coat, the
>swelled cravat, the sleek trousers, the tasselled cane – in short, the whole
>tournure and turn-out of the male exquisites, would do honour to Bond-
>street or the Palais Royal. But the dress of the women is quite another
>affair: although in many instances the Jupe has given way to the regular
>English gown; yet, on fete days, the former reasserts its preponderance,
>as being more in harmony with the general costume. First you have the
>head-dress set off by the varied and brilliant colours of the Madras head
>kerchief, erected into a pyramid, a cone, or castle, according to the fancy
>of the wearer, and spangled over with costly jewels; next a huge pair of
>earrings of massive gold; then several gold and coral necklaces, tastefully
>thrown over the dark shoulders; then the embroidered bodice trimmed
>with gold and silver tinsel; and lastly, the striped jupe of silk or satin,
>unfolding its bright tints and broad train to the breeze."*

According to the mentioned sources especially the women were dressed
like those in the French Antilles. Regarding the clothing in the French
Antilles compare BERNER (1984: 225-227, 309-313).

6.4 House building

Some references to the house building in St. Lucia were made in the
reports of the STIPOENDIARY MAGISTRATES from the years 1844 and
1845:

In January 1844 the STIPENDIARY MAGISTRATE of the 1st district
(Castries, Anse La Raye) reported:

>*"The habits and tastes of the labourers are evidently improving.- They, it
>is true, are content still to dwell in the wattled hut: but there is more
>attention paid to interior comfort; the inner Chamber or Compartment is
>now very generally floored, and partly lined with Boards; beds, seats and
>buffets have become necessary articles of furniture;..."*
>
>(CO 253/82/1: 10/1/1844)

The STIPENDIARY MAGISTRATE of the 4th district (Vieux Fort, Laborie)
wrote:

"I regret, however, I cannot speak favourable of any improvement in their domestic economy.- Their houses or rather huts, thatched with the dried leaves of the cane, are in too many instances miserable filthy dwellings."

(CO 253/82/2: 10/1/1844)

Another report originates from the STIPENDIARY MAGISTRATE of the 3rd district (Soufrière, Choiseul):

"... they divide and separate their coffee or cocoa estates in small establishments, and construct, at distances, cottages, some of which are very neat, built of stone and covered with tiles, but generally of country wood, covered with trash, in which they locate families, to whom they abandon a certain portion of coffee plantations, which the latter are obliged to cultivate and reap for a certain proportion of the produce. These cottages are generally surrounded with enclosures, which allow the tenants fo feed, in the inside, pigs and poultry, ..."

(CO 253/83/5: 13/1/1845)

A detailed and very informative report is contained in the book "Building in St. Lucia" published by REA in the year 1898. REA distinguishes three types of houses:

- "bamboo and grass huts",
- "wooden houses".
- "stone or brick buildings"

"Bamboo and grass huts"

"These are merely one-roomed hovels, about 16 feet by 8 feet, forming the abodes of the poorest class of natives who live in the bush. The framework is made of wood cut from the nearest plantation, roughly squared and fastened together with wooden pins. The walls are constructed of horizontal strips of split bamboo, between which the blades of cocoanut leaves are vertically interlaced. The roof is of steep pitch, hipped at both ends, and thickly thatched with the "trashed" or stripped ribbon-like tops of sugar-cane; the floor is of bare earth, and square apertures take the place of windows. These choice and picturesque specimens of rural villadom are thus referred to as "trash huts", a title that may be interpreted in more senses than one."

"Wooden houses"

"Some of the wooden shanties to be seen in the towns are not better, but they are limited in Castries by a Buildings Bye-Law to 16 feet by 16 feet, as a minimum size on the streets. They are most frequently built in semi-detached fashion, with one or two rooms each, and very narrow passages between, leading to courtyards behind, the space therein being sub-let for smaller tenements by the dwellers in front. This consequently leads to

"overcrowding in unsanitary areas", that bugbear of medical officers of health, though it is said that the local authorities intend to prohibit this practice in future. The framework is of pitch pine, covered with weather boarding; the floors are of wood, while the roofs are also hipped at both ends and covered with shingles, and a bell-cast being invariably given to the eaves aesthetically satisfies the eye. Split bamboos not infrequently form a substitute for eaves-gutters, and walls are often patched up with the sides of old tin cans – a ludicrous sight indeed. These "packing-cases", as they are jeeringly termed, are of the most flimsy construction and it would not be difficult to knock a whole house down, especially as the structure rests on four or more big stones by way of piers, looking as if with open arms they were inviting a gentle breeze to blow them all over. It is no uncommon spectacle to witness one of these negro huts being carried through the streets by less than a dozen men for the purpose of being deposited on fresh site."

For this house the following picture was taken by REA (1898: 16/17):

Richer people lived in one or two storied houses. REA (1898: 32/33 took the following picture:

<u>Stone and brick houses</u> are described by REA as follows:

"Among the most noticeable buildings in Castries are the Government Offices, the new Market, the Colonial Bank, the Gaol, the Asylum, the Grammar School, and the Convent of the Sisters of St. Joseph, the Anglican Church, the Roman Catholic Church, and the Victoria Hospital, about half a mile from the town, with a capacity of 140 beds, and completed in 1887 at a cost of £8.000. These edifices are characterized by architectural neatness rather than by any pretensions to architectural beauty, with the exception of the Roman Catholic Church now in course of erection, built of stone and iron, and calculated to hold 3,000 people, which is in a pseudo-Romanesque style, with crude mouldings and much poverty of detail."

(REA 1898: 19-21)

6.5 Social structure

6.5.1 Introduction

In the first section it is referred to the maintenance of children as well as to the relationships between men and women in general. For the topic "Christian marriages" there is a separate chapter in which especially the time after the abolition of slavery is referred to.

6.5.2 General

In January 1832 planters and merchants of St. Lucia issued a petition in which they protested against the law that the slaves should maintain themselves. From this petition follows that the prevalent family structure of the black population of St. Lucia was the unit "mother/child":

> "In the present state of the Slave Population few families of Slaves have any Father or reputed Father to take charge of and cultivate the land allotted to infant Slaves – and therefore this task must fall on their Mother, ..."

(CO 253/37/2: January 1832)

In March 1836 Governor DUDLEY HILL of St. Lucia wrote:

> "In the present excess of females the male negroes have generally a plurality of wives or reputed wives who they put away at pleasure or from caprice which would not be the case were the sexes more equalized."

(CO 253/51/1: 15/3/1836)

According to this situation most of the mothers in St. Lucia had to maintain their children alone by themselves. During the time of slavery also the slave owners were responsible for the slave children (cp. chapter "4.7.4.1. Maintenance of slaves", pp. 121-133). Since the abolition of slavery only the parents were responsible for their children (children under six years and new born; cp. chapter "4.3. Abolition of slavery and beginning of the emancipation period", p. 58).
The unit "mother/child" is also confirmed by reports of the STIPENDIARY MAGISTRATES from the 1st and 2nd district:

1st district (Castries, Anse La Raye):

> "The condition of the free children generally is bad from the licentious habits of the labouring population few reputed fathers of the children contribute to their support. They are consequently thrown entirely upon the resources of the mothers."

(CO 253/52/7: 1/10/1836)

<u>2nd district (Gros Islet, Dauphin):</u>

"The free children are generally maintained by their parents on the respective Estates and they generally are not neglected. The practice of promiscuous intercourse between the sexes but too frequent here has left many of the children without even a reputed father and consequently dependent on the mother for support."

(CO 253/52/8: 2/10/1836)

Also the STIPENDIARY MAGISTRATES of the 3rd and 4th district reported of the maintenance of the children:

<u>3rd district (Soufrière, Choiseul):</u>

"The free children are healthy, they are supported by their parents, the younger children have some old person to mind them during working hours, they have medical comforts from the Estate and in general are will treated."

(CO 253/52/5: 31/8/1836)

<u>4th district (Vieux Fort, Laborie):</u>

"Free children cannot considered be happy one. The Planters although charitable generally, do not now pay the same attention to the children as formerly and I am sorry to add that the Apprenticed Mothers do not shew that lively interest in their children's welfare which one would suppose."

(CO 253/64/20: 9/2/1838)

According to two reports of the STIPENDIARY MAGISTRATE of the 3rd district from the years 1841 and 1842 there were frequently quarrels between two partners. This had consequences to the maintenance of the children:

"Violent disputes and frequent battles between reputed man and wife, are common, and much of the stipendiary magistrate's time (to whom they fly on all occasions) is occupied in settling these affairs; and I beg to say that it requires much patience to arrange satisfactorily this sort of questions, particularly when they concern the equitable division of the "ménage" and future maintenance of the children."

(CO 253/74/3: Sept. 1841)

"Disputes respecting the maintenance and services of children are, I think, on the increase, and sometimes I find much difficulty in adjudicating between the reputed parents."

(CO 253/76/6: 12/3/1842)

Regarding the general relationship between two partners there is the following report of the STIPENDIARY MAGISTRATE of the 1st district (Castries, Anse La Raye) from the year 1844. The STIPENDIARY MAGISTRATE referred therein to the existing jealousy between the men and that it also led to violence:

"Libertinism is one of the leading propensities of the negro labourers; and the women with whom they cohabit are often most reliable victims of their jealous disposition. Untaught in those high principles of honour by which virtue and fidelity are guarded in more civilized societies, the black man looks upon his wife's constancy and faith as being lasting only so long as she may be kept beyond the reach of his comrades' wooing.

Perpetually tormented by the "green-eyed" monster he resorts to every conceivable expedient for the purpose of deterring his fellows from visiting his hut during his own absence, and thus sparing himself some of the tortures of jealousy. Should the house of a negro be visited during his absence by any male friend the standing order to be observed by the woman reputed as his wife is to refuse him admittance, should he plead hunger, a stool is to be given him at the door, where he must partake of such refreshment as the house affords; to overstep this rule under any pretence whatsoever, is to conjure the most deadly feud between her husband "son homme" and the stranger and call down upon herself the worst treatment that jealousy can impose.

The liar lashing his flanks dwindles into insignificance on a comparison with the infuriated husband. A combat with cutlasses arises, under such circumstance, and even murder has been known to signalize the degradation and odium which the negro inferred from such behaviour on the part of his wife; for the fact of admittance is all the proof necessary to institute the stranger a paramour."

(CO 253/82/5: 3/7/1844)

6.5.3 Christian marriages

According to the CODE DE LA MARTINIQUE slaves could only marry with the consent of their masters:

> "Art. X.-The formalities described by the Ordinance of Blois, as well as by the Declaration of 1639, respecting marriages, to be observed as well with regard to free persons as to Slaves, with this exception, that the consent of the father and mother of the Slave is not necessary, but only that of the Master."
>
> (BPP/ST/71/2: 16/3/1685, p.184)

A report of the PROCUREUR GENERAL, SENESCHAL and PROCUREUR DU ROI of St. Lucia from the year 1823 confirms this law:

> "The laws of Saint Lucia, authorize marriage between Slaves, and only require the consent of the masters. The formalities and religious ceremonies for such marriages, are the same as for those of free persons."
>
> (BPP/ST/68/1: 1/12/1823, p.281)

From a letter of Governor MAINWARING of St. Lucia dated in August 1823 follows that marriages were seldom in St. Lucia:

> "In this colony marriage among Slaves is little common, but that proceeds from the absence of religious instruction, not from any objection on the part of the owners, who would be anxious to encourage it: marriage between Slaves of different estates is not known.
>
> When a marriage does take place the parties come to Castries or Soufrière, and the celebration is performed with the same rites and formalities as if they were free people."
>
> (CO 253/17/3: 25/8/1823)

In the slave law of St. Lucia from the year 1826 the dependence of the slaves from their masters regarding the approval of the masters to the marriage was restricted; also the PROCUREUR GENERAL could give the consent:

> 57: "The owner, his attorney, guardian, or other representative, shall give his consent to the marriage in writing. In case of refusal on the part of the owner or his representative, either of the Slaves desirous of marrying, may petition the Procureur General, who shall, under summary notice to be served upon the owner or representative, requiring him to appear before him on a given day, which shall be within three weeks from the date of the Procureur General's Order and in default of his appearing, or, if on his appearing he should assign an insufficient reason for his refusal, the Procureur General shall grant them his permission to marry without the owner's consent."
>
> (CO 253/22/4: 1/6/1826)

Other stipulations regarding marriage were fixed in this slave law as follows:

> *"Marriages amongst Slaves shall be subject to the same Law as marriages among free persons, the same forms shall be observed with respect to both with the following exceptions.*
>
> *A marriage among Slaves may be celebrated by any Christian Minister, or by any public teacher of Religion, approved by the government, and engaged in no other secular calling than that of a schoolmaster ...*
>
> *The consent of the Father and Mother of the Slaves is dispensed with."*

The available figures regarding marriages between slaves are as follows: In January 1831 the COLONIAL SECRETARY of St. Lucia made a report for the period from January 1st, 1825, to December 31st, 1830:

	Protestants	Catholics	Total
Whites	11	50	61
Free non-whites	8	105	113
Slaves	1	8	9

(CO 253/29/5: 1/1/1831)

According to reports of the PROTECTOR OF SLAVES from June 1826 on the following table was made:

Time period/source		Number of marriages among slaves
(CO 258/5/1-4:	1/6/1826-30/6/1828/ section C)	3
(CO 258/5/5:	1/7/1828-31/12/1828/section B)	-
(CO 258/5/6:	1/1/1829-30/6/1829/ section F)	-
(CO 258/5/7:	1/7/1829-31/12/1829/ "	1
(CO 258/6/1:	1/1/1830-31/3/1830/ "	-
(CO 258/6/2:	1/4/1830-30/9/1830/ section D)	-
(CO 258/7/1:	1/10/1830-31/12/1830/ "	-
(CO 258/8/1:	1/1/1831-30/6/1831/ "	2
(CO 258/9/1:	1/7/1831-5/11/1831/ "	-
(CO 258/10/2:	5/11/1831-31/12/1831/ "	-
(CO 258/11/1:	1/1/1832-30/6/1832/ "	1
(CO 258/12/1:	1/7/1832-31/12/1832/ "	1
(CO 258/13/1:	1/1/1833-30/6/1833/ "	3
(CO 258/14/1:	1/7/1833-31/12/1833/ "	1
(CO 258/15/1:	1/1/1834-1/8/1834/ "	1

	TOTAL	13

According to these figures 13 marriages among slaves took place from June 1st, 1826 to August 1st, 1834.

The real number of the marriages must have been higher. This opinion follows from the following remark of the PROTECTOR OF SLAVES regarding the period from April to September 1830:

> *"The Undersigned begs to state that no Returns of Marriages have been transmitted by the Clergymen of the different Parishes of the Island and he has reason to believe that considerable Negligence exists in this respect.*
>
> *Notice however has been given to these Gentlemen that the Penalties prescribed by Law will be most rigorously enforced in cases of neglect or delay."*

The available figures regarding marriages after the abolition of slavery concern the total population. For giving a survey of the marriages before and after the abolition of slavery the following table and diagram was made. From the BLUE BOOKS, section "Population" figures were available from 1828 to 1871 and from BREEN (1844: 240) for the period from 1833 to 1843:

Source/year BLUE BOOKS	Source/year BREEN 1844: 240	Number of marriages	
(CO 258/24/1: 1828)		20	
(CO 258/25/1: 1829)		17	
(CO 258/26/1: 1830)		18	
(CO 258/27/1: 1831)		19	
(CO 258/28/1: 1832)		16	
(CO 258/29/1: 1833)		57	
	1833		18
(CO 258/30/1: 1834)		24	
	1834		21
(CO 258/31/1: 1835)		36	
	1835		24
(CO 258/32/1: 1836)		46	
	1836		36
(CO 258/33/1: 1837)		44	
	1837		27
(CO 258/34/1: 1838)		46	
	1838		43
(CO 258/35/1: 1839)		53	
	1839		35
(CO 258/36/1: 1840)		83	
	1840		66
(CO 258/37/1: 1841)		78	
	1841		76
(CO 258/38/1: 1842)		146	
	1842		102
(CO 258/39/1: 1843)		171	
	1843		171
(CO 258/40/1: 1844)		164	
(CO 258/41/1: 1845)		163	
(CO 258/42/1: 1846)		136	
(CO 258/43/1: 1847)		171	
(CO 258/44/1: 1848)		150	
(CO 258/45/1: 1849)		183	
(CO 258/46/1: 1850)		176	
(CO 258/47/1: 1851)		241	
(CO 258/48/1: 1852)		231	
(CO 258/49/1: 1853)		138	
(CO 258/50/1: 1854)		906	
(CO 258/51/1: 1855)		167	
(CO 258/52/1: 1856)		184	
(CO 258/53/1: 1857)		137	
(CO 258/54/1: 1858)		90	
(CO 258/55/1: 1859)		91	
(CO 258/56/1: 1860)		90	
(CO 258/57/1: 1861)		98	
(CO 258/58/1: 1862)		105	
(CO 258/59/1: 1863)		109	
(CO 258/60/1: 1864)		87	
(CO 258/61/1: 1865)		220	
(CO 258/62/1: 1866)		85	
(CO 258/63/1: 1867)		75	
(CO 258/64/1: 1868)		89	
(CO 258/65/1: 1869)		129	
(CO 258/66/1: 1870)		418	
(CO 258/67/1: 1871)		157	

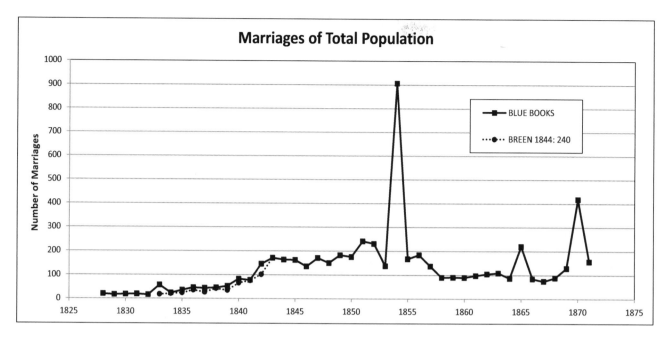

Marriages of Total Population

Legend:
- BLUE BOOKS
- BREEN 1844: 240

According to these figures there is a slight raise in marriages up from 1834 which desultory increases between 1840 and 1843. After this period the figures have great deviations but do not go down to the level existing during the time of slavery and emancipation. The high number of marriages in the year 1854 was mentioned in a letter of Governor POWER dated in June 1855 in which he pointed to a cholera epidemic which according to his opinion was the reason of the great number of marriages:

> *"Though the Cholera produced great afflictions it was not wholly unproductive of good; Concubinage, the master evil of St. Lucia, has been crushed by it, I trust for ever – marriages within the year."*

(CO 253/116/1: 4/6/1855)

Here the Governor probably meant the influence of the church which encouraged the people to marry and intimidated them because of the cholera epidemic.

The great number of marriages in the year 1870 cannot be explained according to the available sources.

Regarding the marriages of the black population of St. Lucia after the end of the emancipation period the reports of the STIPENDIARY MAGISTRATES give valuable information regarding the period from 1841 to 1844. The following extracts inform of a raise in marriages:

1st district (Castries, Anse La Raye):

"The improved taste and habits of the Labourers are becoming more perceptible and are conspicuously made manifest in their desire for marriage and their greater care and anxiety for the welfare of their Children."

(CO 253/78/2: 24/12/1842)

2nd district (Gros Islet, Dauphin):

"I may premise that the observations made are mainly directed to the state of the Second District, although I have every reason to believe the same are applicable to almost every other district of the island …

Marriage amongst the emancipated labourers is more resorted to, and more attention is paid to the early and regular baptism of their children."

(CO 253/73/1: 2/4/1841)

"The desire of establishing themselves respectable by marriage is daily in the increase, …"

(CO 253/82/6: 16/2/1844)

3rd district (Soufrière, Choiseul):

"Marriage is always of frequent occurrence, …"

(CO 253/79/3: 1/8/1843)

4th district (Vieux Fort, Laborie):

"Marriages are becoming more and more frequent amongst the labourers"

(CO 253/78/6: Dec. 1842)

5th district (Micoud, Praslin, Dennery):

"There has been a progressive improvement in the general character and condition of the peasantry, since the dissolution of the apprenticeship; marriage, formerly but little known among them, is now of common occurrence, …"

(CO 253/74/5: 17/9/1841)

"The Marriages in this District are far from being as frequent, or as numerous as in the 4th district which I have left, although the population in both are nearly alike.

Nevertheless, it is not the less obvious that the Labourers here begin to evince a repugnance to that state of concubinage which has so long predominated in the intercourse of the sexes in this Colony."

(CO 253/79/5: 7/8/1843)

The greater part of the people who married were couples who already lived together and mostly had children:

2nd district (Gros Islet, Dauphin):

> *"The desire of establishing themselves respectable by marriage is daily in the increase, tho' hitherto it has been almost exclusively confined to those persons who have been living previously together as man & wife, and who have had by such connections children whom they seek to legitimate, and with the females especially the term M a d a m entitles them a degree of respect which they are fond of."*

(CO 253/82/6: 16/2/1844)

3rd district (Soufrière, Choiseul):

> *"Of the few marriages which do take place, the majority is contracted between old people who for long periods have cohabited together; ..."*

(CO 253/74/3: Sept. 1841)

5th district (Micoud, Praslin, Dennery):

> *"... and the greatest number of marriages that have taken place, have been between those who had been cohabiting together, and many of them with a numerous offspring; ..."*

(CO 253/74/5: 17/9/1841)

Graphic representation of the mentioned districts:

(Division of districts extracted from a map of St. Lucia from the year 1847 – BPP/CG/4/1: 1847, p.518)

To the situation that the greater part of the newly married people are couples who already lived together and mostly had children refers also BREEN in his in 1844 published book. Regarding the number of marriages in the period from 1833 to 1843 (cp. p.384) he wrote:

> *"… these marriages mostly occur between persons who have long cohabited together, and wish to take advantage of the lex loci to have their children legitimated; whereas the younger people still commonly cling to concubinage, or yield themselves unreservedly to a promiscuous intercourse."*
>
> (BREEN 1844: 241)

Further reports of the STIPENDIARY MAGISTRATES are:

4th district (Vieux Fort, Laborie):

> *"Marriages now very generally considered by them as be essential towards assuring their domestic peace, and claim to respectability."*
>
> (CO 253/82/2: 10/1/1844)

5th district (Micoud, Praslin, Dennery):

> *"… there is another motif …, it is the increased degree of respectability which the married men and women acquire in the Society of their class. The title of M a d a m bestowed only upon the married woman is not a little flattering to their unity and amour proper."*
>
> (CO 253/82/7: 12/1/1844)

The STIPENDIARY MAGISTRATE of the 5th district referred the greater wish to marry to religious instructions:

> *"… and particularly the dread of those future sufferings which are represented during their religious instructions by the ministers as being reserved for those who lead a life of immorality, have a great influencer upon their minds, and in most cases may be taken as the determining cause of their marriage; …"*

The marriage ceremonies were described as follows:

3rd district (Soufrière, Choiseul):

> *"… the married couple as well as the assistants, both males and females, who are always very decently, and often richly decorated; …"*
>
> (CO 253/79/3: 1(8/1843)

4th district (Vieux Fort, Laborie):

"Since my short residence amongst them, I have witnessed three or four of such marriages on which occasion great decorum was observed, not to the exclusion, however, of good humoured gaiety and a liberal display of dress and luxury."

(CO 253/79/4: 5/8/1843)

According to a report of the STIPENDIARY MAGISTRATE of the 1st district (Castries, Anse La Raye) dated in January 1844 among the labourers the wish to marry declined whereas the former FREE NON-WHITES preferred to marry:

"Marriage does not seem to increase amongst the labouring classes. – For the first year or two after emancipation, wedlock appeared to increase. But the novelty seems to have lost its charm. No sooner now, does a newly freed tradesman, or labourer, become prosperous in his pecuniary affairs, then he takes another mistress & I can safely answer, that a large proportion of the men of this description in the town of Castries, have more than one establishment. – This state of things I attribute, partly to the many bad examples, set by those who call themselves the better classes – partly to their little respect in advantage which legitimacy obtains in this Colony – partly to the demoralizing tendencies of the two sexes working in common in the Field Gangs, - and partly to the scarcity of labour, … - in facts, in more than one instance, have I known planters to cry down and discourage marriage, on the score that it is that the married woman kept themselves more to the household duties and seldom hired out their Services in the Field labour. I am happy to say, that these observations do not apply to what may be considered the middling classes of this Colony.

I mean the anciently free coloured people, who have evinced a vast improvement of late years in this respect. – Some few years ago a coloured girl preferred being the Mistress of a white man, to becoming the legitimate partner of one of her own class; it is not so now. – Marriages and intermarriages have become the rule, and not the exception, and it is delightful to see, that as the education, wealth, commercial and political importance of this Class of people have augmented, so have their respect for and observance of the best and surest ties of civilized Society increased."

(CO 253/82/1: 10/1/1844)

In general marriages after the end of the emancipation period concerned only the minority of the black population of St. Lucia. This mainly follows from BREEN's book (1844: 167) in which he designated the majority of the relationships between men and women of St. Lucia's black population as "promiscuous intercourse". According to the above mentioned sources of this section it can be assumed that the prevalent family structure "mother/child" as well as the polygynous not long-term relationships between partners existed also after the emancipation period, although not in this extension as during the period of slavery.

6.5.4 Summary

At the time of slavery the prevalent family structure in St. Lucia was the unit "mother/child". Men preferred polygynous relationships which were not of long term. Marriages among slaves were seldom. Till the year 1826 slaves could only marry with the consent of their masters. Then in the slave law of St. Lucia from the year 1826 the dependence of the slaves from their masters regarding the approval of the masters to the marriage was restricted; also the PROCUREUR GENERAL could give the consent.

Regarding the FREE NON-WHITES it is to mention that they liked to marry.

After the end of the emancipation period the number of marriages (concerning the total population) raised till the year 1843; especially till 1840. After that year a raising or declining trend could not be noticed.

According to the available reports regarding the time period from 1841 to 1844 the greater part of the people who married were couples who already lived together and mostly had children. Other reasons for marriages were the legitimation of their children, the desire of the women to be designated as "Madam" which meant a higher social status and the influence of religious instructions.

Among the former FREE NON-WHITES marriages were more preferred than earlier.

Although after the emancipation period there was a general raise in the number of the marriages, the greater part of St. Lucia's black population didn't enter into long term relationships. Therefore the prevalent family structure could also be assumed as unit "mother/child".[28]

Education and maintenance of the children was mostly cared for by the mothers.

---

[28] According to Univ.-Prof. Dr. K.R. WERNHART – research in St. Lucia in the years 1982 and 1983 – and Univ. Prof. Dr. M. KREMSER – research in St. Lucia up from the year 1982 – (both from the Institute of Ethnology, Vienna) also many mothers lived alone with their children in St. Lucia and formed the family unit in those days.

6.6 Christianity in St. Lucia

6.6.1 Introduction

As St. Lucia was colonized in the 18th century mainly by the French (cp. chapter "1.2. History of settlement and policy", pp.17-19), the Catholic Church was established in the colony at that time.

In the first section of this chapter the development of the Catholic Church from the 18th century and the development of the Protestant Church from the beginning of the 19th century are described. The main source was GACHET (1975: 13-112).

The second part of this chapter refers to the influence of Christianity – mainly the Catholicism –to the black population of St. Lucia in the 19th century. It is mainly based on archive material.

6.6.2 The development of Christianity in St. Lucia

In the year 1749 the first priest arrived in St. Lucia. He was a Franciscan. With him came two secular priests who were Jesuits. Already in the year 1770 there were eleven parishes in St. Lucia. The districts Gros Islet, Castries, Anse-La-Raye and Soufrière were Dominican parishes. The districts Choiseul, Laborie, Vieux Fort, Micoud, Praslin, Dennery and Dauphin were Franciscan parishes.

As in the year 1790 the Church in France was declared independent from the Holy See by the Civil Constitution of the clergy, promulgated on August 24th, and all the members of the clergy were asked to swear allegiance to the Constitution under pain of deposition from office, many bishops and priests refused to take the oath and became known as "Refractory Bishops and Priests". On March 1st, 1793, perpetual banishment was decreed against the refractory clergy.

The effects of these events gained a slow foothold in St. Lucia. Till 1792 there were some nine priests in St. Lucia. As in the year 1794 the British took over the island only three priests lived on it. GACHET supposes the official suppression of religion at the end of March 1795. He mentions a notarial act, certifying the death of Dame Negret on 17th April 1796, and informing of the existence of revolutionary tribunals in 1795. GACHET (1975: 70) quotes this act as follows:

> *"During that period the Catholic religion was despised or ignored, the churches were desecrated and used as stores or prisons, and the ministers of the altar could hardly appear in public without incurring some danger from the insurgent negroes and some furious individuals who had come from Europe to stir up people against them."*

When the British finally took over the island in 1803 the Catholics of St. Lucia were guaranteed the unrestricted exercise of their religious worship. This was confirmed by the Treaty of Paris in 1814.

Between the years 1803 and 1820 the number of priests who resided in St. Lucia varied between three and five. They were beneath exclusively Catholic priests, as the first Protestant priest arrived in St. Lucia in the year 1819. The work of the priests was not easy at that time. GACHET (1975: 89) wrote:

> "The priests of the period under review were greatly overworked. They had to travel frequently and the roads were bad. Most of them travelled from parish to parish by canoe."

In the period from 1820 to 1826 the number of the priests varied between two and three and in the period from 1827 to 1837 between three and five. Up from 1838 beneath every of the nine parishes were administered by a priest. Many of them were French.

(GACHET 1975: 13-112)

According to a letter of Governor DUDLEY HILL of St. Lucia in the year 1838 there were only 200 Protestants in the colony. The majority of the population of St. Lucia was designated as Catholics. Finally he mentioned that "no other sect or Religious Worship" existed in the colony (CO 253/64/21: 2/4/1838).

This situation is confirmed by a letter of Governor TORRENS of St. Lucia from the year 1846:

> "A remarkable feature in this society is the absence of sectarianism. No dissenting minister or sectary has ever had footing here. In this respect, perhaps, St. Lucia is a singular instance among the British West Indian possessions. This may partly account for the quiescent conduct of the people. To all outward appearance the community is divided between the Church of England and the Roman Catholic faith."

(CO 253/85/1: 4/1/1846)

In the year 1871 the population of St. Lucia was divided into the following confessions of faith according to the "St. Lucia Handbook" dated in the year 1901 (GARRAWAY 1901: 47):

Confession	Number of persons	%
Roman Catholic	29.592	93,62
Anglican	1.803	5,70
Wesleyan	46	0,15
Prespyterian	12	0,04
Morovian	12	0,04
Mohammedan	131	0,41
Hindu	13	0,04
Other denominations	1	0,00
	31.610	100,00

The majority were the Catholics with 93.6 %. The existence of Mohammedans and Hindus is explainable by the Indian immigration to St. Lucia starting at 1859 (cp. chapter "5.4.5. Indian Immigrants", pp.344-345).

6.6.3 The influence of Christianity on the black population of St. Lucia in the first half year of the 19th century

As already mentioned in the preceding section there was a lack of priests in St. Lucia from the beginning of the 19th century till the end of the emancipation period. To this situation pointed also Governor BLACKWELL of St. Lucia in August 1824 as follows:

> "I have found in the Quarters of Choiseul, Laborie, and Vieux Fort, Catholic Churches in excellent order and which are at all times kept open for private devotion, tho' they have no Curés to officiate in them. The want of Catholic Clergymen is much felt throughout the Island, and the Inhabitants during my late tour have strongly expressed to me the disadvantages under which, themselves, and their Negroes, labour from this want."

(CO 253/18/2: 6/8/1824)

But he also mentioned:

> "I must here observe that upon most of the Plantations, prayers are regularly read to the Negroes assembled for that purpose both morning and evening."

The same situation was described by Governor STEWART of St. Lucia in 1829:

> "In the present state of perfect ignorance of the Negroes of every principle and feeling of religion, a few zealous good clergymen, Protestants and Catholics, would be of greater benefit than Schoolmasters, who only teach, what may be called, the mechanical art of reading, while, it would be the duty of Clergymen to visit the plantations, and the slaves in their houses, and teach them the first principles of religious and moral duties; and thus lay a good foundation for future acquirements in reading: Unfortunately,

however, this Colony is at present much in want of zealous conscientious Clergymen, capable, or willing to attend to the fatiguing duties (as they consider it) of visiting and instructing the poor people; and until proper clergymen of character can be procured, all my exertions or those of others in authority, will avail little. When Clergymen are the most active at jovial meetings – conspicuous on many occasions, but never in their own clerical duties, and when clergymen have been brought before Criminal Courts, and severely find for cruelty to their slaves and servants; neither the precept nor example of such men can be of the least use: Indeed, the example is most injurious, and a scandal to morals."

(CO 253/26/6: 29/9/1829)

In his report for the months from October to December 1830 the PROTECTOR OF SLAVES wrote:

"It is painful to declare that the State of Religion among the Slave Population is at very low ebb."

(CO 258/7/1: 1/10/1830-31/12/1830, section GO)

Regarding the average attendance of the church there is the following table of the CHIEF SECRETARY's OFFICE concerning the period from 1825 to 1830:

	WHITES	FREE NON-WHITES	SLAVES	TOTAL
Protestants:	14	14	2	30
Catholics (Castries):	30	370	-	400
(Soufrière):	-	-	-	400

(CO 253/29/6: 1/1/1831)

According to a letter of Governor BUNBURY of St. Lucia dated in May 1837 the above described situation didn't change in the emancipation period:

"I found an almost total apathy on the part of the Planters to afford religious or moral instruction to the Apprenticed Labourers, who, I am sorry to say, generally speaking, remain in a perfect state of ignorance; ..."

(CO 253/55/2: 19/5/1837)

After the end of the emancipation period this situation changed completely. In the reports of the STIPENDIARY MAGISTRATES of the early forties it is referred to crowded churches, especially on Sundays and feast days. Extracts of these reports are as follows:

1st district (Castries, Anse La Raye):

"The chief ambition of the labouring population now is to dress themselves and their children, and conduct themselves in a manner that would even surpass our European peasantry; on Sundays and fete days the church is actually crowded with these persons, many of whom come a considerable distance from the country to attend the mass."

(CO 253/74/1: 1/10/1841)

2nd district (Gros Islet, Dauphin):

"The attendance of the Peasantry at divine Service continues regular, and their conduct praiseworthy, and although the Church is spacious, and capable of affording accommodation for about a thousand persons, it seldom happens that there is sufficient room for all who attend, consequently many are frequently obliged to remain outside.

(CO 253/82/6: 16/2/1844)

3rd district (Soufrière, Choiseul):

"The attendance of the Peasantry at Divine Worship, here as elsewhere is really regular and praiseworthy; on Sundays and Festivals the Roman Catholic Churches are always crowded;"

(CO 253/79/3: 1/8/1843)

"On days of great religious fetes, the Roman-catholic church is not sufficiently large to contain the congregation who desire to attend Divine service; the consequence arises, that a considerable number are obliged to remain outside the walls of the church during the celebration of the service."

(CO 253/83/5: 13/1/1845)

4th district (Vieux Fort, Laborie):

In this District there are two Roman Catholic Churches, from four to five hundred persons can be accommodated in each of these Churches and they are generally well attended, especially on Sundays or particular feast days of the Church. The labourers are particularly exact in their attendance on divine Service and the observance of all the religious obligations of their Church is on all occasions exemplary."

(CO 253/82/2: 10/1/1844)

5th district (Micoud, Praslin, Dennery):

"The attendance of the labourers at church, and their desire to contract marriage, continues to increase. The two Roman Catholic churches in the district are numerously attended, and I have been informed that the number of communicants of both sexes of the labouring class is rapidly augmenting."

(CO 253/83/7: 2/7/1845)

To another point referred the STIPENDIARY MAGISTRATE of the 3rd district (Soufrière, Choiseul) dated in September 1841:

> *"It is the custom in the Roman Catholic churches of this Island to put up the sittings to public auction once a year. The last annual sale took place last Sunday in this parish, and about 100 places were purchased by the newly freed, at prices varying from two to six dollars, mostly by women, who, I am sadly afraid, go to church principally to display their finery."*

(CO 253/74/3: Sept. 1841)

From the reports of the STIPENDIARY MAGISTRATES follows further that the black population of St. Lucia supported the church either with money or with their working power.

In September 1841 the STIPENDIARY MAGISTRATE of the 5th district (Micoud, Praslin, Dennery) reported:

> *"In the quarter of Dennery there is a small chapel, and a church is being erected at Micoud; a Roman Catholic clergyman visits there parishes alternately; the negroes are very regular in their devotional duties, and have contributed largely, both in labour and money, towards the erection of the church; in fact to them is mainly to be attributed the maintenance of the curate, who receives no fixed stipend from the Government, nor is there any law to oblige them to contribute."*

(CO 253/74/5: 17/9/1841)

Also the STIPENDIARY MAGISTRATE of the 1st district referred to this support:

> *"The Roman Catholic Church at Anse Laraye, at the extremity of the district nearly, has been recently rebuilt and fitted up for the purpose of Divine Worship, almost entirely at the expense of the labouring population, by voluntary contributions; and they have further subscribed funds to procure from France the usual pompous ornaments and sacred vases generally used in the Roman Catholic Churches."*

(CO 253/83/8: 17/1/1845)

In this connection compare chapter "6.2. The flower festivals LA ROSE and LA MARGUERITE: Sources of the 19th century", p. 369-370). In it the strong relationship of the LA ROSE and LA MARGUERITE societies to the church is mentioned. As at that time almost all black labourers were members of these societies (cp. p. 369), it can be assumed that the mentioned supports were initiated by these societies.

Regarding religious instructions by the church there is a report of the STIPENDIARY MAGISTRATE of the 4th district (Vieux Fort, Laborie) from the year 1843:

"Preparatory to entering upon the state of matrimony they are subjected by the Priest to a service of religious instruction, the solemnity of which, seldom fails to impress their minds with the primary elements, and principles of their religion. This preparatory course is performed either publicly by the Priest himself, or privately, by enlightened and devout persons, chosen by him for the purpose and then independently of this instruction preliminary to marriage, there exists another course, the object of which is to prepare such of the Labourers as may be disposed to seek admittance to the Holy communion. This instruction is also administered openly in the Church after Divine service by the Parish Priest, or in private dwellings by charitable, and pious individuals, to whom the Communicant pays some trifling compensation. There are fixed days for the examination of the candidates for admittance to this first communion, and questions simplified and adapted to their understanding, are then proposed to them upon subject of religion, the knowledge of their duty to God, the Sovereign, their employers, and to one another: their admission to the Holy Table being made dependent upon the degree of correctness, and rectitude with which they are able to answer these questions; I was myself present at one of these public instructions, and, I confess, was surprised at the intelligence, piety, and devotion of the candidates. I have also attended at the Church on the occasion of a first communion at Vieux Fort, counted a great number of Labourers in attendance, and I was informed by the Curé that out of 26 communicants, 18 were plantation labourers, males and females."

(CO 253/78/6: Dec. 1842)

According to BREEN (1844: 248) only the educated people could profit by religious instructions. He wrote as follows:

"...: and as for religious instruction, it is only made available to those that can supply the want of it – the educated classes, who can purchase and read religious books; while it is almost totally beyond the reach of the poor, unlettered Negro. Some of the priests are zealous and attentive; but their zeal and attention are confined within the walls of the church. They catechise and instruct on the week-days, but the Negro cannot quit his work. They preach on the Sundays and holydays, but then the church is crowded, and the devotee who has a seat and understands French may profit by the sermon, while the peasant, who stands at the door, either does not hear one word, or, if he hears, does not understand. What prevents the clergy from visiting the estates during the hours of cessation from work, and conversing with the labourers in their own dialect? In former times the Christian missionary was to be seen travelling in every direction in search of spiritual patients, and he deemed it not derogatory to his calling to court acquaintance with the lowest haunts of ignorance and vice: but in these days of selfishness and sound, he is castled up in towns and cities, surrounded by the fashionable follies of the rich, inaccessible to the vulgar vices of the poor."

6.6.4 Summary

In the 18th century the Catholic Church was established in St. Lucia which was well represented by Franciscan and Jesuits. Owing to the pursuit of the French clergy in connection with the French revolution the number of the priests was reduced in St. Lucia at the turn from the 18th to the 19th century to a minimum. As at the beginning of the 19th century the British took over St. Lucia there was a lack of priests in the colony. This situation was not altered by the British till the end of the emancipation period.

According to several reports the slaves had beneath no religious instruction. It was only mentioned that prayers were regularly read to the slaves assembled for that purpose at the plantations. Beside the lack of priests also the ignorance of the planters to afford religious instruction to their labourers was referred to.

After the end of the emancipation period this situation changed completely. There were enough priests, the churches were crowded, especially on Sundays and feast days. From some reports follows further that the black population of St. Lucia supported the church either with money or with their working power.

Although Christianity especially the Catholicism was well represented in St. Lucia after the end of the emancipation period according to the opinion of the author the black population of St. Lucia, especially the peasantry, was only superficial influenced by Christianity. This opinion is founded as follows:

- Little religious influence to the slave population from the beginning of the 19th century till 1838 and the therefrom resulting establishment of African beliefs
- A report of the STIPENDIARY MAGISTRATE dated in September 1841 in which it was stated that the women went to church principally to display their finery
- BREENS opinion that only the educated people could profit by religious instructions

6.7 Education

6.7.1 School education

Already from the second half of the 18th century there were French private schools in St. Lucia. The first British school was an Anglican institution which was closed some years after their foundation (1828) in Castries. The real beginning of school foundations in St. Lucia is to be dated in the time after the abolition of slavery. On June 11th, 1838, the first MICO - school was opened in Castries (GACHET 1975: 121-122).

The designation of this school refers to a Lady MICO who had, in 1670, bequeathed her estate of£1.000 to her nephew on condition that he married one of his six cousins. If he declined, as he did, the money was to go to the ransom of any poor Christian seaman captured by the Barbary pirates of North Africa. But the Barbary pirates had by then been brought under control, so that Lady MICO's second provision had proved fruitless too. The money was invested and left to accumulate; by the time of emancipation the sum had grown to£120.000. The abolitionist Thomas Fowell Buxton applied for it to be used for the education of ex-slaves on the grounds that this was close to the intention of Lady MICO; his application was allowed by the Court of Chancery, which deals with such matters in England (AUGIER/GORDON/HALL/RECKORD: 179-180).

Further foundations of these MICO – schools took place in St. Lucia in the year 1838 on the estates Rivière Dorée, Roseau and Troumassé, in February 1839 at Gros Islet, in April 1839 at Laborie, in June 1839 at Vieux Fort and in August 1841 at Soufrière.

These MICO-schools, on which British teachers educated, were declined by the Catholic clergy of St. Lucia because they saw a danger for the faith of the Catholic children (GACHET 1975: 122-123).

This situation of the MICO-schools was also mentioned in the reports of the STIPENDIARY MAGISTRATES of the early forties. Original extracts of these reports are as follows:

<u>1st district (Castries, Anse La Raye):</u>

> *"There are two schools of the Mico establishment, and two other small schools in the town of Castries; the former are more attended, being almost gratis, and the education in English, which they are desirous of learning; the Roman Catholic clergy are generally opposed to these establishments, and in some instances have prevented children from attending, and at the same time they do not afford any similar institutions for the instruction of the lower classes."*

(CO 253/74/1: 1/10/1841)

2nd district (Gros Islet, Dauphin):

"A branch of the Mico Institution is established in Gros Islet. The number of children attending the school is now 32. Many more were formerly enrolled, but have been since withdrawn by their parents, acting under the influence of the parish priest."

(CO 253/74/2: 20/9/1841)

3rd district (Soufrière, Choiseul):

"There are no new institutions, save and except one of the Mico schools, which was established in the town of Soufrière in July, 1840. In spite of the difficulties which the teacher, Mr. A. Johnstone, had to contend with from his imperfect knowledge of the French language, and from the opposition on the part of the Roman Catholic clergy, it has flourished better and done more good than any other school in the island."

(CO 253/74/3: Sept. 1841)

4th district (Vieux Fort, Laborie):

"Catholic Clergy: ignorant of the English language decidedly French in their tastes and opinions, and fearing the instillation of religious Doctrines foreign to their Church, they are jealous of the interference of the Mico teachers in the education of the children of their congregation; ..."

(CO 253/82/2: 10/1/1844)

Numbers of children attending "day schools" are available according to the reports of the STIPENDIARY MAGISTRATES for the period from 1845 to 1850 as follows:

Source/time period	number of scholars	% of total population
(CO 258/16/3: 1/7/1845-31/12/1845, p.3)	452	2,14
(CO 258/16/4: 1/1/1846-30/6/1846, p.68)	535	2,52
(CO 258/16/5: 1/7/1846-31/12/1846, p.134)	526	2,52
(CO 258/16/6: 1/1/1847-30/6/1847, p.195)	594	2,21
(CO 258/16/1: 1/7/1847-31/12/1847, p.259)	659	3,14
(CO 258/16/7: 1/1/1848-30/6/1848, p.320)	870	4,14
(CO 258/16/2: 1/7/1848-31/12/1848, p.380)	884	4,21
(CO 258/17/19: 1/1/1849-30/6/1848, p.2)	-	-
(CO 258/17/2: 1/7/1849-31/12/1849, p.41)	827	3,93
(CO 258/17/3: 1/1/1850-30/6/1850, p.101)	906	4,31

According to this table the share of the scholars in comparison to the total population was very low.

From a report of the PUBLIC LIBRARY of St. Lucia dated in the year 1854 follows that only 7.77% of the population could write and 10.9% read (CO 253/114/2: 28/2/1854).

In the year 1859 the first public Catholic school was established in St. Lucia. In 1862 a second followed (GACHET 1975: 141).

Owing to the strong opposition of the Catholic clergy the MICO-schools had to be closed in the second half of the 19th century in St. Lucia (DES VOEUX 1903: I, 190).

6.7.2 Establishment of the first library in St. Lucia

By an Ordinance of June 18th, 1847, (CO 255/5/1: 18/6/1847, p.52) stipulations for the establishment of a public library and museum were fixed.

On April 19th, 1848, the newspaper ST. LUCIA GAZETTE published the rules and regulations for this library. The first four clauses of these stipulations were as follows:

> "Rules and regulations of the SAINT LUCIA LIBRARY AND MUSEUM
>
> 1.The Books, Maps, &c. collected by Donations or otherwise, may be referred to within the Library and Museum, by all the Inhabitants of St. Lucia; and Subscribers (see Regulation No. 4) may personally introduce Strangers.
>
> 2.Daily admittance will be allowed to the Library and Museum, between the hours of 9 and 10 in the morning, and 3 and 5 in the afternoon, except on Sundays and Holidays.
>
> 3.Strict silence to be preserved in the Library and Museum.
>
> 4.With a view of rendering the Library of the most extensive public utility, Books (not being Books of reference) may be taken out of the Library by Persons making an Annual Subscription according to the following Scale:-
>
> Subscribers of 6s. per annum, to be allowed 1 work at a time.
> Subscribers of 12s. per annum, to be allowed 2 works at a time.
>
> All subscriptions to be paid in advance, to entitle persons to the benefit thereof. The first subscription to be considered as paid on the 1st January last."
>
> (N/CO 253/92/1: 19/4/1848)

In May 1848 Governor DARLING of St. Lucia informed the STIPENDIARY MAGISTRATES, the priests as well as the "Leading Inhabitants of the Island" of the library with the following circular:

> "I entertain a hope that, with a very moderate degree of public support, the ST. LUCIA LIBRARY AND MUSEUM may be made an important instrument in creating and fostering a taste for literature, and in diffusing useful practical information amongst the Inhabitants of the Colony at large.
>
> No means, I am confident, will more conduce to the rapid improvement of the social and political condition of the People, than those which directly tend to raise their intellectual standard.
>
> The Institution has met with a fair share of encouragement among the Residents in the Town of Castries; but I would gladly see its operation extended to the other Towns and Villages of the Island, as well as to the Rural Districts.
>
> I beg to enclose a few copies of the Rules and Regulations adopted by the Trustees, by which you will observe, not only that the Institution itself is open to all the Inhabitants of St. Lucia, but that the trifling annual contribution of six shillings will entitle a Subscriber to the use of Books from the circulating department of the Library; and I am satisfied, that care will be taken by the Trustees, so to arrange the period allowed for the perusal of works, as to render them available to Residents in the Country.
>
> It is almost unnecessary to say, that the Library will comprise Works in both the French and English Languages.
>
> I hope I shall not be disappointed in relying, as I venture to do, upon your co-operation, as well by supporting the Institution yourself, as by making generally known the popular advantages it is intended to afford, and by using your influence with others to promote its prosperity."

(CO 253/92/1: May 1848)

In the year 1852 already about 1.500 books were at the library (N/CO 258/2/1: 19/3/1852, p.113).

7 Summary and result

The aim of my thesis was to establish a dynamic ethno-historical cultural picture of the black population of St. Lucia under British dominion before and after the abolition of slavery in the 19th century. It could be shown that the abolition of slavery in the year 1834 respectively 1838 (end of emancipation period) caused essential changes in the living conditions of the black population of St. Lucia, especially in the social and economic scope. At the abolition of slavery about 70% of the total population of St. Lucia were declared from the status of a slave to a free inhabitant. In the following review the situation before and after the abolition of slavery is shown.

7.1 British slave policy in St. Lucia

As the British conquered St. Lucia in the year 1803, they took over the French slave laws which were part of the CODE DE LA MARTINIQUE. These French laws were translated into English and renewed in some cases by British enactments (ordinances, proclamations) and valid up to the year 1826.

According to a movement in Britain to ameliorate the living conditions of the slaves the British government took measures in the colonies. The first suggestions of amelioration reached the colonial government in St. Lucia in the year 1832 by a letter of the SECRETARY OF STATE BATHURST. These suggestions became law in St. Lucia on June 1st, 1826. Further extensive amelioration laws were enacted in St. Lucia in the years 1830 (April 20th) and 1831 (December 24th).

Between the slave owners of St. Lucia and the British colonial government respectively the British government in London were discussions about the amelioration measures whereas the slave owners of St. Lucia often protested very vehemently against the directed measures. But because of the political system of St. Lucia the amelioration measures were enforced by the British government with ORDERS IN COUNCIL.

On August 1st, 1834, the abolition of slavery took place in St. Lucia. On it a four-year emancipation period followed.

7.2 Population

At the beginning of the 19th century the number of the black population of St. Lucia was about 15.000: 13.500 slaves and 1.500 free blacks and people of mixed colour. Till the abolition of slavery there was a slight increase in the black population and the people of mixed colour which concerned mainly the free persons amounting about 3.900. After the end of the emancipation period the black population including people of mixed colour increased essentially (1851: 23.300 and 1871: 30.773 persons).

The number of the whites was at the beginning of the 19th century as well as at the time of the abolition of slavery about 1.200. Then their number decreased. A census of the year 1871 informs of 837 whites.

At about 1800 the main part of the population lived in the area of Soufrière (21%). In the year 1835 Soufrière still showed a high portion of population (22%), but also Castries had become with a portion of 22% a main settlement area.

Finally it is to mention that there was a surplus of women in St. Lucia as well as before and after the abolition of slavery.

7.3 Economic

At the beginning of the 19th century the export produces of St. Lucia were cotton, sugar, coffee and cocoa. Then there was a change. Cotton which was the main export produce lost in significance. Also the export figures of coffee and cocoa fell. The main export produce became sugar. After the end of the emancipation period cotton had totally lost its significance, also the export figures of coffee had further decreased. Only cocoa gained a little in significance. The export of sugar, which was already the main export produce, has risen essentially from about 1860.

The common economic situation in St. Lucia from the end of the 18th century to the emancipation period was a miserable one. As reasons for this there were stated events of war at the end of the 18th century (the struggle for St. Lucia between the French and the British), a lack of slaves, hurricanes as well as legal measures by the British Colonial Government for ameliorating the situation of the slaves. In the emancipation period there was a slight improvement of the economic situation which further improved in the second half of the 19th century.

After the end of the emancipation period there was for a short time a lack of labourers on the estates because many former APPRENTICES didn't continue to work. Further complaints of the planters referred to unsatisfactory execution of the work as well as to the high wages they had to pay to the labourers. This situation had a negative effect on the agriculture of St. Lucia and there was a decline in sugar exports. But already in the second half of the year 1839 there was a general amelioration of the labour situation on the estates. It is stated that the labourers were attracted by the high wages which were paid. In the year 1846 Governor TORRENS of St. Lucia reported of a successful change in the labour system from slavery to free labour.

The METAIRIE-system – a special kind of a tenancy whereby instead of paying a rent the crop yield is divided in a certain portion between proprietor and leaseholder – was the first time applied in St. Lucia at the beginning of the forties. From the late forties till about 1855 its significance increased. In the second half of the fifties the METAIRIE-system became more and more uneconomic because of the good economic situation of the island and at the beginning of the sixties it was only found on few estates in St. Lucia.

To the use of the plough in St. Lucia it is to mention that till about 1845 the plough was not used very much. The general implement was the hoe. But up from the year 1845 the use of the plough progressed generally.

7.4 General situation and way of life of the black population of St. Lucia

At the beginning of the 19th century there were the following restricting slave laws in St. Lucia:

-   Slaves were considered as moveables and as such liable to mortgage.
-   Slaves could possess nothing independent of their masters.
-   Assemblies of slaves of different estates were only possible with the sanction of the PROCUREUR DU ROI.
-   Slaves were not allowed to be appointed to office or to any public situation or to be concerned in commerce. They were further not allowed to compose or distribute remedies or to undertake the cure of any description of disorder with the exception of the bite of serpents.
-   They were forbidden to sell certain products as for example sugar canes, coffee or cotton. Other products like fruits or vegetables could only be sold with the consent of their masters.
-   Slaves were not allowed to possess arms of any kind, except they were sent out shooting by their masters.
-   Slaves could not be parties in civil matters, either as plaintiffs or defendants. Their evidence in court was used except for or against their masters.

Owing to the movement for the amelioration of the living conditions of the slaves the above mentioned restrictions were commuted as follows:

-   With the law of June 1826 the slaves got the right to possess property.
-   Up from the year 1832 slaves were allowed to assemble with the consent of their masters.

- Up from the year 1826 it was possible for slaves to compose or distribute remedies or to undertake the cure of any description of disorder with the consent of their master.
- With the slave law of 1826 the general prohibition of selling certain products as sugar cane, coffee or cotton was abolished; but the consent of the slaves' master was necessary. With an Ordinance of June 1832 the purchase of sugar, coffee, cocoa, rum and molasses was allowed till a certain volume.

The beneficent clauses for slaves at the beginning of the 19th century were:

- Masters were to supply each slave with provisions, clothes as well as looked after medically.
- Slave owners were prohibited to put their slaves to torture, to mutilate or kill them, but they were permitted to flog them or to put them in chains.
- Slaves had the right to make their complaint to the PROCUREUR DU ROI.
- Masters of twenty years of age and over could manumit their slaves.
- When slaves were sold, families were not to be broken up.

The new laws concerning the amelioration of their living condition of the slaves referred to

- Better regulations regarding the maintenance of the slaves as well as the possibility for the slaves to maintain themselves with self-grown produces.
- Relief concerning the punishment regulations and
- The right of the slave to buy his freedom also against the will of his master.

Apart from the legal situation of the slaves it is to mention:

In spite of the legal prohibition for the slaves to possess property it was common in St. Lucia that they possessed little property. Slaves could earn money by selling cultivated produces, fish as well as logwood and by trade activities; especially up from the year 1826 when they got the legal right to possess property.

Regarding the maintenance of the slaves it is to mention that owing to the bad financial and economic situation of the slave owners the general maintenance of the slaves was often very difficult. But reports of the twenties refer also to a good maintenance situation. Short before the abolition of slavery the majority of the slaves maintained themselves with self-cultivated produces.

If a slave complained because of improper treatment or bad maintenance in most of the cases he was treated disadvantageously.

After the end of the emancipation period among the former slaves there was the trend to live independently from the estates on small grounds. At that time the existing town and villages extended, also new villages were established. The former slaves worked on the one hand on the estates and on the other hand they cultivated provisions or raised cattle by themselves.

The nourishment of these people was based on self-cultivated provisions and salted fish or meat.

As leisure-time activities dancing, narrating and celebrating feasts were mentioned.

Already in the middle of the forties an independent peasantry had developed which rose in the following time.

7.5 Miscellaneous to the period of slavery

Slave imports to St. Lucia up from the war period at the end of the 18th century till the abolition of slave trade on January 1st, 1808, were very small. They came directly from Africa or from other Caribbean islands.

Regarding the situation of runaway slaves in St. Lucia it is to mention that it was easy form them to hide themselves in the interior of the island because of the non-development of the densely wooded mountain ranges by the colonial government. Furthermore there was the possibility for runaway slaves to get shelter from free inhabitants. This practice was very common. In spite of severe punishments fixed by law the running away of slaves in St. Lucia was very common. The colonial government had no control over this situation. Sporadically slaves fled from St. Lucia to Martinique.

The free population of St. Lucia – besides the white inhabitants - during the period of slavery were FREE NON-WHITES and refugees from Martinique.

The part of the FREE NON-WHITES rose from the year 1772 with 4% to 27% in the year 1835. Till the years 1826 respectively 1829 they were legally restricted in contrary to the whites. For example they were not to be employed in any public office or they could not use names which were similar to those of whites. Regarding the property it is to mention that the most of them were in a relatively good financial situation. Especially this group made a social rise within the society of St. Lucia after the abolition of slavery.

The slave refugees from Martinique arrived essentially in the period from 1830 till the end of the emancipation period (1838) in St. Lucia. The estimates vary between 600 and 800 refugees. These refugees preferred a way of life independent from the estates. This was possible because they have got their freedom by arriving on the island.

7.6 The immigrations after the abolition of slavery

Owing to a lack of labourers already in the emancipation period but especially from the end of the forties labourers were brought to St. Lucia. In the period from 1836 to 1842 Europeans immigrated. From about 1840 to 1848 immigrants from Barbados arrived. These above mentioned immigration were not significant for St. Lucia. The real immigration period in St. Lucia started in the year 1849. Totally 1.298 African immigrants arrived in the island in the years 1849, 1850 and 1862. These immigrants were Africans liberated from slaves' ships and who were taken on board in Sierra Leone or in St. Helena. The planters of St. Lucia were in generally satisfied with them. They had a good labour morale and were healthy. In the course of the time most of these African immigrants merged with the local black population.

The immigration of Indians started in the year 1859 and ended in the year 1893. In this period more than 4.000 contract labourers arrived in St. Lucia. After the expiration of their contracts most of these immigrants returned to their homeland.

Further African immigration refugees from Martinique are to mention. They came to St. Lucia in the years 1858 and 1859. But their number was very low.

7.7 Special subjects

In the 19th century OBEAH was wide spread in St. Lucia, although the general practice of it was prohibited by several proclamations and ordinances. Punishments were whipping and confinement.

The societies LA ROSE and LA MARGUERITE consisted as well as before and after the abolition of slavery in 1834, whereby it is to note that during the period of slavery their assemblies and feasts were essentially restricted.

Regarding clothes it is to mention that after the emancipation period the black population of St. Lucia preferred expensive material. The type was the same as that in the French Antilles.

House building: In the country bamboo and grass huts were built. In villages and towns wooden houses were preferred. Especially richer people lived in one or two storied houses. There were also some stone houses, but mostly for public and governmental use.

The prevalent family structure of the black population of St. Lucia at the time of slavery was the unit "mother/child". Men preferred polygynous relationships which were not of long-term. Christian marriages occurred seldom. Although after the emancipation period there was a common increase in Christian marriages, the majority of the black population didn't enter into long-term relations. I therefore assume that after the abolition of slavery the prevalent family structure was also the unit "mother/child".

The influence of Christianity on the slave population was little in the 19th century. Reasons were a lack of priests as well as the lack of interest by the resident priests and planters for religious instruction. Although after 1838, the end of the emancipation period, the Christian influence intensified essentially, it had only superficial effects on the black population. A survival of African beliefs, mainly of slaves and immigrants who came to St. Lucia in the 19th century, was consequently easily possible.

Regarding school education it is to note that the real beginning of school foundations in St. Lucia is to be dated in the time after the abolition of slavery. On June 11th, 1838, the first MICO-school was opened in Castries. These MICO-schools, on which British teachers educated, were declined by the Catholic clergy of St. Lucia because they saw therein a danger for the faith of the Catholic children. In the year 1859 the first public Catholic school was established in St. Lucia. In 1862 a second followed. Owing to the strong opposition of the Catholic clergy the MICO-schools had to be closed in the second half of the 19th century in St. Lucia.

The attendance of school was very low at the emancipation period. From a report of the year 1854 follows that only about 8% of the total population could write and about 11% could read.

The aim of my thesis, to show that the abolition of slavery in the year 1834 respectively 1838 (end of emancipation period) caused essential changes in the living conditions of the black population of St. Lucia, especially in the social and economic scope, was achieved. I wanted to represent the written sources and to write a history of the black population of St. Lucia in the 19th century regarding cultural, social, legal and economic aspects. It shall help to discover the origin of the today's living black population of St. Lucia, shall show the sufferings of their ancestors and how they have managed to survive.

8 Sources

8.1 Book publications

BREEN, Henry, H.
    1844   St. Lucia: Historical, Statistical & Descriptive, London

COLERIDGE, Henry, Nelson
    1826   Six Months in the West Indies in 1825, London

COMINS, D.W.D.
    1893   Note on Emigration, From the East Indies to St. Lucia, Calcutta

DES VOEUX, William, G.
    1903   My Colonial Service in British Guiana, St. Lucia, Trinidad, Fiji, Australia, New-Foundland, and Hong Kong with Interludes, 2 volumes, London

INHABITANT OF ST. LUCIA
    1832   Mr. Jeremie's Pamphlet, London

JEREMIE, John, Esq.
    1831   Four Essays on Colonial Slavery, London

MARTIN, R. Montgomery, Esq.
    1851-57   The British Colonies; their History, Extent, Condition and Resources, 4 volumes, London

REA, J.T.
    1898   Building in St. Lucia, Inverness

STURGE J./HARVEY T.
    1838   The West Indies in 1837; being the Journal of a visit to Antigua, Montserrat, Dominica, St. Lucia, Barbados, and Jamaica, London

8.2 Documents of the PUBLIC RECORD OFFICE

CO 253/2/1   Letter of Governor PREVOST, St. Lucia, to the SECRETARY OF STATE in London, dated 22/11/1798

CO 253/2/2   Letter of Governor PREVOST, St. Lucia, to the SECRETARY OF STATE in London, dated 2/2/1799

CO 253/2/3   "State of the population of the Island of St. Lucia for the Year 1799 as by the Denombrements of the respective Districts", signed by Governor PREVOST, 1799

     Enclosure to
     Letter of Governor PREVOST, St. Lucia, to the SECRETARY OF STATE PORTLAND in London, dated 12/11/1799

CO 253/2/4   Letter of Governor PREVOST, St. Lucia, to the SECRETARY OF STATE PORTLAND in London, dated 19/6/1799

CO 253/2/5   Letter of Governor PREVOST, St. Lucia, to the SECRETARY OF STATE PORTLAND in London, dated 12/11/1799

CO 253/2/6   "Account specifying the total number of Negroes born, and who have died since 1796", SECRETARY'S OFFICE, 1799

     Enclosure to
     Letter of Governor PREVOST, St. Lucia, to the SECRETARY OF STATE PORTLAND in London, dated 12/11/1799

CO 253/2/7   Letter of the SECRETARY OF STATE PORTLAND, London, to Governor PREVOST in St. Lucia, dated 6/7/1799

     Enclosure to
     Letter of Governor PREVOST, St. Lucia, to the SECRETARY OF STATE PORTLAND in London, dated 4/9/1799

CO 253/2/8   Letter of Governor PREVOST, St. Lucia, to the SECRETARY OF STATE PORTLAND in London, dated 4/9/1799

CO 253/3/1   "State of the Population of the Island of St. Lucia, signed by Governor BRERETON, dated in 1803

     Enclosure to
     Letter of Governor BRERETON, St. Lucia, to the SECRETARY OF STATE HOBART in London, dated 10/7/1803

CO 253/3/2   Letter of Governor BRERETON, St. Lucia, to the SECRETARY OF STATE GAMDEN in London, dated 24/7/1805

CO 253/3/3   Letter of Governor BRERETON, St. Lucia, to the SECRETARY OF STATE WINDHAM in London, dated 21/9/1806

CO 253/3/4   Letter of Governor BRERETON, St. Lucia, to the SECRETARY OF STATE HOBART in London, dated 14/11/1803

CO 253/3/5   Letter of Governor BRERETON, St. Lucia, to the SECRETARY OF STATE CASTLEREACH in London, dated 20/11/1805

CO 253/7/1   "Réponses aux questions faites par ordre de son Altesse Royale le
                     Prince Régent sur la petition du Parlement du 2 Juillet 1811", signed
                     by the PROCUREUR GENERAL, dated 30/11/1811

                     Enclosure to
                     Letter of Governor WOOD, St. Lucia, to the SECRETARY OF STATE in
                     London, dated 10/1/1812

CO 253/7/2   "Tableau Comparatif de la population de Ste. Lucie des années 1807
                     & 1810", signed by the PROCUREUR GENERAL, dated 30/11/1811

                     Enclosure to
                     Letter of Governor WOOD, St. Lucia, to the SECRETARY OF STATE in
                     London, dated 10/1/1812

CO 253/7/3   "Pétition de les membres de la Cour d'Appel de Sainte-Lucie aux
                     Parlement des royaumes Unis de la Grande-Brétagne et d'Irlande",
                     dated 8/1/1812

                     Enclosure to
                     Letter of Governor WOOD, St. Lucia, to the SECRETARY OF STATE in
                     London, dated 10/1/1812

CO 253/7/4   Proclamation of Governor MYERS, dated 10/12/1804

                     Enclosure to
                     Letter of Governor WOOD, St. Lucia, to the SECRETARY OF STATE in
                     London, dated 10/1/1812

CO 253/8/1   ORDER IN COUNCIL, London, dated 24/9/1814, (printed)

                     Enclosure to
                     "Miscellaneous 1813 & 1814"

CO 253/10/1   Letter of the Slave Registrar ROBERTSON, St. Lucia, to the
                     SECRETARY OF STATE BATHURST in London, dated 3/12/1816

                     Enclosure to
                     "Miscellaneous – 1816"

CO 253/10/2   Letter of Governor DOUGLASS, St. Lucia, to the SECRETARY OF
                     STATE BATHURST in London, dated 16/10/1816

CO 253/11/1   Letter of Governor SEYMOUR, St. Lucia, to the SECRETARY OF
                     STATE BATHURST in London, dated 20/1/1817

CO 253/11/2   Report of the Members of the PRIVY COUNCIL (Estimate of the
                     Losses sustained by the Inhabitants of St. Lucia by the Hurricane of
                     the 21st October 1817, collected from the Returns of the
                     Commissaries of Quarters), signed by the COLONIAL SECRETARY of
                     St. Lucia, 1817
                     Enclosure to
                     Letter of Governor O'HARA, St. Lucia, to the SECRETARY OF STATE
                     BATHURST in London, dated 10/11/1817

CO 253/11/3   Extract of a court report, signed by Governor SEYMOUR,
                     dated 9/1/1817

Enclosure to
Letter of Governor SEYMOUR, St. Lucia, to the
SECRETARY OF STATE BATHURST in London, dated 3/10/1817

CO 253/11/4   Letter of Governor SEYMOUR, St. Lucia, to the
SECRETARY OF STATE BATHURST in London, dated 3/10/1817

CO 253/12/1   "Comparative Statements of Colonial Produce exported from
St. Lucia in the six months ending July 31, 1817 to 1818", signed by
the COLONIAL SECRETARY SHAW, dated 31/7/1818

Enclosure to
Letter of Governor KEANE, St. Lucia, to the SECRETARY OF STATE
BATHURST in London, dated 27/7/1818

CO 253/12/2   Letter of Governor O'HARA, St. Lucia, to the SECRETARY OF STATE
BATHURST in London, dated 18/4/1818

CO 253/13/1   Letter of Governor KEANE, St. Lucia, to the SECRETARY OF STATE
BATHURST in London, dated 27/10/1819

CO 253/14/1   Letter of Governor KEANE, St. Lucia, to the SECRETARY OF STATE
BATHURST in London, dated 1/11/1820

CO 253/14/2   Report of the PRIVY COUNCIL, St. Lucia, dated 10/6/1819

Enclosure to
Letter of Governor KEANE, St. Lucia, to the SECRETARY OF STATE
BATHURST in London, dated 29/3/1820

CO 253/14/3   "Statement of the losses occasioned in the Island of Saint Lucia by
the Hurricane and Floods of the 13th, 14th and 15th October 1819,
SECRETARY'S OFFICE, dated 12/4/1820

Enclosure to
Letter of Governor KEANE, St. Lucia, to the SECRETARY OF STATE
BATHURST in London, dated 29/3/1820

CO 253/14/4   "General Alphabetical Account or Abstract of the triennial Returns of
Personal Slaves made and registered at the triennial Registration of
Slaves in the year 1819, signed by the slave registrar J.M.S.,
dated 15/2/1819

Enclosure to
Letter of Governor KEANE, St. Lucia, to the SECRETARY
OF STATE BATHURST in London, dated 24/11/1820

CO 253/14/5   Letter from the PROCUREUR DU ROI, Castries, to Governor KEANE
of St. Lucia, dated 29/1/1819

Enclosure to
Letter of Governor KEANE, St. Lucia, to the SECRETARY OF STATE
BATHURST in London, dated 6/2/1820

CO 253/14/6   Letter of the COLONIAL SECRETARY SHAW, Castries, to the
PROCUREUR DU ROI of St. Lucia, dated 1/2/1819

Enclosure to

	Letter of Governor KEANE, St. Lucia, to the SECRETARY OF STATE BATHURST in London, dated 6/2/1820
CO 253/15/1	"General Statement of the sums paid into the Colonial Treasury on account of the Revenue and of the Expenses incurred for the Public Service during the year 1820", SECRETARY'S OFFICE, 1820
	Enclosure to Letter of Governor MAINWARING, St. Lucia, to the SECRETARY OF STATE BATHURST in London, dated 6/10/1821
CO 253/16/1	Report of the CUSTOM HOUSE of St. Lucia, dated 1/10/1822
	Enclosure to Letter of Governor MAINWARING, St. Lucia, to the SECRETARY OF STATE BATHURST in London, dated 11/10/1822
CO 253/17/1	Petition of the Members of the PRIVY COUNCIL of St. Lucia, dated 8/8/1823, (printed)
	Enclosure to Letter of Governor MAINWARING, St. Lucia, to the SECRETARY OF STATE BATHURST in London, dated 8/8/1823
CO 253/17/2	Letter of Governor MAINWARING, St. Lucia, to the SECRETARY OF STATE BATHURST in London, dated 11/8/1823
CO 253/17/3	Letter of Governor MAINWARING, St. Lucia, to the SECRETARY OF STATE BATHURST in London, dated 25/8/1823
CO 253/18/1	Letter of Governor BLACKWELL, St. Lucia, to the SECRETARY OF STATE BATHURST in London, dated 15/5/1824
CO 253/18/2	Letter of Governor BLACKWELL, St. Lucia, to the SECRETARY OF STATE BATHURST in London, dated 6/8/1824
CO 253/18/3	Report of the CUSTOM HOUSE of St. Lucia, dated 12/9/1823
	Enclosure to Letter of Governor BLACKWELL, St. Lucia, to the SECRETARY OF STATE BATHURST in London, dated 7/5/1824
CO 253/18/4	Petition of the "Free Coloured" to Governor MAINWARING, St. Lucia, dated 15/1/1824
	Enclosure to Letter of Governor MAINWARING, St. Lucia, to the SECRETARY OF STATE BATHURST in London, dated 16/4/1824
CO 253/18/5	Letter of Governor MAINWARING, St. Lucia, to the SECRETARY OF STATE BATHURST in London, dated 16/4/1824
CO 253/19/1	Table of Population from 1812 to 1821, SECRETARY'S OFFICE, dated 8/8/1825
	Enclosure to Letter of Governor BLACKWELL, St. Lucia, to the SECRETARY OF STATE BATHURST in London, dated 10/8/1825

CO 253/19/2	Letter of Justice JEREMIE, St. Lucia, to Governor BLACKWELL of St. Lucia, dated 18/2/1825
	Enclosure to Letter of Governor BLACKWELL, St. Lucia, to the SECRETARY OF STATE BATHURST in London, dated 19/2/1825
CO 253/20/1	Petition of the NON FREE-WHITES to Governor BLACKWELL, St. Lucia, dated 31/7/1824
	Enclosure to Letter of Governor BLACKWELL, St. Lucia, to the SECRETARY OF STATE BATHURST in London, dated 8/11/1825
CO 253/22/1	Letter of Governor MAINWARING, St. Lucia, to the SECRETARY OF STATE BATHURST in London, dated 9/2/1826
CO 253/22/2	"Return of Manumissions from 1821 to 1825", CUSTOM HOUSE, St. Lucia, dated 1/6/1826
	Enclosure to Letter of Governor MAINWARING, St. Lucia, to the SECRETARY OF STATE BATHURST in London, dated 1/6/1826
CO 253/22/3	Petition of the NON FREE-WHITES to Governor MAINWARING, St. Lucia, dated 9/3/1826
	Enclosure to Letter of Governor MAINWARING, St. Lucia, to the SECRETARY OF STATE BATHURST in London, dated 23/4/1826
CO 253/22/4	Slave Law of St. Lucia, dated 1/6/1826 (passed by the PRIVY COUNCIL on 8/2/1826)
	Enclosure to Letter of Governor MAINWARING, St. Lucia, to the SECRETARY OF STATE BATHURST in London, dated 9/2/1826
CO 253/23/1	"Pétition des certains Planteurs de St. Lucie à la Seigneure Goderich", dated 28/7/1827,
	Enclosure to Letter of Governor MAINWARING, St. Lucia, to the SECRETARY OF STATE GODERICH in London, dated 28/7/1827
CO 253/23/2	"Return of the number of Slaves, imported and exported from the 1st Jan. 1821", signed by the Slave Registrar STEPHENS, 1827
	Enclosure to Letter of Governor MAINWARING, St. Lucia, to the SECRETARY OF STATE GODERICH in London, dated 7/7/1827
CO 253/23/3	Letter of Justice JEREMIE, St. Lucia, to Governor MAINWARING of St. Lucia, dated 17/4/1827
	Enclosure to Letter of Governor MAINWARING, St. Lucia, to the SECRETARY OF STATE GODERICH in London, dated 7/7/1827

CO 253/24/1	Letter of Justice JEREMIE, St. Lucia, to the SECRETARY OF STATE HORTON in London, dated 28/7/1827
	Enclosure to "Miscellaneous" –Section "Mr. Jeremie"
CO 253/26/1	Letter of Governor STEWART, St. Lucia, to the SECRETARY OF STATE MURRAY in London, dated 15/9/1829
CO 253/26/2	Letter of Governor STEWART, St. Lucia, to the SECRETARY OF STATE MURRAY in London, dated 10/3/1829
CO 253/26/3	Petition of "certains Planteurs et Propriétaires de St. Lucie", to the Governor of St. Lucia, dated in June 1829
	Enclosure to Letter of Governor STEWART, St. Lucia, to the SECRETARY OF STATE MURRAY in London, dated 25/6/1829
CO 253/26/4	Letter of Governor STEWART, St. Lucia, to the SECRETARY OF STATE MURRAY in London, dated 25/6/1829
CO 253/26/5	Report of Justice JEREMIE, St. Lucia, dated 30/5/1829
	Enclosure to Letter of Governor STEWART, St. Lucia, to the SECRETARY OF STATE MURRAY in London, dated 12/6/1829
CO 253/26/6	Letter of Governor STEWART, St. Lucia, to the SECRETARY OF STATE in London, dated 29/9/1829
CO 253/26/7	Report of Peter MUTER, Member of the PRIVY COUNCIL of St. Lucia, dated 30/5/1829
	Enclosure to Letter of Governor STEWART, St. Lucia, to the SECRETARY OF STATE MURRAY in London, dated 12/6/1829
CO 253/26/8	"ORDER IN COUNCIL repealing the Laws whereby Free Persons of African Birth or descent are subjected to certain disabilities", London, dated 15/1/1829
CO 253/29/1	Enclosure to "Miscellaneous" – Section "Council Office" "Abstract of the Condition and particular Management of Plantations in the 1st District, Castries, commission of the 1st District", dated 31/3/1830
	Enclosure to Letter of Governor BOZON, St. Lucia, to the SECRETARY OF STATE GODERICH in London, dated 30/6/1831
CO 253/29/2	Letter of Governor BOZON, St. Lucia, to the SECRETARY OF STATE GODERICH in London, dated 18/8/1831
CO 253/29/3	Letter of Governor BOZON, St. Lucia, to the SECRETARY OF STATE GODERICH in London, dated 28/6/1831

CO 253/29/4	Letter of Governor BOZON, St. Lucia, to the SECRETARY OF STATE GODERICH in London, dated 11/7/1831
CO 253/29/5	"Return of the numbers of Marriages legally solemnized between Slaves, Free Blacks or Coloured Persons in the Colony of St. Lucia between the 1st Jan. 1825 and the 31st Dec. 1830", Castries, SECRETARY'S OFFICE, dated 1/1/1831
	Enclosure to Letter of Governor FARQUHARSON, St. Lucia, to the SECRETARY OF STATE in London, dated 1/1/1831
CO 253/29/6	"Return of different Places of Worship in connexion with the Established Church, and with all other Religious Bodies, in the Colony of St. Lucia, from 1st January 1825 to 31st December 1830", Castries, SECRETARY'S OFFICE, dated 1/1/1831
	Enclosure to Letter of Governor FARQUHARSON, St. Lucia, to the SECRETARY OF STATE in London, dated 1/1/1831
CO 253/30/1	"Petition of the Proprietors, Planters, Merchants and other Inhabitants of St. Lucia" to the SECRETARY OF STATE GODERICH, dated 31/10/1831
	Enclosure to Letter of Governor MALLET, St. Lucia, to the SECRETARY OF STATE GODERICH in London, dated 13/11/1831
CO 253/30/2	Report of three Members of the PRIVY COUNCIL of St. Lucia to Governor MALLET, dated 27/9/1831
	Enclosure to Letter of Governor MALLET, St. Lucia, to the SECRETARY OF STATE GODERICH in London, dated 1/10/1831
CO 253/30/3	Letter of Governor MALLET, St. Lucia, to the SECRETARY OF STATE GODERICH in London, dated 29/10/1831
CO 253/37/1	Proclamation of Governor BOZON, St. Lucia, dated 18/1/1832, (printed)
	Enclosure to Letter of Governor BOZON, St. Lucia, to the SECRETARY OF STATE GODERICH in London, dated 24/1/1832
CO 253/37/2	"Remonstrance" of Merchants and Planters to Governor CARTER, St. Lucia, dated in January 1832
	Enclosure to Letter of Governor CARTER, St. Lucia, to the SECRETARY OF STATE GODERICH in London, dated 28/1/1832
CO 253/37/3	Petition of Merchants of St. Lucia to Governor BOZON of St. Lucia, Dated 4/1/1832

Enclosure to
Letter of Governor BOZON, St. Lucia, to the
SECRETARY OF STATE GODERICH in London, dated 5/1/1832

CO 253/37/4   Protest of "Planters, Merchants and other Inhabitants of the Island of St. Lucia", dated 4/1/1832

Enclosure to
Letter of Governor BOZON, St. Lucia, to the
SECRETARY OF STATE GODERICH in London, dated 5/1/1832

CO 253/37/5   "The Memorial of the Managers and Others having the Administration of Estates in St. Lucia", to Governor BOZON, dated in January 1832

Enclosure to
Letter of Governor BOZON, St. Lucia, to the
SECRETARY OF STATE GODERICH in London, dated 24/1/1832

CO 253/38/1   Petition of William Muter, Member of the PRIVY COUNCIL of St. Lucia, to the SECRETARY OF STATE in London, dated 30/4/1832

Enclosure to
Letter of Governor FARQUHARSON, St. Lucia, to the
SECRETARY OF STATE GODERICH in London, dated 30/4/1832

CO 253/39/1   Petition of "Merchants and Householders of St. Lucia" to Governor FARQUHARSON, Castries, dated 15/5/1832

Enclosure to
Letter of Governor FARQUHARSON, St. Lucia, to the
SECRETARY OF STATE in London, dated in June 1832

CO 253/39/2   Letter of Governor FARQUHARSON, St. Lucia, to the SECRETARY OF STATE GODERICH in London, dated 25/7/1832

CO 253/39/3   Letter of Governor FARQUHARSON, St. Lucia, to the SECRETARY OF STATE GODERICH in London, dated 4/7/1832

CO 253/39/4   Letter of Governor FARQUHARSON, St. Lucia, to the SECRETARY OF STATE GODERICH in London, dated 3/5/1832

CO 253/39/5   Report of the CUSTOM HOUSE of St. Lucia, dated 4/7/1832

Enclosure to
Letter of Governor FARQUHARSON, St. Lucia, to the
SECRETARY OF STATE in London, dated 4/7/1832

CO 253/39/6   Report of the CUSTOM HOUSE of St. Lucia, dated 30/7/1832

Enclosure to
Letter of Governor FARQUHARSON, St. Lucia, to the
SECRETARY OF STATE GODERICH in London, dated 30/8/1832

CO 253/39/7   Report of the CUSTOM HOUSE of St. Lucia, dated 25/8/1832

	Enclosure to Letter of Governor FARQUHARSON, St. Lucia, to the SECRETARY OF STATE GODERICH in London, dated 30/8/1832
CO 253/39/8	Letter of Governor FARQUHARSON, St. Lucia, to the SECRETARY OF STATE GODERICH in London, dated 30/8/1832
CO 253/40/1	Letter from Vice Chairman ROBINSON, PRIVY COUNCIL, St. Lucia, to Governor FARQUHARSON of St. Lucia, dated 19/9/1832
	Enclosure to Letter of Governor FARQUHARSON, St. Lucia, to the SECRETARY OF STATE GODERICH in London, dated 25/9/1832
CO 253/40/2	Extract of a protocol of the PRIVY COUNCIL of St. Lucia, signed by the COLONIAL SECRETARY LOWEN, dated 20/8/1832
	Enclosure to Letter of Governor FARQUHARSON, St. Lucia, to the SECRETARY OF STATE GODERICH in London, dated 16/9/1832
CO 253/40/3	"Return of Manumissions granted in St. Lucia between 1817 and the 31st Dec. 1830", CUSTOM HOUSE, Castries, signed by Governor FARQUHARSON, dated 4/10/1832
	Enclosure to Letter of Governor FARQUHARSON, St. Lucia, to the SECRETARY OF STATE GODERICH in London, dated 5/10/1832
CO 253/40/4	Proclamation of Governor FARQUHARSON, St. Lucia, dated 11/9/1832, (printed)
	Enclosure to Letter of Governor FARQUHARSON, St. Lucia, to the SECRETARY OF STATE GODERICH in London, dated 20/9/1832
CO 253/40/5	Letter of Governor FARQUHARSON, St. Lucia, to the Governor of Martinique, dated 11/9/1832
	Enclosure to Letter of Governor FARQUHARSON, St. Lucia, to the SECRETARY OF STATE GODERICH in London, dated 20/9/1832
CO 253/40/6	Proclamation of Governor FARQUHARSON, St. Lucia, dated 31/10/1832
	Enclosure to Letter of Governor FARQUHARSON, St. Lucia, to the SECRETARY OF STATE GODERICH in London, dated 3/11/1832
CO 253/40/7	Letter of Governor FARQUHARSON, St. Lucia, to the SECRETARY OF STATE GODERICH in London, dated 1/11/1832
CO 253/40/8	Letter of Governor FARQUHARSON, St. Lucia, to the SECRETARY OF STATE GODERICH in London, dated 3/11/1832
CO 253/40/9	Report of the Planter J.P. Noel, St. Lucia, dated 29/11/1832

Enclosure to
Letter of Governor FARQUHARSON, St. Lucia, to the
SECRETARY OF STATE GODERICH in London, dated 29/11/1832

CO 253/40/10   Report of the Planter James Scott, St. Lucia, dated 30/11/1832

Enclosure to
Letter of Governor FARQUHARSON, St. Lucia, to the
SECRETARY OF STATE GODERICH in London, dated 29/11/1832

CO 253/40/11   Letter of Governor FARQUHARSON, St. Lucia, to the
Governor of Martinique, dated 25/9/1832

Enclosure to
Letter of Governor FARQUHARSON, St. Lucia, to the
SECRETARY OF STATE GODERICH in London, dated 5/10/1832

CO 253/43/1   Report of the FIRST PRISON JUDGE MALLET, St. Lucia,
dated 3/1/1833

Enclosure to
Letter of Governor FARQUHARSON, St. Lucia, to the
SECRETARY OF STATE GODERICH in London, dated 3/1/1833

CO 253/43/2   Report of the CHIEF JUSTICE BIRRELL, St. Lucia, dated 3/1/1833

Enclosure to
Letter of Governor FARQUHARSON, St. Lucia, to the
SECRETARY OF STATE GODERICH in London, dated 3/1/1833

CO 253/43/3   Protocol about "A general Meeting of the Proprietary Body of
St. Lucia, Castries, dated 28/1/1833, (printed)

Enclosure to
Letter of Governor FARQUHARSON, St. Lucia, to the
SECRETARY OF STATE GODERICH in London, dated 23/2/1833

CO 253/43/4   Letter of Governor FARQUHARSON, St. Lucia, to the
SECRETARY OF STATE GODERICH in London, dated 23/2/1833

CO 253/43/5   Letter of Governor FARQUHARSON, St. Lucia, to the
SECRETARY OF STATE GODERICH in London, dated 7/3/1833

CO 253/43/6   "Notes of the Proceedings on the Trial of Donald Shaw, late Manager
on the Grande Anse Plantation", dated 6/2/1833

Enclosure to
Letter of Governor FARQUHARSON, St. Lucia, to the
SECRETARY OF STATE GODERICH in London, dated 8/4/1833

CO 253/43/7   Report of the PROVISIONAL PROCUREUR GENERAL of St. Lucia to
Governor FARQUHARSON, Castries, dated 3/12/1832

Enclosure to
Letter of Governor FARQUHARSON, St. Lucia, to the
SECRETARY OF STATE GODERICH in London, dated 4/1/1833

CO 253/43/8	Letter of Governor FARQUHARSON, St. Lucia, to the SECRETARY OF STATE GODERICH in London, dated 31/1/1833
CO 253/44/1	Letter of Governor FARQUHARSON, St. Lucia, to the SECRETARY OF STATE in London, dated 26/6/1833
CO 253/44/2	Letter of Governor FARQUHARSON, St. Lucia, to the SECRETARY OF STATE in London, dated 2/8/1833
CO 253/44/3	Report of the PROTECTOR OF SLAVES, St. Lucia, dated 23/3/1833
	Enclosure to Letter of Governor FARQUHARSON, St. Lucia, to the SECRETARY OF STATE in London, dated 26/5/1833
CO 253/44/4	Letter of Governor FARQUHARSON, St. Lucia, to the PROTECTOR OF SLAVES in St. Lucia, dated 12/4/1833
	Enclosure to Letter of Governor FARQUHARSON, St. Lucia, to the SECRETARY OF STATE GODERICH in London, dated 1/5/1833
CO 253/44/5	Report of the examining Magistrate of St. Lucia to the SECRETARY OF STATE GODERICH in London, dated 1/5/1833
	Enclosure to Letter of Governor FARQUHARSON, St. Lucia, to the SECRETARY OF STATE GODERICH in London, dated 1/5/1833
CO 253/44/6	Letter of Governor FARQUHARSON, St. Lucia, to the SECRETARY OF STATE GODERICH in London, dated 1/5/1833
CO 253/46/1	Letter of Governor DUDLEY HILL, St. Lucia, to the SECRETARY OF STATE SPRING RICE in London, dated 1/8/1834
CO 253/46/2	Letter of Governor DUDLEY HILL, St. Lucia, to the SECRETARY OF STATE SPRING RICE in London, dated 1/10/1834
CO 253/46/3	Letter of Governor DUDLEY HILL, St. Lucia, to the SECRETARY OF STATE SPRING RICE in London, dated 26/8/1834
CO 253/46/4	Letter of Governor DUDLEY HILL, St. Lucia, to the SECRETARY OF STATE SPRING RICE in London, dated 3/11/1834
CO 253/46/5	Letter of Governor DUDLEY HILL, St. Lucia, to the SECRETARY OF STATE SPRING RICE in London, dated 28/11/1834
CO 253/46/6	Letter of Governor DUDLEY HILL, St. Lucia, to the SECRETARY OF STATE SPRING RICE in London, dated 4/11/1834
CO 253/48/1	"Petition of Planters and other Persons", St. Lucia, to Governor DUDLEY HILL, dated 17/1/1835
	Enclosure to Letter of Governor DUDLEY HILL, St. Lucia, to the SECRETARY OF STATE in London, dated 8/2/1835

CO 253/49/1	"Return of the Number and Nature of the Punishments inflicted on the Apprenticed Labourers in the Colony of St. Lucia by the Special or Stipendiary Magistrates from 1st Aug. 1834 to 31st July 1835 inclusively", St. Lucia, 1835
	Enclosure to Letter of Governor DUDLEY HILL, St. Lucia, to the SECRETARY OF STATE GLENELG in London, dated 15/9/1835
CO 253/49/2	Letter of Governor DUDLEY HILL, St. Lucia, to the SECRETARY OF STATE GLENELG in London, dated 23/11/1835, (printed)
CO 253/49/3	Circular letter of Governor DUDLEY HILL, St. Lucia, to the STIPENDIARY MAGISTRATES, dated 28/7/1834, (printed)
	Enclosure to Letter of Governor DUDLEY HILL, St. Lucia, to the SECRETARY OF STATE GLENELG in London, dated 15/9/1835
CO 253/49/4	"Return of all Apprenticed Labourers discharged from the Apprenticeship from 1st Aug. 1834 to 1st Aug. 1835", SECRETARY'S OFFICE, in September 1835
	Enclosure to Letter of Governor DUDLEY HILL, St. Lucia, to the SECRETARY OF STATE GLENELG in London, dated 15/9/1835
CO 253/49/5	Letter of Governor DUDLEY HILL, St. Lucia, to the SECRETARY OF STATE GLENELG in London, dated 2/9/1835, (printed)
CO 253/49/6	Letter of the SECRETARY OF STATE GLENELG, London, to the Governor of St. Lucia, DUDLEY HILL, dated 15/2/1836, (printed)
	Enclosure to Letter of Governor DUDLEY HILL, St. Lucia, to the SECRETARY OF STATE GLENELG in London, dated 2/9/1835
CO 253/49/7	Letter of Governor DUDLEY HILL, St. Lucia, to the SECRETARY OF STATE GLENELG in London, dated 7/8/1835, (printed)
CO 253/51/1	Letter of Governor DUDLEY HILL, St. Lucia, to the SECRETARY OF STATE GLENELG in London, dated 15/3/1836
CO 253/51/2	Letter of the Bishop of Barbados, Daniel MacDonnel, Barbados, to Governor DUDLEY HILL of St. Lucia, dated 12/5/1836
	Enclosure to Letter of Governor DUDLEY HILL, St. Lucia, to the SECRETARY OF STATE GLENELG in London, dated 1/6/1836
CO 253/52/1	Report of the STIPENDIARY MAGISTRATE of the 1st district, Castries, dated in September 1836
	Enclosure to Letter of Governor DUDLEY HILL, St. Lucia, to the SECRETARY OF STATE GLENELG in London, dated 5/9/1836

CO 253/52/2	Report of the STIPENDIARY MAGISTRATE of the 2nd district, Soufrière, dated 2/9/1836
	Enclosure to Letter of Governor DUDLEY HILL, St. Lucia, to the SECRETARY OF STATE GLENELG in London, dated 5/9/1836
CO 253/52/3	Report of the STIPENDIARY MAGISTRATE of the 3rd district, Vieux Fort, dated 31/10/1836
	Enclosure to Letter of Governor DUDLEY HILL, St. Lucia, to the SECRETARY OF STATE GLENELG in London, dated 3/11/1836
CO 253/52/4	Letter of Governor DUDLEY HILL, St. Lucia, to the SECRETARY OF STATE GLENELG in London, dated in December 1836
CO 253/52/5	Report of the STIPENDIARY MAGISTRATE of the 3rd district, Vieux Fort, dated 31/8/1836
	Enclosure to Letter of Governor DUDLEY HILL, St. Lucia, to the SECRETARY OF STATE GLENELG in London, dated 5/9/1836
CO 253/52/6	Letter of Governor DUDLEY HILL, St. Lucia, to the SECRETARY OF STATE GLENELG in London, dated 3/11/1836
CO 253/52/7	Report of the STIPENDIARY MAGISTRATE of the 1st district, Castries, dated 1/10/1836
	Enclosure to Letter of Governor DUDLEY HILL, St. Lucia, to the SECRETARY OF STATE GLENELG in London, dated 7/10/1836
CO 253/52/8	Report of the STIPENDIARY MAGISTRATE of the 2nd district, Soufrière, dated 2/10/1836
	Enclosure to Letter of Governor DUDLEY HILL, St. Lucia, to the SECRETARY OF STATE GLENELG in London, dated 7/10/1836
CO 253/52/9	Letter of Governor DUDLEY HILL, St. Lucia, to the SECRETARY OF STATE GLENELG in London, dated 19/9/1836
CO 253/54/1	Report of the STIPENDIARY MAGISTRATE of the 1st district, Castries, dated 1/2/1837
	Enclosure to Letter of Governor DUDLEY HILL, St. Lucia, to the SECRETARY OF STATE GLENELG in London, dated 8/2/1837
CO 253/54/2	Report of the STIPENDIARY MAGISTRATE of the 3rd district, Vieux Fort, dated in February 1837
	Enclosure to Letter of Governor DUDLEY HILL, St. Lucia, to the SECRETARY OF STATE GLENELG in London, dated 8/2/1837

CO 253/54/3	Report of the STIPENDIARY MAGISTRATE of the 1st district, Castries, dated 1/3/1837
	Enclosure to Letter of Governor DUDLEY HILL, St. Lucia, to the SECRETARY OF STATE GLENELG in London, dated 4/3/1837
CO 253/55/1	Report of the STIPENDIARY MAGISTRATE of the 2nd district, Soufrière, dated 1/5/1837
	Enclosure to Letter of Governor BUNBURY, St. Lucia, to the SECRETARY OF STATE GLENELG in London, dated 11/5/1837
CO 253/55/2	Letter of Governor BUNBURY, St. Lucia, to the SECRETARY OF STATE GLENELG in London, dated 19/5/1837
CO 253/56/1	"Supplementary Instructions for the guidance of the Special Justices in the Colony of St. Lucia", Castries, from Governor BUNBURY, dated 4/9/1837
	Enclosure to Letter of Governor BUNBURY, St. Lucia, to the SECRETARY OF STATE GLENELG in London, dated 26/9/1837
CO 253/56/2	Report of the STIPENDIARY MAGISTRATE of the 1st district, Castries, dated 1/9/1837
	Enclosure to Letter of Governor BUNBURY, St. Lucia, to the SECRETARY OF STATE GLENELG in London, dated 6/9/1837
CO 253/56/3	Letter of Governor BUNBURY, St. Lucia, to the SECRETARY OF STATE GLENELG in London, dated 8/9/1837
CO 253/57/1	Report of the STIPENDIARY MAGISTRATE of the 2nd district, Gros Islet, dated 1/12/1837
	Enclosure to Letter of Governor BUNBURY, St. Lucia, to the SECRETARY OF STATE GLENELG in London, dated 12/12/1837
CO 253/57/2	Report of the STIPENDIARY MAGISTRATE of the 3rd district, Soufrière, dated 1/12/1837
	Enclosure to Letter of Governor BUNBURY, St. Lucia, to the SECRETARY OF STATE GLENELG in London, dated 12/12/1837
CO 253/61/1	Petition of "Planters, Merchants and other Inhabitants of St. Lucia" to the Queen of England, dated 24/5/1838, (printed)
	Enclosure to Letter No. 22
CO 253/61/2	Letter of Governor MEIN, St. Lucia, to the GENERAL GOVERNOR MacGREGOR in London, dated 28/5/1838, (printed)
	Enclosure to Letter No. 22

CO 253/62/1   Report of the STIPENDIARY MAGISTRATE of the 2nd district,
               Gros Islet, dated 3/8/1838

               Enclosure to Letter No. 54

CO 253/62/2   Report of the STIPENDIARY MAGISTRATE of the 3rd district,
               Soufrière, dated 2/8/1838

               Enclosure to Letter No. 54

CO 253/62/3   Report of the STIPENDIARY MAGISTRATE of the 4th district,
               Vieux Fort, dated 1/8/1838

               Enclosure to Letter No. 54

CO 253/62/4   Report of the STIPENDIARY MAGISTRATE of the 5th district,
               Micoud, dated 4/8/1838

               Enclosure to Letter No. 54

CO 253/62/5   Letter of Governor MEIN, St. Lucia, to the
               General Governor MacGREGOR in Barbados, dated 4/8/1838

               Enclosure to Letter No. 49

CO 253/62/6   Report of the STIPENDIARY MAGISTRATE of the 1st district,
               Castries, dated 8/6/1838

               Enclosure to Letter No. 38

CO 253/62/7   Report of the STIPENDIARY MAGISTRATE of the 2nd district,
               Gros Islet, dated 7/6/1838

               Enclosure to Letter No. 38

CO 253/62/8   Report of the STIPENDIARY MAGISTRATE of the 3rd district,
               Soufrière, dated 18/6/1838

               Enclosure to Letter No. 38

CO 253/62/9   Report of the STIPENDIARY MAGISTRATE of the 4th district,
               Vieux Fort, dated 14/6/1838

               Enclosure to Letter No. 38

CO 253/62/10   Report of the STIPENDIARY MAGISTRATE of the 5th district,
               Micoud, dated 2/6/1838

               Enclosure to Letter No. 38

CO 253/64/1   Circular letter of the GOVERNMENT OFFICE, St. Lucia, to the
               STIPENDIARY MAGISTRATES, dated 22/3/1838, (printed)

               Enclosure to
               Letter of Governor MEIN, St. Lucia, to the
               SECRETARY OF STATE GLENELG in London, dated 22/4/1838

CO 253/64/2   Report of the STIPENDIARY MAGISTRATE of the 1st district, Castries, dated 10/4/1838, (printed)

Enclosure to
Letter of Governor MEIN, St. Lucia, to the
SECRETARY OF STATE GLENELG in London, dated 22/4/1838

CO 253/64/3   Report of the STIPENDIARY MAGISTRATE of the 2nd district, Gros Islet, dated 8/4/1838, (printed)

Enclosure to
Letter of Governor MEIN, St. Lucia, to the
SECRETARY OF STATE GLENELG in London, dated 22/4/1838

CO 253/64/4   Report of the STIPENDIARY MAGISTRATE of the 3rd district, Soufrière, dated 28/3/1838, (printed)

Enclosure to
Letter of Governor MEIN, St. Lucia, to the
SECRETARY OF STATE GLENELG in London, dated 22/4/1838

CO 253/64/5   Report of the STIPENDIARY MAGISTRATE of the 4th district, Vieux Fort, dated 9/4/1838, (printed)

Enclosure to
Letter of Governor MEIN, St. Lucia, to the
SECRETARY OF STATE GLENELG in London, dated 22/4/1838

CO 253/64/6   Report of the STIPENDIARY MAGISTRATE of the 5th district, Vieux Fort, dated 28/3/1838, (printed)

Enclosure to
Letter of Governor MEIN, St. Lucia, to the
SECRETARY OF STATE GLENELG in London, dated 22/4/1838

CO 253/64/7   Report of the STIPENDIARY MAGISTRATE of the 1st district, Castries, dated 2/6/1838

Enclosure to
Letter of Governor MEIN, St. Lucia, to the
SECRETARY OF STATE GLENELG in London, dated 30/6/1838

CO 253/64/8   Report of the STIPENDIARY MAGISTRATE of the 2nd district, Gros Islet, dated 4/6/1838

Enclosure to
Letter of Governor MEIN, St. Lucia, to the
SECRETARY OF STATE GLENELG in London, dated 30/6/1838

CO 253/64/9   Report of the STIPENDIARY MAGISTRATE of the 5th district, Vieux Fort, dated 1/6/1838

Enclosure to
Letter of Governor MEIN, St. Lucia, to the
SECRETARY OF STATE GLENELG in London, dated 30/6/1838

CO 253/64/10   Report of the STIPENDIARY MAGISTRATE of the 3rd district,

Soufrière, dated 1/6/1838

Enclosure to
Letter of Governor MEIN, St. Lucia, to the
SECRETARY OF STATE GLENELG in London, dated 30/6/1838

CO 253/64/11   Report of the STIPENDIARY MAGISTRATE of the 4th district,
Vieux Fort, dated 1/6/1838

Enclosure to
Letter of Governor MEIN, St. Lucia, to the
SECRETARY OF STATE GLENELG in London, dated 30/6/1838

CO 253/64/12   Report of the STIPENDIARY MAGISTRATE of the 4th district,
Vieux Fort, dated 2/7/1838

Enclosure to
Letter of Governor MEIN, St. Lucia, to the
SECRETARY OF STATE GLENELG in London, dated 23/7/1838

CO 253/64/13   Letter of Governor BUNBURY, St. Lucia, to the
SECRETARY OF STATE GLENELG in London, dated 7/2/1838

CO 253/64/14   Letter of Governor BUNBURY, St. Lucia, to the
SECRETARY OF STATE GLENELG in London, dated 31/1/1838

CO 253/64/15   Report of the STIPENDIARY MAGISTRATE of the 2nd district,
Gros Islet, dated 6/3/1838

Enclosure to
Letter of Governor MEIN, St. Lucia, to the
SECRETARY OF STATE GLENELG in London, dated 21/3/1838

CO 253/64/16   Report of the STIPENDIARY MAGISTRATE of the 4th district,
Vieux Fort, dated 1/3/1838

Enclosure to
Letter of Governor MEIN, St. Lucia, to the
SECRETARY OF STATE GLENELG in London, dated 21/3/1838

CO 253/64/17   Report of the STIPENDIARY MAGISTRATE of the 2nd district,
Gros Islet, dated in January 1838

Enclosure to
Letter of Governor MEIN, St. Lucia, to the
SECRETARY OF STATE GLENELG in London, dated 20/2/1838

CO 253/64/18   Report of the STIPENDIARY MAGISTRATE of the 4th district,
Vieux Fort, dated 1/5/1838

Enclosure to
Letter of Governor MEIN, St. Lucia, to the
SECRETARY OF STATE GLENELG in London, dated 14/5/1838

CO 253/64/19   Letter of Governor BUNBURY, St. Lucia, to the
SECRETARY OF STATE GLENELG in London, dated 2/3/1838

CO 253/64/20	Report of the STIPENDIARY MAGISTRATE of the 4th district, Vieux Fort, dated 9/2/1838 Enclosure to Letter of Governor BUNBURY, St. Lucia, to the SECRETARY OF STATE GLENELG in London, dated 20/2/1838
CO 253/64/21	Letter of Governor DUDLEY HILL, St. Lucia, to the SECRETARY OF STATE GUY in London, dated 2/4/1838
CO 253/65/1	Order in Council, London, dated 15/2/1838 Enclosure to "Miscellaneous" – Section "Council"
CO 253/67/1	Report of the COLONIAL TREASURER from the year 1839, St. Lucia Enclosure to Letter No. 33
CO 253/67/2	Letter of Governor EVERARD, St. Lucia, to the General Governor MacGREGOR in Barbados, dated 20/6/1839 Enclosure to Letter No. 33
CO 253/67/3	Report of the STIPENDIARY MAGISTRATE of the 2nd district, Gros Islet, dated 5/4/1839 Enclosure to Letter No. 33
CO 253/67/4	Report of the STIPENDIARY MAGISTRATE of the 4th district, Vieux Fort, dated 9/4/1839 Enclosure to Letter No. 33
CO 253/67/5	Proclamation of Governor EVERARD, dated 16/5/1839, (printed) Enclosure to Letter No. 33
CO 253/67/6	Report of the STIPENDIARY MAGISTRATE of the 1st district, Castries, dated 3/6/1839 Enclosure to Letter No. 33
CO 253/68/1	Report of the STIPENDIARY MAGISTRATE of the 1st district, Castries, dated 5/11/1839 Enclosure to Letter No. 77
CO 253/68/2	Report of the STIPENDIARY MAGISTRATE of the 2nd district, Gros Islet, dated 1/11/1839 Enclosure to Letter No. 77
CO 253/68/3	Report of the STIPENDIARY MAGISTRATE of the 3rd district, Soufrière, dated in August 1839 Enclosure to Letter No. 56

CO 253/68/4   Report of the STIPENDIARY MAGISTRATE of the 3rd district, Soufrière, dated 4/11/1839

Enclosure to Letter No. 77

CO 253/68/5   Report of the STIPENDIARY MAGISTRATE of the 4th district, Vieux Fort, dated 3/9/1839

Enclosure to Letter No. 62

CO 253/68/6   Report of the STIPENDIARY MAGISTRATE of the 5th district, Micoud, dated 3/8/1839

Enclosure to Letter No. 56

CO 253/68/7   Report of the STIPENDIARY MAGISTRATE of the 1st district, Castries, dated 31/7/1839

Enclosure to Letter No. 56

CO 253/68/8   Report of the STIPENDIARY MAGISTRATE of the 2nd district, Gros Islet, dated 17/8/1839

Enclosure to Letter No. 56

CO 253/70/1   Report of the STIPENDIARY MAGISTRATE of the 5th district, Micoud, dated 7/3/1840

Enclosure to Letter No. 23

CO 253/71/1   Letter of Mr. King, Belle Plaine (3rd district) to the STIPENDIARY MAGISTRATE of the 3rd district, dated 1/10/1840

Enclosure to Letter No. 55

CO 253/71/2   Report of the STIPENDIARY MAGISTRATE of the 3rd district, Soufrière, dated 16/8/1840

Enclosure to Letter No. 51

CO 253/71/3   Report of the STIPENDIARY MAGISTRATE of the 5th district, Micoud, dated 3/7/1840

Enclosure to Letter No. 42

CO 253/71/4   Letter of Governor EVERARD, St. Lucia, to the General Governor MacGREGOR in Barbados, dated 9/10/1840

Enclosure to Letter No. 57

CO 253/73/1   Report of the STIPENDIARY MAGISTRATE of the 2nd district, Gros Islet, dated 2/4/1841, (printed)

Enclosure to Letter No. 26

CO 253/73/2   Report of the STIPENDIARY MAGISTRATE of the 3rd district, Soufrière, dated 10/5/1841

Enclosure to Letter No. 27

CO 253/73/3   Report of the STIPENDIARY MAGISTRATE of the 3rd district, Soufrière, dated 1/3/1841

Enclosure to Letter No. 20

CO 253/73/4   Report of the STIPENDIARY MAGISTRATE of the 4th district, Vieux Fort, dated 1/5/1841, (printed)

Enclosure to Letter No. 27

CO 253/73/5   Report of the STIPENDIARY MAGISTRATE of the 1st district, Castries, dated 3/4/1841, (printed)

Enclosure to Letter No. 26

CO 253/74/1   Report of the STIPENDIARY MAGISTRATE of the 1st district, Castries, dated 1/10/1841, (printed)

Enclosure to Letter No. 26

CO 253/74/2   Report of the STIPENDIARY MAGISTRATE of the 2nd district, Gros Islet, dated 20/9/1841, (printed)

Enclosure to Letter No. 26

CO 253/74/3   Report of the STIPENDIARY MAGISTRATE of the 3rd district, Soufrière, dated in September 1841, (printed)

Enclosure to Letter No. 26

CO 253/74/4   Report of the STIPENDIARY MAGISTRATE of the 4th district, Vieux Fort, dated 15/9/1841, (printed)

Enclosure to Letter No. 26

CO 253/74/5   Report of the STIPENDIARY MAGISTRATE of the 5th district, Micoud, dated 17/9/1841, (printed)

Enclosure to Letter No. 26

CO 253/74/6   Report of the STIPENDIARY MAGISTRATE of the 2nd district, Gros Islet, dated 2/8/1841, (printed)

Enclosure to Letter No. 20

CO 253/74/7   Report of the STIPENDIARY MAGISTRATE of the 4th district, Vieux Fort, dated 1/6/1841, (printed)

Enclosure to Letter No. 5

CO 253/74/8	Report of the STIPENDIARY MAGISTRATE of the 1st district, Castries, dated 2/6/1841, (printed) Enclosure to Letter No. 5
CO 253/74/9	Report of the STIPENDIARY MAGISTRATE of the 5th district, Micoud, dated 2/6/1841, (printed) Enclosure to Letter No. 5
CO 253/74/10	Report of the STIPENDIARY MAGISTRATE of the 3rd district, Soufrière, dated 12/7/1841, (printed) Enclosure to Letter No. 11
CO 253/74/11	Report of the STIPENDIARY MAGISTRATE of the 3rd district, Soufrière, dated 7/6/1841, (printed) Enclosure to Letter No. 5
CO 253/74/12	Report of the STIPENDIARY MAGISTRATE of the 3rd district, Soufrière, dated 7/8/1841, (printed) Enclosure to Letter No. 20
CO 253/74/13	Report of the STIPENDIARY MAGISTRATE of the 2nd district, Gros Islet, dated in November 1841 Enclosure to Letter No. 33
CO 253/76/1	Report of the STIPENDIARY MAGISTRATE of the 5th district, Micoud, dated 2/4/1842 Enclosure to Letter No. 22
CO 253/76/2	Report of the STIPENDIARY MAGISTRATE of the 4th district, Vieux Fort, dated 10/5/1842 Enclosure to Letter No. 26
CO 253/76/3	Report of the STIPENDIARY MAGISTRATE of the 5th district, Micoud, dated 1/2/1842 Enclosure to Letter No. 7
CO 253/76/4	Report of the STIPENDIARY MAGISTRATE of the 5th district, Micoud, dated 1/3/1842 Enclosure to Letter No. 7
CO 253/76/5	Report of the STIPENDIARY MAGISTRATE of the 4th district, Vieux Fort, dated 1/1/1842 Enclosure to Letter No. 3
CO 253/76/6	Report of the STIPENDIARY MAGISTRATE of the 3rd district, Soufrière, dated 12/3/1842 Enclosure to Letter No. 7

CO 253/76/7	Report of the STIPENDIARY MAGISTRATE of the 1st district, Castries, dated 3/6/1842
	Enclosure to Letter No. 35
CO 253/78/1	Letter from Governor GRAYDON, St. Lucia, to the General Governor GREY in Barbados, dated 20/12/1842 Enclosure to Letter No. 7
CO 253/78/2	Report of the STIPENDIARY MAGISTRATE of the 1st district, Castries, dated 24/12/1842
	Enclosure to Letter No. 22
CO 253/78/3	Report of the STIPENDIARY MAGISTRATE of the 2nd district, Gros Islet, dated 21/12/1842
	Enclosure to Letter No. 22
CO 253/78/4	Report of the STIPENDIARY MAGISTRATE of the 3rd district, Soufrière, dated in December 1842
	Enclosure to Letter No. 22
CO 253/78/5	Report of the STIPENDIARY MAGISTRATE of the 5th district, Micoud, dated 30/12/1842
	Enclosure to Letter No. 22
CO 253/78/6	Report of the STIPENDIARY MAGISTRATE of the 4th district, Vieux Fort, dated in December 1842
	Enclosure to Letter No. 22
CO 253/78/7	"Return of the Number of Immigrants into the Island of St. Lucia, from the 1st day of August 1834, to the 30th April 1843", 1843, signed by the COLONIAL SECRETARY HANLEY, (printed)
	Enclosure to Letter No. 27
CO 253/79/1	Report of the STIPENDIARY MAGISTRATE of the 1st district, Castries, dated 27/7/1843
	Enclosure to Letter No. 48
CO 253/79/2	Report of the STIPENDIARY MAGISTRATE of the 2nd district, Gros Islet, dated 1/8/1843
	Enclosure to Letter No. 48
CO 253/79/3	Report of the STIPENDIARY MAGISTRATE of the 3rd district, Soufrière, dated 1/8/1843
	Enclosure to Letter No. 48
CO 253/79/4	Report of the STIPENDIARY MAGISTRATE of the 4th district, Vieux Fort, dated 5/8/1843
	Enclosure to Letter No. 48

CO 253/79/5	Report of the STIPENDIARY MAGISTRATE of the 5th district, Micoud, dated 7/8/1843
	Enclosure to Letter No. 48
CO 253/81/1	Letter from Governor CLARKE, St. Lucia, to the General Governor GREY in Barbados, dated 30/3/1844
	Enclosure to Letter No. 52
CO 253/81/2	Letter from Governor TORRENS, St. Lucia, to the General Governor GREY in Barbados, dated 15/10/1844
	Enclosure to Letter No. 57
CO 253/81/3	Proclamation of Governor TORRENS, dated in October 1844, (printed)
	Enclosure to Letter No. 57
CO 253/82/1	Report of the STIPENDIARY MAGISTRATE of the 1st district, Castries, dated 10/1/1844
	Enclosure to Letter No. 23
CO 253/82/2	Report of the STIPENDIARY MAGISTRATE of the 4th district, Vieux Fort, dated 10/1/1844
	Enclosure to Letter No. 23
CO 253/82/3	Report of the STIPENDIARY MAGISTRATE of the 3rd district, Soufrière, dated 10/1/1844
	Enclosure to Letter No. 23
CO 253/82/4	Report of the STIPENDIARY MAGISTRATE of the 4th district, Vieux Fort, dated 2/7/1844
	Enclosure to Letter No. 48
CO 253/82/5	Report of the STIPENDIARY MAGISTRATE of the 1st district, Castries, dated 3/7/1844
	Enclosure to Letter No. 48
CO 253/82/6	Report of the STIPENDIARY MAGISTRATE of the 2nd district, Gros Islet, dated 16/2/1844
	Enclosure to Letter No. 23
CO 253/82/7	Report of the STIPENDIARY MAGISTRATE of the 5th district, Micoud, dated 12/1/1844
	Enclosure to Letter No. 23

CO 253/82/8   Report of the STIPENDIARY MAGISTRATE of the 5th district, Micoud, dated 3/7/1844

Enclosure to Letter No. 48

CO 253/83/1   Letter from Governor TORRENS, St. Lucia, to the General Governor GREY in Barbados, dated 3/3/1845, (printed)

Enclosure to Letter No. 12

CO 253/83/2   Report of the STIPENDIARY MAGISTRATE of the 4th district, Vieux Fort, dated 10/1/1845, (printed)

Enclosure to Letter No. 12

CO 253/83/3   Report of the STIPENDIARY MAGISTRATE of the 2nd district, Gros Islet, dated 5/7/1845, (printed)

Enclosure to Letter No. 31

CO 253/83/4   Report of the STIPENDIARY MAGISTRATE of the 3rd district, Soufrière, dated 1/7/1845, (printed)

Enclosure to Letter No. 31

CO 253/83/5   Report of the STIPENDIARY MAGISTRATE of the 3rd district, Castries, dated 13/1/1845, (printed)

Enclosure to Letter No. 12

CO 253/83/6   Report of the STIPENDIARY MAGISTRATE of the 2nd district, Gros Islet, dated 12/1/1845, (printed)

Enclosure to Letter No. 12

CO 253/83/7   Report of the STIPENDIARY MAGISTRATE of the 5th district, Micoud, dated 2/7/1845, (printed)

Enclosure to Letter No. 31

CO 253/83/8   Report of the STIPENDIARY MAGISTRATE of the 1st district, Castries, dated 17/1/1845, (printed)

Enclosure to Letter No. 12

CO 253/83/9   Report of the STIPENDIARY MAGISTRATE of the 5th district, Micoud, dated 10/1/1845, (printed)

Enclosure to Letter No. 12

CO 253/83/10   Report of the STIPENDIARY MAGISTRATE of the 1st district, Castries, dated 14/7/1845, (printed)

Enclosure to Letter No. 31

CO 253/83/11   Report of the STIPENDIARY MAGISTRATE of the 4th district,
Vieux Fort, dated 1/7/1845, (printed)

Enclosure to Letter No. 31

CO 253/85/1   Letter from Governor TORRENS, St. Lucia, to the
General Governor GREY in Barbados, dated 4/1/1846, (printed)

Enclosure to Letter No. 12

CO 253/91/1   Petition from 225 Inhabitants of St. Lucia (Planters and Merchants),
St. Lucia, dated 21/10/1847 to the Queen of England

Enclosure to Letter No. 28

CO 253/92/1   Circular letter of Governor DARLING, St. Lucia, to the
STIPENDIARY MAGISTRATES, Priests and "leading Inhabitants of the

Island" dated in May 1848, (printed)

Enclosure to Letter No. 51

CO 253/92/2   "Sketch of the town of Castries", 1849

Enclosure to
Letter of Governor DARLING, St. Lucia, to the
General Governor COLEBROOKE in Barbados, dated 26/1/1849

Enclosure to Letter No. 24

CO 253/93/1   Letter of Governor DARLING, St. Lucia, to the
SECRETARY OF STATE in London, dated 28/5/1848

Enclosure to "Mai 28"

CO 253/97/1   "Report on the Immigrants by the Ship Una of Liverpool which
arrived at Saint Lucia from Sierra Leone on the 6. February 1849",
Castries, GOVERNMENT IMMIGRATION AGENT, dated 16/2/1849

Enclosure to Letter No. 12

CO 253/97/2   Letter of Governor DARLING, St. Lucia, to the
General Governor COLEBROOKE in Barbados, dated 7/2/1849

Enclosure to Letter No. 11

CO 253/97/3   Letter of Governor PINE, Sierra Leone, to
Governor DARLING of St. Lucia, dated 12/1/1849

Enclosure to Letter No. 11

CO 253/97/4   Letter of Governor DARLING, St. Lucia, to the
General Governor COLEBROOKE in Barbados, dated 21/2/1849

Enclosure to Letter No. 12

CO 253/97/5   Letter of Governor COLEBROOKE, Barbados, to the SECRETARY OF
STATE GREY in London, dated 26/2/1849 – Letter No. 12

CO 253/97/6   "Government Notice", signed by the COLONIAL SECRETARY
                   HANLEY, dated 6/2/1849, (printed)

                   Enclosure to Letter No. 11

CO 253/98/1   "Petition of the principal landed Proprietors and Merchants",
                   St. Lucia, to the SECRETARY OF STATE GREY in London,
                   dated 3073/1849

                   Enclosure to Letter No. 39

CO 253/99/1   Letter of Governor DARLING, St. Lucia, to the General
                   Governor COLEBROOKE in Barbados, dated 15/6/1849, (printed)

                   Enclosure to Letter No. 55

CO 253/100/1   "Names of Estates to which African Immigrants ex Ship "Una" have
                   been allotted with the number located on each estate", signed by
                   the STIPENDIARY MAGISTRATE of the 1st district, Castries,
                   dated in February 1849

                   Enclosure to Letter No. 103

CO 253/100/2   "Return of African Immigrants per "Una" specifying their Tribes and
                   Sexes, compiled from the Special Magistrates' Reports", signed by
                   Act. Col. Secretary DRYSDALE, Castries, 1849

                   Enclosure to Letter No. 103

CO 253/102/1   Letter of Governor DARLING, St. Lucia, to the
                   General Governor COLEBROOKE in Barbados, dated 30/3/1850

                   Enclosure to Letter No. 27

CO 253/102/2   Report of the STIPENDIARY MAGISTRATE of the 2nd district,
                   Gros Islet, dated 7/3/1850

                   Enclosure to Letter No. 27

CO 253/102/3   "Report on the Immigrants by the Ship Tropic which arrived at
                   Castries, St. Lucia from Sierra Leone on the 4th January 1850",
                   Government Immigration Agent, Castries, dated 9/1/1850

                   Enclosure to Letter No. 8

CO 253/102/4   Letter of Governor DARLING, St. Lucia, to the
                   General Governor COLEBROOKE in Barbados, dated 19/1/1850

                   Enclosure to Letter No. 8

CO 253/103/1   Letter of Governor DARLING, St. Lucia, to the General
                   Governor COLEBROOKE in Barbados, dated 29/4/1850, (printed)

                   Enclosure to Letter No. 32

CO 253/103/2   "Report on the Immigrants by the Ship "Tuskar" which arrived at Saint Lucia from St. Helena on the 11th May 1850", Castries, Government Immigration Agent, dated 20/5/1850

Enclosure to Letter No. 38

CO 253/103/3   Report of the Doctor of the ship William Mc.Gill, Castries, dated in May 1850

Enclosure to Letter No. 38

CO 253/103/4   Letter of Governor MENDS, St. Lucia, to the General Governor COLEBROOKE in Barbados, dated 23/5/1850

Enclosure to Letter No. 38

CO 253/104/1   "An Ordinance Promoting African Immigration into the Colony of Saint Lucia and the Industry of the Immigrants", of Governor DARLING, St. Lucia, dated 2/5/1850, (printed)

Enclosure to Letter No. 58

CO 253/105/1   Report of the STIPENDIARY MAGISTRATE of the 1st district, Castries, dated 11/10/1850

Enclosure to Letter No. 97

CO 253/105/2   Report of the STIPENDIARY MAGISTRATE of the 2nd district, Gros Islet, dated 26/10/1850

Enclosure to Letter No. 97

CO 253/105/3   Report of the STIPENDIARY MAGISTRATE of the 5th district, Micoud, dated 3/10/1850

Enclosure to Letter No. 97

CO 253/112/1   "Distribution Returns of African Immigrants from 1st Jan. to 30th June 1853" signed by the STIPENDIARY MAGISTRATES of the several districts, Castries, 1853

Enclosure to Letter No. 45

CO 253/112/2   Report of the STIPENDIARY MAGISTRATE of the 2nd district, Gros Islet, dated 10/8/1853

Enclosure to Letter No. 45

CO 253/113/1   Letter of Governor POWER, St. Lucia, to the General Governor COLEBROOKE in Barbados, dated 4/12/1853

Enclosure to Letter No. 57

CO 253/114/1   Letter of Governor POWER, St. Lucia, to the General Governor COLEBROOKE in Barbados, dated 20/6/1854

Enclosure to Letter No. 21

CO 253/114/2 — Report of the "St. Lucia Library and Commercial Reading Room", Castries, dated 28/2/1854

Enclosure to Letter No. 15

CO 253/116/1 — Letter of Governor POWER, St. Lucia, to the General Governor COLEBROOKE in Barbados, dated 4/6/1855

Enclosure to Letter No. 33

CO 253/123/1 — Report of the STIPENDIARY MAGISTRATE of the 2nd district, Gros Islet, dated 13/4/1858

Enclosure to Letter No. 27

CO 253/123/2 — Letter of Governor BREEN, St. Lucia, to the General Governor HINCKS in Barbados, dated 4/5/1858

Enclosure to Letter No. 27

CO 253/123/3 — Letter of Governor BREEN, St. Lucia, to the General Governor HINCKS in Barbados, dated 23/8/1858

Enclosure to Letter No. 50

CO 253/123/4 — Letter of Governor BREEN, St. Lucia, to the General Governor HINCKS in Barbados, dated 1/9/1858

Enclosure to Letter No. 52

CO 253/123/5 — Letter of Governor BREEN, St. Lucia, to the General Governor HINCKS in Barbados, dated 16/9/1858

Enclosure to Letter No. 61

CO 253/125/1 — Report of the STIPENDIARY MAGISTRATE of the 3rd district, Soufrière, dated 12/10/1859

Enclosure to Letter No. 64

CO 253/125/2 — Report of the STIPENDIARY MAGISTRATE of the 3rd district, Soufrière, dated 22/11/1859

Enclosure to Letter No. 71

CO 253/128/1 — Letter of Governor BREEN, St. Lucia, to the General Governor HINCKS in Barbados, dated 25/5/1861

Enclosure to Letter No. 29

CO 253/130/1 — Letter of Governor GRANT, St. Lucia, to the General Governor WALKER in Barbados, dated 30/6/1862

Enclosure to Letter No. 49

CO 253/130/2	Report of the IMMIGRATION AGENT Mc. LEOD, Castries, dated 15/2/1862
	Enclosure to Letter No. 8
CO 253/130/3	Report of the IMMIGRATION AGENT Mc. LEOD, Castries, dated 17/2/1862
	Enclosure to Letter No. 8
CO 253/130/4	"Return of the Assignments of the male adult Liberated Africans ex Ship "Ulysses"", Castries, signed by the IMMIGRATION AGENT Mc. LEOD, dated 3/3/1862
	Enclosure to Letter No. 12
CO 253/130/5	"Return of the Assignments of the male adult Liberated Africans ex Barque "Damietta"", Castries, signed by the IMMIGRATION AGENT Mc. LEOD, dated 3/3/1862
	Enclosure to Letter No. 12
CO 253/131/1	Report of the IMMIGRATION AGENT Mc. LEOD, Castries, dated 16/9/1862
	Enclosure to Letter No. 74
CO 253/132/1	Report of the IMMIGRATION AGENT Mc. LEOD, Castries, dated 31/3/1863
	Enclosure to Letter No. 110
CO 253/134/1	Report of the IMMIGRATION AGENT Mc. LEOD, Castries, dated 3/2/1864
	Enclosure to Letter No. 117
CO 253/135/1	Report of the IMMIGRATION AGENT JENNINGS, Castries, dated 13/8/1864
	Enclosure to Letter No. 214
CO 253/136/1	Report of the IMMIGRATION AGENT CHADWICK, Castries, dated 30/1/1865
	Enclosure to Letter No. 240
CO 253/136/2	Letter of Governor GRANT, St. Lucia, to the General Governor MUNDY in Barbados, dated 29/4/1865
	Enclosure to Letter No. 257
CO 253/136/3	Report of the IMMIGRATION AGENT CHADWICK, Castries, dated 10/2/1866
	Enclosure to Letter No. 306

CO 253/138/1   Report of the IMMIGRATION AGENT CHADWICK, Castries, dated 28/1/1867

Enclosure to Letter No. 357

CO 253/139/1   Report of the IMMIGRATION AGENT CHADWICK, Castries, dated 2/8/1867

Enclosure to Letter No. 390

CO 253/140/1   Report of the IMMIGRATION AGENT CHADWICK, Castries, dated 25/2/1868

Enclosure to Letter No. 430

CO 253/140/2   Report of the IMMIGRATION AGENT CHADWICK, Castries, dated 14/8/1868

Enclosure to Letter No. 476

CO 253/145/1   Letter of Governor DES VOEUX, St. Lucia, to the General Governor RAWSON in Barbados, dated 18/11/1870

Enclosure to Letter No. 71

CO 253/148/1   "An Ordinance for the repression of Obeah and other kindred practices", of Governor DES VOEUX, dated 6/12/1871 (printed)

Enclosure to
Letter of General Governor RAWSON, Barbados, to the
SECRETARY OF STATE KIMBERLEY in London, dated 5/1/1872

CO 253/148/2   Letter of Governor DES VOEUX, St. Lucia, to the General Governor RAWSON in Barbados, dated 16/11/1871

Enclosure to
Letter of General Governor RAWSON, Barbados, to the
SECRETARY OF STATE KIMBERLEY in London, dated 5/1/1872 (No.I)

CO 255/1/1   Proclamation of Governor MAINWARING, St. Lucia, dated 1/6/1826, p.164

CO 255/1/2   ORDER IN COUNCIL "Amending the Slave Law passed in St. Lucia on 8th February 1826" of Governor MAINWARING, St. Lucia, dated 24/4/1827

CO 255/1/3   ORDER IN COUNCIL "fixing the Sum to be paid for the Capture of runaway Negroes", of Governor KEANE, St. Lucia, dated 8/4/1820, p.22

CO 255/1/4   ORDER IN COUNCIL "Establishing a permanent detachment for the suppression of marronage", of Governor MAINWARING, St. Lucia, dated 7/6/1826, p.166

CO 255/1/5	"Ordinance respecting and amending several laws relating to Free Persons of Colour" of Governor MAINWARING, St. Lucia, dated 8/2/1826, p.140
CO 255/2/1	"Proclamation carrying into effect the Order in Council of 2nd day of Nov. 1831", of Governor BOZON, St. Lucia, dated 24/12/1831, p.106
CO 255/2/2	Proclamation of Governor DUDLEY HILL, St. Lucia, dated 1/8/1834, p.268
CO 255/2/3	Proclamation of Governor DUDLEY HILL, St. Lucia, dated 16/8/1834, p.276
CO 255/2/4	Proclamation of Governor FARQUHARSON, St. Lucia, dated 3/1/1833 (printed), p.181
CO 255/2/5	Ordinance "Establishing a Savings Bank", of Governor FARQUHARSON, St. Lucia, dated 13/8/1832, p.146
CO 255/2/6	Ordinance "for defining the offences committed by slaves, and for punishing the same; and also describing the Modes of Punishment", of Governor FARQUHARSON, St. Lucia, dated 16/6/1832, p.133
CO 255/2/7	"An ordinance for fixing and determining the number of hours per week which shall be allotted to praedial apprenticed labourers for the cultivation of the provision grounds and also for regulating the apportionment of the 45 hours per week during which praedial apprenticed labourers are required by law to work for the benefit of their employers", of Governor DUDLEY HILL, St. Lucia, dated 1/8/1834, p.272
CO 255/2/8	Proclamation "Describing the Nature of such Punishments as FEMALE SLAVES are liable to endure", of Governor FARQUHARSON, St. Lucia, dated 26/5/1832, (printed), p.124
CO 255/2/9	Proclamation "Describing certain Regulations to be observed in the Punishment of FEMALE SLAVES by the PILLORY", of Governor FARQUHARSON, St. Lucia, dated 24/4/1833, (printed), p.199
CO 255/2/10	"An Ordinance for repressing the practice of harbouring runaway slaves", of Governor CARTER, St. Lucia, dated 3/3/1834, p.257
CO 255/2/11	Proclamation of Governor DUDLEY HILL, St. Lucia, dated 25/7/1834, pp. 264/266
CO 255/2/12	"An Ordinance for preventing the Slaves of certain Cantons in St. Lucia from effecting their escape to the Island of Martinique or elsewhere", of Governor FARQUHARSON, St. Lucia, dated 25/11/1833, p.231
CO 255/3/1	Proclamation of Governor BUNBURY, St. Lucia, dated 13/2/1838, (printed), p.131
CO 255/3/2	"An Ordinance For the Termination of the Existing System of Apprenticeship within the Island of Saint Lucia, and for Providing for such sick and infirm Apprentices as shall be emancipated on the first day of August, 1838", of General Governor MacGREGOR, St. Lucia, dated 13/7/1838, (printed), p.138

CO 255/3/3	Proclamation of Governor BUNBURY, St. Lucia, dated 4/12/1837, p.121
CO 255/5/1	"An Ordinance For Establishing a Public Library and Museum in the Town of Castries" of Governor DARLING, St. Lucia, dated 18/6/1847, p.52
CO 256/1/1	Protocol of the PRIVY COUNCIL of St. Lucia, dated 21/7/1823
CO 256/1/2	Protocol of the PRIVY COUNCIL of St. Lucia, dated 22/4/1822
CO 256/1/3	Protocol of the PRIVY COUNCIL of St. Lucia, dated 7/5/1822
CO 256/1/4	Protocol of the PRIVY COUNCIL of St. Lucia, dated 22/7/1822
CO 256/2/1	Protocol of the PRIVY COUNCIL of St. Lucia, dated 20/4/1830
CO 256/2/2	Protocol of the EXECUTIVE AND LEGISLATIVE COUNCIL of St. Lucia, dated 31/10/1832
CO 256/2/3	Protocol of the EXECUTIVE AND LEGISLATIVE COUNCIL of St. Lucia, dated 11/11/1833

CO 258/5/1	Report of the PROTECTOR OF SLAVES for the period from 1/6/1826 to 31/12/1826
CO 258/5/2	Report of the PROTECTOR OF SLAVES for the period from 1/1/1827 to 30/6/1827
CO 258/5/3	Report of the PROTECTOR OF SLAVES for the period from 1/7/1827 to 31/12/1827
CO 258/5/4	Report of the PROTECTOR OF SLAVES for the period from 1/1/1828 to 30/6/1828
CO 258/5/5	Report of the PROTECTOR OF SLAVES for the period from 1/7/1828 to 31/12/1828
CO 258/5/6	Report of the PROTECTOR OF SLAVES for the period from 1/1/1829 to 30/6/1829
CO 258/5/7	Report of the PROTECTOR OF SLAVES for the period from 1/7/1829 to 31/12/1829
CO 258/5/8	Letter of Governor STEWART, St. Lucia, to the SECRETARY OF STATE MURRAY in London, dated 10/11/1829 Enclosure to Report of the PROTECTOR OF SLAVES for the period from 1/1/1829 to 30/6/1829
CO 258/6/1	Report of the PROTECTOR OF SLAVES for the period from 1/1/1830 to 31/3/1830

CO 258/6/2	Report of the PROTECTOR OF SLAVES for the period from 1/4/1830 to 30/9/1830
CO 258/6/3	Letter of the SECRETARY OF STATE GODERICH, London, to Governor BOZON, St. Lucia, dated 15/11/1831
CO 258/7/1	Enclosure to Report of the PROTECTOR OF SLAVES for the period from 1/4/1830 to 30/9/1830 Report of the PROTECTOR OF SLAVES for the period from 1/10/1830 to 31/12/1830
CO 258/8/1	Report of the PROTECTOR OF SLAVES for the period from 1/1/1831 to 30/6/1831
CO 258/9/1	Report of the PROTECTOR OF SLAVES for the period from 1/7/1831 to 5/11/1831
CO 258/10/1	Report from London from the year 1832
	Enclosure to Report of the PROTECTOR OF SLAVES for the period from 5/11/1831 to 31/12/1831
CO 258/10/2	Report of the PROTECTOR OF SLAVES for the period from 5/11/1831 to 31/12/1831
CO 258/11/1	Report of the PROTECTOR OF SLAVES for the period from 1/1/1832 to 30/6/1832
CO 258/12/1	Report of the PROTECTOR OF SLAVES for the period from 1/7/1832 to 31/12/1832
CO 258/13/1	Report of the PROTECTOR OF SLAVES for the period from 1/1/1833 to 30/6/1833
CO 258/14/1	Report of the PROTECTOR OF SLAVES for the period from 1/7/1833 to 31/12/1833
CO 258/15/1	Report of the PROTECTOR OF SLAVES for the period from 1/1/1834 to 1/8/1834
CO 258/16/1	Report of the STIPENDIARY MAGISTRATE of the 1st district for all districts for the period from 1/7/1847 to 31/12/1847
CO 258/16/2	Report of the STIPENDIARY MAGISTRATE of the 1st district for all districts for the period from 1/7/1848 to 31/12/1848
CO 258/16/3	Report of the STIPENDIARY MAGISTRATE of the 1st district for all districts for the period from 1/7/1845 to 31/12/1845
CO 258/16/4	Report of the STIPENDIARY MAGISTRATE of the 1st district for all districts for the period from 1/1/1846 to 30/6/1846
CO 258/16/5	Report of the STIPENDIARY MAGISTRATE of the 1st district for all districts for the period from 1/7/1846 to 31/12/1846

CO 258/16/6	Report of the STIPENDIARY MAGISTRATE of the 1st district for all districts for the period from 1/1/1847 to 30/6/1847
CO 258/16/7	Report of the STIPENDIARY MAGISTRATE of the 1st district for all districts for the period from 1/1/1848 to 30/6/1848
CO 258/16/8	Report of the STIPENDIARY MAGISTRATE of the 2nd district, Gros Islet, for the period from 1/7/1845 to 31/12/1845
CO 258/16/9	Report of the STIPENDIARY MAGISTRATE of the 3rd district, Soufrière, for the period from 1/7/1845 to 31/12/1845
CO 258/16/10	Report of the STIPENDIARY MAGISTRATE of the 4th district, Vieux Fort, for the period from 1/7/1845 to 31/12/1845
CO 258/16/11	Report of the STIPENDIARY MAGISTRATE of the 3rd district, Soufrière, for the period from 1/1/1846 to 30/6/1846
CO 258/16/12	Report of the STIPENDIARY MAGISTRATE of the 3rd district, Soufrière, for the period from 1/7/1847 to 31/12/1847
CO 258/16/13	Report of the STIPENDIARY MAGISTRATE of the 2nd district, Gros Islet, for the period from 1/1/1846 to 30/6/1846
CO 258/16/14	Report of the STIPENDIARY MAGISTRATE of the 1st district, Castries, for the period from 1/1/1848 to 30/6/1848
CO 258/16/15	Report of the STIPENDIARY MAGISTRATE of the 1st district, Castries, for the period from 1/7/1848 to 31/12/1848
CO 258/16/16	Report of the STIPENDIARY MAGISTRATE of the 2nd district, Gros Islet, for the period from 1/7/1848 to 31/12/1848
CO 258/17/1	Report of the STIPENDIARY MAGISTRATE of the 1st district, Castries, for the period from 1/7/1850 to 31/12/1850
CO 258/17/2	Report of the STIPENDIARY MAGISTRATE of the 1st district for all districts for the period from 1/7/1849 to 31/12/1849
CO 258/17/3	Report of the STIPENDIARY MAGISTRATE of the 1st district for all districts for the period from 1/1/1850 to 30/6/1850
CO 258/17/4	Report of the STIPENDIARY MAGISTRATE of the 2nd district, Gros Islet, for the period from 1/7/1852 to 31/12/1852
CO 258/17/5	Report of the STIPENDIARY MAGISTRATE of the 1st district, Castries, for the period from 1/1/1849 to 30/6/1849
CO 258/17/6	Report of the STIPENDIARY MAGISTRATE of the 2nd district, Gros Islet, for the period from 1/1/1849 to 30/6/1849
CO 258/17/7	Report of the STIPENDIARY MAGISTRATE of the 4th district, Vieux Fort, for the period from 1/1/1849 to 30/6/1849
CO 258/17/8	Report of the STIPENDIARY MAGISTRATE of the 4th district, Vieux Fort, for the period from 1/7/1849 to 31/12/1849

CO 258/17/9	Report of the STIPENDIARY MAGISTRATE of the 4th district, Vieux Fort, for the period from 1/1/1850 to 30/6/1850
CO 258/17/10	Report of the STIPENDIARY MAGISTRATE of the 1st district, Castries, for the period from 1/1/1850 to 30/6/1850
CO 258/17/11	Report of the STIPENDIARY MAGISTRATE of the 2nd district, Gros Islet, for the period from 1/1/1850 to 30/6/1850
CO 258/17/12	Report of the STIPENDIARY MAGISTRATE of the 4th district, Vieux Fort, for the period from 1/7/1850 to 31/12/1850
CO 258/17/13	Report of the STIPENDIARY MAGISTRATE of the 2nd district, Gros Islet, for the period from 1/7/1851 to 31/12/1851
CO 258/17/14	Report of the STIPENDIARY MAGISTRATE of the 3rd district, Soufrière, for the period from 1/7/1851 to 31/12/1851
CO 258/17/15	Report of the STIPENDIARY MAGISTRATE of the 4th district, Vieux Fort, for the period from 1/7/1851 to 31/12/1851
CO 258/17/16	Report of the STIPENDIARY MAGISTRATE of the 1st district, Castries, for the period from 1/1/1853 to 30/6/1853
CO 258/17/17	Report of the STIPENDIARY MAGISTRATE of the 1st district, Castries, for the period from 1/7/1853 to 31/12/1853
CO 258/17/18	Report of the STIPENDIARY MAGISTRATE of the 1st district for all districts for the period from 1/7/1853 to 31/12/1853
CO 258/17/19	Report of the STIPENDIARY MAGISTRATE of the 1st district for all districts for the period from 1/7/1853 to 31/12/1853
CO 258/18/1	BLUE BOOK for 1821
CO 258/19/1	BLUE BOOK for 1822
CO 258/20/1	BLUE BOOK for 1823
CO 258/21/1	BLUE BOOK for 1824
CO 258/23/1	BLUE BOOK for 1827
CO 258/24/1	BLUE BOOK for 1828
CO 258/25/1	BLUE BOOK for 1829
CO 258/26/1	BLUE BOOK for 1830
CO 258/27/1	BLUE BOOK for 1831
CO 258/28/1	BLUE BOOK for 1832
CO 258/29/1	BLUE BOOK for 1833
CO 258/30/1	BLUE BOOK for 1834
CO 258/31/1	BLUE BOOK for 1835

CO 258/32/1	BLUE BOOK for 1836
CO 258/33/1	BLUE BOOK for 1837
CO 258/34/1	BLUE BOOK for 1838
CO 258/35/1	BLUE BOOK for 1839
CO 258/36/1	BLUE BOOK for 1840
CO 258/37/1	BLUE BOOK for 1841
CO 258/38/1	BLUE BOOK for 1842
CO 258/39/1	BLUE BOOK for 1843
CO 258/40/1	BLUE BOOK for 1844
CO 258/41/1	BLUE BOOK for 1845
CO 258/42/1	BLUE BOOK for 1846
CO 258/43/1	BLUE BOOK for 1847
CO 258/44/1	BLUE BOOK for 1848
CO 258/45/1	BLUE BOOK for 1849
CO 258/46/1	BLUE BOOK for 1850
CO 258/47/1	BLUE BOOK for 1851
CO 258/48/1	BLUE BOOK for 1852
CO 258/49/1	BLUE BOOK for 1853
CO 258/50/1	BLUE BOOK for 1854
CO 258/51/1	BLUE BOOK for 1855
CO 258/52/1	BLUE BOOK for 1856
CO 258/53/1	BLUE BOOK for 1857
CO 258/54/1	BLUE BOOK for 1858
CO 258/55/1	BLUE BOOK for 1859
CO 258/56/1	BLUE BOOK for 1860
CO 258/57/1	BLUE BOOK for 1861
CO 258/58/1	BLUE BOOK for 1862
CO 258/59/1	BLUE BOOK for 1863
CO 258/60/1	BLUE BOOK for 1864

CO 258/61/1   BLUE BOOK for 1865

CO 258/62/1   BLUE BOOK for 1866

CO 258/63/1   BLUE BOOK for 1867

CO 258/64/1   BLUE BOOK for 1868

CO 258/65/1   BLUE BOOK for 1869

CO 258/66/1   BLUE BOOK for 1870

CO 258/67/1   BLUE BOOK for 1871

8.3 Printed documents of the OFFICIAL PUBLICATIONS LIBRARY

OPL/C.S./F 246/1   "An Ordinance to amend the Ordinance No. 7, of the second day of May, one thousand eight hundred and fifty, entitled "An Ordinance for promoting African Immigration into the Colony of Saint Lucia and the industry of the Immigrants", of Governor BREEN, St. Lucia, dated 21/7/1858,
In: Saint Lucia: Ordinances enacted by His Excellency the Lieutenant-Governor; no. 1 of 1853 – no. 17 of 1935

OPL/C.S./F 246/2   "An Ordinance to amend the Laws now in force in this Island, relating to African Immigration", of Governor Macnamara Dix, St. Lucia, dated 31/3/1862,
In: Saint Lucia: Ordinances enacted by His Excellency Lieutenant-Governor, no. 1 of 1853 – no. 17 of 1935

BPP/BP/I/1   "A Bill to prevent the Importation of Slaves", Bd. I, 1806, p.273

BPP/CG/4/1   "Topographical Map of Saint Lucia", 1847, p.518

BPP/CG/9/1   "Statement of Staple Exports from St. Lucia, from 1839 to 1856 inclusive", signed by "Her Majesty's Treasurer" M'HUGH, dated 15/4/1857, p.81

BPP/ST/61/1   "Accounts of Exports from several West Indian Islands to St. Lucia (1799-1801)", p.57-59

BPP/ST/61/2   "Accounts of all Vessels which arrived in the British West Indies from Africa with Slaves (1799-1801)", p.52

BPP/ST/61/3   "Accounts of Arrivals in the West Indies from Africa Negroes imported and exported, (1802-1804)", p.423-428

BPP/ST/61/4   "Account of Negroes imported from the Coast of Africa (1805)", p.445

BPP/ST/68/1   Letter of the SECRETARY OF STATE BATHURST, London, to all Governors of the British Colonies, dated 9/7/1832 as well as the answer of the PROCUREUR GENERAL, SENESCHAL, and PROCUREUR DU ROI of St. Lucia, dated 1/12/1823, p.278

BPP/ST/71/1   Letter of Governor BLACKWELL, St. Lucia, to the
SECRETARY OF STATE BATHURST in London,
Dated 25/10/1825, p.178

BPP/ST/71/2   Extract of the CODE DE LA MARTINIQUE: "MARTINIQUE CODE",
signed by the SECRETARY SHAW, St. Lucia, dated 24/10/1825,
(1685-1819), p.184-212

BPP/ST/77/1   ORDER IN COUNCIL, London, dated 2/2/1830, p.27

BPP/ST/77/2   "Second Supplementary Ordinance to His Majesty's Order in Council,
establishing a Consolidated Slave Law, of Governor FARQUHARSON,
St. Lucia, dated 3/5/1830, p.368

BPP/ST/79/1   ORDER IN COUNCIL, London, dated 2/11/1831, p.93

8.4 Newspapers

N/BL/ND/C.misc. 425 (2)
"State of the Colony"
In: The Independent Press, Bd. I, no. 1, St. Lucia,
dated 4/9/1839

N/CO 28/171/1   "Expected Immigrants"
In: St. Lucia Palladium and Public Gazette, St. Lucia,
dated 17/8/1849
Enclosure to letter no. 7

N/CO 253/46/1   Speech of Governor DUDLEY HILL of St. Lucia,
In: Saint Lucia Gazette, St. Lucia, dated 30/7/1834, Vol. 3, no. 114,

Enclosure to
Letter of Governor DUDLEY HILL, St. Lucia, to the
SECRETARY OF STATE SPRING RICE in London, dated 1/8/1834

N/CO 253/92/1   "Rules and Regulations of the SAINT LUCIA LIBRARY AND MUSEUM"
In: St. Lucia Gazette, St. Lucia, dated 19/4/1848
Enclosure to letter no. 51

N/CO 253/123/1   "The Kroomen again"
In: St. Lucia Palladium and Public Gazette, St. Lucia,
dated 10/7/1858
Enclosure to letter no. 44

N/CO 258/1/1   "Local Matters"
In: The Palladium and St. Lucia Free Press, St. Lucia, Vol. I, no. 13,
dated 15/9/1838, p.2

N/CO 258/1/2   Article about the labour situation,
In: The Palladium and St. Lucia Free Press, St. Lucia, Vol. I, no. 14,
dated 22/9/1838, p.3

N/CO 258/1/3   Article about the labour situation,
In: The Palladium and St. Lucia Free Press, St. Lucia, Vol. I, no. 20,
dated 4/10/1838, p.6

N/CO 258/1/4 "The Country"
In: The Palladium and St. Lucia Free Press, St. Lucia, Vol. I, no. 26, dated 15/12/1838, p.20

N/CO 258/1/5 Article about the economic situation,
In: The Palladium and St. Lucia Free Press, St. Lucia, Vol. II, no. 40, dated 5/10/1839, p.73

N/CO 258/1/6 "State of the Island"
In: The Palladium and St. Lucia Free Press, St. Lucia, Vol. II, no. 51, dated 21/12/1839, p.89

N/CO 258/1/7 "St. Lucia Agricultural Report, May 2, 1846"
In: St. Lucia Palladium and Public Gazette, St. Lucia, Vol.IX, no.405, dated 9/5/1846, p.408

N/CO 258/1/8 "Local Matters"
In: The Palladium and St. Lucia Free Press, St. Lucia, Vol.VI, no.231 dated 5/1/1843, p.272

N/CO 258/1/9 Article about OBEAH
In: The Palladium and St. Lucia Free Press, St. Lucia, Vol.IV, no.139 dated 3/4/1841, p.186

N/CO 258/1/10 Two articles about OBEAH,
In: The Palladium and St. Lucia Free Press, St. Lucia, Vol.IV, no.141 dated 17/4/1841, p.190

N/CO 258/1/11 "Quembois"
In: The Palladium and St. Lucia Free Press, St. Lucia, Vol.IV, no.140 dated 10/4/1841, p.188

N/CO 258/1/12 "INQUEST NEGLECTED"
In: The Palladium and St. Lucia Free Press, St. Lucia, Vol.IV, no.179 dated 6/1/1842, p.227

N/CO 258/1/13 "Coroner's Inquest"
In: The Palladium and St. Lucia Free Press, St. Lucia, Vol.V, no.225 dated 24/11/1842, p.264

N/CO 258/1/14 "The Roses" and the "Marguerittes"
In: The Palladium and St. Lucia Free Press, St. Lucia, Vol.IV, no.162 dated 11/9/1841, p.209

N/CO 258/1/15 "Les Marguerites"
In: The Palladium and St. Lucia Free Press, St. Lucia, Vol.V, no.209 dated 4/8/1842, p.251

N/CO 258/1/16 "The Roses"
In: The Palladium and St. Lucia Free Press, St. Lucia, Vol.V, no.217 dated 29/9/1842, p.257

N/CO 258/1/17 Article about LA ROSE and LA MARGUERITE,
In: St. Lucia Palladium and Public Gazette, St. Lucia, Vol. VIII, no.366, dated 7/8/1845, p.365

N/CO 258/1/18 "Coroner's Inquest"
In: The Palladium and St. Lucia Free Press, St. Lucia, Vol.IV, no.137 dated 20/3/1841, p.182

N/CO 258/2/1   "The Public Library and Reading Room"
                In: St. Lucia Palladium and Municipal Gazette of Castries, St. Lucia,
                Vol. XV, dated 19/3/1852, p.118

N/OPL/LG   "Petition of the Proprietors, Merchants, Planters ...", St. Lucia,
                dated 27/3/1832, In: The London Gazette, dated 29/5/1832, p.1219

8.5 Literature

ANTHONY, Patrick, A.B.,
    s.a. 1965   Study Notes; Historical Notes of the West Indies, Castries
                In: File No. 24, Folk Research Centre, Castries

    1970   Religion and Culture in St. Lucia, Castries

    1975   The Folk Research Centre, St. Lucia, - A Case Study,
                Missiology Seminar Antigua, 12-15th May, Castries

    1979   The Literature on the Flower Festivals of St. Lucia,
                In: Bulletin of Folk Research Centre, Vol. 1, No. 1, June, Castries,
                pp.7-14

ASHDOWN, Peter,
    1983   Caribbean History in Maps, London/New York,
                3rd edition (ISBN 0 582 765412)

AUGIER F.R./GORDON S.C./HALL D.G./RECORD M.,
    1983   The Making of the West Indies, Longman Group Limited, Harlow,
                (ISBN 0 582 76304 5)

BERNER, Dominique,
    1984   Bericht über die afro-karibische Kultur in Martininique und
                Guadeloupe im 19. Jahrhundert anhand deutschsprachigen Archiv-
                und Bibliotheksmaterials im Vergleich zur historisch-französischen
                Dokumentation. Ein Beitrag zur Ethnohistorie der Karibik,
                Dissertation an der Grund- und Integrativwissenschaftlichen
                Fakultät, Wien

BRANFORD, Eric, M.,
    1973   „Legalise Obeah for Cultural Uplift"
                In: The Voice of St. Lucia, November, St. Lucia

BROCK, Colin,
    1984   Saint Lucia – Caribbean Communities, A Social Studies Series for
                Secondary Schools, London/Basinstoke, 5th edition,
                (ISBN 0 333 197801 1)

BROWNE, W.A.,
    1899   Money, Weights & Measures of the chief commercial Nations in the
                World, with the British Equivalents, London

CLAYPOLE, William/ROBOTTOM, John,
    1983   Caribbean Story, Book One: Foundations, Longman Group Limited,
                Harlow, 3rd edition (ISBN 0 582 76543 X)

CROWLEY, Daniel, J.,
　　　1955　　　　　Festivals of the Calendar in St. Lucia
　　　　　　　　　　In: Caribbean Quaterly, Vol.IV, No.2, dated 4th December,pp.99-121

　　　1958　　　　　La Rose and La Marguerite Societies in St. Lucia
　　　　　　　　　　In: Journal of American Folklore 71, (Oct.-Dec. 1958), pp.541-551

CURTIN, P.D.
　　　1972　　　　　The Atlantic Slave Trade: A Census, Maadison

CUST, Robert, Needham,
　　　1883　　　　　A Sketch of the Modern Languages of Africa, London

DIZ, Jabetz,
　　　1933　　　　　Adolphe – one of the most terrible of Obeah-men
　　　　　　　　　　In: Canada-West Indies Magazine 22 (2), January, pp. 53-55

DOOKHAN, Isaac
　　　1981　　　　　A Post-Emancipation History of the West Indies, Collins-England,
　　　　　　　　　　5th edition, (ISBN 0 00 329350 5)

　　　1983　　　　　A Pre-Emancipation History of the West Indies, Collins-England,
　　　　　　　　　　10th edition, (ISBN 0 00 329335 I)

DURHAM H./LEWISOHN F.
　　　1971　　　　　St. Lucia – Tours and Tales, Wilmington

FRIESINGER H./DEVAUX R.
　　　1983　　　　　Vorbericht über die österreichischen Ausgrabungen auf St. Lucia,
　　　　　　　　　　Westindien (Mit einem Beitrag von A.J. Clark), Vienna

GACHET, Charles F.M.I.
　　　1975　　　　　A History of the Roman Catholic Church in St. Lucia, Trinidad

　　　1901　　　　　The St. Lucia Handbook, Directory and Almanac, London

HIRSCHBERG, Walter,
　　　1965　　　　　Völkerkunde Afrikas, Mannheim

　　　1974　　　　　Die Kulturen Afrikas,
　　　　　　　　　　In: Handbuch der Kulturgeschichte, Vol. 2, Frankfurt/Main

HUGHES, Alister,
　　　1973　　　　　„Legalising OBEAH"
　　　　　　　　　　In: The Voice of St. Lucia, 21st November, St. Lucia

ISICHEI, Elizabeth,
　　　1977　　　　　History of West Africa since 1800, London

JESSE, Rev. Charles, F.M.I.
　　　1964　　　　　Outlines of St. Lucia's History, Castries, 2nd edition

　　　1968　　　　　Sketch for a life of H.H. BREEN, F.S.A. (1805-1881) – Registrar,
　　　　　　　　　　Administrator and First Mayor of Castries -, St. Lucia

　　　1973　　　　　"Obeah"
　　　　　　　　　　In: The Voice of St. Lucia, November, St. Lucia

KOELLE, S.W.
    1963   Polyglotta Africana, Sierra Leone
                    (Reprint – 1st edition 1854)

KUBIK, Gerhard,
    1981   Extensionen afrikanischer Kulturen in Brasilien, 2nd part
                    In: Wiener Ethnohistorische Blätter, Heft 22, Vienna

SIMMONS, Harold, F.C.
    1853   The Flower Festivals of St. Lucia,
                    In: The Voice of St. Lucia, dated 27/8/1853, St. Lucia

SZALAY, Miklos
    1983   Ethnologie und Geschichte, Berlin

WERNHART, Karl, R.
    1971   Die Ethnohistorie und ihre Quellengattungen,
                    In: Sonderdruck aus den Mitteilungen der Anthropologischen
                    Gesellschaft in Wien, Vol. 101, pp.53-60

    1981   Kulturgeschichte und Ethnohistorie als Strukturgeschichte
                    In: Grundfragen der Ethnologie, Berlin, pp. 233-252

WESTERMANN D./BRYAN M.A.
    1970   Handbook of African Languages, Part II:
                    Languages of West Africa, London

WIRZ, Albert,
    1984   Sklaverei und Kapitalistisches Weltsystem, Frankfurt am Main

---

Miscellaneous:

ENCYCLOPAEDIA BRITANNICA, Chicago/London/Toronto 1768
EVERYMAN'S ENCYCLOPAEDIA, Vol. 8, London/Melbourne/Toronto 1978
GRAND LAROUSSE Encyclopédique, Paris 1962
ÖSTERREICHISCHER ATLAS FÜR HÖHERE SCHULEN, Vienna 1975, 101. Edition
ST. LUCIA YEAR BOOK 1982, Castries
THE CARIBBEAN HANDBOOK 1983/84, London/Antigua 1983
THE OXFORD ENGLISH DICTIONARY, Oxford 1969
WORLD TRAVEL MAP "Africa", Edinburgh 1975

9 Biography of the Author Dr. Ernestine Kolar

I was born in Vienna, Austria in 1955. After finishing an economical college I married my husband Hans. I worked some years in the economy. In 1980 I started studying social and cultural anthropology at the University in Vienna and finished with my theses "ST. LUCIA: SKLAVEREI, EMANZIPATION UND FREIHEIT" in the year 1985.

I got one daughter and started working in the adult education. In the early nineties I elaborated an English version of my theses. It was, like the German one, a paper version written with a typewriter. The diagrams were drawn on paper. This English paper version was brought to St. Lucia and I thank Msgr. Patrick A.B. Anthony for proofreading.

In 2015 I retired and started looking for the English paper version. In December 2017 I went to St. Lucia and found it in the Folk Research Centre in St. Lucia where Msgr. Patrick A.B. Anthony had stored it in the library. I brought it to Vienna and started to type it in my laptop.

Regrettably on March 25th 2018 the Folk Research Centre with all the collected material burnt down. My English version of my thesis would have been lost forever.

In Vienna I continued typing my thesis and made new diagrams for which I thank my husband for helping. Also I updated a few points in the introductions to some chapters. The main part of my thesis is detailed original quotations from the correspondence of the British government in the 19th century. These texts, of course, didn't change during the last 39 years and therefore I hope that my work is a fruitful distribution to the history of St. Lucia.

Contact: ernestine.kolar.st.lucia@outlook.com

Printed in Great Britain
by Amazon